THE PHILOSOPHY

OF ILLUMINATION

Suhrawardī

The Philosophy of Illumination

حكمة الاشراق

A New Critical Edition of the Text of Ḥikmat al-ishrāq
with English Translation, Notes, Commentary, and Introduction by

John Walbridge & Hossein Ziai

Brigham Young University Press • Provo, Utah • 1999

Library of Congress Cataloging-in-Publication Data is available.

ISBN 978–0–8425–2457–6 (cloth)

PRINTED IN THE UNITED STATES OF AMERICA.

2 3 4 5 6 7 8 9 09 08 07 06 05 04

TO OUR PARENTS

John and Mary Lou Walbridge
and the late Dr. Mahmoud Ziai and Ozra Moshiri Ziai

از صدای سخن عشق ندیدم خوشتر
یادگاری که در این گنبد دوار بماند

Never didst I hear a sound more beautiful than love.
'Tis memory eternal, unchanging,
as the wheel of life does turn.

Contents

Part One
The Rules of Thought, in Three Discourses

Part Two

On the Divine Lights, the Light of Lights,
and the Bases and Order of Existence,
in Five Discourses

Foreword to the Series

The Islamic Translation Series: Philosophy, Theology, and Mysticism (hereafter ITS) is designed not only to further scholarship in Islamic studies but, by encouraging the translation of Islamic texts into the technical language of contemporary Western scholarship, to assist in the integration of Islamic studies into Western academia and to promote global perspectives in the disciplines to which it is devoted. If this goal is achieved, it will not be for the first time: Historians well know that, during the so-called Middle Ages, a portion of the philosophical, scientific, and mathematical wealth of the Islamic tradition entered into and greatly enriched the West. Even Christian theology was affected, as is brilliantly evidenced in the works of St. Thomas Aquinas and other scholastics.

Manuscripts submitted to ITS for consideration are, of course, evaluated without regard to the religious, methodological, or political preferences of the translators or to their gender or national origins. The translator of each text, not the editors of the series nor the members of the advisory board, is solely responsible for the volume in question.

On behalf of Daniel C. Peterson, the executive editor, and members of the advisory board, I wish to express deep appreciation to the cosponsoring institutions—the Institute for the Study and Preservation of Ancient Religious Texts at Brigham Young University and the Foundation for Interreligious Diplomacy (and its director, Charles Randall Paul)—for their gracious support of this project.

—Parviz Morewedge
Editor in Chief
Rutgers, The State University of New Jersey

◆ ◆ ◆

Brigham Young University and its Institute for the Study and Preservation of Ancient Religious Texts are pleased to sponsor and publish the Islamic Translation Series: Philosophy, Theology, and Mysticism (ITS). We wish to express our appreciation to the editor in chief of ITS, Parviz Morewedge, for joining us in this important project. We are especially grateful to James L. and Beverley Sorenson of Salt Lake City for their generous support, which made ITS possible, and to the Ashton Family Foundation of Orem, Utah, which kindly provided additional funding so that we might continue.

Islamic civilization represents nearly fourteen centuries of intense intellectual activity, and believers in Islam number in the hundreds of millions. The texts that will appear in ITS are among the treasures of this great culture. But they are more than that. They are properly the inheritance of all the peoples of the world. As an institution of The Church of Jesus Christ of Latter-day Saints, Brigham Young University is honored to assist in making these texts available to many for the first time. In doing so, we hope to serve our fellow human beings, of all creeds and cultures. We also follow the admonition of our own tradition, to "seek . . . out of the best books words of wisdom," believing, indeed, that "the glory of God is intelligence."

—Daniel C. Peterson
Executive Editor
Brigham Young University

◆ ◆ ◆

A NOTE ON SPELLING

In this work, terms of Arabic derivation found in *Webster's Third New International Dictionary* generally follow the first spelling given therein and are treated as regular English words. Otherwise, Arabic or Persian words and proper names have been transliterated following, with few exceptions, the standard recommended by the *International Journal of Middle East Studies.*

Acknowledgments

We would like to express our thanks to the Tehran University Central Library, the Beinecke Rare Books and Manuscripts Library at Yale University, and the Special Collections of the library of the University of California at Los Angeles for copies of manuscripts in their collections.

Ed Macierowski, Parviz Morewedge, and Paul Vincent Spade read the manuscript at various times and gave us advice and encouragement. We are most grateful for the exceptional care given to a difficult manuscript by the editorial staff of the Islamic Translation Series at Brigham Young University and by its managing editor, Daniel C. Peterson.

Finally, we would like to acknowledge the encouragement and forbearance of our families and especially our wives, Linda Walbridge and Mahasti Ziai.

—John Walbridge
Hossein Ziai

Translators' Introduction

Suhrawardī: The Master of Illumination

In the year 579 A.H./1183 C.E. a ragged young man dressed in the garb of a dervish (an Islamic mystic) came wandering into the city of Aleppo.[1] So unprepossessing was his appearance that he was at first mistaken for a donkey driver.[2] He was Shihāb al-Dīn Abū al-Futūḥ Yaḥyā ibn Ḥabash ibn Amīrak al-Suhrawardī.[3] He was born around 549 A.H./1154 C.E., perhaps in the village of Suhraward, near Zanjān in northwestern Iran.[4] Nothing is known of his family background, but he evidently went first to Marāgha, a nearby city, where he studied philosophy and theology with Majd al-Dīn al-Jīlī, who also taught philosophy to the famous theologian Fakhr al-Dīn al-Rāzī (b. 543 or 544 A.H./1148–50 C.E., d. 606 A.H./1209 C.E.).[5] He next studied in either Isfahan or Mārdīn with Fakhr al-Dīn al-Mārdīnī (d. 594 A.H./1198 C.E.), who is said to have predicted Suhrawardī's death. He studied logic with Zahīr al-Fārisī, who taught him the *Baṣāʾir* (Insights) of ʿUmar ibn Sahlān al-Ṣāwī (fl. 540 A.H./1145 C.E.). Al-Ṣāwī's logic differed significantly from Aristotelian logic, particularly in its abandonment of the nine-part division of the organon in favor of a simpler two-part division into semantics and proof theory, which is later reflected in Suhrawardī's reorganization of the logical corpus.

Suhrawardī seems to have spent his twenties traveling in northern Syria and Anatolia, where he is mentioned as having been in Diyarbakr and Mīyafāriqīn, presumably with the intention of attaching himself to courts. He seems to have already developed a reputation as a Sufi mystic and rising philosopher. A few anecdotes survive from this period, picturing him as an eccentric but brilliant ascetic.

Sometime before coming to Aleppo, he made his fundamental philosophical shift, rejecting the Avicennan Peripatetic philosophy he had studied in his youth and setting himself the task of reviving the earlier philosophical tradition of the Ancients. This change was, he said, occasioned by a dream in which Aristotle appeared to him, revealing the doctrine later known as "knowledge by presence" and asserting the superiority of the Ancients and certain of the Sufis over the Peripatetics. It was also through mystical experience that Suhrawardī claimed to have become convinced of the existence of Platonic Forms.[6]

By the time Suhrawardī arrived in Aleppo in 1183, he was already formulating his new philosophical system. His largest philosophical work, *Al-mashāri^{c} wa al-muṭāraḥāt,* was completed that year. The work presented here, *Ḥikmat al-ishrāq,* was completed two years later, on 15 September 1186. That evening at sunset the sun, the dark moon, and the five visible planets came together in the western sky in a magnificent conjunction in the constellation of Libra. But soon the stars turned against Suhrawardī.

These were dramatic years in Syria. Nine years earlier the death of the Amīr Nūr al-Dīn, the ruler of Syria, had opened the way for Saladin, already ruler of Egypt, to add Muslim Syria to his empire. Saladin, a pious Sunni Muslim, had absorbed something of the crusading spirit of his Christian enemies. Saladin saw orthodox Islam as under threat from two directions. Outside, of course, were the Christian Crusaders, who held the holy city of Jerusalem and its shrines. But Islam was also menaced internally by the esoteric Isma^{c}ili Shi^{c}a. Saladin had already destroyed the Shi^{c}ite Fatimid state in Egypt, restoring the dominance of Sunni Islam there. Now, as master of Syria, he neutralized another branch of Isma^{c}ili Shi^{c}ism—the "Assassin" order in its almost impregnable castles. He forced their leader, the "Old Man of the Mountain," to sign a treaty with him. Aleppo fell to Saladin with the fall of northern Mesopotamia in 1183, and he put it into the hands of the prince al-Malik al-Ẓāhir, one of his teenaged sons, to give the young man some experience of government.

Suhrawardī had come to Aleppo in the year of its fall to Saladin, and the young philosopher soon attracted attention there. He was reportedly a charismatic teacher and gathered a circle of students fascinated to hear his novel philosophical views and to share in his mystical exercises and experiences. He was reportedly adept in the magical crafts, and a gem that he miraculously produced won him access to the prince-governor. Soon the prince was Suhrawardī's devoted disciple. His ascendancy over the prince soon aroused the jealousy of the Muslim jurists of the city, especially the brothers Jahbal, resident faqihs at the Nūrīya Madrasa.

The complaints reached the ears of the grim Saladin, who was facing his own problems. In 1187, four years after Suhrawardī's arrival in Aleppo, Saladin had destroyed the Kingdom of Jerusalem at the Battle of the Horns of Hattin. The disaster, with the attendant loss of Jerusalem, roused Christendom. The counterattack came four years later, in 1191, in the form of the Third Crusade, led by the two kings Richard the Lion-hearted of England and Philip Augustus of France. That same year Saladin ordered Suhrawardī put to death. The events are probably related. Though the sources are confused, it seems that Saladin became alarmed at the influence Suhrawardī had acquired over his son—an alarm that was fanned by the more orthodox clergy of Aleppo. Suhrawardī, a Platonist, evidently sought to train the young prince to be a philosopher-king—and he was accused of claiming to be a prophet himself. Even before he came to Aleppo, he had had dealings with several rulers in Anatolia; these contacts may have been attempts to carry out the implicit political program of his Illuminationist philosophy. Saladin had met philosopher-kings before—the Fatimid caliphs in Egypt and the Old Man of the Mountain with his murderous followers—and he did not like them. He could not take the chance that Aleppo, with its location strategic for both Saladin and the Crusaders, might revolt or even make common cause with the Crusaders. Saladin sent repeated orders that the troublesome philosopher be executed. Eventually, the reluctant prince obeyed, some said by leaving Suhrawardī to die of hunger.[7]

The Illuminationist Philosophy

The nature of the "Illuminationist philosophy" has long been a matter of controversy. As early as the thirteenth century, Shams al-Dīn Shahrazūrī (d. after 1288) could write, "The philosophy of illumination *(ḥikmat al-ishrāq)* is the philosophy based upon illumination *(ishrāq)*, which is unveiling *(kashf)*, or the philosophy of the easterners, which is to say, the Persians." He adds, helpfully,

> It amounts to the same thing since their philosophy is based on unveiling and intuition *(al-kashf wa al-dhawq)* and so is related to the illumination that is the manifestation of the intelligible lights, of their first principles, and their emanation of illuminations upon the perfected souls when they are abstracted from bodily matter. The Persians relied in their philosophy upon intuition and unveiling. The ancient philosophers of Greece did the same, with the exception of Aristotle and his school, who relied only upon reasoning and syllogism.[8]

Shahrazūrī captures both the essential features of the Illuminationist philosophy and the most important controversy concerning its nature. Suhrawardī's philosophy differs from that of the Islamic Peripatetics like Avicenna in giving a fundamental epistemological role to immediate and atemporal intuition. Intuition plays an essential role, both on the basic level of sensation and in the form of direct mystical awareness of the supersensible entities that Suhrawardī in the present book calls "immaterial lights." His philosophy is explicitly—often stridently—anti-Peripatetic and is identified with the pre-Aristotelian sages, particularly Plato. Like the Neoplatonists of Roman times, he is convinced that this wisdom was also expressed, though generally in symbolic form, by the ancient sages of other nations, notably the Egyptians, as represented by Hermes Trismegistus, and the ancient Persian sages and righteous kings.[9] Controversy, already prefigured in the passage just quoted, exists concerning the degree to which Suhrawardī's philosophy should be seen as Persian. Considered another way, the dispute concerns whether Suhrawardī's thought should be looked at primarily as an attempt to construct a philosophical system or as mysticism and gnosticism.

Suhrawardī himself identifies two periods in his thought, divided by the dream of Aristotle revealing the key doctrine of knowledge by presence and by his acceptance of the reality of the Platonic Forms. Works written before that time were Peripatetic in doctrine; later works reflected his Illuminationist thought. For our purposes, Suhrawardī's works can be divided into four classes—a system that can be supported from the analysis of his works given in the introduction to *The Philosophy of Illumination.*

1. *Juvenilia.* Suhrawardī wrote a number of philosophical works prior to the development of his distinctive philosophical views, perhaps as exercises.

2. *Persian and mystical works.* He also wrote a large number of shorter works in Arabic and Persian dealing with mystical topics. The best known are the allegories, mostly in Persian prose. There are also prayers.

3. *The mature "Peripatetic" works.* These are three medium to large philosophical compendia: *Al-talwīḥāt* (Intimations), *Al-muqāwamāt* (Apposites), and *Al-mashāri*ᶜ *wa al-muṭāraḥāt* (Paths and havens). They are written in the conventional Avicennan philosophical language but criticize the Peripatetics on many points.

4. *Ḥikmat al-ishrāq* (The philosophy of illumination), the work presented here.

The interrelations among these works have been a subject of some controversy, reflecting differing interpretations of the nature of Suhrawardī's philosophical project. Among Western scholars there have been two major approaches. The great French orientalist Henry Corbin saw Suhrawardī's project as an "Oriental theosophy." The "Peripatetic" works were thus either purely propædeutic or a middle phase of his thought. Among the philosophical works, *The Philosophy of Illumination* stands alone as representative of Suhrawardī's mature thought. What is important in that work is the metaphysics of light and darkness and, in general, the mythological elements of Suhrawardī's thought. The allegories and the mystical works are likewise seen as representative of the final and highest stage of his thought. Suhrawardī's primary cultural identification is with ancient Iran. Insofar as Corbin's interpretation has premodern roots, they are in the Zoroastrian-oriented philosophy of the Illuminationists of Mughal India. Corbin's interpretation is expressed not just in his studies of Suhrawardī but also in his translations and even his critical editions of Suhrawardī's works. The use of renderings like "theosophy" and "oriental" indicate the fundamentally mythological focus of Corbin's interests and interpretations. His translation of *The Philosophy of Illumination* omits the logic, and his editions of the three "Peripatetic" (or, perhaps it would be more accurate to say, anti-Peripatetic) works omit the logic and physics of each work and contain only the sections on metaphysics.[10] Such methods inevitably downplay the strictly philosophical aspects of Suhrawardī's thought.[11]

Others—and we are among them—see Suhrawardī's program as fundamentally philosophical and consider the "mature Peripatetic" works to be part of the same philosophical program as *The Philosophy of Illumination.* In such an interpretation, Suhrawardī's logical and metaphysical critique of the Peripatetics is central to his philosophical enterprise. Suhrawardī is presenting what is fundamentally a philosophy—albeit one with a place provided for the use of allegory and mystical experience—and is thus to be interpreted and judged in philosophical terms. The corpus of texts on *The Philosophy of Illumination* are thus ordered in the following manner: the *Intimations;* the *Apposites;* the *Paths and Havens;* and finally the best-known, which also bears the name of the new system as its title, *The Philosophy of Illumination.* This same order—as well as the necessity of studying every part of each text (logic, physics, and metaphysics) for a complete understanding of the philosophy of illumination—is corroborated by Shahrazūrī in his comprehensive Illuminationist commentary, *Sharḥ ḥikmat al-ishrāq.*[12] The allegorical works, though of literary interest, are seen as primarily elementary and semipopular works and not central to the Illuminationist philosophy.[13]

This approach to Suhrawardī, in which the major "Peripatetic" works and *The Philosophy of Illumination* are seen as a coherent interdependent corpus, is endorsed by the example of the later Iranian philosophical tradition, which almost always discusses Suhrawardī using conventional Avicennan terminology and takes as its point of departure precisely those points where Suhrawardī attacks Avicenna and the Islamic Peripatetics: the primacy of quiddity, the Platonic Forms, the epistemology of presence, the rejection of Aristotelian definition, and related issues. In terms of *The Philosophy of Illumination,* these are issues that derive from the section on logic and the "discursive philosophy" that Corbin and his followers have tended to ignore.[14] Suhrawardī referred to discursive philosophy, one of two constituents of "perfect" philosophy, in terms such as *baḥth, al-ḥikma al-baḥthiyya, ṭarīq al-mashshā'īn,* and *madhhab al-mashshā'īn.* "Intuitive philosophy," the other half, has priority in establishing the principles of philosophy. The terms used—such as *dhawq, al-ḥikma al-dhawqiyya,* and *al-ʿilm al-ḥuḍūrī, al-ʿilm al-shuhūdī*—all indicate intuitive philosophy but differ when used in a technical context. The distinction is made by Aristotle in *Posterior Analytics,* 1.1–2, where he gives priority to "primary immediately known premises" in science. All too often, intuitive philosophy is interpreted as a "mystical experience." The combination of discursive and intuitive philosophy into one consistent system—the philosophy of Illumination—was Suhrawardī's major achievement in the eyes of the medieval biographers and commentators on Illuminationist texts.[15]

The argument of *The Philosophy of Illumination* will be summarized below, but it is appropriate to say something here about the principal distinctive doctrines of Suhrawardī and his school.

First is the doctrine of *knowledge by presence.* Suhrawardī stressed that all knowledge involves some sort of direct, unmediated confrontation of the knower and the known. In general, he rejected intermediary mechanisms as ways of explaining various sorts of knowledge. At the lowest level, this involved a rejection of both the extramission and intramission theories of vision and of similar theories to explain the other senses. At the level of logic, he rejected Peripatetic essential definition, arguing that essences could only be known through direct acquaintance. At the highest level, intuition was the means by which supersensible entities could be known. Knowledge by presence was also invoked to solve the notorious Peripatetic difficulty of God's knowledge of particulars.

Second is the doctrine of *primacy of quiddity.* Though Suhrawardī himself apparently did not use the term, later interpreters categorized his ontology as "primacy of quiddity" *(aṣālat al-māhīya),* in contrast to Mullā Ṣadrā's assertion of the "primacy of existence" *(aṣālat al-wujūd).* This issue arises from Avicenna's famous distinction of the quiddity and the existence of a real thing. Suhrawardī argued that the existence of a valid mental distinction did not imply the corresponding existence of a real distinction in concrete things. In other words, such metaphysical entities as existence, necessity, unity, and so on were *iᶜtibārāt ᶜaqlīya,* "beings of reason," and only concrete individual entities really existed.

Finally, it is clear that Suhrawardī himself saw the question of the Platonic Forms as being the issue that united him and the Ancients against the Peripatetics. Since he saw the forms not as epistemological entities but as metaphysical explanations for order in the world, he framed the issue in terms of the number of immaterial intellects. The Peripatetics, by whom he mainly meant Avicenna, accepted a hierachy of only ten such intellects. The Illuminationists believed there were a great many more, many of them equal in rank but different in kind.

The history of the Illuminationist School

A comprehensive history of the Illuminationist school has yet to be written. Except for the few years of Suhrawardī's stay in Aleppo, the school never existed as an organized, institutionalized group comparable to the Pythagoreans, the early Platonists, or the Ismaᶜili philosophers. Suhrawardī stresses in *The Philosophy of Illumination* that proper understanding of the book is dependent on *al-qāʾim bi al-kitāb,* "he who arises with the Book," Suhrawardī's designated successor and interpreter. That there should have been such a person is implicit in his system. Shahrazūrī comments that Suhrawardī's wanderings were motivated by a search for such an intellectual peer but adds that he never found one.[16] However, Suhrawardī's disciples were scattered with his death and we seem to know the names of none of them—with, of course, the exception of al-Malik al-Ẓāhir. Suhrawardī's books circulated widely after his death, but without an accompanying oral tradition of intepretation.

The first prominent advocate of Suhrawardī's philosophy was Shahrazūrī, who flourished in the mid-thirteenth century. Though he was the author of several widely read works, he remains a rather mysterious figure. Contrary to some reports, he certainly was not a direct student of Suhrawardī, nor was he taught by one; apart from the disparity of dates, he makes clear in the introduction to his commentary on *The Philosophy of Illumination* that his knowledge of Suhrawardī came from books.

Shahrazūrī is best known for three works: the commentary just referred to; a widely read but unpublished philosophical encyclopedia entitled *Al-shajara al-ilāhīya* (The divine tree); and a biographical dictionary of ancient and Islamic philosophers on Illuminationist principles, *Nuzhat al-arwāḥ* (The consolation of spirits).[17]

Shahrazūrī's commentary on *The Philosophy of Illumination* was the basis of the commentary by Quṭb al-Dīn Shīrāzī (d. 1311), a well-known scientist who was a student of Naṣīr al-Dīn al-Ṭūsī. His commentary incorporated and superseded that of Shahrazūrī and came to be the vehicle through which *The Philosophy of Illumination* was understood in later Islamic philosophy. Suhrawardī's influence is also predominant in Quṭb al-Dīn's popular Persian philosophical encyclopedia, *Durrat al-tāj* (The pearly crown).[18]

Another early expounder of the Illuminationist philosophy was the Jewish convert to Islam, Ibn Kammūna, whose *Al-jadīd fī al-ḥikma* (The new philosophy) is a version of the Illuminationist philosophy and who wrote a commentary on another of Suhrawardī's works, *Al-talwīḥāt.*[19] The next two centuries are something of a blank. Although commentaries were written on Suhrawardī's works by Ghiyāth al-Dīn Dashtakī and Jalāl al-Dīn Dawwānī around the beginning of the sixteenth century, little is known about the philosophy of this period.

The major revival of the Illuminationist philosophy is associated with the so-called "School of Isfahan" of the late sixteenth and seventeenth centuries and a curious revival of interest in Zoroastrian lore in Mughal India at about the same time. The interest in Suhrawardī shown by the members of the School of Isfahan was largely philosophical. The great exponent of Suhrawardī's views was Mīr Dāmād (d. 1040 A.H./1631 C.E.). His student Mullā Ṣadrā, generally considered the most significant Islamic philosopher of the later period, broke with Mīr Dāmād and the Illuminationist tradition on certain significant points, the most important issue being the reality and primacy of existence. Whereas Suhrawardī and his followers had considered existence to be *iʿtibārī,* a "being of reason" produced by the mind's activity, Mullā Ṣadrā held that there was a deeper sort of existence to which Suhrawardī's critique of Avicenna did not apply. Thus, in the later tradition of Iranian philosophy, it may fairly be said that there are two wings of the Illuminationist tradition: one faithful to Suhrawardī on the issue of the primacy of quiddity; and the other, led by Mullā Ṣadrā, that criticized Suhrawardī on major points but still defined itself in terms of issues that Suhrawardī had first set out. Since Mullā Ṣadrā, Iranian philosophers have largely been divided into those who supported and those who rejected Mullā Ṣadrā's critique of Suhrawardī, with the supporters of Mullā Ṣadrā generally in the ascendant. Both schools exist in Iran to this day, and *The Philosophy of Illumination* is still taught in the theological academies.

In Mughal India, the mythological aspects of Suhrawardī's writings appealed to a group of Iranian and Parsi intellectuals led by one Ādhar Kaywān, a Zoroastrian priest. For them, Suhrawardī, with his allusions to the doctrines of light and darkness among the ancient Persians, provided an intellectually respectable form of Zoroastrian wisdom—one that was expressed in such productions of this school as the *Dasātīr* and the *Dabistān al-madhāhib*. A more philosophical expression of the Indian school is found in Hirawī's Persian commentary on *The Philosophy of Illumination*.[20]

In the Western parts of the Islamic world, however, Suhrawardī's philosophy had little influence, though a paraphrase of parts of *The Philosophy of Illumination* is found in a work of the Nasrid vizier Lisān al-Dīn ibn al-Khaṭīb (d. 776 A.H./1375 C.E.).[21] On medieval European philosophy, it probably had no influence at all.

Argument of *The Philosophy of Illumination*

The Philosophy of Illumination[22] consists of an introduction and two parts: logic (in three "discourses"), and the science of lights (in five). The arrangement is related to that of more conventional works of philosophy but differs in certain important respects. A philosophical compendium in the tradition of Avicenna would typically consist of four parts: logic, physics, mathematics, and metaphysics. Suhrawardī omits the middle two in *The Philosophy of Illumination* and omits mathematics in all his works.

The introduction identifies the purpose of the work, its intended audience, its specific subject matter, and its relations to the work of earlier philosophers. Its subject is the "science of lights"—a science that Suhrawardī first learned through mystical exercises. These experiences were reinforced later by logical proofs and confirmed by the parallel experiences of the Ancients, especially Plato, who generally expressed their philosophical views more or less symbolically. It was written at the same time he was writing works in the Peripatetic style, but its method is simpler and easier for the student. The introduction states that philosophers can practice discursive philosophy, intuitive philosophy, or both. The philosopher who has mastered both kinds is the natural ruler in this world, regardless of whether he actually possesses political power.

The philosophers who possess only intuitive philosophy are superior to those who possess only discursive philosophy. The reader of this book must have reached a certain level of mystical attainment, warns Suhrawardī; if he has not, he should confine himself to the books in the Peripatetic mode, which do not presume mystical experience.

In "Part One: The Rules of Thought," Suhrawardī gives an extremely simplified account of logic, "a small number of very useful rules . . . sufficient for the intelligent and for those who seek illumination." It is, in turn, divided into discourses on concepts and definitions, proofs, and fallacies. His exposition of elementary logic is deliberately simple—even simple-minded—and uses many nonstandard logical terms, often ordinary-sounding expressions like "general meaning" *(al-maᶜnā al-ᶜāmm)* for "universal." It is, among other things, a sort of parody of traditional logic, in which the venerable and abstract discipline is revealed to be no more than common sense wrapped up in complicated terms. His exposition of logic has important philosophical content, however, and the neologisms of his logic turn out to have subtle differences from the Peripatetic terms they replace, reflecting his distinctive philosophical views.

In the first discourse, on semantics, Suhrawardī rejects the Aristotelian notion of essential definition. Such definitions were supposed to reveal the essence of natural universals by listing the proximate genus and the differentia. He argues that such definitions are not actually possible. If the definition is successful, it presumes that the hearer already knows the genus and differentia; if so, the hearer must already have known the essence of the thing. If he does not know the genus and differentia, the definition will only be empty words. In other words, he who knows the thing does not need the definition; if he does not know the thing, the definition will not teach him what it is. Moreover, he can never be certain that all the essential differentia have actually been included. Suhrawardī argues that things must be known through direct experience, and definitions can do no more than point out what is being talked about. The rejection of essential definition thus wounds the heart of the Peripatetic notion of science.

In the second discourse, on proofs, in the course of an elementary summary of the doctrine of syllogism and scientific demonstration, Suhrawardī attacks the complex structure of the Peripatetic modal syllogism. He argues that for any scientific purpose the modal proposition can be reduced to a universal necessary affirmative proposition with modality, quantification, and negation incorporated into the terms of the proposition. For example, "It is possible that any man is literate" may be reformulated as

"It is necessary that all men are contingently literate." Similarly, "Necessarily no man is a stone" becomes "Necessarily every man is non-stone." By this means all syllogisms can be reduced to one, a modalized iterated form of Barbara: "Necessarily all A are B, and necessarily all B are C; therefore, necessarily all A are C."

The third discourse deals with fallacies in three sections. The first two sections are an elementary survey of common fallacies and how to avoid them. They have some interest, since the discussions contain criticisms of Peripatetic philosophical argumentation. The third section is central to Suhrawardī's philosophical enterprise, since it contains refutations of ten specific Peripatetic doctrines, forming a compendium of Suhrawardī's principal philosophical disagreements with the Peripatetics. He calls these discussions "judgments" *(ḥukūmāt).* His use of this section on sophisms to discuss substantive issues of physics and metaphysics is similar to the practice of medieval European natural philosophers, for whom books on sophismata came to be considered the appropriate place for discussing disputed questions of natural philosophy and metaphysics.

The section has an introduction "establishing certain technical terms." He does somewhat more than define terms, however, giving substantive discussions of substance and accident, necessity and contingency, cause, and possible and impossible infinities. The philosophical principles he establishes here are used extensively both in the critique of the Peripatetics that follows it and in his own metaphysics of light in the second half of the book. Among the important ideas introduced here are: (1) that "contingency" means to be necessary by a cause; (2) that a cause is ontologically but not temporally prior to its effect; (3) that a cause may be composite and include conditions and the removal of impediments; and (4) that an ordered, simultaneous, actual infinity is impossible but that an infinity that does not have these three properties is possible.

The first judgment deals with "beings of reason" *(iᶜtibārāt ᶜaqlīya),* which are concepts such as existence, necessity, contingency, unity, duality, color in general, privations, relations, and substantiality. Unlike concrete attributes like blackness, these attributes have no being outside the mind and are actually products of our thought about things. Suhrawardī complains that the Peripatetics have improperly reified such ideas and as a result have created insoluble third-man problems. The second judgment reiterates his criticism of the Peripatetic essential definition and adds a brief attack on the doctrine of the categories. As with the Stoics, a reduced five-fold set of categories are said to be the subject of physics.

The problem of the number of categories *(ḥaṣr al-maqūlāt)* was a lasting problem bequeathed to philosophers such as Mullā Ṣadrā.

The third, fourth, and fifth judgments attack Peripatetic hylomorphism, the doctrine that bodies are a combination of matter and form. He argues that the positing of matter distinct from body is unnecessary and that body is simply self-subsistent magnitude. (His doctrine probably derives from the *Timæus,* for Plato's "receptacle" was often understood in both antiquity and the Middle Ages as space.) Included here is an attack on the Aristotelian notion of form and secondary substance. In these sections Suhrawardī deals with a variety of physical questions, including compression and rarefaction, heat, the elements, and the nature of species. There are also separate refutations of atomism and the possibility of vacuum.

The sixth judgment deals with the Peripatetic proofs of the immortality of the soul. In this case he does not disagree with the doctrine of the immortality of the soul but does hold that the specific arguments used by the Peripatetics to establish it are invalid, primarily due to their inadequate doctrines of causality and contingency.

The seventh judgment concerns the Platonic Forms and the related question—in Suhrawardī's system, at least—of whether a simple effect can have a composite cause. He confines himself to answering the traditional Peripatetic arguments against the forms and defends his own theory of composite causes, a theory that will later be a necessary underpinning of his version of the theory of forms.

The eighth and ninth judgments deal with vision and criticize both major theories of vision: imprinting and visual rays. Suhrawardī argues here for his theory of vision by presence, whereby vision occurs by the presence of a lighted object before a sound eye without the movement of anything between the object and the eye. This theory of vision he later generalizes into the theory of knowledge by presence. The tenth judgment extends this theory to sounds, criticizing the view that sound is reducible to vibrations in the air.

"Part Two: On the Divine Lights" is the metaphysics of *The Philosophy of Illumination.* The first discourse establishes his basic metaphysical concepts—light, darkness, independence, and dependence—and their interrelations. Light is that which is evident or manifest in itself and makes other things evident. There are four classes of beings: self-subsistent light, which is self-conscious and is the cause of the other classes of beings; accidental light, which includes both physical light and some accidents in immaterial light; dusky substances, which are material bodies; and dark accidents, which include both physical accidents and some accidents in immaterial lights. Immaterial light cannot be seen by vision. All conscious beings are immaterial lights, aware of themselves directly. Immaterial lights differ by intensity, not by species. Immaterial lights are the causes of all other beings and in turn are caused by other, more intense immaterial lights. The sequence ends in an uncaused light, the Light of Lights, which is the counterpart of Avicenna's Necessary Existent, or God.

The second discourse is a cosmogony explaining how all other beings come into existence from the Light of Lights. The Light of Lights, being perfectly simple, can have only one direct effect: a single light called the "Proximate Light" that differs from it only in intensity. Likewise, the first material object must be a single, homogenous sphere encompassing everything else. The circular motions of the spheres must be the result of their being alive, and thus they must be moved by an immaterial light. The outermost sphere cannot come to be directly from the Light of Lights; rather, it exists by virtue of a dark accident in the Proximate Light or some lesser light. Because the light that is its cause has two relations to the Light of Lights—independence, by virtue of its luminosity, and dependence, by virtue of its being caused—it can bring into being both another immaterial light and a body, the sphere. Since all the lights are manifest to each other, the lower they are in the hierarchy of being, the more accidental multiplicity the lights can contain. Rays of light do not represent the separation of something from the light but, rather, the creation of an accident in the thing illumined. The complexity of the interactions of the immaterial lights is shown by the apparent disorder of the fixed stars.

Unlike Avicenna, who posited a hierarchy of only ten intellects, each of a different ontological rank, Suhrawardī allows the possibility of lights of equal intensity that differ in accidents. The lights of this "horizontal order" are the causes of the species and natural kinds of the sublunar world—the Platonic Forms, or the "archetypes of the talismans." There are also immaterial lights directly controlling physical bodies: the souls. God's knowledge of particulars is simply the presence of everything else to the Light of Lights—the highest example of Suhrawardī's knowledge by presence. The general principle that everything on a lower ontological plane must have a cause on a higher ontological plane is called "the most noble contingency" and is a fundamental principle of Suhrawardī's system. These lower lights may have composite causes.

The knowledge of the existence of these innumerable immaterial lights is one of the products of Suhrawardī's mystical experiences and can be confirmed by the testimony of the great sages of the past, both Greek and oriental. The Platonic Form, thus, is not equivalent to the universal of logic but is an immaterial mind that is the cause of the species of which it is the archetype. As one descends the ontological ladder, the immaterial lights grow dimmer and more complex until one reaches lights such as human souls, whose power is finite.

The third discourse deals with the activity of the lights and, in particular, the relationship among the immaterial lights, the motions of the spheres, and temporal events in the sublunar world. Simply put, the eternal circular movements of the spheres are the intermediary by which the timeless and unchanging complexity of the immaterial lights is expressed in the physical world.

The fourth discourse deals with physical topics. First, Suhrawardī reformulates the traditional four elements in terms of the opaque, the translucent, and the subtle, rejecting fire as an independent element. Next, he demonstrates that all motions ultimately originate in lights. Finally, he deals with the topics of traditional psychology: the temporal origin of the soul, the senses, the relationship between the rational and animal souls, and the number and nature of the inner senses, which he incorporates into his theory of knowledge by presence.

The fifth discourse deals with religious topics. Suhrawardī first discusses reincarnation, explaining it with a quote attributed to the Buddha and then giving an unconvincing refutation. The view discussed is that the soul is first born into human beings and then is reborn into animals until its evil moral qualities are expunged. Whatever his real views on reincarnation, he firmly asserts the immortality of the soul and the salvation of pure souls through their escape to the world of lights. Lesser souls are rewarded or punished in the world of suspended images. Evil in this world is not the direct product of the Light of Lights but is, rather, a concomitant of the motions of the spheres. This world is the best and only possible world, and there is much less evil here than good. Prophecy, true dreams, and the like are possible because the forms of events are inscribed in some way in the spheres and are accessible to human beings under special conditions. There are a variety of such experiences, including the music of the spheres; and the prophets, saints, and magicians have the power to bring the forms of things into being from the world of image. At this point Suhrawardī interjects two ecstatic utterances in praise of the mystics and prophets and assuring people that God will answer their prayers. He next gives a list of mystical experiences involving light. He closes with an exhortation to his disciples to study this book carefully.

The edition and translation

The present volume is the outcome of a plan that we made in Cambridge, Massachusetts, in 1983, to translate *The Philosophy of Illumination.* Other projects and commitments delayed the completion of the translation for some years. We had completed a second draft of the translation when the Islamic Translation Series was established. This new publication series offered us the opportunity to incorporate a revised edition of the Arabic text of *The Philosophy of Illumination* into a bilingual edition.

The translation

Apart from the general goal of making an important Islamic philosophical text available to English-speaking readers, this project should be seen as part of our larger project to explicate the philosophical nature of the Illuminationist tradition. As we have already remarked, Western scholars have tended to see Suhrawardī as a mystic, a "gnostic," or a "theosopher." In order to demonstrate, therefore, the existence of a well-defined systematic side to the philosophy of illumination, we have made the attempt to provide the nonspecialist reader with a balanced and philosophically meaningful English translation of the entire text of *The Philosophy of Illumination,* including its neglected but philosophically essential section on logic.[23]

Therefore, we have tried to translate the text into philosophically rigorous contemporary American English with as little deviation from the literal sense as possible. Technical terms are translated consistently, as far as we are able. Whenever possible, we have used the terminology that is standard in translations and analyses of Greek and medieval European philosophy. In a few places, Suhrawardī's terminology does not translate neatly into standard terms; these problems are discussed in the notes as they occur. We have tried to avoid colorful but speculative renderings like "theosophy" and "oriental." This is especially true because we have almost always deferred to the judgment of the early commentators Shahrazūrī and Quṭb al-Dīn Shīrāzī as to the meaning of the text. Their interpretations seem to us to be almost always sound, philosophically well informed, and temperate; and they do not, in general, support the more lurid renderings. We have not annotated heavily and have not identified Suhrawardī's usually anonymous quotations except for those from the Qurʾān. When he cites "the followers of the Peripatetics," he is usually referring to Avicenna.

The title we have chosen, *The Philosophy of Illumination,* reflects these principles. *Ḥikma* is literally translated as "wisdom," but in Arabic it also came to replace *falsafa* for "philosophy." This was partly because there is a tendency in Arabic for native Arabic words to supplant loan words, but it was also because *falsafa* had come to have connotations of atheism and materialism. Suhrawardī is using *ḥikma* in a general sense of "philosophy," as is shown by such expressions as *ḥakīm baḥḥāth* to refer to philosophers of the Peripatetic style. *Ishrāq* means either "the rising of the Sun" or "Illumination" and is used in the second sense in this book.

There are two exceptions to these policies. First, in the first and second discourses of the logic, Suhrawardī uses a deliberately nonstandard set of logical terms. We have devised our own set of nonstandard logical terms literally translating his. Where he uses the usual terms, as he often does, we use conventional terminology. Second, in some passages Suhrawardī uses a high-flown religio-poetic Arabic, particularly in the introduction and the concluding discourses. We have translated these into a slightly archaic liturgical English and have been a little looser in the translation where no philosophical point seemed to be at issue.

We occasionally translate variants in the notes if the variant differs significantly in meaning from the reading we follow—mostly they do not—and the variant is clearly more than the idiosyncratic reading of a single manuscript. In most cases, this means that the notes document cases where the meaning of our text differs significantly from that of Corbin's edition.

The edition

Suhrawardī has been exceptionally well served by the editors of his text, going back to the scholars of the seventh A.H./thirteenth C.E. century, who fixed the two major recensions of *The Philosophy of Illumination.* The textual tradition is documented by a series of excellent manuscripts, both of the text in isolation and of the two early commentaries. As we prepared the edition, we found that the textual problems we faced were documented as early as Quṭb al-Dīn's commentary. It is a pleasure to acknowledge a debt incurred over eight centuries to the previous editors who so carefully and skillfully preserved this text: Shahrazūrī, whose commentary preserves the older "Persian" tradition of the text; the unknown thirteenth-century editor whose "corrected" text is preserved in Quṭb al-Dīn's commentary; Quṭb al-Dīn himself, who carefully documented the textual traditions available to him; the obscure nineteenth-century scholar Muḥammad-Aḥmad, who edited and copied the fine Yale manuscript of Shahrazūrī's commentary; his contemporary Asadu'llāh Harātī and Muḥammad ibn ᶜAbd al-ᶜAlī al-Darjazīnī, the editor and copyist of the magnificent lithograph of Quṭb al-Dīn's commentary; and finally Henry Corbin, whose edition of *The Philosophy of Illumination* has been the basis for most modern study of the work. It is sobering to realize that, despite the pretensions of modern scholarship, we and Corbin have done little more than reproduce the editions of *The Philosophy of Illumination* preserved in the commentaries of Shahrazūrī and Quṭb al-Dīn respectively—and where modern translations have deviated from the interpretive tradition established by Shahrazūrī, it has almost certainly been for the worse.

During Ziai's research for his text-edition of Shahrazūrī's *Sharḥ ḥikmat al-ishrāq,* he identified manuscripts of the text and the two main Arabic commentaries unknown to Corbin when he had worked on his edition. Corbin's edition, he discovered, represents a corrected and regularized text produced by an unknown seventh/thirteenth-century editor and best attested in the commentary of Quṭb al-Dīn Shīrāzī. We refer to this edition as the "corrected" text. It is this version of the text that is generally known to scholars because it was the basis of Quṭb al-Dīn's commentary, which was the version generally studied even before the publication of its lithograph edition, and because Quṭb al-Dīn's commentary was the main basis of Corbin's edition. The text preserved in Shahrazūrī's commentary represents a different tradition, which we refer to as the "Persian" recension. In truth, the differences between the two early versions are minimal. The Persian recension is looser in its Arabic grammar and contains a number of minor variants that are obvious slips of the pen. The grammatical lapses are in things like agreement in case and gender—notorious weak points for Persians writing or speaking another language. The slips of the pen generally concern fine philosophical points, usually only noticeable after the kind of examination necessary to translate or comment on the text; the sentence looks right on first examination, but when one thinks about it there is obviously something wrong. In the corrected recension—the version represented by the Corbin edition and the lithograph of Quṭb al-Dīn's commentary—the Arabic grammatical lapses tend to be corrected and the slips of the pen are usually fixed. In some cases, however, the Persian recension is clearly superior, as in its use of *anāʾīya,* "ego," in place of the corrected recension's more familiar *anānīya.*[24] Quṭb al-Dīn states that he had used a manuscript copied from a copy read to Suhrawardī, a standard scholarly method of correcting a manuscript. This is evidently the manuscript referred to throughout the commentary as *ba^{c}ḍ al-nusakh,* whose readings almost always agree with those of the Persian recension. Quṭb al-Dīn was aware of the formal authority of this manuscript, but he evidently preferred the corrected recension with its greater number of manuscripts and its grammatical and philosophical clarity.

We believe that the most probable explanation for the existence of two distinct, very early textual traditions is that the Persian recension represents *The Philosophy of Illumination* as Suhrawardī wrote it. The grammatical and textual lapses reflect Suhrawardī's Persian background and the unsettled and hurried conditions under which he wrote. At some point—presumably in the mid-thirteenth century C.E., when Suhrawardī's works had become popular—an unknown scholar prepared a new and corrected edition of the work in which some, though hardly all, of the grammatical irregularities were dealt with and the slips of the pen were carefully corrected, resulting in a text that is grammatically adequate and philosophically excellent.

Thus, we believe that our text represents an older recension, though not one that differs dramatically from the familiar text of Quṭb al-Dīn and Corbin. It is based on Corbin's text but deviates from it to follow the older Persian tradition of the text. Indeed, since the corrections made by the unknown editor of the corrected text are generally well informed and judicious, in a sense our text is inferior to that of Corbin—although, if we are right, it is closer to what Suhrawardī actually wrote. It also corrects some errors in the Corbin edition—both typographical errors and cases where pieces of commentary have been included in the text. Deviations from Corbin are always noted in the critical apparatus. We have not duplicated Corbin's apparatus, so those interested in the full documentation of the text will need to consult both our edition and Corbin's and will probably wish to consult Quṭb al-Dīn and Shahrazūrī as well. We have followed Corbin's edition in such matters as paragraph divisions and numbering. Section titles usually, though not always, follow Corbin. Where they do not, they are generally taken—sometimes with abridgement—from Quṭb al-Dīn. We have used modern Arabic orthography and punctuation.

In general, Corbin tends to use masculine forms of verbs, a practice not uncommon in dotted medieval manuscripts such as ل (described below). Since masculine and feminine verbs often differ only in the dotting, we have changed them in accordance with the rules of Arabic grammar but have not given them as variants in the notes.

Manuscript sources

Manuscripts and editions of the text of Ḥikmat al-ishrāq

ط: Henry Corbin's text-edition of Suhrawardī's *The Philosophy of Illumination,* in *Opera Metaphysica et Mystica* (1952; reprint, Tehran: Bibliothèque Iranienne, 1977), 2:1–260. This edition is based on the lithographed edition of Quṭb al-Dīn Shīrāzī's *Sharḥ ḥikmat al-ishrāq* and on several manuscripts described by Corbin (French introduction, 71–79), including س, which is described below. This edition represents the corrected recension described above and differs from the Persian recension of تح and ل mostly only in respect to minor textual variants, all indicated in the notes to the present edition. Many of the discrepancies are additions to Suhrawardī's text taken from Quṭb al-Dīn's commentary (described below), where the text *(matn)* and commentary *(sharḥ)* are often distinguished only by a line drawn over the passages of the text. This common device in running commentaries is used in manuscripts and the lithograph of Quṭb al-Dīn's commentary. In many cases, however, the lithograph edition erroneously extends the line over the commentary, which probably led Corbin to consider the commentator's additions as parts of the text. A careful examination of manuscript يش resolves the few ambiguities, which are recorded in the notes to the present edition.

يو: Los Angeles, UCLA, Special Collections: Minasian Collection of Arabic and Persian Manuscripts, no. M1111. The manuscript is 18 by 12.5 cm, consisting of 139 folios, 15 lines per page, written in a scribal *naskh* script. It has been briefly described by M. T. Dānish-Pazhūh in *Fihrist-i nuskhahā-yi Dānishgāh-e UCLA,* p. 214, who dates it to the eighth/fourteenth century. The copy is not complete, consisting of almost all of Part One minus the last section (corresponding to numbered sections 1–105). This copy differs from the text part of ل in only a limited number of cases, all noted in the present edition. This copy, however, helps to establish the text of *The Philosophy of Illumination* and to separate Quṭb al-Dīn's *sharḥ* from the *matn.*

Manuscripts of Shahrazūrī's Sharḥ ḥikmat al-ishrāq

As noted above, this commentary contains the Persian recension of the text.

تح: Tehran University, Central Library, Collection of Manuscripts, no. 2981. The oldest manuscript of the work available to us, it was produced in the late decades of the seventh/thirteenth century and is not among those used by Corbin in his edition. It has 212 folios, each 20.5 by 13.5 cm with 19 lines of text. It is incomplete, including Shahrazūrī's commentary only on the second *qism* of *The Philosophy of Illumination*. It is most probably one of the several copies used in the production of ل, with which it is almost identical. This manuscript has been given primary status in the preparation of Part Two of the present text-edition, but only in close association firstly with ل and secondly, in a few problematic cases (mostly due to ink smears from facing folios), with س. Some of its folios have been exchanged at a later date; it was a common practice in medieval manuscript collections to replace damaged or missing folios of a work. Thus, there are two distinct styles of calligraphy and two types of paper utilized. All but 9 of the 212 folios are written in a scribal *naskh* style characteristic of late seventh/thirteenth and early eighth/fourteenth centuries. Folios covering the beginning of Part Two to the end of Discussion 2, Chapter 11 (corresponding to section numbers 107–72, plus the *sharḥ*) are written in this hand. The next six folios are written in a scribal *ta^c^līq*, a near-cursive *nasta^c^līq* resembling calligraphic styles used only from the eleventh/seventeenth centuries on. These corrections cover the *sharḥ* on Discussion 2, Chapter 11, plus portions of paragraph number 172 of the *matn* plus its *sharḥ*. The rest of the manuscript is in the older scribal *naskh* style, with the exception of one folio that covers paragraphs 266–71, plus the two final folios of the work, which are in the same later scribal *ta^c^līq* style. This means that the colophon, bearing the date 727 A.H. (1326–27 C.E.) as the completion of the copy, is in the later hand. However, our assumption is that the "repairs" were made based on a copy dated 727 A.H. This date is consistent with the older portions of the manuscript, and these portions are consistent in style and format with other manuscripts of that period. For example, the Āstān-i Quds manuscript of Ibn Kammūna's *Al-tanqīhāt fī sharḥ al-talwīhāt,* a commentary on another work of Suhrawardī, which was intended as a textbook for the Niẓāmīya Madrasa in Baghdad, is dated 703 A.H./1303 C.E. and is in a similar scribal *naskh*.

ل : New Haven, Yale University, Beinecke Rare Books and Manuscripts Library: Landberg Collection, no. 7. It is briefly described in *Arabic Manuscripts in the Yale University Library,* compiled by Leon Nemoy (New Haven, Conn.: 1957), 125. This manuscript is 25.5 by 19 cm, consisting of 239 folios with 25 lines per page. It is written in a superbly executed *naskh* calligraphy typical of many finely produced manuscripts and lithograph printings from nineteenth-century Iran. It was completed on Saturday, the 4th of Jumādā al-Ākhar, 1296 A.H./1879 C.E., by

Muḥammad-Aḥmad. This manuscript is not a simple "scribal copy" but is a carefully edited and collated copy based on an unspecified number of manuscripts. On numerous pages, "variants" are given in the margins in the following forms: *nuskha, fī nuskha, fī akthar al-nusakh.* In many instances the "editor" offers his opinion on possible alternative, "more correct" readings of difficult or ambiguous passages by adding "perhaps . . . is more correct" *(wa laᶜalla . . . aṣaḥḥ).* In several instances the note "Collation was completed with the original up to this point" *(balagha muqābala ᶜalā aṣlihi)* is added on the margin, indicating that when a segment was completed it was read against the sources used in the preparation of the manuscript and that two or perhaps more persons were involved in its production. The copy is indeed very well produced, with few orthographic or other errors. We have used this edition as the principal copy for Part One of the present text-edition. In a few instances we have followed Corbin's edition where its reading was clearly superior to that of تح and ل; but in general, تح and ل, supported by س (described below), establish the present edition of *The Philosophy of Illumination.*

س : Istanbul, Saray Ahmet III, no. 3230. The manuscript is 26.5 by 15 cm, consisting of 367 folios, 19 lines per page, written in a handsome scribal *taᶜlīq* script. It bears the stamp of Bāyazīd II (ninth/fifteenth century). This manuscript was first identified and described by Helmut Ritter[25] and was one of the manuscripts used by Henry Corbin in his text-edition of Suhrawardī's *The Philosophy of Illumination.* There is a near-total agreement between س and ل, which leads us to believe that س was copied from a manuscript—say, م—that was a basis of the carefully edited and collated manuscript ل.

Editions and manuscripts of *Quṭb al-Dīn Shīrāzī's* Sharḥ ḥikmat al-ishrāq

Quṭb al-Dīn's commentary employs the corrected recension followed by Corbin in his edition. Quṭb al-Dīn, however, also had access to at least one manuscript copied from a manuscript that had been read to Suhrawardī, representing the Persian recension. He systematically notes their divergences, which are, in general, the more important differences between our edition and that of Corbin.

يش: Los Angeles, UCLA, Special Collections: Minasian Collection of Arabic and Persian Manuscripts, No. M881. The manuscript is 20.5 by 11.5 cm, consisting of 324 folios, 19 lines per page, written in a scribal *naskh* and *taḥrīrī naskh* scripts. It has been briefly described by

M.-T. Dānish-Pazhūh in *Fihrist-i nuskhahā-yi Dānishgāh-e yū sī il ay,* 250, and is dated 881 A.H./1476 C.E. The manuscript is very carefully copied and collated, with variants noted as: *nuskha, fī nuskha, fī akthar al-nusakh, fī ba*ᶜ*ḍ al-nusakh.* In a few instances, descriptions and explanations are added on the margins by the scribe himself, indicating that it had been produced by a learned editor. This manuscript is almost identical with the lithograph edition of copy ش, described below, but is in many ways a better copy since it is mostly free from ش's orthographical errors.

ش: Tehran, lithograph edition, 1315 A.H./1897 C.E. The edition is 25 by 17 cm, in 564 pages, with 19 lines per page. It is written in a superb *naskh* by the calligrapher Muḥammad ibn Mīrzā ᶜAbd al-ᶜAlī Darjazīnī. Mūlla Ṣadrā's *Ta*ᶜ*līqāt* ᶜ*alā sharḥ ḥikmat al-ishrāq,* plus al-Fārābī's *Al-jam*ᶜ *bayn ra*ʾ*yayn al-ḥakīmayn* are printed on the margins. Evidently, يش had been one of the copies used in the preparation of ش, and the two are here employed to establish the *matn* of *The Philosophy of Illumination* in the present edition. Variants are given in the notes.

In sum, the manuscripts ل, س, تح, and يو form a consistent, closely related family representing the Persian recension of the text. The Corbin edition ط, the Tehran lithograph of Quṭb al-Dīn's commentary ش, and the manuscript يش represent the corrected edition.

Finally, while a widely employed standard for printing Arabic texts has not yet been established, a brief note on orthography and style is here given:

(1) In general, we have not added all *shaddas, hamzat al-qaṭ*ᶜ*as,* or extensive vocalization, following common practice in modern Arabic editions, except to avoid ambiguity. For example, a *shadda* is added to the definite verbal noun of form 3 of the geminated verb m-s-s, التّماس, to distinguish it from the indefinite verbal noun of form 8 of the verb l-m-s, التماس. *Hamzat al-qaṭ*ᶜ*as* are added to verbal nouns of the verbs a-m-r, a-kh-dh, and so on, as was done in medieval manuscripts. Passive voices of verbs are indicated, and the common practice of adding a *ḍamma* to the feminine singular *ukhrā* is observed.

(2) Of the possible forms ههنا, هيهنا, and هاهنا, the latter is the one used most widely in the manuscript traditions named here, though not consistently so. We have chosen هاهنا but have not given variants in the notes.

(3) The name Plato appears both as افلاطن and افلاطون. We have chosen افلاطون but have not given variants.

(4) Persian names and loan words have been vocalized, e.g.: أُرديبِهِشت, خُرْداد.

(5) The Persian term اسفندارمذ also appears as اسفندارمد; we have chosen اسفندارمذ but have not given variants.

(6) The name جابرص (a "city" in هورقليا) also appears as جابرس in the same manuscript, and the variation has been retained.

List of abbreviations in the *apparatus criticus*

ل Manuscript of Shahrazūrī's *Sharḥ ḥikmat al-ishrāq,* Yale University, Beinecke Rare Books and Manuscripts Library, Landberg Collection, no. 7.

س Manuscript of Shahrazūrī's *Sharḥ ḥikmat al-ishrāq,* Istanbul, Saray Ahmet III, no. 3230.

تح Manuscript of Shahrazūrī's *Sharḥ ḥikmat al-ishrāq,* Tehran University, Central Library, Collection of Manuscripts, no. 2981.

ط Printed text of Suhrawardī's *Ḥikmat al-ishrāq,* ed. Henry Corbin, in *Opera Metaphysica et Mystica* (1952; reprint, Tehran: Bibliothèque Iranienne, 1977), 2:1–260.

يو Manuscript of Suhrawardī's *Ḥikmat al-ishrāq,* UCLA, Minasian Collection of Arabic and Persian Manuscripts, no. M1111.

يش Manuscript of Quṭb al-Dīn Shīrāzī's *Sharḥ ḥikmat al-ishrāq,* UCLA, Minasian Collection of Arabic and Persian Manuscripts, no. M881.

ش Lithograph edition of Quṭb al-Dīn Shīrāzī's *Sharḥ ḥikmat al-ishrāq,* Tehran, 1315 A.H. [1897].

م Explanations given by us in the notes.

ص Page.

س Line.

ح Margin of a manuscript, or notes in printed texts.

[ ] When used in the text, these indicate an addition to the text that we deemed necessary for consistency in syntax; when used specifically in section headings, they indicate additions to the text by Corbin based on Quṭb al-Dīn's *Sharḥ ḥikmat al-ishrāq* and at times modified by us for consistency; and when used in the notes, they indicate explanations added by us, as distinguished from textual variants and from references to Qurʾānic passages used in the text.

Shahrazūrī's Introduction

When Corbin published his edition and his translation of The Philosophy of Illumination, *he included the introduction to Shahrazūrī's commentary as an introduction to Suhrawardī's text. What Shahrazūrī has to say about the text is of considerable interest, since it set the agenda for all later interpretation of the work; we have therefore included a slightly abridged translation of Shahrazūrī's introduction here. Since the Arabic text is readily available in Corbin's edition and in Ziai's edition of Shahrazūrī's* Sharḥ ḥikmat al-ishrāq, *we have not reprinted it here.*

◆ ◆ ◆

O God, the Subtle! Make easy the path and do not make it hard.
In the Name of God, the Merciful, the Compassionate!

Exalted art Thou, O emanating Source of pre-eternal bounty, Giver of order to eternal existence, Bestower of noble and holy essences, Perfector of precious human souls, Mover of the celestial spheres by their everlasting and exalted longings, Joiner of the lower pillars by lofty active powers. From those pairs and mixtures Thou didst create forms straight and curved, loose and interwoven—mineral, plant, and animal all together. Then didst Thou complete creation with man, that creature both joyful and oppressed. Blessed be Thou in the glorious splendor of Thine unmoved unity. Exalted art Thou in the divine grandeur of Thine imperishable singleness. . . .

Now, the purpose for which the rational soul descended from the lofty world of the intellect to this dark and lowly world was to become perfected by true science and knowledge, for it does not at first have these. Since it can only acquire these sciences by long toil and effort, it requires the cooperation of the body and its faculties. The body requires for its subsistence food, clothing, shelter, and the pleasant things associated with them. It is necessary that these things be selected, limited, and acquired in moderation, lest they lead the soul into one of the extremes of deficiency or excess, thus, in the first instance, defeating the purpose for which the bodily pleasures were created, becoming the cause that strengthens the attachment and inclination of the soul to the world of exile, and destroying its perfection. In the second instance, the body—whose survival is a cause by which the perfection that leads to divine union is acquired—will be harmed. Therefore, we need ethics, directly and indirectly, because preoccupation with the external and internal senses and with desire and anger is a veil for the soul and will, in that state, prevent it from acquiring the sciences. Even if they are attained, love for this lowly world will become firmly fixed in the substance of the soul, and its attachment to the world will strengthen. That love will cause pains for a long period of time and prevent the pure enjoyment of the intellectual pleasures. [But] if, when the soul is separated from the body, the realities of existents are fully inscribed within it, it will break the connection to the lower world and its weakness and will carry them up to the company on high. There it will attain its full reward, enjoying the bliss of the pre-eternal beauty and the happiness of unending splendor, for it will have acquired the correspondence bringing about union. [As] it has been said, "Lineage is a condition of association." [But] if the soul is in the opposite condition when it is separated from the body, its fate will be the opposite.

You are aware that human perfection consists in the theoretical sciences, that the science of practical wisdom is also theoretical, and that improvement of character is acquired by turning the soul away from distractions and by purifying it from hindrances in order to become perfected. Therefore, human happiness is conditioned on acquiring sciences. The sciences are divided into two primary classes: the first is true sciences and the second customary or linguistic sciences. By "true sciences" I mean those that do not change because their subject does not change, for the change in a science is due to the change in its subject. If the subject of the science is unchanging, the science will also be unchanging—for example, the sciences treating of the Creator, the intellects and souls, the spheres, the universals, and the elements and their compounds. The customary or linguistic sciences are the opposite of the true sciences and are those that change with the alteration of their subjects, such as grammar, lexicography, poetics, rhetoric, epistolography, and other such literary sciences. These change and alter with the destruction of peoples and religions and the languages associated with these sciences. The most important cause for their disappearance is the fall of the empires belonging to those peoples and religious communities and their subjugation by their enemies. In our age, Greek grammar, poetics, and epistolography have vanished, along with the customary sciences of the Persians, Egyptians, Babylonians, and other ancient nations. As for the science of law, which is political science, it has not vanished completely, but some of its branches have fallen into desuetude and its regulations have been changed and altered as it moved from nation to nation. The same is true of the science of jurisprudence.[1] There is, however, a mystery in this to which we will refer later, God willing.

Now that you know this, you ought also to know that true perfection can only be attained by true knowledge, for true knowledge is unchanging. Thus, the soul can behold the unchanging object of that knowledge after separation from the body. That which is changeable cannot be beheld after separation from the body, so it cannot be the means for the attainment of true perfection, though it might be the means for the attainment of estimative[2] perfection. In short, we know that happiness is conditioned on true sciences and not on the other sort. Next, the true sciences are divided into two classes: first, revealed and intuitive and, second, discursive and speculative.

The first class consists of those in which the spiritual and incorporeal entities are beheld directly and are known neither by thought and the linking of syllogistic proofs nor by the devising of an essential or descriptive definition. Instead, they are known by successive, differing rays of light stealing the soul from the body so that they can be seen, suspended and incorporeal, and that which is above them can be seen with the divine providence. Very few of the philosophers attain this intuitive philosophy, for it is acquired only by some virtuous individual divine philosophers. Among them were the Ancients who came in the time before Aristotle—Agathadæmon, Hermes, Empedocles, Pythagoras, Socrates, Plato, and other learned Ancients whose learning and precedence are attested by the different nations. Though they devoted their efforts to the intuitive philosophy, they did not lack the speculative; for their investigations, writings, and hints were of use to Aristotle, the master of speculation, who corrected and expanded them. For this reason the First Teacher [Aristotle] said, "The early philosophers did true philosophy. Though they may have erred in some physical matters, they excelled in solving questions of theology."[3] The Moderns—those who have come since Aristotle—are weak in their intuitive philosophy, for Aristotle has distracted them with speculation and rules, with refutation and rebuttal, questions and answers, and other such matters that keep them from acquiring intuitive philosophy. This is especially true when speculative philosophy is combined with a love of leadership. Thus, speculative thought has continually increased and intuition diminished and grown rare up to nearly our own time. After such a long time, the paths of their wayfaring have become overgrown; they are no longer able to attain direct vision of the incorporeal lights, and their souls cannot attain subtleness, whether in the separation that follows the destruction of the body or before separation. The proofs have been erased before them, and they can no longer see clearly the other path to their goal.

The steady decline of intuitive philosophy continued until our age, when one man arose [who was] prepared for intuitive philosophy and dissatisfied with pure speculation. He sought to acquire some portion of the true philosophy as it ought to be known. It was difficult for him, for the path leading an individual to that goal had been forgotten. His quest was blocked and troubled, until the star of happiness arose and the morn of philosophy dawned from the horizon of certitude. The lights of realities shone from the all-highest spot with the manifestation of our master. He is the king of reality and the guide on the path, the place where subtle truths become evident, the source of the emanation of realities, the mine of wisdom, the master of spiritual resolve. He was strengthened by the Kingdom and joined himself to the world of might. He was the remnant of the pious forefathers, the prince of the learned of the latter generation, the most learned of the Ancients and Moderns, quintessence of philosophers and divine sages: Shihāb al-Milla wa al-Ḥaqq wa al-Dīn al-Suhrawardī—may God make holy his soul and let the spirit flow over his resting place! He began to reform that which had been corrupted, bringing back to light that which had been effaced by the centuries, explaining in detail what the Ancients had summarized, commenting on what they had hinted at and told in symbols, unlocking that which had been closed up and made difficult, and reviving what had been dead and forgotten. He girded up the loins of effort to devote himself to the earliest sages, defending them and refuting those who criticized them. He went to every length to understand their views—with open eyes and well informed, not blindly or in confusion. His tools were the revelations occurring after rigorous and saintly spiritual exercises and sound and complete speculative investigations—may God be pleased with him!—for he was indeed a master of both philosophies, the intuitive and the speculative, penetrating deeply into both. Indeed, no one apprehends the peaks he scaled or the depths he plumbed. You will know this for yourself when we come to our careful study of his words and our attempt to explain his aspirations and being. He spoke of noble and hidden matters, precious mysteries locked away in treasuries, which we have heard no other mortal mention. No one else has appeared with the like, neither the philosophers nor the mystics. That is a proof that his feet were firm in wisdom and that his arm was long in philosophy, that his heart was steadfast in revelation and intuition in the science of the lights, as he said:

> The verses of love's prophethood became manifest to me.
> Before me they were sealed, but in my time they were noised abroad.[4]

You will only understand all of this if you find this path and learn some of its mysteries and states.

All the books of this great man are noble and profitable, but especially the book *The Philosophy of Illumination*—that treasury of wonders, laden with rare subtleties and useful points. On the science of theology or other sciences no book greater than it has been seen on the face of the earth, nor one nobler, sounder, more complete, or more exact. It is of great import, a noble work; but it is a hidden treasure, a rolled-up scroll. It is reached by paths reserved to it alone. Few are they who walk these paths or know them. It is not easy for most scholars who come after him to follow these paths to the book or to unravel its symbols. Such scholars are preoccupied with the affairs of the world and are too fond of and too accustomed to the words of the Peripatetics. Inevitably, this book has remained neglected and unheeded due to the difficulty of its style and the subtlety of its method. But God eased for us the marvels and wonders contained in it and unveiled to us its realities and subtle truths. To the enlightened gaze both lean and fat are manifest, and by something else both the subtle and the plain. For a long time we were stingy with the secrets of this book and revealed them to no one. We hid them and did not give them away generously. This was not out of a coarse miserliness but because of the obscurity of the style, the subtlety of its depths and investigations, and the lack of sincere students and learned individuals prepared to study it. It was due also to the death of knowledge and philosophy, to the dearth of people of learning and intellect, and the depression of the bazaar of philosophy in this age. Nevertheless, in my many journeys and wanderings through the lands and at the urgings of the receptive, the learned, and those with pure souls and high spiritual aspirations, I learned of this excellent man and was seized with a desire to know about him and study his books and his words. The intelligent were very anxious to acquire his wise sayings and exquisite poems. There were many requests to learn his paths and methods, especially those of his book *The Philosophy of Illumination.* This book should only be begun after following all the paths of knowledge and completely mastering the popular philosophy and the conventional sciences, for it is a summary of philosophy and the quintessence of knowledge, a treasury of wonders and registry of marvels. Neither I nor anyone else had found a sounder book than it for theology and mystical science. Since such was the case, I decided to compose a comprehensive commentary on its fundamental and derivative teachings, containing the principles of both intuitive and speculative philosophy. In this commentary I would correct both the superficial and the excess. I would include the discourses and sections, seeking thereby to clarify its obscurities and difficulties, to make clear the solution to its subtle points and texts, to reveal the meaning of its symbols and hints, and to investigate its principles and allusions. In my commentary I would seek to determine the reality, to hit upon the truth, to record the proof, and to ease the path for the wayfarers to the court of holiness and the presence of the Friend—those who strive to reach the divine presence, who ascend the stairway to heaven, hoping for that generous recompense and handsome reward, for the mention that gives immortality, for eternal reward. . . .

بسم الله الرحمن الرحيم

In the name of God, the Compassionate, the Merciful

[Suhrawardī's Introduction]

(1) O God, glorious is Thy mention and mighty Thy holiness. Great is Thy friend, exalted Thy majesty, and lofty Thy station. Blessings and salutation be upon all Thy chosen ones and Thy messengers, and specifically upon Muḥammad, the chosen one, the lord of mankind, he whose intercession will be heeded on Judgment Day. Enable us, then, by Thy light to be among those who have attained and who remember Thy blessings and are thankful for Thy bounty.

(2) Know, my brethren, that your frequent demands that I record the philosophy of illumination[1] have finally overcome my reluctance. Were it not for an incumbent obligation, a prior word, and a command given from a place, disobedience to which will lead to straying from the path, I would not have felt obliged to step forward and openly reveal it, for the difficulty therein is known to you. But you went on, my friends—may God direct you toward what He loves and approves of—begging me to write you a book in which I would tell what I have obtained through my intuition[2] during my retreats and visions. In every seeking soul there is a portion, be it small or great, of the light of God. Every one who strives has intuition, be it perfect or imperfect. Knowledge did not end with one people, so that the doors of heaven are shut behind them and the rest of the world is denied the possibility of obtaining more. Rather, the Giver of knowledge,[3] who stands at the "clear horizon, is not stingy with the unseen" [Qurʾān 81:23–24]. The most evil age is the one in which the carpet of striving has been rolled up, in which the movement of thought is interrupted, the door of revelations bolted, the path of visions blocked.

بِسْمِ اللّٰهِ الرَّحْمٰنِ الرَّحِيمِ

[المقدمة للسهروردى]

(١) جلّ ذكرك اللّهمّ وعظم قدسك وعزّ جارُك وعلت سُبحُاتك وتعالى جدّك! صلّ على مصطفيك واهل رسالاتك عموما، وخصوصا على محمد المصطفى سيد البشر والشفيع المشفّع فى المحشر، عليه وعليهم السلام. واجعلنا بنورك من الفائزين ولاٰلائك من الذاكرين ولنعمائك من الشاكرين.

(٢) وبعد، اعلموا اخوانى ان كثرة اقتراحكم فى تحرير «حكمة الاشراق» اوهن١ عزمى فى الامتناع وازال٢ ميلى الى الاضراب عن الاسعاف. ولولا حق لزم وكلمة سبقت وأمر ورد من محل يُفضى عصيانه الى الخروج عن السبيل لما كان لى داعية الاقدام على اظهاره، فان فيه من الصعوبة ما تعلمون؛ وما زلتم يا معشر صحبتى، وفّقكم الله لما يحبّ ويرضى، تلتمسون منّى ان اكتب لكم كتابا اذكر فيه ما حصل لى بالذوق فى خلواتى ومنازلاتى. ولكل نفس طالبة قسط من نور الله قلّ او كثر، ولكل مجتهد ذوق نقص او كمل؛ وليس العلم وقفا على قوم ليغلق بعدهم باب الملكوت ويمنع المزيد عن العالمين، بل واهب العلم الّذى هو «بالافق المبين، وما هو على الغيب بضنين»؛٣ وشر القرون ما طوى فيه بساط الاجتهاد وانقطع فيه سير الافكار وانحسم باب المكاشفات وانسدت طرق المشاهدات.

١

٥

١٠

١٥

(3) Before I wrote this book and during the times when interruptions prevented me from working on it, I wrote other books in which I have summarized for you the principles of the Peripatetics according to their method. Among these books is the short work known as *Intimations of the Tablet and the Throne*. Many principles are summarized in it, despite its brevity. Then there is my book *The Flashes of Light*.[4] I have also composed other works, some in my youth. But the present work has another method and provides a shorter path to knowledge than their method does. It is more orderly and precise, less painful to study. I did not first arrive at it through cogitation; rather, it was acquired through something else. Subsequently I sought proof for it, so that, should I cease contemplating the proof, nothing would make me fall into doubt.

(4) In all that I have said about the science of lights and that which is and is not based upon it,[5] I have been assisted by those who have traveled the path of God. This science is the very intuition of the inspired and illumined Plato, the guide and master of philosophy, and of those who came before him from the time of Hermes, "the father of philosophers," up to Plato's time, including such mighty pillars of philosophy as Empedocles, Pythagoras, and others.[6] The words of the Ancients are symbolic[7] and not open to refutation. The criticisms made of the literal sense of their words fail to address their real intentions, for a symbol cannot be refuted. This is also the basis of the Eastern[8] doctrine of light and darkness, which was the teaching of Persian philosophers such as Jamasp, Frashostar, Bozorgmehr,[9] and others before them. It is not the doctrine of the infidel Magi, nor the heresy of Mani, nor that which leads to associating other gods with God—be He exalted above any such anthropomorphism![10]

Do not imagine that philosophy has existed only in these recent times. The world has never been without philosophy or without a person possessing proofs and clear evidences to champion it. He is God's vicegerent on His earth. Thus shall it be so long as the heavens and the earth endure. The ancient and modern philosophers differ only in their use of language and their divergent habits of openness and allusiveness. All speak of three worlds,[11] agreeing on the unity of God. There is no dispute among them on fundamental questions. Even though the First

(٣) وقد رتّبت لكم قبل هذا الكتاب وفى اثنائه عند معاوقة القواطع عنه كتبا على طريقة المشّائين ولخّصت فيها قواعدهم ومن جملتها المختصر المرسوم بـ«التلويحات اللوحية والعرشية» المشتمل على قواعد كثيرة ولخّصت فيه القواعد مع صغر حجمه، ودونه «اللمحات». وصنّفت غيرهما، ومنها ما رتّبته فى أيام الصبى. وهذا سياق آخر وطريق اقرب من تلك الطريقة واضبط وانظم[٤] واقلّ اتعابا فى التحصيل. ولم يحصل لى اولا بالفكر، بل كان حصوله بأمر آخر؛ ثم طلبت الحجة حتى لو قطعت النظر عن الحجة مثلا، ما كان يشككنى فيه مشكك.

(٤) وما ذكرتُه من علم الانوار وجميع ما يبتنى عليه وغيره يساعدنى عليه كل من سلك سبيل الله عزّ وجلّ وهو ذوق امام الحكمة ورئيسها افلاطون صاحب الايد والنور؛ وكذا من قبله من زمان والد الحكماء هرمس الى زمانه من عظماء الحكماء واساطين الحكمة، مثل انباذقلس وفيثاغورس وغيرهما. وكلمات الاولين مرموزة وما ردّ عليهم وان كان يتوجه على ظاهر اقاويلهم لم يتوجه على مقاصدهم، فلا ردّ على الرمز. وعلى هذا تبتنى قاعدة الشرق فى النور والظلمة التى كانت طريقة حكماء الفرس، مثل جامسف وفرشاوشير[٥] وبزرجمهر[٦] ومن قبلهم. وهى ليست قاعدة كفرة المجوس والحاد مانى وما يفضى الى الشرك بالله تعالى وتنزه. ولا تظنّ ان الحكمة فى هذه المدة القريبة كانت لا غير، بل العالم ما خلا قطّ من[٧] الحكمة وعن شخص قائم بها عند الحجج والبيّنات، وهو خليفة الله فى ارضه، وهكذا تكون ما دامت السموات والارض. والاختلاف بين متقدّمى الحكماء ومتأخّريهم إنّما هو فى الالفاظ واختلاف عاداتهم فى التصريح والتعريض. والكل قائلون بالعوالم الثلاثة متفقون على التوحيد لا نزاع بينهم فى اصول المسائل.

Teacher [Aristotle] was very great, profound, and insightful, one ought not exaggerate about him so as to disparage his master. Among them are the messengers and lawgivers such as Agathadæmon, Hermes, Asclepius, and others.

(5) The ranks of philosophers are many, and they fall into these classes: a divine philosopher proficient in intuitive philosophy[12] but lacking discursive philosophy; a discursive philosopher lacking intuitive philosophy; a divine philosopher proficient in both intuitive philosophy and discursive philosophy; a divine philosopher proficient in intuitive philosophy but of middle ability or weak in discursive philosophy; a philosopher proficient in discursive philosophy but of middle ability or weak in intuitive philosophy; a student of both intuitive philosophy and discursive philosophy; a student of only intuitive philosophy; and a student of only discursive philosophy. Should it happen that in some period there be a philosopher proficient in both intuitive philosophy and discursive philosophy, he will be the ruler by right and the vicegerent of God. Should it happen that this not be the case, then rulership will belong to a philosopher proficient in intuitive philosophy but of middle ability in discursive philosophy. Should these qualities not coincide, rulership belongs to a philosopher who is proficient in intuitive philosophy but who lacks discursive philosophy.[13] The world will never be without a philosopher proficient in intuitive philosophy. Authority on God's earth will never belong to the proficient discursive philosopher who has not become proficient in intuitive philosophy, for the world will never be without one proficient in intuitive philosophy—one more worthy than he who is only a discursive philosopher—for the vicegerency requires direct knowledge. By this authority I do not mean political power. The leader with intuitive philosophy may indeed rule openly,[14] or he may be hidden—the one whom the multitude call "the Pole."[15] He will have authority even if he is in the deepest obscurity. When the government is in his hands, the age will be enlightened; but if the age is without divine rule, darkness will be triumphant. The best student is the student of both intuitive philosophy and discursive philosophy. Next is the student of intuitive philosophy, and then the student of discursive philosophy.

والمعلم الأوّل، وان كان كبير القدر عظيم الشأن بعيد الغور تام النظر، لا يجوز المبالغة فيه على وجه يفضى الى الازدراء[٨] باستاذه.[٩] ومن جملتهم جماعة من ارباب[١٠] السفارة والشارعين مثل اغاثاذيمون وهرمس واسقلينوس وغيرهم.

(٥) والمراتب كثيرة وهم على طبقات، وهى هذه: حكيم الهى متوغّل فى التأله عديم البحث؛ حكيم بحّاث عديم التأله؛ حكيم الهى متوغّل فى التأله والبحث؛ حكيم الهى متوغّل فى التأله متوسط فى البحث او ضعيفه؛ حكيم متوغّل فى البحث متوسط[١١] التأله او ضعيفه؛ طالب للتأله والبحث؛ طالب للتأله فحسب؛ طالب للبحث فحسب. فان اتفق فى الوقت متوغّل فى التأله والبحث، فله الرئاسة وهو خليفة الله، وان لم يتفق فالمتوغّل فى التأله المتوسط فى البحث. وان لم يتفق فالحكيم المتوغّل فى التأله عديم البحث.[١٢] ولا تخلوا الارض من[١٣] متوغّل فى التأله ابدا. ولا رئاسة فى ارض الله للباحث المتوغّل فى البحث الّذى لم يتوغّل فى التأله، فان المتوغّل فى التأله لا يخلوا عنه العالم[١٤] وهو أحق من الباحث فحسب، اذ لا بد للخلافة من التلقى ولست اعنى بهذه الرئاسة التغلب، بل قد يكون الامام المتأله مستوليا ظاهرا،[١٥] وقد يكون خفيا، وهو الّذى سمّاه الكافة «القطب»، فله الرئاسة وان كان فى غاية الخمول. واذا كانت السياسة بيده، فيكون[١٦] الزمان نوريا؛ واذا خلا الزمان عن تدبير الهى، كانت الظلمات غالبة. واجود الطلبة طالب التأله والبحث، ثم طالب التأله ثم طالب البحث.

(6) This book of ours is for the student of both intuitive philosophy and discursive philosophy. There is nothing in it for the discursive philosopher not given to, and not in search of, intuitive philosophy. We only discuss this book and its symbols with the one who has mastered intuitive philosophy or who seeks it. The reader of this book must have reached at least the stage in which the divine light has descended upon him—not just once, but regularly. No one else will find any profit in it. So, whoever wishes to learn only discursive philosophy, let him follow the method of the Peripatetics, which is fine and sound for discursive philosophy by itself. We have nothing to say to such a person, nor do we discuss Illuminationist principles with him.[16] Indeed, the system of the Illuminationists cannot be constructed without recourse to luminous inspirations, for some of their principles are based upon such lights. Should Illuminationists fall into doubt about these principles, they will overcome it by climbing the ladder of the soul.[17] Just as by beholding sensible things we attain certain knowledge about some of their states and are thereby able to construct valid sciences like astronomy, likewise we observe certain spiritual things and subsequently base divine sciences upon them. He who does not follow this way knows nothing of philosophy and will be a plaything in the hands of doubts.

We have reduced the famous "tool"[18] that guards thought from error to a small number of very useful rules. These are sufficient for the intelligent and for those who seek illumination. Whoever wishes to learn the details of this science—which is merely a tool—should consult the more detailed books.[19]

The present work is divided into only two parts.[20]

(٦) وكتابنا هذا لطالبى التأله والبحث، وليس للباحث الّذى لم يتأله او لم يطلب التأله فيه نصيب. ولا نباحث فى هذا الكتاب ورموزه إلاّ مع المجتهد المتأله او الطالب للتأله واقلّ درجات القارى[١٧] لهذا الكتاب ان يكون قد ورد عليه البارق الالهى وصار وروده ملكة له، وغيره لا ينتفع به اصلا. فمن اراد البحث وما فيه[١٨] فعليه بطريقة المشائين، فانها حسنة للبحث وحده محكمة، وليس لنا معه كلام ومباحثة فى القواعد الاشراقية؛ بل الاشراقيون لا ينتظم امرهم دون سوانح نورانية[١٩] فان من هذه القواعد ما تتبنى عليه هذه[٢٠] لانوار حتى ان وقع لهم فى الاصول شك يزول عنهم بالسلم المخلّعة. وكما انّا شاهدنا المحسوسات وتيقّنا بعض احوالها ثم بنينا عليها علوما صحيحة، كالهيئة وغيرها، فكذا نشاهد من الروحانيات اشياء ثم نبنى عليها العلوم الالهية.[٢١] ومن ليس هذا سبيله فليس من الحكمة فى شىء وستلعب به الشكوك.

والآلة المشهورة الواقية للفكر جعلناها ههنا مختصرة مضبوطة بضوابط قليلة العدد كثيرة الفائدة[٢٢] وهى كافية للذكى ولطالب الاشراق. ومن اراد التفصيل فى العلم الّذى هو الآلة فليرجع الى الكتب المفصّلة.

ومقصودنا فى هذا الكتاب ينحصر فى قسمين.

PART ONE

The Rules of Thought, in Three Discourses

The First Discourse

Knowledge and definition [comprising seven rules]

Rule one

[On how the word signifies the meaning[1]]

(7) The use of a word to signify its whole conventional meaning is called "intended signification." Its use to signify part of the meaning is called "implicit signification." Its use to signify a concomitant of the meaning is called "concomitant signification."[2] Signification by intention includes concomitant signification, because nothing in existence is without concomitants.[3] It does not have to include signification by implication, because some things do not have parts. The general does not signify the specific in its specificity. If someone says, "I saw an animal," he may also say, "I did not see a man," but he cannot say, "I did not see a body, or something that moves by volition."

القسم الأوّل

فى ضوابط الفكر

وفيه ثلاث مقالات

المقالة الأولى
فى المعارف والتعريف

وفيها[١] ضوابط سبعة.

الضابط الأوّل

[فى دلالة اللفظ على المعنى]

(٧) هو ان اللفظ دلالته على المعنى الّذى وُضع بازائه هى دلالة القصد، وعلى جزء المعنى دلالة الحيطة، وعلى لازم المعنى دلالة التطفّل؛ ولا تخلوا دلالة قصد عن متابعة دلالة تطفّل اذ ليس فى الوجود ما لا لازم له؛ ولكنها قد تخلوا[٢] عن دلالة الحيطة،[٣] اذ من الاشياء ما لا جزء له، والعام لا يدلّ على الخاص بخصوصه. فمن قال «رأيت حيوانا» فله ان يقول «ما رأيت انسانا»، ولا يمكنه ان يقول «ما رأيت جسما» او «متحركا بالارادة» مثلا.

Rule two

[On the division between conception and assent][4]

(8) If you apprehend a thing absent from you, you can only apprehend it—in that sense appropriate to this context—by having an image[5] of its reality in you. If you know something without having some trace occur in you, then the states before knowing and after are identical. If you have a trace of it that does not correspond to [the thing], then you have not known it as it is. Therefore, there must be some correspondence in what you know. That trace in you is the image. We call the meaning that can validly correspond to the many the "general meaning." The word that signifies it is the "general word," such as the word "man" and its meaning. If what the word signifies cannot in itself be conceived to be multiple, then it is called "the individualizing meaning," and the word that signifies it is called the "individualizing word," such as the name Zayd and its meaning. A meaning that is included in something else is called "the inferior meaning" in relation to that thing.[6]

Rule three

[On quiddities]

(9) A "reality"[7] is either "simple"—having no parts in the mind—or "not simple"—having parts. For example, [an] animal is compounded from body and something that causes it to live.[8] The first—that is, body—is the "general part"[9] because, if it is taken in the mind with "animal," "body" is more general than "animal" and "animal" is lower in relation to it. The second is the "specific part" of the thing and belongs to it alone.[10] The meaning specific to the thing may be equal to the thing (such as capacity for speech[11] in man) or may be more specific than the thing (such as being male to man). The reality may have "separable accidents," such as actual laughter in man, or may have "concomitant accidents."[12]

الضابط الثانى

[فى مقسّم التصوّر والتصديق]

(٨) هو ان الشئ الغائب عنك اذا ادركته فإنمّا ادراكه، على ما يليق لهذا الموضع، هو بحصول مثال حقيقته فيك. فان الشئ الغائب ذاته اذا علمته، ان لم يحصل منه أثر فيك فاستوى حالتا ما قبل العلم وما بعده؛ وان حصل منه أثر فيك ولم يطابق فما علمته كما هو، فلا بدّ من المطابقة من جهة ما علمت، فالأمر الّذى فيك مثاله. والمعنى الصالح فى نفسه لمطابقة الكثيرين اصطلحنا عليه بـ«المعنى العام» واللفظ الدال عليه هو «اللفظ العام»، كلفظ الانسان ومعناه؛ والمفهوم من النفس اذ لم يتصوّر فيه الشركة لنفسه اصلا هو «المعنى الشاخص»، والنفس ايضا هى عليه باعتباره يسمّى اللفظ الشاخص، كاسم زيد ومعناه. وكل معنى يشمله غيره فهو بالنسبة اليه سميّناه «المعنى المنحط».

الضابط الثالث

[فى الماهيات]

(٩) هو ان كل «حقيقة» فاما «بسيطة»، وهى التى لا جزء لها فى العقل، او «غير بسيطة»، وهى التى لها جزء كالحيوان، فانّه مركب من جسم وشئ يوجب حياته؛ والأوّل «جزء عام»، اى اذا أُخذ هو والحيوان فى الذهن كان هو، اى الجسم، اعم من الحيوان والحيوان منحط بالنسبة اليه؛ والثانى هو «الجزء الخاص» الّذى لا يكون إلاّ له. والمعنى الخاص بالشئ يجوز ان يساويه، كاستعداد النطق للانسان، ويجوز ان يكون اخص منه، كالرجولية له. والحقيقة قد تكون لها «عوارض مفارقة»، كالضحك بالفعل للانسان، وقد تكون لها «عوارض لازمة».

The complete concomitant is the concomitant related essentially to the reality—for example, the relation of the three angles to the triangle. Even in the imagination, it is impossible to avoid predicating the three angles to the triangle. The reason for the triangle having three angles cannot be some other cause; for, were this the case, the three angles might or might not attach to the triangle. In that case, there could be a real triangle without three angles—which is absurd.[13]

Rule four

[On the difference between essential and separable accidents]

(10) If you wish to distinguish what adheres in a reality necessarily and essentially from what adheres in it through an efficient cause, you must contemplate the reality alone and avert your gaze from everything else. That which it would be absurd to remove from the reality is dependent on the reality and is necessitated and caused by the reality itself. If its cause were something other than the reality, it could either adhere in or be removed from the reality. Among the signs of the part is that it is thought prior to thinking the whole and that it plays a role in giving reality to the whole. A part by which a thing is described—for example, animality for man—is called "essential" by the followers of the Peripatetics. About such things, we will mention only what is necessary. The thought of the accident,[14] concomitant or separate, is posterior to the thought of the reality, and the reality plays a role in realizing its existence. The accident may be more general than the thing (like the ability to walk in relation to man) or may be specific to it (such as ability to laugh in relation to man).

Rule five

[Stating that the universal is not existent outside the mind]

(11) The "universal meaning" has no reality outside the mind. If it had, it would have an identity by which it would be distinguished from everything else and which would not be shared. It would thus become a

واللازم التام ما يجب نسبته الى الحقيقة لذاتها، كنسبة الزوايا الثلاث للمثلث[٤] فانها ممتنعة الرفع فى الوهم؛ وليس ان فاعلا جعل المثلث ذا زوايا ثلاث، اذ لو كان كذا لكانت ممكنة اللحوق واللالحوق بالمثلث، وكان يجوز تحقق المثلث دونها، وهو محال.

الضابط الرابع

[فى الفرق بين الاعراض الذاتية والمفارقة]

(١٠) هو ان كل حقيقة اذا اردت ان تعرف ما الّذى يلزمها لذاتها بالضرورة دون الحاق فاعل وما الّذى يلحقها من غيرها، فانظر الى الحقيقة وحدها واقطع النظر عن غيرها، فما يستحيل رفعه عن الحقيقة وهو تابع للحقيقة فموجبه وعلته نفس الحقيقة، اذ لو كان الموجب غيرها لكان ممكن اللحوق والرفع. والجزء من علاماته تقدم تعقله على تعقل الكل، وان له مدخلا فى تحقق الكل. والجزء الّذى يوصف به الشئ، كالحيوانية للانسان ونحوها، سمّاه اتباع المشائين «ذاتيا»، ونحن نذكر فى هذه الاشياء ما يجب. والعرض[٥] اللازم او المفارق يتأخر عن الحقيقة تعقله، والحقيقة لها مدخل مّا فى وجوده. والعرض قد يكون اعم من الشئ، كاستعداد المشى للانسان، وقد يختص به، كاستعداد الضحك للانسان.

الضابط الخامس

[فى انّ الكلى ليس بموجود فى الخارج]

(١١) هو ان «المعنى العام» لا يتحقق فى خارج الذهن اذ لو تحقق لكان له هوية يمتاز بها[٦] عن غيره لا يتصور فيها الشركة،[٧] فصارت

specific thing, whereas it has been supposed to be universal—which is a contradiction.

If the universal meaning applies to many equally, like "four" to its instances, it is called a "continuous universal." If it can apply to the thing more or less completely, as white applies to snow and ivory and other things in which it is more or less present, then it is called the "differing meaning." When many names are said of one named thing, they are called "synonymous." When many objects are named by one name and it is not used with a single meaning, we call its examples "equivocal." If a name is used with other than its meaning due to some resemblance, proximity, or concomitance, we call it "metaphorical."

Rule six
[On human knowledge]

(12) Man's knowledge is either innate or not innate. When an unknown thing cannot be made known by pointing it out or bringing it to mind and it is something that cannot be attained by the true visions of the great sages, then knowledge of it must depend on things leading to it that are in an order and that are ultimately based on innate knowledge. Otherwise, knowledge of anything that man desires to know will depend on previously obtaining an infinite number of things, and he will not even be able to obtain the first step in knowledge—which is absurd.

Rule seven
[On definition and its conditions]

(13) If something is to be defined for someone who does not know it, the definition must consist of parts that are specific to the thing—either by each part being specific to the thing, or by some part being specific to it, or by their combination.[15] A definition must be by something more apparent than the thing defined, not by something of only the same clarity or

شاخصة وقد فرضت عامة، وهو محال. والمعنى العام، اما ان يكون وقوعه على الكثيرين بالسواء، كالاربعة على شواخصها، ويسمّى «العام المتساوق»؛[٨] واما ان يكون على سبيل الأتمّ والانقص، كالابيض على الثلج والعاج وسائر ما فى[٩] الأتمّ والانقص نسمّيه «المعنى المتفاوت». واذا تكثّرت الاسماء لمسمّى واحد سُمّيت «مترادفة». واذا تكثّرت مسمّيات اسم واحد لا يكون وقوعه عليها بمعنى واحد مثله، سُمّيت «مشتركة». والاسم اذا أُطلق فى غير معناه لمشابهة او لمجاورة او ملازمة يُسمّى «مجازيا».

الضابط السادس

[فى المعارف الانسان]

(١٢) هو ان معارف الانسان فطرية او غير فطرية. والمجهول اذا لم يكفه التنبيه والاخطار بالبال وليس مما يتوصل اليه بالمشاهدة الحقة التى للحكماء العظماء، لا بدّ له من معلومات موصلة اليه ذات ترتيب موصل اليه[١٠] منتهية فى التبيُن الى الفطريات، والا يتوقف كل مطلوب للانسان على حصول ما لا يتناهى قبله ولا يحصل له أوّل علم قط، وهو محال.

الضابط السابع

[فى التعريف وشرائطه]

(١٣) هو ان الشئ اذا عُرّف لمن لا يعرف فينبغى ان يكون التعريف بأمور تخصه اما لتخصيص الآحاد او لتخصيص[١١] البعض او للاجتماع. والتعريف لا بدّ وان يكون باظهر من الشئ، لا بمثله او بما[١٢] يكون

by something more obscure than it or by something that is itself only known by means of the thing being defined. Thus, it is not correct to define "father" as "possessor of a son," because father and son are equally known or unknown: whoever knows one also knows the other. Moreover, a condition for that by means of which a thing is defined is that it be known prior to the thing defined and not concurrently with it. It is incorrect to say, "Fire is an element that resembles the soul," because the soul is something more obscure than fire. Likewise, it is incorrect to say, "The Sun is a heavenly body that rises every day," because the day is only known by the period of time marked by the rising Sun. The definition of the reality cannot be just the substitution of a word,[16] because such a substitution is only useful to someone who knows the reality but is uncertain about the meaning of the word. The definitions of relatives should mention the cause that brings about the relation. The definition of derivatives should mention that from which the derivation is made together with something else, depending on the places of the derivation.[17]

A section [on real essential definitions]

(14) Someone[18] uses the term "essential definition" for a formula indicating the quiddity of a thing. Such a formula indicates the essentials and the aspects internal to the reality of the thing. The formula that makes the reality known by externals is called "description." Consider the example of body. Some people affirm that body has parts, but some are uncertain, and others deny the existence of parts altogether.[19] (You will later learn what such parts are.) However, for the multitude such parts are not in the concept of the thing named. Indeed, the name signifies only the sum total of the concomitants of its concept. Consider also water and air. Even if there is a proof that these have non-sensible parts, some people will still not accept it. Those parts, thus, have nothing to do with their understanding of water and air. Even if a body is as we have explained it to be and is part of a corporeal reality, people will only conceive those parts apparent to them. It is those aspects that are meant by the name—both by the one who coined the name and by them. Now, if this is the case with sensible things, how much more will this be so for something of which nothing can be sensed at all! Further, consider that

اخفى منه او يكون لا يعرف الشئ[١٣] إلاّ بما عُرّف به. فقول القائل فى تعريف الاب «انه هو الّذى له الابن» غير صحيح، فانهما متساويان فى معنى[١٤] المعرفة والجهالة، ومن عرف احدهما عرف الآخر؛ ومن شرط ما يُعرف به الشئ ان يكون معلوما قبل الشئ لا مع الشئ؛ او يقال «النار هى الاسطقس الشبيه بالنفس» والنفس اخفى من النار. وكذا قولهم «ان الشمس كوكب يطلع نهارا» والنهار لا يُعرف إلاّ بزمان طلوع الشمس. وليس تعريف الحقيقة مجرد تبديل اللفظ، فان تبديل اللفظ إنمّا ينفع لمن عرف الحقيقة والتبس عليه معنى اللفظ. والاضافيات ينبغى ان تُؤخذ فى حدودها السبب الموقع للاضافة، والمشتقات تُؤخذ ما منه الاشتقاق مع أمر مّا فى حدّها على حسب مواضع الاشتقاق.

فصل [فى الحدود الحقيقية]

(١٤) اصطلح بعض الناس على تسمية القول الدال على ماهية الشئ «حدّا» ويكون دالا على الذاتيات والأمور الداخلة فى حقيقته، ومعرّف الحقيقة بالعوارض[١٥] من الخارجيات «رسما». واعلم ان الجسم، مثلا، اذا اثبت له مثبت جزء يشك فيه بعض الناس وينكره بعضهم، كما ستعرف ذلك الجزء، فالجماهير لا يكون عندهم ذلك الجزء من مفهوم المسمّى، بل لا يكون الاسم إلاّ لمجموع لوازم تصوره ثم ان كل واحد من الماء، مثلا، والهواء اذا ثبت ان له اجزاء غير محسوسة يُنكرها بعض الناس؛ فتلك الاجزاء عندهم لا مدخل لها فيما يفهمون فيه. وكل حقيقة جرمية اذا كان الجسم احد اجزائها وحاله كما سبق، فما تصوّر الناس منها إلاّ أمورا ظاهرة عندهم هى المقصود بالتسمية للواضع ولهم. فاذا كان حال المحسوسات كذا، فكيف حال ما لا يحسّ شئ منه اصلا! ثم

there is something possessed by man which makes him human. This thing is unknown to the multitude and even to the elite among the Peripatetics, for the latter define man as "rational animal." But the capacity for reasoning is accidental and posterior to the reality of man. But the soul—which is the principle of these things[20]—can only be known through concomitants and accidents. If this is so for the soul, the thing closest to a man, how much more difficult will it be to know other things! However, we will say later what is necessary about this question.

An Illuminationist principle
[in refutation of the Peripatetic theory of definitions]

(15) The Peripatetics admit that the general and specific essentials of the thing must be mentioned in its essential definition. "Genus" is the name for the general essential that is not part of another general essential belonging to the universal reality explained by the answer to the question, "What is it?"[21] They call the essential specific to that thing the "differentia." (But there is another way of using these two in definition, which we have explained elsewhere in our books.)[22] Further, the Peripatetics stipulate that the unknown can only be obtained through the known. However, the essential specific to the thing is unknown to one who is ignorant of it everywhere else. But if it is known through something other than the thing defined, it will not be specific to the thing defined. If the essential is specific to the thing and is neither evident to sensation nor known, it will remain unknown, as will the thing defined. And if that essential specific to it is to be defined, it might be by things more general—which would not define it—and not by things specific to it. It could not be defined by what is specific to it, since its case would be the same as above. Thus, the only recourse is to use matters that are either sensible or evident in another way and that are specific to the thing collectively. You will learn the gist of this in what follows.

Even if someone enumerates the essentials he knows, he cannot be sure that he has not overlooked the existence of some other essential. Thus, an inquirer or an opponent may challenge the person who constructs a definition, and that person will be unable to reply, "Were there another attribute, I would have known about it," for there are more attributes that are not evident. And it is not sufficient to say, "If the

ان الانسان اذا كان له شئ به تحققت انسانيته وهو مجهول للعامة والخاصة من المشائين حيث جعلوا حدّه «الحيوان الناطق» واستعداد النطق عرضى تابع للحقيقة والنفس التى هى مبدأ هذه الاشياء لا تعلم إلاّ باللوازم والعوارض ولا اقرب الى الانسان من نفسه وحاله كذا، فكيف يكون حال غيره على انا نذكر فيه ما يجب؟

قاعدة اشراقية [فى هدم قاعدة المشائين فى التعريفات]

(١٥) سلّم المشاؤون ان الشئ يذكر فى حدّه الذاتى العام والخاص؛ فالذاتى العام، الّذى ليس بجزء لذاتى عام آخر للحقيقة الكلية التى يتغير بها جواب ما هو، يسمّى «الجنس»؛ والذاتى الخاص بالشئ سمّوه «فصلا». ولهذين نظم فى التعريف غير هذا، قد ذكرناه فى مواضع اخرى من كتبنا. ثم سلّموا ان المجهول لا يتوصل اليه إلاّ من المعلوم، فالذاتى الخاص للشئ ليس بمعهود لمن يجهله فى موضع آخر فانه ان عهد فى غيره لا يكون خاصا به. واذا كان خاصا به، وليس بظاهر للحس وليس بمعهود، فيكون مجهولا معه. فاذا عُرف ذلك الخاص ايضا، ان عرف بالأمور العامة دون ما يخصه فلا يكون تعريفا له، والجزء الخاص حاله على ما سبق. فليس العود الى أمور محسوسة او ظاهرة من طريق آخر، ان كان يخص الشئ جملتها بالاجتماع، وستعلم كنه هذا فيما بعد. ثم من ذكر ما عرف من الذاتيات لم يؤمن وجود ذاتى آخر غفل عنه وللمستشرح او المنازع ان يطالبه بذلك. وليس للمعرِّف حينئذ ان يقول «لو كانت صفة

thing had had another essential, we would have been unable to know its quiddity without it," since the answer can be made, "The reality is known only when all its essentials are known." Thus, if the possibility exists that another essential has not been apprehended, there can be no certainty about the knowledge of the reality of the thing. Thus, it is clear that it is impossible for a human being to construct an essential definition in the way the Peripatetics require—a difficulty which even their master [Aristotle] admits.[23] Therefore, we have definition only by means of things that specify by conjunction.

أُخرى لاطلّعت عليها»، اذ كثير من الصفات غير ظاهرة. ولا يكفى ان يقال «لو كان له ذاتى آخر ما عرفنا الماهية دونه». فيقال: إنمّا تكون الحقيقة عُرفت اذا عُرفت جميع ذاتياتها. فاذا انقدح جواز ذاتى آخر لم يُدرك لم يكن معرفة الحقيقة متيّقنة. فتبين ان الاتيان على الحدّ كما التزم به المشاؤون غير ممكن للانسان وصاحبهم اعترف بصعوبة ذلك. فاذن ليس عندنا إلاّ تعريفات بأمور تخص بالاجتماع.

The Second Discourse

On proofs and their principles, comprising [seven] rules

Rule one

[In description of propositions and syllogisms]

(16) A "proposition" is an expression whose speaker may be told that he speaks the truth or falsehood. A "syllogism" is an expression composed of propositions that, when accepted, imply essentially another expression. The simplest proposition is the "categorical[1] proposition," one which contains a judgment as to whether or not one of two things is the other—for example, "Man is (or is not) animal." The thing judged is called the "subject," and that which is judged to be the case is called the "predicate." A single proposition is made from two propositions when each one ceases to be a proposition and the two are connected. If they are connected by implication, it is called a "conditional compound proposition"—for example, "If the Sun is shining, then it is day." The part connected to the conditional particle is called the "antecedent," and the part

المقالة الثانية
فى الحجج ومباديها
وهى تشتمل على ضوابط

الضابط الأوّل

[فى رسم القضية و القياس]

(١٦) هو ان «القضية» قول يمكن ان يقال لقائله انه صادق فيه او كاذب. و«القياس» هو قول مؤلف من قضايا اذا سلمت لزم عنه لذاته قول آخر. والقضية التى هى ابسط القضايا هى «الحملية» وهى قضية حُكم فيها بان احد الشيئين هو الآخر او ليس، مثل قولك[1] «الانسان حيوان او ليس». فالمحكوم عليه يسمّى «موضوعا»، والمحكوم به يسمّى «محمولا». وقد يجعل من القضيتين قضية واحدة، بان يخرج كل واحدة منهما عن كونها قضية ويربط بينهما. فان كان الربط بلزوم تسمّى «شرطية متصلة»، كقولهم «ان كانت الشمس طالعة فالنهار موجود» وما قُرن به حرف الشرط من جزئيها يُسمّى «المقدّم»، وما قرن به حرف الجزاء يُسمّى «التالى». وان اردنا ان نجعل منها قياسا، ضممنا اليها قضية حملية لاستثناء عين المقدم ليلزم منه عين التالي، كقولنا «لكن الشمس طالعة، فيلزم ان يكون النهار موجودا»؛ او لاستثناء نقيض التالى لنقيض المقدّم،

connected to the particle of implication is called the "consequent." To construct a syllogism from a conditional proposition, we add a categorical proposition that affirms the antecedent and thereby implies the consequent. Thus, "The Sun is shining" implies, "It is day."[2] If we can add the contradictory of the consequent, we imply the contradictory of the antecedent. Thus, "It is not day" implies, "The Sun is not shining."[3] This is because whenever there exists that which implies something, then necessarily that which is implied also exists. If that which is implied is not the case, then that which implied it must also not be the case. However, we cannot construct a syllogism either by adding the contradictory of the antecedent or [by] affirming the consequent.[4] This is because the consequent may be more general than the antecedent, as in, "If this is black,[5] then it is a color." The negation and falsehood of the more specific does not imply the negation and falsehood of the more general, nor does the affirmation and truth of the more general imply the affirmation and truth of the more specific. Rather, the affirmation and truth of the more specific implies the affirmation and truth of the more general, and the negation and falsity of the more general implies the negation and falsity of the more specific. When the connection between two categorical propositions is by alternation,[6] the compound proposition is called a "disjunctive conditional"—for example, "Either this number is even or it is odd." It may have more than two parts.[7] Such a proposition is true if all its parts cannot be true and all its parts cannot be false. In order to make a syllogism from a disjunctive conditional, one may affirm some part of the proposition, thereby implying the contradictory of what remains.[8] If it has many parts, affirming the contradictory of one part implies the disjunction of the remaining parts.[9]

A conjunctive proposition may be compounded of two conjunctives: "If the Sun is shining, then it is day; then if the Sun has set, it is night." A disjunctive may also be compounded of two conjunctive conditionals: "Either, if the Sun is shining, then it is day; or, if the Sun has set, then it is night." Many other combinations are possible. Anyone with talent, after learning the laws, will have no difficulty with such combinations. Conditional propositions may be reduced to categorical propositions by stipulating the implication or alternation. Thus, we can say, "The rising of the Sun implies that it is day; or it excludes the night." The conditionals may thus be reduced to categorical propositions.

كقولك[2] «لكن ليس النهار موجودا، فليست الشمس طالعة». فانه اذا وُجد الملزوم، فبالضرورة يكون اللازم قد وُجد؛ واذا ارتفع اللازم، يكون الملزوم قد ارتفع، ولا يستثنى نقيض المقدّم ولا عين التالى، فانه قد يكون التالي اعم من المقدّم، كقولك[3] «ان كان هذا اسود،[4] فهو لون». فلا يلزم من رفع الاخص وكذبه رفع الاعم وكذبه. ولا من وضع الاعم وصدقه وضع الاخص وصدقه، بل إنمّا يلزم من وضع الاخص وصدقه وضع الاعم وصدقه، ومن رفع الاعم وكذبه رفع الاخص وكذبه. وان كان الربط بين الحمليتين بعناد يسمّى «شرطية منفصلة»، كقولنا «اما ان يكون هذا العدد زوجا واما ان يكون فردا». ويجوز ان تكون[5] اجزائها اكثر من اثنين. والحقيقة هى التى لا يمكن اجتماع اجزائها ولا الخلوّ عن اجزائها. وان اريد ان يجعل منها قياس، يستثنى فيها عين ما يتفق. فيلزم نقيض ما بقى، كان واحدا او اكثر، او نقيض ما يتّفق فيلزم عين ما بقى. وان كانت ذات اجزاء كثيرة واستثنى نقيض واحد، فتبقى منفصلة فى الباقى. وقد تركب[6] منفصلة من متصلتين، كقولهم «ان كان كلّما كانت الشمس طالعة، فالنهار موجود، كلّما كانت الشمس غاربة، فالليل موجود». وقد تركب[7] منها منفصلة، كقولنا «اما ان يكون اذا كانت الشمس طالعة، فالنهار موجود؛ واما ان يكون كانت الشمس غاربة، فالليل موجود» والتصرفات كثيرة. ومن كان له قريحة لا يصعب عليه مثل هذه التركيبات بعد معرفة القانون. واعلم ان الشرطيات يصح قلبها الى الحمليات،[8] بان يصرّح باللزوم او العناد، فنقول «طلوع الشمس يلزمه وجود النهار» او «يعانده الليل». فكانت[9] الشرطيات محرّفة عن الحمليات.

Rule two

[On the classes of propositions]

(17) When one says, "If . . . then . . ." or "Either . . . or . . ." in a conditional proposition, one ought to add "always" or "sometimes" to quantify the proposition. Otherwise, it will be indefinite and may cause errors. Thus, in the categorical proposition "Man is animal," one must specify whether every man is such or only some. Humanity itself requires neither exhaustiveness—otherwise, a single individual would not be human—nor specificity but, rather, is compatible with both.[10] Thus, one must specify whether a judgment is exhaustive or not so as to avoid errors in quantification.[11] We call propositions whose subjects are individual "particular propositions," such as "Zayd is literate."[12] Examples of propositions whose subjects are inclusive and in which the judgment applies to all members of the class are "All men are animals," or, in negation, "No man is stone." For every proposition there is an affirmation and a negation—that is, an assertion and a denial. Examples of propositions whose subject is specified by "some" are "Some animals are (or are not) human." The term that removes indefiniteness is called the "quantification sign": "all," "some," and the like.[13] A quantified proposition is definite. We call the general definite proposition the "universal proposition." We call a proposition whose judgment is specified by "some" the "existential indefinite proposition."

In an existential indefinite conditional proposition we say, for example, "It may be that if . . . then . . . ," or "Either . . . or . . . ." There is also indefiniteness in "some," for the individual things may be many. Let that "some" in a syllogism be given a name—C, for example. Thus, it can be said, "All C is such and such," and the proposition will become definite, so removing the misleading indefiniteness. The existential proposition is not useful except in certain cases of conversion and the contradictory.

Likewise, in conditionals, if it is said, "If Zayd is in the sea, then he is drowning," let it be specified and thus made universal. It should then

الضابط الثانى

[فى اقسام القضايا]

(١٧) هو ان الشرطية اذا قيل فيها «اذا كان»، كان او «اما واما»، فيصلح ان يكون دائما او فى بعض الاوقات، فتعيّن؛ والا يكون مهملا مغلّطا. وفى الحملية اذا قيل «الانسان حيوان»، فتعيّن ان كل واحد من الانسان كذا او بعض جزئياته. فان الانسانية لذاتها لا تقتضى الاستغراق، اذ لو اقتضت ما كان الشخص الواحد انسانا، ولا ايضا تقتضى التخصيص، بل هى صالحة لهما. فلعيّن ان الحكم هل هو مستغرق او غير مستغرق، حتى لا يكون اهمالا مغلّطا. فالقضية التى موضوعها شاخص نسمّيها «شاخصة»، كقولك «زيد كاتب». والتى موضوعها شامل وعُيّن فيها الحكم على كل واحد، هى كقولنا «كل انسان حيوان» او[١٠] «لا شئ من الناس بحجر» فى السلب. فان لكل قضية ايجابا وسلبا، اى اثباتا ونفيا. وفيما يتخصص بالبعض، هى كقولنا[١١] «بعض الحيوان انسان» او «ليس» ويسمّى اللفظ المخرج من الاهمال «سورا»، مثل «كل» و«بعض» وغيرهما. والقضية المسوّرة محصورة، والحاصرة الكلية سميّناها «القضية المحيطة»، والتى عُيّن فيها الحكم على البعض «مهملة بعضية».

وفى المهملة البعضية الشرطية نقول «قد يكون اذا كان او اما» والبعض فيه اهمال ايضا، فان ابعاض الشئ كثيرة. فليجعل لذلك البعض فى القياسات اسم خاص وليكن مثلا جيم. فيقال «كل جيم كذا» لتصير[١٢] القضية محيطة، فيزول عنها الاهمال المغلّط ولا ينتفع بالقضية البعضية إلاّ فى بعض مواضع العكس والنقيض وكذا فى الشرطيات، كما يقال «قد يكون اذا كان زيد فى البحر، فهو غريق» فليتعيّن ذلك الحال ولتجعل

be said, "Whenever[14] Zayd is in the sea and does not have a boat and does not know how to swim, then he is drowning." It cannot be denied that "some" is by nature indefinite.

When you do research in the sciences, you will find no questions in which the nature of a particular thing is sought in its indefiniteness unless the "some" is determined. If things are done in accordance with what we are saying, then only universal propositions will remain, for the particular propositions are not investigated in the sciences. At the same time, the rules governing propositions will become fewer, clearer, and easier.

(18) Know that every categorical proposition must have a subject and a predicate and that the relation between them is assent or denial. It is only by virtue of their relation that a proposition is a proposition. The word that indicates this relation is called the "copula." It may be omitted in some languages and something else that indicates the relation be substituted for it—as in Arabic, where one can say either, "Zayd literate," or, "Zayd he literate."[15]

Negative propositions are those in which negation cuts the copula. In Arabic, negation must precede the copula to negate it, as when they say, "Zayd not he literate." However, if the negation is connected to the copula in such a way as to become part of either the subject or the predicate, the affirmative nature of the copula will remain. Thus, when it is said in Arabic, "Zayd is nonliterate," the affirmative copula remains and the negation has become part of the predicate. Such affirmative propositions are called "infinite."[16]

In languages other than Arabic, whether or not the negative particle precedes the copula may not determine affirmation or negation. Instead, so long as there is a copula and the negation is part of the subject or predicate, then the proposition itself will remain affirmative, unless the negation cuts the copula. When you say, "All non-even numbers are odd," then oddness has been affirmed of every number described as non-even and, thus, the proposition will remain affirmative.

A mental affirmative judgment can only apply to something established in the mind. An affirmative proposition concerning something that exists outside the mind must likewise apply to something that exists outside the mind.

مستغرقة. فيقال «كلّما كان زيد فى البحر وليس له فيه مركب وسباحة، فهو غريق»، وكون طبيعة البعض مهملة لا تنكر. واذا تفحّصت عن العلوم لا تجد فيها مطلوبا يُطلب فيه حال بعض الشئ مهملا دون ان يُعيّن ذلك البعض. فاذا عُمل على ما قلنا، لا تبقى القضية إلاّ محيطة، فان الشواخص لا تطلب حالها فى العلوم وحينئذ تصير احكام القضايا اقلّ واضبط واسهل.

(١٨) واعلم ان كل قضية حملية من حقها ان يكون فيها موضوع ومحمول، ونسبة بينهما صالحة للتصديق والتكذيب؛ وباعتبار تلك النسبة صارت القضية قضية. واللفظة الدالّة[١٣] على تلك النسبة تسمّى «الرابطة»، وقد تحذف فى بعض اللغات ويورد بدلها هيئة مّا مشعرة بالنسبة، كما يقال فى العربية «زيد كاتب»؛ وقد تورد كما قيل «زيد هو كاتب». والسالبة هى التى تكون سلبها قاطعا للروابط،[١٤] وفى العربية ينبغى ان يكون السلب متقدّما على الرابطة لينفيها، كقولهم «زيد ليس هو كاتبا». واذا ارتبط السلب ايضا بالرابطة فصار جزء أحد جزئيها فالرابط الايجابى بُعد باق، كما يقال فى العربية «زيد هو لا كاتب» فان الرابط[١٥] باق، وقد يسير[١٦] السلب جزء المحمول، والقضية موجبة تُسمّى «معدولة». وفى غير العربية قد لا يُعتبر تقدّم الرابطة وتأخّرها فى السلب والايجاب، بل ما دام الرباط حاصلا والسلب سواء كان جزء المحمول او الموضوع هى موجبة إلاّ ان يكون السلب قاطعا لها. اذا قلت «كل لا زوج فهو فرد» فهو ايجاب الفردية على جميع الموصوفات باللازوجية، فتكون موجبة. والحكم الموجب الذهنى لا يثبت إلاّ على ثابت ذهنى. والموجب على انه فى العين لا يكون إلاّ على ثابت عينى.[١٧] والشرطيات ايضا ان تكثّرت السلوب فيها والربط اللزومى، او العنادى

Moreover, if there is more than one negation in a conditional proposition and the relation of implication or disjunction remains unchanged, then the proposition itself will be affirmative. If a negation is negated, the result will be affirmative.[17] If you say, "Not all men are literate," then you may be able to say, "Some man is literate," since the negation only applies to the part. When it is said, "It is not the case that no man is literate," then it is correct to say, "Some man is literate." A connective conditional proposition is negated by denying the implication, and a disjunctive conditional is negated by denying the disjunction.

Rule three

[On modalities in propositions]

(19) The relation of the predicate of a categorical proposition to its subject either must exist (in which case it is called "the necessary") or must not exist ("the impossible") or may either exist or not exist ("the possible" or "the contingent"). An example of the first is "Man is animal"; of the second, "Man is stone"; and of the third, "Man is literate." By "possible," most people mean that which is not impossible. For when they say "not impossible," they mean by it the possible, and when they say "not possible" they mean by it the impossible.[18] However, this is not our usage, for what is not contingent according to this usage may be either what has to exist or what cannot exist. If the necessity or impossibility of something depends on something else, and if that other thing is removed, then neither the necessity nor the impossibility remains, and the thing is contingent in itself.

The contingent is necessary by virtue of that which necessitates it and is impossible on condition of the nonexistence of that which necessitates its existence. When one examines the thing itself in the two states of existence and nonexistence, it is contingent.

(20) Know that when we say, "All C are B," it means that each and every thing described by C is described by B. This is because when you say, "All C are B," you will understand that the concept C is a general meaning. You then make explicit that it refers to the particulars in C

باق، فالقضية موجبة. والسلب اذا دخل على سلب من غير اعتبار جال آخر، يكون ايجابا. واذا قلت «ليس كل انسان كاتبا» يجوز ان يكون البعض كاتبا، فالّذى يتيقن فيه سلب البعض فحسب، واذا قيل «ليس لا شئ من الانسان كاتبا» يجوز ان لا يكون البعض كاتبا وسلب المتصلة برفع اللزوم، وسلب المنفصلة برفع العناد.

الضابط الثالث

[فى جهات القضايا]

(١٩) هو ان الحملية نسبة محمولها الى موضوعها وموضوعها الى محمولها اما ضرورى الوجود ويسمّى «الواجب»، او ضرورى العدم ويسمّى «الممتنع»، او غير ضرورى الوجود والعدم وهو «الممكن». فالاول، كقولك «الانسان حيوان»؛ والثانى، كقولك «الانسان حجر»؛ والثالث، كقولك «الانسان كاتب». والعامة قد يعنون بالممكن ما ليس بممتنع فاذا قالوا «ليس بممتنع» عنو به الممكن، واذا قالوا «ليس بممكن» عنوا به الممتنع. وهذا غير ما نحن فيه، فان ما ليس بممكن هو قد يكون ضرورى الوجود وقد يكون ضرورى العدم بهذا الاعتبار، وما يتوقف وجوده وامتناعه على غيره فعند انتفاء ذلك الغير لا يبقى وجوبه وامتناعه، فهو ممكن فى نفسه، والممكن يجب بما يوجب وجوده ويمتنع بشرط لا يكون موجب[١٨] وجوده، وعند تجرد النظر الى ذاته فى حالتى وجوده وعدمه ممكن.

(٢٠) واعلم انّا اذا قلنا «كل ج ب» ليس معناه إلاّ انّ كل واحد واحد مما يوصف بـ«ج» يوصف بـ«ب» لأنك اذا قلت «كل ج ب» عرفت ان مفهوم الجيم معنى عام ثم تعرضت للشواخص التى تحته

by saying "each and every," because the meaning is not C as a whole: You can say, "Any man can fit in a single house," but you cannot say, "All men can fit in a single house." When, for example, you see a proposition such as "All sleepers may awaken," you will realize that the meaning of "all sleepers" is not "one who sleeps qua being asleep," because in such a case it is not possible to imagine someone actually sleeping being described as awake. Rather, what is meant here is that every individual who is described as asleep may sleep and wake up. Likewise, when we say, "Every father is prior to his son," it does not mean that he is so insofar as he is a father but as an individual who is described as being a father. Further, when you say, "All things that move necessarily change," you should know that each and every thing described as moving is not necessarily changing because of its own essence, but because it is moving. Thus, its necessity depends on a condition and it is contingent in itself. By "necessary," we mean only that which it has by virtue of its own essence. That which is necessary on condition of a time or state is contingent in itself.[19]

An Illuminationist doctrine [on the reduction of all propositions to the necessary affirmative]

(21) Since the contingency of the contingent, the impossibility of the impossible, and the necessity of the necessary are all necessary, it is better to make the modes of necessity, contingency, and impossibility parts of the predicate so that the proposition will become necessary in all circumstances. You would thus say, "Necessarily all humans are contingently literate, necessarily animals, or impossibly stones." Such a proposition is called the "definitely necessary."[20] In the sciences we investigate the contingency or impossibility of things as part of what we are investigating. We can make no definitive and final judgment except concerning that which we know necessarily. Even for that which is only true sometimes, we use the definitely necessary proposition. In the case of "breathing at

بقولك «كل واحد واحد» اذ ليس معناه جميع الجيم، اذ يمكنك ان تقول «كل انسان تسعه دار واحدة» ولا يمكنك ان تقول «جميع الناس تسعهم دار واحدة». واذا رأيت فى القضايا مثل قولك «كل نائم يجوز ان يتيقظ» مثلا، دريت ان مقتضى قولنا «كل نائم» ليس النائم من حيث هو نائم فانه مع النوم لا يتصوّر ان يوصف باليقظة، بل الشخص الموصوف بانه نائم هو الّذى يجوز ان ينام ويستيقظ. وكذا اذا قلنا «كل اب متقدم على الابن» ليس معناه من حيث هو، بل الشخص الموصوف بانه اب. واذا قلت «كل متحرك بالضرورة متغير»، لك ان تعلم ان كل واحد واحد مما يوصف بانه متحرك ليس بضرورى له لذاته ان يتغير، بل لأجل كونه متحركا. فضرورته متوقفة على شرط، فيكون ممكنا فى نفسه. ولا نعنى بالضرورى إلاّ ما يكون لذاته، فحسب. واما ما يجب بشرط من وقت وحال فهو ممكن فى نفسه.

حكمة اشراقية [فى بيان ردّ القضايا كلها الى الموجبة الضرورية البتّاتة]

(٢١) لما كان الممكن امكانه ضروريا والممتنع امتناعه ضروريا والواجب وجوبه ايضا كذا،[١٩] فالاولى ان تجعل الجهات من الوجوب وقسيميه اجزاء للمحمولات حتى تصير القضية على جميع الاحوال ضرورية، كما تقول «كل انسان بالضرورة هو ممكن ان يكون كاتبا او يجب ان يكون حيوانا او يمتنع ان يكون حجرا». فهذه هى الضرورة البتّاتة. فانا اذا طلبنا فى العلوم امكان شئ او امتناعه، فهو جزء مطلوبنا. ولا يمكننا ان نحكم حكما جازما بتّة إلاّ بما يعلم انه بالضرورة كذا. فلا نورد من القضايا إلاّ البتّاتة حتى اذا كان من الممكن ما يقع فى كل واحد

some time," it would be correct to say, "All men necessarily breathe at some time." That men necessarily breathe at some time is always an attribute of man. That they necessarily do not breathe at some time is also a necessary attribute of a man at all times, even at the time when he is breathing. However, this is different from literacy. While literacy is necessarily contingent, it is not necessary that it be actualized at some time. If the proposition is necessary, the mode of the copula alone is sufficient for us; or it is posited to be definite without including another mode in the predicate—for example, when you say, "All men are definitely animal." In other modal propositions, whenever they are to be made definite, the mode must be included in the predicate. We do not need to employ negation once we have specified the modes, for complete negation is the necessary and is included in the affirmative type, as we have mentioned. The same holds true for the impossible and for the contingent.[21]

Know that a proposition is not a proposition by virtue of affirmation only: it may be one by virtue of negation as well. Negation is also an intellectual judgment, regardless of whether it is conceived as exception or denial, for it is a judgment in the mind that is not pure denial, an affirmation insofar as it is a judgment that that denial is the case. A thing must be either denied or affirmed. Negation and affirmation in the intellect are mental judgments whose state is something else. Thus, when the intelligible is not judged to be in some state, then it is itself neither negated nor confirmed by another but, rather, is in itself either confirmed or denied. Concerning this point, we shall have something to add later. When the mode of a proposition is not specified, then it remains indefinite in mode, and it will cause many mistakes. So you should refrain from using indefinite modals as you would refrain from using a proposition in which the quantity of the subject is indefinite.[22]

Rule four

[On contradiction and its definition]

(22) Contradiction is when two propositions differ only by affirmation or negation. It thus follows that they cannot both be true or both be false. The subject, predicate, relations, and modalities must not differ in

وقتا مّا كالتنفس، صحّ ان يقال «كل انسان بالضرورة هو متنفس وقتا مّا». وكون الانسان ضرورى التنفس وقتا مّا أمراً يلزمه ابدا، وكونه ضرورى اللاتنفس فى وقت مّا غير ذلك الوقت ايضا أمر يلزمه ابدا وهذا زائد على الكتابة فانها وان كانت ضرورية الامكان، ليست ضرورية الوقوع وقتا مّا واذا كانت القضية ضرورية، كفانا جهة الربط فحسب، او تعرض كونها بتّاتة دون ادخال جهة اخرى فى المحمول، مثل ان تقول «كل انسان هو بتّة حيوان» وفى غيره اذا جعلت بتّاتة، لا بدّ من ادراج الجهة فى المحمول، ولنا ان نتعرض للسلب بعد ان[٢٠] تعرضنا للجهات، فان السلب التام هو الضرورى، وقد دخل تحت الايجاب اذا اورد الامتناع على ما ذكرنا وكذا الامكان.

واعلم انّ القضية ليست هى باعتبار مجرّد الايجاب قضية، بل وباعتبار السلب ايضا، فانّ السلب ايضا حكم عقلى سواء عُبّر عنه بالرفع او بالنفى. فانّه حكمُ فى الذهن ليس بانتفاء محض، وهو اثبات من جهة انّه حكم بالانتفاء؛ والشئ لم يخرج من الانتفاء والثبوت. وامّا النفى والاثبات فى العقل، فهما احكام ذهنية، حاليهما شئ آخر. فالمعقول، اذا لم يحكم عليه بحالٍ مّا، فليس بمنفى ولا بمثبت، بل هو فى نفسه امّا منتفٍ، او ثابت؛ وله تتمّة سنذكرها. والقضية اذالم يتعين فيها جهة، فهى مهملة الجهات، وكثر فيها الخبط. فلتُحذف مهملة الجهات كما حُذفت مهملة كمية الموضوع.

الضابط الرابع

[فى التناقض وحدّه]

(٢٢) هو انّ التناقض اختلاف قضيتين بالايجاب والسلب لا غير. ثم يلزم منه ان لا يجتمعا صدقا ولا كذبا. فينبغى ان يكون الموضوع والمحمول والشرط والنسب والجهات فيهما غير مختلفة وفى القضايا

the two. In the case of universal propositions, there is no need for additional conditions; for we deny exactly what we had affirmed, as in the definite proposition “Every A necessarily is contingently B,” whose contradiction is “Every A is not necessarily contingently B.” It is the same in other cases. When we say, “No [A is B],” its contradiction will be “It is not the case that no [A is B] nothing.” In this way, in the two propositions we negate the very same thing we affirm. However, when the universal affirmative is negated, some particular is certainly negated but some other may still be affirmed.[23] When a universal negative proposition is negated, it follows that some particular is affirmed, but some other particular may still be negated. The proposition that is specific to a particular has no contradictory with respect to the particular. Statements such as “Some animal is human” and “It is not the case that some animal is human” are not correct, since the existential proposition is indefinite in conception. The particular that is human may not be the same particular that is not human. In such a case, the subject of the two propositions is not the same. However, if we specify the particular and give it a name—as we mentioned, a way to make it universal—then it will be the same as above. Indeed, there is no need for the detailed explications of the Peripatetics: if you remember this, you may dispense with most of their elaborate explanations.

Rule five

On conversion

(23) Conversion is making the entire subject of the proposition the predicate and the predicate the subject while keeping the quality and the truth or falsity of the proposition the same. You know that when you say, “All men are animals,” you cannot say, “and all animals are men.” The same is true in every proposition whose subject is more specific than its predicate. But at least the following is true: Suppose that something is described as being A and is described as being B—let this thing be C, for example. Then, since something of A is B (whether all or some of it) then something of B (all or some) must be described as A, so that C will be described by both A and B.

المحيطة لا نحتاج[٢١] الى زيادة شرط، بل نسلب ما اوجبناه بعينه، كقولنا فى القضية البتّاتة «كل فلان بالضرورة هو ممكن ان يكون بهمانا». فنقيضه[٢٢] «ليس بالضرورة كل فلان هو ممكن ان يكون بالضرورة بهمانا». وهكذا يكون[٢٣] فى غير هذه. واذا قلنا «لا شئ» نقيضه «ليس لا شئ» وقد سلبنا ما اوجبنا بعينه فى القضيتين، إلاّ انه لزم من سلب الاستغراق فى الايجاب تيقن سلب البعض مع جواز الايجاب فى البعض، ومن سلب الاستغراق فى السلب تيقن الايجاب فى البعض وجواز سلب البعض. والقضية التى خصصت بالبعض لم يكن لها من البعض نقيض، كقولك «بعض الحيوان انسان، ليس بعض الحيوان انسانا» وإنمّا لا يصحّ هذا لان البعض مهمل التصوّر، فيجوز ان يكون البعض الّذى هو انسان غير البعض الّذى ليس بانسان، فلم يكن موضوع القضيتين واحد. ولكن اذا عيّنا البعض[٢٤] وجعلنا له اسما، كما ذكرنا من جعله مستغرقا، كان على ما سبق. ولعله لا يحتاج الى تعمق المشائين، واذا حفظت هذا استغنيت عن كثير من تطويلاتهم.

الضابط الخامس

فى العكس

(٢٣) والعكس[٢٥] هو جعل موضوع القضية بكليته محمولا والمحمول موضوعا مع حفظ الكيفية وبقاء الصدق والكذب بحالهما. وتعلم أنّك اذا قلت «كل انسان حيوان» لا يمكنك ان تقول «وكل حيوان انسان»، وكذا كل قضية موضوعها اخصّ من محمولها. ولكن لا اقلّ من ان يوجد شئ هو موصوف بانّه فلان وموصوف بانّه بهمان، ولكن ج مثلا، فاذا كان شئ من فلان بهمان، كان كله او بعضه، فلا بدّ من ان يكون شئ مما يوصف بانه

When we say, "Necessarily all men are contingently literate," its converse will be "Necessarily something that is contingently literate is a man." The other modes besides contingency also move with the predicate when it is converted. The converse of the necessary definite affirmative proposition is itself a necessary definite affirmative proposition, whatever the mode may be.

Universal and particular propositions are converted in such a way that something of the predicate is described by the subject without quantity. If [it is true that] "Necessarily no man is stone," then "Necessarily no stone is man." Otherwise, if one of the things described by either the subject or the predicate should also be described by the other, then it will be impossible to assert the falsity of only one of the propositions, and both propositions will be false.[24]

If the contingency is part of the predicate of the definite necessary proposition and the negation is with the predicate, the negation will also be moved in conversion, as in the statement "Necessarily all men are contingently nonliterate." Its converse will be the definite affirmative: "Necessarily something that is contingently nonliterate is a man." Many Peripatetics have been prone to err about this. For example, if you single out the particular in the proposition "It is not the case that some animals are man" and make the proposition universal, it will be converted to our expression. However, if you make the negation part of the predicate and say, "Some animal is non-man," it will convert into "Some non-man is animal," or else it will not convert at all. Your statement "Nothing of the throne is on the king" cannot be converted without changing it completely. Thus, you cannot say, "Nothing of the king is on the throne." You must change it to "Nothing of that which is on the king is a throne." The word "on" must be transported because it is part of the predicate here.

Conversion, contradiction, negatives, and indefinite particular propositions are mentioned here merely for instruction. We will not need them hereafter.

بهمان يوصف بانه فلان كان كله او بعضه، فانّ الجيم موصوف بكليهما؛ واذا قلنا «بالضرورة كل انسان هو ممكن ان يكون كاتبا»، فعكسه «بالضرورة بعض ما يمكن ان يكون كاتبا فهو انسان». وكذا غير الامكان من الجهات فينقل مع المحمول. وعكس الضرورية البتّاتة الموجبة الضرورية بتّاتة موجبة مع ایّ جهة كانت. فللمحيطة وللجزئية انعكاس على انّ شيئا من المحمول يوصف بالموضوع مهملا. واذا كان بالضرورة لا شئ من الانسان بحجر فلا شئ من الحجر بانسان بالضرورة؛ والا ان وُجد من موصوفات احدهما ما يوصف بالآخر، ما وقع الاقتصار على كذب احدهما، بل كذب كليهما.[٢٦] والضرورية البتّاتة اذا كان الامكان جزء محمولها، فان كان معها سلب، ينتقل ايضا كقولهم «بالضرورة كل انسان هو ممكن ان لا يكون كاتبا». فهى بتّاتة موجبة عكسها «بالضرورة شئ مما يمكن ان لا يكون كاتبا فهو انسان». وقد يخبط فيه كثير من المشائين. وفى مثل قولك «ليس بعض الحيوان انسانا» اذا عيّنت ذلك البعض وجعلته كليا لانعكس على ما قلنا؛ او تجعل السلب جزء المحمول فتقول «بعض الحيوان هو غير انسان» فينعكس الى «بعض غير الانسان حيوان»، والا لا ينعكس. وقولك «لا شئ من السرير على الملك» لا ينبغى ان تعكسه دون النقل بالكلية، فلا تقول «لا شئ من الملك على السرير»، بل «لا شئ مما على الملك بسرير». فلفظة «على» لا بدّ من نقلها، اذ هى جزء المحمول هاهنا وايراد العكس والنقيض والسوالب والمهملات البعضية إنمّا كان للتنبيه لا لحاجتنا اليه فيما بعد.

Rule six

[On what pertains to the syllogism]

(24) A syllogism has at least two propositions. If one of the propositions includes the entire conclusion, the proposition is conditional and another proposition is posited or denied. This is the "exclusive syllogism." If one proposition corresponds to part of the conclusion, then the other proposition must correspond to the other part. The syllogism in this case is called "conjunctive."[25] No single syllogism consists of more than two propositions because the conclusion has only two parts. Since each of the two premises corresponds to one part of the conclusion, it is impossible to add a third. As for conditionals, in the case of exclusive syllogisms, only the exclusion will remain.[26] Indeed, it is possible to have many syllogisms, all of which establish the premises of a syllogism. When a proposition becomes part of a syllogism, it is called a "premise." In a conjunctive syllogism, both premises must share something called the "middle term." Both the subject and the predicate of the premise are called "terms." The middle term may be in the predicate of one of the premises and the subject of the other, or it may be in the subject of both or the predicate of both. The two terms other than the middle are called the "extremes." The conclusion is obtained from the two terms with the middle omitted. When the repeated term—that is, the middle—is the subject of the first premise and the predicate of the second premise,[27] it is an implausible figure whose validity as a syllogism is not intuitively obvious and is thus omitted. The perfect conjuctive syllogism is that in which the middle term is the predicate of the first premise and the subject of the second. This is the most perfect mood.[28]

An Illuminationist doctrine [on negations]

(25) Know that the difference between negation in an affirmative proposition and the negation that severs the relation of affirmation is that

الضابط السادس

[فى ما يتعلّق بالقياس]

(٢٤) هو انّ القياس لا يكون اقلّ من قضيتين فان القضية الواحدة ان اشتملت على كل النتيجة فهى شرطية، لا بدّ فيها من وضع او رفع قضية أُخرى وهو القياس الاستثنائى. وان ناسبت جزء المطلوب، فلا بدّ مما يناسب الجزء الآخر فيكون قضية اخرى ويُسمّى حينئذ القياس «اقترانيا». ولا قياس واحد من اكثر من قضيتين، فانّ المطلوب ليس له إلاّ جزءان. فاذا ناسب كل واحد من القضيتين جزءا فلا امكان لانضمام الثالثة. وفى الشرطية لم يبق إلاّ الاستثناء فى الاستثنائيات، بل يجوز ان تكون قياسات كثيرة مبيّنة لمقدمتى قياس واحد. والقضية اذا صارت جزء القياس تسُمّى «مقدمة». ولا بدّ من اشتراك مقدمتى الاقترانى فى شئ يسُمّى «الحدّ الاوسط»، وكل واحد من موضوع المقدمة ومحمولها يسُمّى «حدّا». والشركة لا بدّ وان تقع فى محمول احديهما وموضوع الاخُرى او موضوعهما او محمولهما وغير الاوسط من الحدين يسُمّى «طرفا». والنتيجة تحصل من الطرفين وينحذف الاوسط. واذا كان الحدّ المتكرر، اعنى الاوسط، موضوع المقدمة الاولى ومحمول الثانية فهو السياق البعيد الّذى لا يتفطن لقياسيته من نفسه، فحذف. والتام من الاقترانيات ما يكون الاوسط محمول الاولى فيه وموضوع الثانية، وهو السياق الأتمّ: وهاهنا.

دقيقة اشراقية [فى السلب]

(٢٥) اعلم ان الفرق بين السلب اذا كان فى القضية الموجبة، وبين السلب اذا كان قاطعا للنسبة الايجابية، هو ان الأوّل لا يصحّ على المعدوم، اذ لا

the first cannot apply to the nonexistent, since the affirmation must apply to something that can be affirmed. In the second, the denial may apply to that which can be denied.[29] However, this distinction only applies to propositions about individuals and does not apply to universal propositions or other quantified propositions. When you say, "All men are non-stone," or "No man is stone," you are making a judgment about each and every thing that can be described as "man" in the propositions, whereas the negation applies only to stoniness. Thus, all individuals that can be described as being "man" must exist for the description to be correct. Since there is no longer a distinction, negation in a universal proposition ought to be made part of either the predicate or the subject, so that we will only have affirmative propositions and no error will occur when we distribute the parts in premises of syllogisms. Indeed, negation does play a role in the making of a negative proposition—since it is part of the assent, as we have said—and is made part of the affirmative proposition. How could it be otherwise when you know that affirming impossibility allows us to dispense with the negation of the necessary and that the negation and the affirmation of a contingent proposition are the same?

The most perfect figure is the single mood: "Necessarily all C are B, and necessarily all B are A; therefore, necessarily all C are A." Should the first premise be particular, then we will make it exhaustive, as mentioned before—as, for example, "Some animals are rational," and "All rational beings are capable of laughter." Let us give a name to the particular without considering the predication of rationality, though rationality accompanies the particular. Let this be D. Thus, it can be said, "All D are rational, and all rational beings are so-and-so," according to what we said before. Now we no longer need to say, "Some animals are D" as another premise, because D is the name of that animal, and how can a thing's name be predicated of it? If there should be a negation, we shall make it a part, as before, and say, "All men are animals, and all animals are non-stone; therefore, all men are non-stone."

There is no need to multiply the moods of syllogism, rejecting some and accepting others. Further, since the last term leads to the first term by means of the middle, the modes in the definite necessary proposition are

بدّ للاثبات من ان يكون على ثابت بخلاف الثانى، فان النفى يجوز عن المنفى. ولكن هذا الفرق إنمّا يكون فى الشخصيات لا فى القضايا المحيطة وجملة المحصورات. فانك اذا قلت «كل انسان هو غير حجر» او «لا شئ من الانسان بحجر» هو حكم على كل واحد من الموصوفات بالانسانية فيهما، والسلب إنمّا هو للحجرية. فلا بد وان تكون الموصوفات بالانسانية متحققة حتى يصحّ ان تكون موصوفة بها. فاذا زال الفرق، فيجعل[٢٧] السلب فى المحيطة جزء المحمول او الموضوع حتى لا يكون لنا قضية إلاّ موجبة، ولا يقع الخبط فى نقل الاجزاء فى مقدمات الاقيسة، ولانّ السلب له مدخل فى كون القضية السالبة قضية، اذ هو جزء التصديق على ما سبق، فنجعله جزءا للموجبة، كيف وقد دريت انّ ايجاب الامتناع يغنى عن ذكر السلب الضرورى، والممكن ايجابه وسلبه سواء.

والسياق الأتمّ ضرب واحد، وهو «كل ج ب بتّة وكل ب ا بتّة»، فينتج «كل ج ا بتّة». واذا كانت المقدمة جزئية، فنجعلها مستغرقة، كما سبق، مثل «ان يكون بعض الحيوان ناطقا» و«كل ناطق ضاحك» مثلا. فلنجعل لذلك البعض مع قطع النظر عن الناطقية اسما وان كان معها، وليكن د؛ فيقال «كل د ناطق وكل ناطق كذا» على ما سبق. ثم لا نحتاج الى ان نقول «وبعض الحيوان د» على انّه مقدمة اُخرى لانّ د اسم ذلك الحيوان، فكيف يحمل عليه اسمه؟ وان كان ثَمّ سلب، فلنجعل جزءا كما مضى. فيقال «كل انسان حيوان» و«كل حيوان فهو غير حجر» ينتج «كل انسان هو غير حجر»؛ فلا يحتاج الى تكثير ضروب وحذف بعض واعتبار بعض. ثم لما كان الطرف الاخير يتعدى الى الطرف الأوّل بتوسط الاوسط، فالجهات فى القضية الضرورية البتّاتة تجعل جزء

made part of the predicate in one or both of the premises, thus leading to the major. For example, "All men are necessarily contingently literate, and all contingently literate beings are necessarily animals by necessity (or contingently walkers), therefore, all men are necessarily animals by necessity (or contingently walkers)."[30]

There is no need here to elaborate any further concerning the composite moods. Rather, the Illuminationist rule will suffice. The other two figures[31] are appendages of this figure. In this respect, there is a principle:

A principle [of Illumination relating to the second figure]

(26) Whenever there are two universal propositions with different subjects, and the predicate of one cannot be affirmed of the other in all respects, or in some one respect, then it is known with certainty that if one of the two subjects could be conceived to be included under the other, it would have been possible for the predicate of the other to be predicated of it. Therefore, it is impossible for one of the two to be described by the other, regardless of which one is made the subject of the conclusion and which one is made the predicate. The conclusion will be definite and necessary, asserting the impossibility of predicating its predicate[32] [on the other subject] or the necessity of negation therein. So affirmations and negations will be made parts of the predicate, as in: "All men are necessarily contingently literate," and "All stones are necessarily impossibly literate." We thus know that "All men necessarily are impossibly stones." So, in this specific mood, it is not a condition that the predicates be the same in every aspect. They need only be the same in that which they share apart from the mode that is made part of the predicate, and it is thus permissible for the two modes of the two premises to be different.[33] They differ from the first figure in that these two statements are propositions such that what is impossible for the subject of one of the two is possible for the subject of the other. For each of the propositions, what is possible for the subject of one is impossible for the subject of the other. Their two subjects are necessarily incompatible, yielding the conclusion that these two statements are propositions whose

المحمول فى المقدمتين او فى احداهما، فعدى الى الاصغر، مثل «كل انسان بالضرورة هو ممكن الكتابة» و«كل ممكن الكتابة فهو بالضرورة واجب الحيوانية او ممكن المشى»، ينتج «ان كل انسان بالضرورة واجب الحيوانية او ممكن المشى». ولا يحتاج الى تطويل كثير فى المختلطات، بل الضابط الاشراقى مقنع، والسياقان الآخران ذنابتان لهذا السياق. وهاهنا:

قاعدة [فى قاعدة الاشراقيين فى الشكل الثانى]

(٢٦) وهى انّه اذا كانت قضيتان محيطتان مختلفتا الموضوع يستحيل اثبات محمول احديهما على الأُخرى من جميع الوجوه او من وجه واحد فيعلم يقينا انّه لو كان احدهما مما يتصور ان يدخل تحت الآخر ما استحال عليه محموله. فيمتنع اذن ان يوصف احدهما بالآخر ايُّهما جُعل موضوعا فى النتيجة، وايُّهما حمل هاهنا، فالنتيجة ضرورية بتّاتة لامتناع حمل[٢٨] محمولها او وجوب السلب فيها فما يكون فى المقدمتين من جهات او سلب سلوب[٢٩] فتُجعل جزءا من المحمول،[٣٠] مثل قولك «كل انسان بالضرورة ممكن الكتابة» و«كل حجر بالضرورة فهو ممتنع الكتابة». فنعلم انّ الانسان بالضرورة ممتنع الحجرية وحينئذ لا يشترط اتحاد المحمول ايضا فى جميع الوجوه فى هذا السياق خاصة، بل إنمّا تعتبر الشركة فيها وراء الجهة المجعولة جزء المحمول، ويجوز تغاير جهتى القضيتين فيه ومخرجه من السياق الأوّل: ان هذين القولين قضيتان استحال على موضوع احديهما ما امكن على موضوع الأُخرى وكل قضيتين استحال على موضوع احديهما ما امكن على موضوع الاخُرى، فموضوعهما بالضرورة متباينان؛ فهذان القولان

subjects are necessarily different. Likewise, if the predicate of one definite proposition has a contingent relation and [the predicate of] the other a necessary relation, then a necessary relation is impossible for the first and contingency is impossible for the other. Likewise, if the predicate of one has a contingent relation and [the predicate of] the other a relation of impossibility, it is as we had said before.

Should there be a particular proposition in this figure, then we will transform it into a universal, as mentioned before. It is not necessary for us to do this for each and every premise in the sciences. Rather, if we learn the law here and apply it in every case to any two premises that we encounter, we will know what their status is. We can thus leave lengthy discussions to the logicians who deal with moods, exposition, and mixed forms.

Conditionals also may be discussed in the same way. Should the subjects of the two premises be such that one of the two may correctly be included in the other, then that which is predicated necessarily of the particulars of one will be the same as that which is contingent or impossible for the particulars of the other premise. And in this way, the contradictory of the consequence will imply the contradictory of the antecedent.

A principle [of Illumination relating to the third figure]

(27) When we find a single thing described by two predicates, we know that at least one thing from one of the predicates is necessarily described by the other predicate. For example, if "Zayd is animal," and "Zayd is man," then we know that "Some animal is man," and "Some man is animal," whatever else may be the case. Should this specific thing be a general meaning, then we will make the proposition exhaustive, as in "All men are animal, and all men are rational." This will then be confined to a specific thing described by both, and it will follow that something from one of the two is the other. When a particular thing is described by one or both of the predicates and is specified and made universal, then the case will be the same.[34] The negation should be made part of the predicate and transferred to the conclusion. The middle term will be described by the two extremes[35] in every place of this figure without

موضوعهما بالضرورة متباينان.[٣١] وكذا اذا كان فى البتّاتة محمول احديهما ممكن النسبة وفى الاخرى واجب النسبة، فان وجوب النسبة يمتنع على الأوّلى والامكان على الاخرى. وكذا[٣٢] اذا كان محمول احداهما واجب النسبة والآخر[٣٣] ممتنع النسبة فكان على ما قلنا. وان كان فى هذا السياق جزئية فلتُجعل كلية، كما سبق. ولسنا نوجب ان نعمل فى آحاد مقدمات العلوم هذا العمل، بل اذا علمنا القانون هاهنا، فلكل مقدمتين صادفناهما على هذا القانون، علمنا ان حالهما كما سبق، وتركنا التطويل على اصحابه فى الضروب والبيان والخبط. ولهذا خرج من الشرطيات من انه لو كان موضوعا هاتين المقدمتين ما يصح دخول احدهما فى الآخر فما وجب على جزئيات احدهما ما امكن على جزئيات الآخر او امتنع؛ ويستثنى نقيض التالى لنقيض المقدم.

قاعدة [فى قاعدة الاشراقيين فى الشكل الثالث]

(٢٧) واذا وجدنا شيئا واحدا معينا ووُصف بمحمولين، علمنا ان شيئا من احد المحمولين موصوف بالمحمول الآخر ضرورة، مثل «ان يكون زيد حيوانا وزيد انسانا»، علمنا ان شيئا من الحيوان انسان بل وشيئا[٣٥] من الانسان حيوان على اى طريق كان. واذا كان هذا الشئ المعيّن معنى عاما فيُجعل مستغرقا، كقولك[٣٦] «كل انسان حيوان وكل انسان ناطق»، فصار هذا الحصر لشئ معين موصوف بالأمرين فيلزم ان يكون شئ من احدهما هو الآخر. واذا كان بعض من شئ موصوفا باحد المحمولين او كليهما وعُيّن فجُعل مستغرقا، فكان[٣٧] هذا حاله، ويُجعل السلب ايضا جزء المحمول، فينقل الى النتيجة، ويكون الاوسط موصوفا بالطرفين فى جميع المواضع فى هذا السياق دون الحاجة الى

requiring a negative proposition. And if both premises contain negations, then the two negations should be made part of the two predicates. One should say, "All men are non-birds, and all men are non-horses." The conclusion will be affirmative: "Something described as a non-bird is a non-horse." If one of the premises is universal and the other is not, it is permissible if the subjects overlap. This is because the particular is itself included in "all." In this way, it is certain that some one thing is described by both predicates, implying that some one thing described by one predicate is also described by the other. It does not follow that everything described by one of the predicates is described by the other in this figure. This is because either both predicates or one of them may be more general than the subject that is the middle term and more general than the extreme. Therefore, it is not necessary that each single one of the two be described by the other, but it will be necessary that something of the one be described by the other.

Since we have made the modalities and negations of the premises parts of the predicate, we are able to dispense with many moods and mixed forms. The validity of the syllogism will depend only on this: the certainty that one thing is described by two things. It differs from the first figure in that the two statements are propositions within each of which is something described by each predicate and within which is something described by both predicates. Therefore, an individual described by one predicate is also described by the other. This is all there is to these two propositions, and we can dispense with lengthy discussions.

A section on conditionals[36]

(28) Conjunctive syllogisms are composed of conditionals, as in the compound proposition, "Whenever the Sun has risen, then it is day; and whenever it is day, then the stars are hidden."[37] The conditions and terms are treated in the way discussed above.[38] A syllogism may also be composed of a conditional and a categorical proposition. The common term

سالب. واذا كان المقدمتان فيهما السلبان فجُعل السلبان جزء المحمولين، صحّ ايضا، كما فى قولك «كل انسان هو لا طير[٣٨] وكل انسان هو لا فرس» جائت النتيجة موجبة، وهى ان شيئا مما يوصف بانه «لا طير» هو «لا فرس». وان كانت احدى المقدمتين مستغرقة والأُخرى غير مستغرقة بعد الشركة فى الموضوع، يجوز، فان دخل البعض[٣٩] فى الكل فيتيّقن كون الشئ[٤٠] واحدا موصوفا بالمحمولين ويلزم اتصاف شئ من احد المحمولين بالآخر. ولا يلزم اتصاف كل واحد من المحمولين بالآخر فى هذا السياق، فان المحمولين او احدهما ربما يكون اعم من الموضوع الّذى هو الاوسط والطرف الآخر، فلا يلزم اتصاف كل احدهما بالآخر، بل شئ من احدهما هو الآخر؛ واذا جعلنا الجهات والسلوب اجزاء المحمول فى المقدمتين حصل الاستغناء عن ضروب كثيرة ومختلطات. ومداره على أمر واحد وهو تيّقن اتصاف شئ واحد بشيئين؛ ومخرجه من الشكل الأوّل هو انّ هذين القولين قضيتان فيهما شئ مّا وُصف بكلى المحمولين؛ وكل قضيتين فيهما شئ مّا وُصف بكلى المحمولين، فبعض من موصوفات[٤١] احد المحمولين يوصف بالآخر. فهذان القولان هكذا حالهما وقد انحذف عنّا التطويلاة.

فصل فى الشرطيات

(٢٨) والشرطيات تؤلّف[٤٢] منها قياسات اقترانية، كقولك فى المتصلات «كلّما كانت الشمس طالعة فالنهار موجود، وكلّما كان النهار موجودا فالكواكب خفية» ينتج «كلّما كانت الشمس طالعة فالكواكب خفية». والشرائط والحدود حالهما[٤٣] كما سبق. وقد يتركب قياس من شرطية وحملية كقولك،[٤٤] فيما اذا كانت الشركة بينهما فى

may be[39] in the consequent and the categorical in the major, as in "If all C are B, then all E are D, but all E are A." The conclusion will be a compound conditional proposition whose antecedent will be the minor antecedent of the syllogism itself, and its consequent will be the result of the combination of the consequent and the categorical, as in "If all C are B, then all E are A."

A section [on reductio ad absurdum*]*

(29) The syllogism that shows the truth of the conclusion by proving the falsity of its contradictory is called *reductio ad absurdum.* It is composed of two syllogisms, one categorical and one exclusive, as in "If it is false that no C is B, then some C are B, and all B are A." If the premise is true, then the conclusion will be: "If it is false that no C is B, then some C are A." You could, if you want, make these propositions universal propositions, as we saw before, by making universal the contradictory of the desired conclusion, which is the consequent of the conditional. Next, the contradictory of the consequent will be excluded so that the contradictory of the antecedent will be the result, which is: "It is not false that no C is B; rather, it is true." In *reductio ad absurdum,* it is clear that an absurd conclusion cannot be inferred from true premises or their combination. The contradictory of the desired conclusion implies the absurdity.

Rule seven

[On the matter of demonstrative syllogisms]

(30) In true sciences, only demonstration is used. Demonstration is a syllogism composed of premises known with certainty. The premises that we know with certainty may be "primary," meaning those to which assent is given merely by conceiving their terms and whose truth no one can deny after their terms have been understood. Examples are the judgments that the whole is greater than the part, that two things equal to the same thing are themselves equal, and that "black" and "white" cannot be said of the same thing at the same time and place. "Perceived" premises may be known through your outer or inner senses. These

التالى والحملية كبرى، «كلّما كان ج ب فكل ه د، وكل د ا» فتحصل النتيجة شرطية متصلة مقدمها مقدم صغرى القياس بعينه وتاليها نتيجة تأليف التالى والحملية، كقولنا «كلّما كان ج ب فكل ه ا».

فصل [فى قياس الخلف]

(٢٩) والقياس الّذى يتبيّن فيه حقة[٤٥] المطلوب بابطال نقيضه هو قياس الخلف ويتركب من قياسين: اقترانى واستثنائى، كقولك «ان كذب لا شئ من ج ب فبعض ج ب وكل ب ا» على انها مقدمة حقة ينتج على ما قلنا «ان كذب لا شئ من ج ب، فبعض ج ا». وان شئت جعلت هذه محيطة كما سبق بان تجعل نقيض المطلوب، الّذى هو تالى الشرطية، محيطا. ثم يستثنى نقيض التالى، لينتج نقيض المقدم وهو انه «لم يكذب لا شئ من ج ب بل هو صادق». وفى الخلف يتبيّن ان كذب[٤٦] النتيجة المحالة ما لزمت من المقدمة الصادقة ولا من الترتيب، فتعيّن ان يكون لنقيض المطلوب.

الضابط السابع

[فى مواد الاقيسة البرهانية]

(٣٠) هو ان العلوم الحقيقية لا يستعمل فيها إلاّ البرهان، وهو قياس مؤلف من مقدمات يقينية. ثم ما تعلمه يقينا من المقدمات اما ان يكون «اوليا» وهو الّذى تصديقه لا يتوقف على غير تصوّر الحدود، ولا يتأتى لاحد انكاره بعد تصور الحدود، كحكمك انّ «الكل اعظم من الجزء»، وانّ[٤٧] الاشياء المساوية لشئ واحد بعينه[٤٨] متساوية، وانّ السواد والبياض لا يجتمعان فى محل واحد. او يكون «مشاهدا» بقواك الظاهرة او

include sensory data, like the Sun shining, or your knowledge that you have desire and anger. Such perceived premises are not probative for someone else who has not had the same apprehension.

Premises may also be "intuitive." According to Illuminationist principles, intuitive premises are of several kinds. The first are the empirical premises: things observed with such great frequency as to yield certitude and to make one confident that these could not occur by chance—for example, the judgment that being hit with a stick is painful. This conclusion is not reached by induction, for induction is a conclusion about a universal based on its many particulars. Since induction is an expression for this judgment, then we know that our judgment that no man will live if his head is cut off is only a conclusion in relation to the universal based on the many particulars that are actually encountered because one cannot observe the whole. Induction may lead to certitude if there is only one species, as in the example just mentioned; but should they be of different species, then the induction may not lead to certitude. The judgment that all animals move the lower jaw when eating, which is an induction based on what you have observed, may be false, because it is possible that what you have not observed—such as a crocodile[40]—is different from what you have observed.

The second kind of intuitive premise is the "traditional" premise. This is a proposition of which a man can be certain because of the large frequency of testimonies to it, the observed thing itself being contingent and the man himself being confident that there is no collusion. Certitude itself is the evidence that the number of testimonies is sufficient. It is not up to us to set the number at some fixed amount, because certitude is often obtained from a small number.[41] Associations have something to do with all these things, and man acquires an intuition by means of them. Your intuitions are not proof for someone else, because he does not obtain the same thing as you do by way of intuition. Often the estimative faculty of man makes a judgment about something which turns out to be false, such as the denial of the soul, of the intellect, and of the nonspatial existent. It may assist the intellect by supplying premises that imply its converse, whereupon [the intellect] will accept what it had rejected. However, every estimative judgment that contradicts reason is false, and reason never affirms that which implies a contradiction with something else it had deduced.

الباطنة، كالمحسوسات مثل انّ الشمس مضيئة، او كعلمك بان لك شهوة او غضبا؛ ومشاهدتك ليست بحجة على غيرك ما لم يكن له ذلك المشعر والشعور. او يكون «حدسيا».

والحدسيات على قاعدة الاشراق لها اصناف: اولها «المجربات»، وهى مشاهدات مكررة مفيدة بالتكرار يقينا تأمن فيه النفس عن[٤٩] الاتفاق، كحكمك بانّ «الضرب بالخشب مؤلم»، وليس هو من الاستقراء، والاستقراء هو حكم على كلى بما وُجد فى جزئياته الكثيرة. فاذا كان الاستقراء عبارة عن هذا الحكم[٥٠] فنعلم انّ حكمنا على كل انسان «بانه اذا قُطع رأسه لا يعيش» ليس إلاّ حكما على كلى بما صودف فى جزئياته الكثيرة اذ لا مشاهدة للكل، والاستقراء قد يفيد اليقين، اذا اتخذ النوع كما فى المثال المذكور. واذا اختلف، قد لا يفيد اليقين، كحكمك بانّ «كل حيوان يحرّك لدن مضغة فكه الاسفل» استقراءا بما شاهدت ويجوز ان يكون حكم ما لم تشاهده، كالتمساح، بخلاف ما شاهدته.

ومن الحدسيات «المتواترات»، وهى قضايا يحكم بها الانسان لكثرة الشهادات يقينا ويكون الشئ ممكنا فى نفسه وتأمن النفس عن التواطئ واليقين هو القاضى بوفور الشهادات، وليس لنا ان نحصر عددها فى مبلغ معيّن،[٥١] فرُبّ يقين حصل من عدد قليل وللقراين مدخل فى هذه الاشياء كلها يحدس منها الانسان حدسا. وحدسياتك ليست بحجة[٥٢] على غيرك، اذا لم يحصل له من الحدس ما حصل لك. وكثيرا ما يحكم الوهم الانسانى بشئ ويكون كاذبا، كانكاره لنفسه وللعقل وللموجود لا فى جهة، ويساعد العقل فى مقدمات ناتجة لنقيضه؛ فاذا وصل الى النتيجة، رجع عمّا سلّمه. فكل وهمى يخالف العقل فهو باطل والعقل لا يوجب ما يقتضى خلاف مقتضى آخر له.

"Generally accepted" premises are not always known innately.[42] Some of them may be proven to be true—such as the judgment that ignorance is abhorrent—while others are false. A primary premise may also be generally accepted.[43]

Other propositions that may be used as premises are those that are accepted from someone of whom one holds a high opinion.[44] Some premises do not lead to assent but do affect the sentiments; these are called "imaginative," such as the judgment that honey is bitter and induces vomiting.[45] Other propositions trick people and induce doubts in order to create belief in a falsehood. We will mention them later.

Demonstration uses only premises known with certitude—premises either known innately or based on prior innate premises in a valid syllogism.

A section [on analogy]

(31) Analogy does not yield certitude. It is an argument claiming that a predicate[46] is common to two things based on an element being common to them both. Dialecticians identify two methods in this mode. In the first, wherever the common meaning is found, then that predicate is associated with it—and vice versa—so, therefore, they are connected in point in question. However, [the dialecticians] cannot explain why these two should be inseparable in some other circumstances not considered in the proof. In the second method, they enumerate some attributes of that in which the predicate happens to exist. This they call the "root," or the "evidence." They cannot be sure that they have not overlooked some attribute that is the basis of the predicate. Many predicates depend on something of which one becomes aware only later on. [The dialecticians] then assert that all individual things, except that to which the predicate is related in the root, are incapable of causing the predicate because of the absence of the predicate with each one of them in another context. They may also assert that that to which the predicate is related is independent of the attributes in causing the predicate in another context. Though they may try to eliminate everything other than that to which the predicate is related, there is still the continuing probability of its being in the root because of its specificity and individuality—not due to a meaning that may be transcended, and not because of a collection of attributes that is more inclusive, because it certainly contains the cause.

و«المشهورات» قد لا تكون ايضا فطرية؛[٥٣] فمنها[٥٤] ما يتبين بالحجة، كحكمك[٥٥] بان «الجهل قبيح»؛ ومنها باطل. وقد يكون الاولى مشهورا ايضا. ومن القضايا ما قُبل[٥٦] عمن يحسن به الظن ومن القضايا ما يُؤثر لا بتصديق[٥٧] بل بقبض وبسط وسُميّت «المخيلات»، كحكمك بان «العسل مرة متهوعة»؛ ومنها قضايا مزوّرة مشبهة بأمر مروج بالتزوير وسنذكرها. فلا تستعمل فى البرهان[٥٨] إلاّ اليقينى[٥٩] سواء كان فطريا او يبتنى على فطرى فى قياس صحيح.

فصل [فى التمثيل]

(٣١) التمثيل غير مفيد لليقين، وهو ما يُدّعى فيه شمول حكم الأمرين بناء على شمول معنى واحد لهما ثم يقرر اصحاب الجدل هذا النمط بطريقين: احدهما هو انّ المعنى الشامل حيث عُهد كان مقترنا بهذا الحكم، وكذا بالعكس؛ فيقترنان فى محل النزاع وهم فى حيّز الانقطاع عند مطالبة لميّة عدم جواز انفكاكها فى موضع لم يعهده هذا المحتج؛ والثانى هو انّهم يعدّون صفات ما وُجد فيه الحكم بالاتفاق الّذى سموه الاصل او الشاهد ولا ينقطع عنهم احتمال جواز[٦٠] وصف غفلوا عنه هو مناط الحكم. فرُبّ حكم متعلق بشئ لا يطلع عليه إلاّ بعد حين. ثم يثبتون انّ ما وراء ما نُسب اليه الحكم فى الاصل آحاده غير صالحة لاقتضاء الحكم لتخلف الحكم عن كل واحد فى موضع آخر او انّ الّذى نُسب اليه الحكم استقل دون الاوصاف باقتضاء الحكم فى موضع آخر. اما الغاء ما سوى الّذى نُسب اليه الحكم لا يتمشى لبقاء احتمال ان يكون فى الاصل لخصوصه وتشخيصه[٦١] لا لمعنى يجوز ان يتعدى، او لمجموع الاوصاف وهو احوَط لاشتماله على العلة يقينا.

They may work this out two by two or three by three, with every degree of number having some role. It is also possible that what they specify might be divided into two classes in which the predicate is correlated with only one of them and in which the correlation does not exist in the absence of the common element. This is similar to the previous case, in view of the likelihood of neglecting some attribute that is actually the basis of the predicate. The claim that the attribute that [the dialecticians] have specified is independent in another context is of no help to them, in view of the possibility that that attribute is part of one of the two causes and that, to whichever of the two it is adjoined, it implies the predicate. It may also be that a single general predicate may have many causes, as we will mention; so there would also be another attribute in that place along with it, and the whole would collectively necessitate that predicate. The argument would thus regress to the enumeration of the attributes, if they were linked thereafter in a second place. [The dialecticians] reject the possibility of a general predicate being caused in different places by different causes, and they offer proofs against it. However, the basis of their proof is itself analogy, so that they affirm by analogy some of what analogy is based upon. Moreover, if it is possible for a single general predicate to have multiple causes, then their principle—that the cause of the evidence is the cause of the absent thing—must be unsound. The existence of conditions also makes it allowable for a general or particular thing to have alternative conditions and causes. Another of their principles is that that which indicates something in the evidence also indicates it in the absent thing. To this it may be replied that, if the indication of it were essential to the general predicate, then its relation would be the same to both the evidence and the absent thing, and there would be no need for analogy. But if the specificity of the evidence has something to do with the indication or with the establishment of the indication, the previous argument applies to the specificity.[47]

A section [on the division of demonstration into causal and assertoric][48]

(32) The demonstration in which the middle term is the cause of the relation between the major and the minor terms in both the mind and in concrete reality is called "causal." That in which it is the cause of the relation between the two extremes only in the mind—that is, it is the cause only of the assent—is called "assertoric demonstration" because

وعند النزول عند هذا، يجوز ان يكون اثنان اثنان او ثلاثة ثلاثة، وكل مرتبة من العدد له مدخل. وايضا يحتمل انقسام ما عيّنوه الى قسمين لا يلازم إلاّ لاحدهما، ولا يوجد فى محل النزاع؛ وهذا يقرب من الوجه الّذى سبق من احتمال غفلتهم عن وصف هو المناط، ودعوى استقلال الوصف الّذى عيّنوه فى موضع آخر لا ينجعهم لجواز ان يكون ذلك الوصف جزء احدى العلتين الى ايهما ينضم اقتضى الحكم، ويجوز ان يكون لحكم واحد عام اسباب كثيرة كما سنذكره؛ فيكون فى ذلك الموضع معه صفة أُخرى،[٦٢] فيقتضى الكل باجتماع ذلك الحكم، ويعود الكلام الى عدّ الاوصاف ان التزم بعدّها فى الموضع الثانى؛ وهم ينكرون جواز تعليل الحكم العام فى المواضع المتعددة بالعلل المتعددة، ويقيمون الحجة عليه. ثم يرجع حاصل حجتهم الى التمثيل، فيثبتون بالتمثيل بعض ما يبتنى عليه التمثيل، وايضا اذا جاز ان يكون الحكم واحد عام علل، لا تصحّ قاعدتهم ان العلة فى الشاهد علة فى الغائب، وكذا الشرط يجوز ان يكون لشئ عام او مشخص شروط وعلل[٦٣] على سبيل البدل. ومن قواعدهم ايضا انّ ما دلّ على أمر فى الشاهد دلّ على مثله فى الغائب؛ فيُقال ان كانت الدلالة له[٦٤] لذاته على الحكم العام، فنسبتها الى ما فى الشاهد والغائب سواء، فلا حاجة الى التمثيل وان كان لخصوص الشاهد مدخل فى الدلالة او اثبات الدلالة، فالكلام فى اعتبار الخصوص ما سلف.

فصل [فى انقسام البرهان الى برهان لمِ وبرهان اَنَّ]

(٣٢) الحدّ الاوسط قد يكون عليه نسبة الطرفين ذهنا وعينا والبرهان الّذى فيه ذلك يُسمّى «برهان لمِ»؛ وقد يكون على نسبة الطرفين فى الذهن فقط، اى يكون على التصديق فحسب، ويُسمّى

it shows only that the proposition is the case, but not why it is so in itself. It may happen that the middle term is itself caused by the relation in concrete reality but is more apparent to us, such as, "This stick is burning, and everything that is burning must have been touched by fire; therefore, this stick has been touched by fire."[49]

A section [on the questions asked in science][50]

(33) Among the questions asked in science is "What?" which seeks the concept of the thing. "Does . . . ?" seeks one extreme of the contradiction connected with it, its answer being one of the two. "Which?" seeks a distinction. "Why?" seeks the cause of the assent; it may also seek the cause of the thing in concrete reality. These are the principal scientific questions. The secondary questions include, "How is the thing?" the answer to which is called "quality"—for example, "The thing is black (or is white)." The answer to "How much?" is called "quantity" and may be continuous, as with magnitudes, or discrete, as with numbers. "Where?" seeks a thing's relation to its place, and "When?" its relation to its time. "Which?" may be used to make these other questions unnecessary by linking it to what is sought, as in, "In which place is it?" or "In which time is it?" thereby making "where" and "when" extraneous. The question "Who?" seeks to specify that which is known to be rational by essence.

«برهان انّ» لاقتصاد دلالته على انّية الحكم دون لميته فى نفسه. وقد يكون هذا الاوسط معلول النسبة فى الاعيان إلاّ انه اظهر عندنا، كقولك «هذا الخشب محترق وكل محترق مسّته النار، فهذا الخشب مسّته النار».

فصل [فى بيان المطالب]

(٣٣) والمطالب منها «ما»، ويطلب لها مفهوم الشئ؛ و«هَلْ»، ويطلب به احد طرفى النقيض[٦٥] ما قُرن به وجوابه باحدهما؛ و«اَىْ»، ويطلب به التمييز؛ و«لما»، ويطلب به علة التصديق وقد يطلب به علة الشئ فى الاعيان. فهذه هى اصول المطالب العلمية. ومن فروعها «كَيْف» الشئ، وما يقال فى جوابه «كيفية» مثل انّ الشئ اسود وابيض؛ و«كَمْ»، وما يقال فى جتوابه يُسمّى «كمية» كانت متصلة، كالمقادير، او منفصلة، كالاعداد؛ و«اين» الشئ، ويطلب به نسبة الشئ الى مكانه؛ و«متى»، ويطلب به نسبة الشئ الى زمانه. وقد يغنى عنهما «اى» اذا قرن بما يطلب، كما يقال «فى اى مكان هو؟» او «فى اى زمان هو؟» فيغنى «اى»، «عَنْ»، «متَىْ»، و«ايَنْ»، وعلى هذا غيرهما ومن المطالب «مَنْ» الشئ ويطلب به خصوص ما عُرف انه عاقل لذاته.

The Third Discourse

On sophistical refutations and some judgments between the Illuminationists and the Peripatetic doctrine, in [several] sections

Section one

On sophistical refutations[1]

(34) Error may occur in a syllogism because its arrangement is not one of the valid moods that we have mentioned. This may be because the middle term is not shared completely by the second premise, because it is not the same in both, or because it is not predicated of all. For example, to say "All men are animals, and animal is a universal; therefore, all men are universals" is an error due to the indefiniteness of the second premise and because "animal" in the second premise cannot be predicated of all but, rather, is something peculiar to the mental reality and thus is not distributed as a middle term. Other errors occur because one of the two extremes is not used in the conclusion in the same way that it is used in the syllogism. If you bear in mind what has been said before, you will be immune from error in such things.

(35) Errors may occur because of the matter—for example, in begging the question, which is when the conclusion is presupposed in the syllogism in different words. The premise may be less known than the conclusion or similar to it, so that the conclusion proven by the premise

المقالة الثالثة
فى المغالطات وبعض الحكومات
بين احرف اشراقية وبين احرف المشائين

وفيها فصول

الفصل الأوّل

فى المغالطات

(٣٤) انّه قد يقع الغلط فى القياس بسبب ترتيبه وهو ان لا يكون من هيئة ناتجة على ما ذكرنا. ومما يتعلق بذلك لا ينتقل الحدّ الاوسط بالكلية الى المقدمة الثانية او لا يكون متشابها فيهما او لا يكون مقولا على الكل، كقولك «كل انسان حيوان والحيوان عام» لينتج «انّ كل انسان عام»، وهو خطأ قد نشأ من اهمال المقدمة الثانية وكون الحيوان فى المقدمة الثانية غير مقول على الكل، بل هو مختص بالحقيقة الذهنية فلا يتعدى او لا يكون احد الطرفين فى النتيجة على ما ذكر فى القياس. فاذا حفظت ما مضى امنت من الغلط فى هذه الاشياء.

(٣٥) وقد يقع الغلط بسبب المادة، كالمصادرة على المطلوب الأوّل، وهو ان تكون النتيجة بعينها موردة فى القياس مغيرة فى اللفظ وكما تكون المقدمة اخفى من النتيجة او مثلها، فلا يكون تبييّن النتيجة

may equally well prove the premise. The premise may be false because of semantic errors in the use of particles or nouns or ambiguous grammatical forms.

(36) Errors may occur because the negation or the mode is too early or too late or is repeated, as when people suppose that "not necessarily" and "necessarily not" are the same. This is an error, because the first is true of the contingent thing, while the second is not. Likewise, "It does not follow that . . ." is not the same as "It follows that not . . . ." That which is not contingent may be necessary, either in its existence or its nonexistence. This is unlike something that is contingently nonexistent, because such a thing is also contingently existent. If by "contingency" is meant that which is not impossible—"general contingency"—the affirmative cannot be converted to a negative, nor the negative to an affirmative.

If you make the negative particles parts of the subjects or the predicates, as we mentioned before, and do not use a separate particle, and reduce the propositions to affirmative ones, as you are able to do, then you will not have to multiply negations and verbal compounds and will be safe from this fallacy. Negations indeed cause many errors.

(37) Errors may occur because of quantification, such as when the "some" of quantification is used in place of the "some" that refers to the real part,[2] or when "any," "every," and "all" are used interchangeably.[3]

Errors may also occur because of invalid conversion, as when one concludes that all colors are black because all blacks are colors. Errors may also occur by combining what is separate, as when "Zayd is a physician and is good" is taken to imply that Zayd is a good physician, or by separating the compound, such as when "Five is an odd number plus an even" is taken to imply that five is both odd and even. Errors may also occur when someone thinks that one of two concomitants is the other, or that one of them is the cause of the other—such as [the faculties of] being able to laugh and of being literate—not realizing that the only connection between concomitants is some association. This fallacy is very common among those who have not mastered the sciences and who mistake that which is with a thing for that by which the thing is. Such errors often lead

بها اوُلى من تبيّينها بالنتيجة؛ او تكون المقدمة كاذبة، فغلط فيها لاشتباه اللفظ من اداة او اسم[1] او تركيب او تصريف يحتمل الوجوه.

(٣٦) وقد يقع الغلط بسبب تقدم السلوب وتأخرها وتكثرها؛ وكذا الجهات كما يظن انّ قولنا «ليس بالضرورة» و«بالضرورة ليس» سواء وهو خطأ، فان الأوّل يصدق على الممكن دون الثانى؛ وليس قولنا «لا يلزم ان يكون» كقولنا «يلزم ان لا يكون». وما ليس بممكن قد يكون ضرورى العدم او الوجود بخلاف ما هو ممكن ان لا يكون، فانه بعينه ممكن الكون إلاّ ان يعى بالامكان ما ليس بممتنع وهو (الامكان) العام، فانه لا ينقلب موجبة الى سالبة وسالبة الى موجبة واذا جعلت السلوب على ما قلنا اجزاء، او لا يستعمل الزائد وعدلت الى اللفظ الايجابى بحسب طاقتك لئلا كثر السلوب والتراكيب اللفظية، أمنت من هذا الغلط، والسلوب مغلّطة جدا.

(٣٧) وقد يقع بسبب السور، كما يؤخذ «البعض السورى» مكان «البعض» الّذى هو الجزء الحقيقى، وكما يؤخذ كل واحد والجميع كل مكان الآخر.

وقد يقع بسبب ايهام العكس، كمن حكم ان «كل لون سواد» بناء على ان «كل سواد لون»؛ او بسبب تركيب المفصل كقولك «زيد طبيب وجيد»، فيأخذ انه «طبيب جيد»؛ ولتفصيل مركب، كقولك «الخمسة زوج وفرد» فنقول «انها زوج وانها فرد»؛ او بسبب ما يظن انّ احد المتلازمين بعينه هو الآخر، او انّ احدهما علة الآخر ولا يعلم انّ من المتلازمات ما ليس بينهما إلاّ الصحبة، كاستعدادى الضحك والكتابة فى الانسان. وهذه المغالطة كثيرا ما تقع لمن لم يترسّخ فى العلوم فيأخذ ما مع الشئ مكان ما به الشئ. وقد يبتنى على هذا كثير من الدور الفاسد،

to vicious circles. For example, it is said that there can be no fatherhood without there being a child, and no child without fatherhood; therefore, since each depends on the other, there is a circularity. This is erroneous, because they are simultaneous. An impossible dependence would only occur if each existed because of the other, which would imply that each was prior to the other and thus prior to itself.

(38) One scholar has imagined that no two things can be conceived such that each is necessary with respect to the other. This is refuted by the existence of correlative pairs, in which the existence of each of the two things is inconceivable without the other. His proof is that if either one of the two things were independent of the other, then it could exist without the other. If each of the two determines in some way the existence of the other, then each one will depend on the other. If only one of the two determines the existence of the other, then it will be prior to [that which it determines], not equivalent to it. Since the latter is impossible, then [this scholar] cannot hope to construct a proof of it. His proof relates both to the concrete existence of the correlative pair and to the necessity of their being intellected together. However, he often excludes correlative pairs from his rule—which is the fallacy of establishing a rule by some proof and then excluding from the rule, without proof, something whose relation to the proof is the same as something included under the same proof. Our purpose in refuting this doctrine is to guide—not to rebuke—by showing that there may be two fallacies in a single proof. The researcher should be aware of the possibility that two things each have a role in the existence of the other—something inconceivable unless they are correlative. It is not the case that if something has a role in the existence of another, it is prior to it or a cause of it absolutely—nor is having such a role a condition of necessary accompaniment.

(39) Errors may also occur when a specific concomitant of a thing is taken to be a universal so as to establish commonness among several things, such as when someone says, "Black collects vision because it is color," and then says the same about white.[4] Errors may also occur when the actual is taken to be potential, or vice versa; when something essential is taken to be accidental, or vice versa; or when beings of reason[5] and

كما يقال «ان لم تكن الابوّة دون البنوّة والبنوّة دون الابوّة»، فيتوقف كل واحد منهما على الآخر فيكون دورا، وهو فاسد؛ فانّهما يكونان معا، والتوقف الممتنع إنمّا هو[٢] اذا كان كل واحد منهما بالآخر، فيلزم منه تقدم كل واحد منهما على نفسه وعلى المتقدم عليه.

(٣٨) وما ظنّ بعض اهل العلم انه لا يتصوّر ان يكون شيئان كل واحد منهما مع الآخر بالضرورة. لينتقض عليه المتضايفين، فانه لا يتصوّر وجود كل واحد منهما إلاّ مع الآخر بالضرورة. وحجته انّ كل واحد منهما ان استغنى عن الآخر، فيصحّ وجوده دونه؛ وان كان لكل واحد منهما مدخل فى وجود الآخر، فيتوقف كل واحد منهما على الآخر؛ وان كان لاحدهما مدخل فى وجود الآخر فيتقدم عليه فلا معيّة. وهذا اذا مُنع لا يقدر على اقامة الحجة عليه. ثم انّه بعينه متوجه فى المتضايفين فى وجودهما العينى وفى وجوب تعقلهما معا ايضا؛ وربما يستثنى هذا القائل المتضايفين على القاعدة. ومن جملة المغالطات[٣] ان تثبت قاعدة بحجة ويستثنى عنها شئ تكون نسبة الحجة اليه والى غيره، مما يدخل تحت القاعدة سواء، دون حجة وهذا غرضنا فى ايراد هذه المباحثة العلمية، والارشاد لا القدح، ليعلم مغلطتان فى حجة واحدة وليطلع الباحث على جواز ان يكون شيئان لكل واحد منهما مدخل فى وجود[٤] الآخر، فلا يتصوّر إلاّ مع المعية.[٥] وليس من شرط كل ما له مدخل، التقدم والعلية المطلقة ولا من شرط وجوب الصحبة، المدخل.

(٣٩) ومما يوقع به الغلط ان يؤخذ مبنى الأمر فى شئ معنى عاما ليثبت فى مشاركة فيه، كمن يقول «السواد إنمّا يجمع البصر لكونه لونا» ليتعدى الى البياض. وقد يقع الغلط بسبب أخذ ما بالفعل مكان ما بالقوة؛ او[٦] أخذ مكان ما بالقوة مكان ما بالفعل؛ وأخذ مكان[٧] ما بالذات

intellectual predicates are taken to be concrete—such as when someone hears that "Man is a universal" and thinks that its being a universal is something predicated of it as a concrete thing by virtue of its being described by humanity;[6] or when a thing's image is taken in place of the thing itself;[7] or when a part of a thing's cause is taken in place of the cause; or when in *reductio ad absurdum* a thing that is not the cause of the negation of the conclusion is taken to be so. The use of the method of equal priority may also lead to errors when it is applied to different species,[8] as when someone says, "Since both men and fish are alike in being animals, men do not breathe by necessity any more than fish do."[9] This method may also lead to error when it is applied in the realm of chance, as in "Zayd and ᶜAmr are equally likely to be tall, since they are both human; therefore, one of them cannot be taller than the other," since one may not realize that there are reasons unknown to us that necessitate or make impossible contingent matters, as we shall demonstrate later. Within a single species in which individuals differ by perfection and deficiency, this type of argument is not applicable either; for one individual may be in itself worthier of something due to its own perfection. The nature of this perfection will be discussed later.

(40) Errors may occur when something impossible is postulated to exist in order to prove something with respect to the sense in which it is impossible.[10] Errors may occur because of inattention to the sense in which a word is used, as when someone says, "Whiteness is included in the concept of every white thing, and Zayd is white," implying that whiteness is included in the reality of Zayd. The truth is that whiteness is included in the concept of the white thing insofar as it is white, not insofar as it is human or animal or anything else, so it is not possible to include it under the white thing.

(41) Errors may also occur when the usages of technical terms are changed during the argument to respond to objections. For example, "The similar to the similar is similar" is true only if the correspondence holds in all respects. Should the similarity be in only one respect, then the two things will correspond only in that respect. But when they are not similar in the same respect, the conclusion does not follow, for it is possible for something to correspond to something in one respect and to another thing in another. Likewise, two things equal to a thing are equal

وما بالعرض كل واحد منهما مكان الآخر؛ وأخذ الاعتبارات الذهنية والمحمولات العقلية امورا عينية، كمن يسمع انّ الانسان كلى، فيظن انّ كونه كليا أمر يحمل عليه لاتصافه به فى الاعيان؛ وأخذ مثال الشئ مكانه وأخذ جزء العلة مكانها؛ وأخذ ما ليس بعلة الكذب فى الخلف علة له؛ واجراء طريق اللااولوية عند اختلاف النوع، كمن يقول «ليس الانسان بوجوب التنفس اولى من السمك بعد اشتراكهما فى الحيوانية»؛ وكذا اجراء هذا الطريق فى عالم الاتفاقات، كقولك[8] «ليس زيد بالطول اولى من عمرو بعد اشتراكهم فى الانسانية، فلا ينبغى ان يتخصص احدهما به» ولا يعلم انّ هاهنا أسبابا غائبة عنا يجب او يمتنع بها أمور ممكنة، وسنبرهن عليها. وفى النوع الواحد المتفاوت بالكمال والنقص لا يجرى هذا فان بعض اشخاصه قد يكون اولى بأمر لكماله فى نفسه، واما كيفية هذا الكمال فسيأتى فيما بعد.

(٤٠) ومما يوقع الغلط فرض الممتنع موجودا ليبتنى عليه ثبوت شئ من جهة امتناعه. وقد يقع الغلط لقلة المبالات بالحيثيات، كما يقول «كل ابيض داخل فى مفهومه البياض، وزيد ابيض» ليتعدى اليه دخول البياض فى حقيقته، فان البياض داخل فى الابيض من حيث انه ابيض لا من حيث انه انسان او حيوان او غيرهما، فلا يمكن تعديته الى ما تحت الابيض.

(٤١) ومما يوقع الغلط تغيير الاصطلاح فى موضع النقض عن المحل الّذى أُطلق فيما وقع عليه النقض دفعا للنقض. ومن ذلك ما يقال ان مماثل المماثل مماثل، فان هذا لا يلزم إلاّ اذا كانت المماثلة من جميع الوجوه؛ واذا كانت من وجه واحد، فيلزم ايضا ان يكون مماثل المماثل من ذلك الوجه مماثلا. واما اذا لم حد الجهة فلا يلزم اذ يجوز ان يماثل شئ شيئا بأمر ويماثل غيره بأمر آخر. والمساوى للمساوى

provided the equality is in all respects. However, the respects in which they are equal may be different, as when a body is equal in length to one body but equal in width to another. Finding that something is equal in one respect to a thing does not imply that it is equal to something else that is equal to that second thing in another respect. No one, however, can say that "equality" must only be used when there is equality in all respects, because it is possible for two bodies to be equal only in terms of their lengths.

(42) Another error is when the opposite privation is confused with the contrary. Rest, for example, is the nonexistence of motion only in what may move. Blindness is an expression for lack of sight only in a thing that may be conceived as having sight. A stone, which cannot conceivably have sight, cannot be said to be blind.

The rule in understanding privations is that if we can think of the subject—body or man, for example—remaining after the state (motion or sight) has ceased, then we will not need to posit something else that is motionless or blind. Rather, it will suffice to leave the subject as it is and remove something from it. Thus, privation needs no cause, its cause being the absence of the cause of the state. However, if it is confused with the contrary—which is something existential requiring a cause and implying concomitants—errors will occur.

Some names of privations—such as "ineffability" and "uniqueness"—are not conditioned on contingency, because they are names for negations. Others are confined only to part of a species—for example, beardlessness.[11] Others, such as blindness and rest, are conditioned on contingency. However, the particular terms are used in different ways.[12]

Another error is to confuse affirmation and negation with privation and possession. Everything is subject to affirmation and negation, unlike privation and possession. For example, you can say, "The stone does not see," but you cannot say, "The stone is blind."

مساو ايضا، اذا كانت المساواة من جميع الوجوه. واما اذا اختلفت جهات[٩] المساواة، كالجسم الّذى يساوى بطوله جسما وبعرضه جسما آخر، فأخذ مساوى الشئ من وجه لا يلزم ان يساوى لشئ مّا للمساوى الآخر من وجه آخر وليس لاحد ان يدّعى ان المساواة لا يجوز ان تُطلق إلاّ على ان تكون من جميع الوجوه، فانه يجوز ان يكون جسمان متساويان فى الطول[١٠] فقط.

(٤٢) ومن ذلك أخذ العدم المقابل مكان الضد كالسكون، فانه عدم مقابل لانه عدم الحركة فيما يتصوّر فيه الحركة؛ وكذا العمى، فانه عبارة عن انتفاء البصر فى حق من يتصوّر فى حقه البصر، فان الحجر لما لم يتصوّر فى حقه البصر لا يُسمّى اعمى.

والضابط فى معرفة الاعدام: هو انّا اذا استبقينا الموضوع، كالجسم او الانسان مثلا، ورفعنا عنه الملكة كالحركة والبصر، لا يحتاج الى وضع شئ آخر حتى يكون ساكنا او اعمى، بل كفى استبقاء الموضوع ورفع شئ منه.[١١] فالعدم لا يحتاج الى علة، بل علته عدم علة الملكة؛ فاذا أخذ ضدا، فيكون أمراً وجوديا، فيحتاج الى علة ويلزم منه أمور أخرى ويوقع الغلط. ومن اسماء الاعدام ما لا يشترط فيها امكان، كالقدوسية والتفرّد، فهى اسماء للسلوب. ومنها ما لا يطّرد فى نوع واحد، كالمرودية. ومنها ما باعتبار الامكان، كاالاعمى والسكون، والاصطلاحات مختلفة. ومن ذلك أخذ الايجاب والسلب مكان العدم والملكة، فانّ الايجاب والسلب لا يخرج عنهما[١٢] شئ بخلاف العدم والملكة. فلك ان تقول «انّ الحجر ليس ببصير»، ولا تقول «انّه اعمى».

(43) Errors may occur when a general meaning is used differently in different places and one use is mistaken for another. Although this could have been included with the fallacies arising from ambiguous terms, we shall mention it separately, since it is a common error. A general term, as we mentioned, may mean that whose essence does not prevent it from being common to many; or it may be exhaustive, meaning that which applies to each and every case. The truth or affirmation of the first type of general term does not imply the truth or affirmation of its particulars, but its denial or falsehood implies the denial or falsehood of the particulars. The truth of the particular thing corresponding to it implies the truth of the general term, but its falsity does not imply the falsity of the general. The second type of general term is the opposite. Here, the truth of the general implies the truth of the particulars included in it. For example, "All C is B" implies "Some C is B," as well as implying that each individual C is B. However, the falsity [of the general] does not imply the falsity of the particular included in it. As for the particular, the truth of the general is not implied by its truth,[13] but its falsity implies the falsity of the general.[14]

(44) Errors may occur when a quiddity compounded of parts that all resemble each other is identified with the reality of the part. This is only valid in cases other than shapes and certain quantities.[15] Two parts of a circle are similar; but their reality is not the reality of the whole, which is the circle, nor does the circle share their reality. Two results from one and one, but two does not share the reality of one.

Section two

On some rules and solutions to problems

(45) It might be thought that the second [major] premise allows us to dispense with the first premise. Even though we know that every pair is even, "What is inside Zayd's sleeves" is not specifically or actually included in the proposition until it is known that it is a pair through our judgment that this is the case. We can only know that it is a pair through other

(٤٣) ومما يوقع الغلط اجراء اللفظ العام فى المواضع على المعانى المختلفة، فيؤخذ بعضها مكان بعض. وهذا وان كان مندرجا تحت الغلط المنتشئ من اشتباه اللفظ، إلاّ انّه كثير الوقوع فخصصناه بالذكر. والعام قد ذكرنا انّه يُعنى به ما لا تمتنع الشركة لذاته وقد يُعنى به المستغرق، وهو كون الحكم على كل واحد واحد. والعام الأوّل لا يلزم من صدقه واثباته، صدق الخاص واثباته ويلزم من كذبه ونفيه نفى الخاص وكذبه.[١٣] والخاص الّذى بازائه يلزم من صدقه صدق العام، ولا يلزم من كذبه كذب العام. والعام الثانى بعكس هذا، فانه يلزم من صدقه صدق الخاص المندرج فيه، كقولك «كل ج ب» فيصدق «بعض ج ب» ايضا، وكذا كل شخص شخص من ج، ولا يلزم من كذبه كذب الخاص الّذى فيه. واما خاصّه، فلا يلزم من صدقه صدق هذا العام، ولكن يلزم من كذبه كذب هذا العام.

(٤٤) ومما يوقع الغلط أخذ الماهية المركبة من اجزاء متشابهة لكلها حقيقة جزئها. وإنمّا يصحّ هذا فيما وراء الشكل وبعض الكميات، فان قطعتى الدائرة متشابهتان وحقيقتهما غير حقيقة الكل الّذى هو الدائرة ولا تشاركها الدائرة[١٤] فى الحقيقة والاثنان يحصل من واحد وواحد، ولا يتشارك الاثنان مع الواحد فى الحقيقة.

الفصل الثانى

فى بعض الضوابط وحل الشكوك

(٤٥) انه قد يظنّ ان المقدمة الثانية تغنى عن المقدمة الاولى ولا يعلم انا وان علمنا ان كل اثنين زوج لم يندرج تحته[١٥] ما فى كُمّ زيد بخصوصه بالفعل حتى يعلم انه زوج عند حكمنا بهذا، ما لم نعلم انه

knowledge, since the aspect of specificity is not identical with the aspect of generality.[16] This mistake is due to confusing the potential with the actual, because the subject of the first premise is potentially included in the subject of the second premise. It might be thought that it is actually so, but this is wrong.

(46) A well-known fallacy is to ask how you know that the unknown thing which you have learned is what you actually had sought—implying that you must either still be ignorant or that the knowledge already existed, thus allowing you to recognize it.[17] This error is also due to vagueness about existence and modes; for if what is sought is unknown in every respect, it could not be sought—nor could it be sought if it is known in all respects. Rather, it must be known in some respect and unknown in some other respect that may be specified by what we do know. This applies only to propositions and assents. For example, when we ask, "Is the universe contingent?" we are seeking no more than a judgment specified by these concepts. On the other hand, when someone hears the name given to something, seeks to know its meaning, and is told that it corresponds to such-and-such a meaning, he does not acquire knowledge of the thing just by hearing that this is what he had sought. Likewise, when someone conceives of a thing through one of its concomitants and has not actually seen it, he may be in doubt about its other attributes, even after it is described to him. Suppose that someone knows for certain that a bird called "phoenix" exists but has not seen it and seeks to know it specifically. He will know only the general attributes of the bird—that it flies, for example. Only through many people telling him that the other attributes of the bird called "phoenix" are such-and-such can he know it so well that he can say that the attributes mentioned by someone describing it to him all belong to what he seeks and to nothing else.

اثنان بعلم آخر، اذ جهة الخصوص غير جهة العموم. وهذا الشك ينشئ من أخذ ما بالقوة مكان ما بالفعل، فانه لما رأى ان موضوع المقدمة الاولى يندرج تحت موضوع المقدمة[16] الثانية بالقوة ظن انه يندرج بالفعل، فغلط.

(٤٦) ومما اشتهر من المغالطات قول القائل «ان مجهولك اذا حصل فبم تعرف انه مطلوبك؟» فلا بد من بقاء الجهل او وجود العلم به قبله حتى يعرف انه هو. وهذا ايضا لزم من اهمال الوجود والحيثيات. فان المطلوب ان كان من جميع الوجوه مجهولا، لم يُطلب. وكذا ان كان معلوما من جميع الوجوه، بل هو معلوم من وجه مجهول من وجه متخصص بما علمناه. وبهذا إنمّا هو فى القضايا والتصديقات، فانا اذا طلبنا التصديق فى قولنا «العالم هل هو ممكن؟» لم نطلب إلاّ حكما متخصصا بهذه التصورات، فحسب. اما من سمع اسم الشئ فحسب وطلب مفهومه، فقيل له ان هذا وُضع بازاء معنى كذا، لا يحصل له العلم بمجرد السماع ان مطلوبه هو.[17] وكذا من تصّور الشئ بلازم واحد، ولم يشاهده، فقد شك فى بعض الصفات، وان شرح له شارح، فاذا تيقن الانسان وجود طير يقال له «قُقنُس» ولم يشاهده فطلب[18] خصوصه، وهو لا يعلم إلاّ جهة عمومه[19] فيه كالطيرية، مثلا، لم يمكن[20] لاحد ان يعرفه بحيث يعلم ان الصفات التى ذكرها الشارح هى لمطلوبه وان ذلك مطلوبه، إلاّ ان يحصل عنده بضرب من التواتر من اشخاص ان الطائر المسمّى بقُقنُس له صفات كذا وكذا.

A rule [on the constituents of the thing]

(47) The existence of a thing can have alternating contradictory constituents; but the quiddity of something cannot be conceived to have alternating contradictory constituents, since the quiddity would be changed with each one of them.[18] In understanding how the substitution of a constituent is possible, one must first realize that it is not a constituent of the essence. One must be careful to remember that the cause does not embrace all the things taken as differing causes in such a way that the general entity does not exclude the causality of what is other than this. Thus, it would not be valid to claim that this implies multiplicity in the cause.

A rule [on the Universal Rule[19]]:

(48) Know that the universality of a rule stating that something is predicated of something else is disproved by a single instance where that second thing is absent. The universality of a law stating the impossibility of something being predicated of something else is proven by the existence of that thing in a single case. Thus, if someone asserts that every C is necessarily B but finds a single C that is not B, then the universality of the rule is disproved. Likewise, if someone asserts that it is impossible for any C to be B but then finds a single C which is B, then the law will be disproved. However, if someone asserts that any C may be B, this is disproved by neither the existence nor the absence of instances. Thus, should someone claim that some universal is contingently true of another universal—for example, asserting the "B-ness" of C—then he need find only a single instance that is B and another that is not B in order to show that the universal B is not impossible in the nature C (since otherwise no individual C could be described as being B) and that [B] is not necessary [in C] (since in that case no individual C could fail to be B).

Whenever a simple nature has a mental genus—as we shall mention later—it is possible for the genus in the mind to be that nature or a part corresponding to it, insofar as the genus is made specific by the difference of one of the two natures. For example, "being a color" may by its

قاعدة [فى المقوّمات الشئ]

(٤٧) يجوز ان يكون للشئ مقوّمات لوجوده[٢١] مختلفة على سبيل البدل ولا يتصوّر ان يكون لماهيته مقوّمات مختلفة على سبيل البدل،[٢٢] اذ تختلف الماهية بكل واحد منها ولكن يجوز ان يكون للشئ مقوّمات مختلفة لوجوده على سبيل البدل. فمن اراد اثبات تجويز البدل لمقوّم، فليبين انه ليس مقوّما للماهية أوّلا ويحتاط حتى لا تكون العلة ما يعمّ المأخوذات عللا مختلفة، فيستقل الأمر العام بالعلية دونها، ولا يتمشى دعوى التعدد.

قاعدة [فى القاعدة الكلية]

(٤٨) واعلم ان القاعدة الكلية لوجوب شئ على شئ يبطلها عدم ذلك الشئ فى جزء واحد والقاعدة الكلية لامتناع شئ على شئ يبطلها وجود ذلك الشئ فى جزء واحد، كمن حكم ان «كل ج بالضرورة ب» فوجد ج واحدا ليس ب تنتقض به القاعدة الكلية.[٢٣] وكذا من حكم «انّه ممتنع ان يكون كل ج ب» فوجد ج هو ب، فتنتقض قاعدته. ومن حكم «انّ كل ج ب بالامكان» لا يبطل هذه القاعدة وجود او عدم. ومن ادّعى امكان شئ كلى على كلى آخر، مثل البائية على الجيم، كفاه ان يجد جزئيا واحدا منه هو ب وجزئيا آخر ليس بـ«ب»، فيعرف انه لا يمتنع على الطبيعة الجيمية الكلية البائية، والا ما اتصف من اشخاصها واحد بها، ولا يجب، والا ما تعرّى جزئى واحد منها والطبيعة البسيطة اذا كان لها جنس ذهنى، كما سنذكره، يمكن على جنسها فى الذهن ان يكون هى او قسيما لها اى متخصصا بفصل احدهما كاللونية، فانها

nature mean either blackness or whiteness—that is, there is nothing in the mind that prevents color from being specified as one or the other. However, this is not conceivable in concrete reality, because there is no concrete thing that is color without the specification of black or white, as we shall see later. Therefore, what is possible for the universal "color" is not possible for any one color. In the case of the nature of a species, such as humanity, the things that specify the individuals—such as white and black, tall and short—may be applied to the species and to each one of its individuals. If they cannot, it is due to some external factor.[20]

A rule and an apology

(49) Knowing that many books have been written about this science of logic, we have been able to be very brief in this book; but we have discussed fallacies at length so that the student will become familiar with them. Students will find more error than sound reasoning in the proofs advanced by the various schools and sects among men. Therefore, it is just as useful to learn the occasions of error as to learn the rules of correct reasoning.

Negation is existential insofar as it is a denial in the mind and a rational judgment, and the assent is not just an affirmative relation that is broken in the negation. Therefore, assent remains even after negation. This continuing relation of assent during negation is not the ordinary relation of affirmation. Therefore, negation is an existential judgment—that is, it has an existence in the mind even though it itself breaks some other affirmation.[21] We have found that the mode of impossibility will allow us to dispense with necessary negation, that necessity allows us to dispense with impossible negation, that negating and affirming possibility are the same, and that there is no limit to the possible combinations. Thus, in this short book we have limited ourselves to the discussion of affirmative propositions, since we have another purpose in this book. The object of inquiry in the true sciences is something certain. Since the

لطبيعتها ممكنة ان تكون سوادا او بياضا. اى لا مانع لها فى الذهن عن تخصصها باحدهما، وفى الاعيان لا يتصوّر، اذ لا لونية مستقلة فى الاعيان ليمكن لحوق خصوص بياضية وسوادية بها، كما سنذكره. فيمكن على كلى اللون ما لا يمكن على كل لون. والطبيعة النوعية، كالانسانية، يمكن على نوعها سائر ما يتخصص به اشخاصها ويمكن على كل واحد واحد ايضا، مثل السواد والبياض والطول والقصر وان امتنع، فإنمّا يكون لأمر من خارج.

قاعدة واعتذار

(٤٩) إنمّا اقتصرنا فى هذا الكتاب على هذا القدر اعتمادا على الكتب المصنّفة فى هذا العلم، الّذى هو المنطق، واكثرنا فى المغالطات لتدرب الباحث بها فان الباحث يجد الغلط فى حجج طوائف الناس وفرقهم اكثر مما يجد الصحيح. فلا يكون انتفاعه فى التنبيه على مواقع[٢٤] الغلط اقلّ من انتفاعه بمعرفة ضوابط ما هو حق.

ولما كان السلب وجوديا من وجه مّا من حيث هو[٢٥] نفى فى الذهن وحكم عقلى وليس التصديق هو النسبة الايجابية التى يقطعها السلب فحسب، فان التصديق بعد السلب باق، فالنسبة التصديقية الباقية عند السلب غير النسبة الايجابية المشهورة. فالسلب هو حكم وجودى، اى له وجود فى الذهن، وان كان قاطعا لايجاب آخر. ثم وجدنا الامتناع مغنيا عن ذكر السلب الضرورى، والوجوب مغنيا عن ذكر السلب الممتنع، والامكان ايجابه وسلبه سواء؛ وكانت التركيبات الممكنة غير محصورة، اقتصرنا على ذكر الموجب فى هذا المختصر اذ غرضنا فيه أمر آخر. ولما كان فى العلوم الحقيقية المطلوب أمراً يقينيا، وكان

indefinite proposition—that in which no modes are mentioned—does not include the contingent which never occurs, we never say "All C is B" absolutely when it does not apply to some of its particulars; for example, we do not say, "All men are actually literate."[22] The general indefinite proposition, when universal, is not valid except in the six necessary modal propositions that are well known in books of logic,[23] each one of which is necessary because of a specific modal. Therefore, we shall here deal with the necessary modal propositions. There is no benefit in dealing with the indefinite propositions, since the general contingent is broader and more generally valid than they are. The general absolute occurs at some time indicating some necessity in the encompassing proposition, unlike the general contingent. If we consider some general matter or some general mode, we have no need for these indefinite propositions that so easily lead to mistakes. Since no science seeks to know the state of some unspecified part of its subject, except in *reductio ad absurdum,* we can omit any mention of unspecified particulars. The investigator no longer needs to reduce the second and third figures to the first in any scientific question, once he knows the rule in a single place; nor does he need to incorporate the negation or make particular propositions general in all their possible forms, once he knows the rule.

(50) The Peripatetics establish the validity of conversion by ecthesis[24] and *reductio ad absurdum,* though *reductio ad absurdum* in conversion is itself based on ecthesis. If we say that necessarily no C is B, then likewise no B is C, since otherwise it would be true that some B is C. Let us, then, posit a specific thing, which we will call D, which is both C and B. Therefore, something that is described by C is also described by B. However, it has already been said that necessarily no C is B. [The Peripatetics] may establish the validity of the conversion of both the universal affirmative proposition and the particular affirmative proposition by ecthesis, or they may establish their validity by *reductio ad absurdum,* which, in another place, is itself based on ecthesis. The *reductio ad absurdum* in both is based on the conversion of the negative proposition. In the negative proposition, according to what we have said, ecthesis is also necessary. Ecthesis is identical with the third figure, since both seek to prove, for example,

المطلق الّذى لم تذكر فيه جهة لم يتناول من الممكن ما لا يقع ابدا، فانّا لا نقول «كل ج ب مطلقا» اذ لم يقع بعضه ابدا، مثل قولنا «كل انسان كاتب بالفعل».

فالمطلق العام فى المحيطة لا يطّرد إلاّ فى الضروريات الستة المشهورة فى الكتب، ولكل واحد ضرورة بجهة مّا فنتعرض لها ولا فائدة فى المطلق والممكن العام اعمّ منه وأشدّ اطّرادا واطلاقا، فان المطلق العام يتعيّن وقوعه وقتا مّا، وهو مُشعر بضرورة مّا فى المحيطة دون الممكن العام. فاذا عرضنا أمراً عاما او جهة عامة فكفانا الامكان العام، فلا حاجة بنا الى الاطلاق المغلّط ولما لم يطلب فى علم مّا حال بعض موضوعه بعضا غير معين إلاّ فى معرض نقض، حذفناه ذكر البعضيات المهملة. وكما[26] ليس يحتاج الناظر فى كل مطلب من المطالب العلمية الى ردّ السياق الثانى والثالث الى الأوّل بعد ان عرف ضابطه فى موضع واحد، وكذلك لا يحتاج الى ادراج السلوب وتعميم البعضيات فى جميع المواضع بعد ان عرف الضابط.

(٥٠) واعلم ان المشائين ثبتوا العكس بالافتراض والخلف، والخلف ايضا فى العكس يبتنى على الافتراض. فنقول «اذا كان لا شئ من ج ب بالضرورة، فلا شئ من ب ج كذا» والا يصح «بعض ب ج» فنفرضه شيئا معينا وليكن هو «د». فـ«د» يكون هو «ب» وهو «ج» فشئ مما يوصف بـ«ج» يوصف بـ«ب» وقد قيل «لا شئ من ج ب بالضرورة». ثم الموجبة الكلية والجزئية يثبتون عكسيهما بالافتراض وقد يثبتونهما بالخلف، والخلف يبتنى تارة أُخرى على الافتراض. فان الخلف فيهما ابتناؤه على عكس السالبة، وفى السالبة لا بدّ من الافتراض على ما ذكرناه والافتراض بعينه هو الشكل الثالث اذ يطلبون شيئا يحمل

that C-ness and B-ness are predicated of something. Later, they establish the validity of the third figure by reducing it to the first figure by conversion. Therefore, the explanation is circular, explaining a thing by that which explains it! Because *reductio ad absurdum* is a compound syllogism, its use in conversion is not something that people will understand naturally.[25] A person who has not learned the syllogisms and how they are deduced may know through common sense which syllogisms are valid. This will be sufficient for him in all scientific questions. Therefore, there is no need here for lengthy discussions about *reductio ad absurdum.* I do not deny that people find *reductio ad absurdum* useful and that they recognize its soundness, even if they are not aware that it is compounded from two syllogisms—one conjunctive and the other exclusive—and do not know all the details of its uses and are ignorant of how it has been used to prove the validity of conversions. However, there is no need to discuss such things at length.

Further, *reductio ad absurdum* is not sufficient to show that this, and not something else, is conversion. When someone claims that necessarily no C is B, he converts it to "Necessarily it is not the case that some B is C, since otherwise all B would be C." We then posit that the elements in B described by C-ness are D, as you learned before. Thus, an absurdity will follow—that some C is B—though we had assumed that necessarily no C is B. Therefore, the validity of conversion here does not imply that this is the converse. Since *reductio ad absurdum* alone is insufficient and since it is possible to establish the validity of the conversion by some other argument, as we explained, it will not be a problem to drop it. Likewise, in our discussion of the second and third figures of syllogism we will not need to use conversion or *reductio ad absurdum.*

(51) No one should deny that the *reductio ad absurdum* used in conversion is a syllogism, for whoever knows what syllogism and *reductio ad absurdum* are knows also that *reductio ad absurdum* is a syllogism. However, the *reductio ad absurdum* in conversion is also based on exclusive and conjunctive syllogisms, for the conclusion that we are seeking is the conditional proposition "If no C is B, then no B is C." The form of this *reductio ad absurdum* is "If it is true that no C is B, and it is not true that no B is C, then some B is C." The first sentence is the antecedent, and the consequent is "It is true that some B is C." We take this and make it the antecedent in another premise: "If some B is C, then some C is B." We then connect it to the first premise and deduce, "If it is true that no C is B, and it is not true that no B is C, then some C is B." The conjunctive

عليه الجيمية والبائية مثلا. ثم يثبتون الشكل الثالث بردّه الى الأوّل بالعكس، فيدور البيان. ويلزم منه تبيين الشئ بما مبين به. ثم الخلف فى العكس استعماله غير مطبوع، فان الخلف من القياسات المركبة. ومن لم يعرف القياسات واستنتاجها، اذ كفته سلامة القريحة فى معرفة صحّة قياسية فليقنع بذلك فى جميع المطالب العلمية، فلا يحتاج الى تطويل فى قياس الخلف. ولست انكر انّ الانسان ينتفع بالخلف ويعرف صحته، وان لم يعرف[٢٧] كونه مركبا من قياسين، اقترانى واستثنائى، ولم يطّلع على تفاصيل احكامه. وانّ الخلف يعرف منه ويتبيّن به صحة العكوس التى ذكروها، ولكن عن التطويل فى مثل هذه الاشياء استغناء.

ثم انّ الخلف غير كاف فى انّ يتبيّن انّ هذا هو العكس لا غير، فان من ادّعى انّه «اذا كان لا شئ من ج ب بالضرورة»، فانه ينعكس «بالضرورة ليس بعض ب ج»، والا «فكل ب ج»، فيفرض الموصوف بالجيمية من الباء انه دالّ على ما عرفته. فيلزم ان يكون «شئ من الجيم ب» وقد قلنا «بالضرورة لا شئ من ج ب»، هذا محال. فصحّة العكس هكذا بهذا البيان لا يدلّ على انه هو العكس. واذا كان الخلف وحده غير كاف وامكن ان يتبيّن دونه صحة العكس، كما بيّنا، فلا يكون به بأس. وكذا بياننا للشكلين دون الحاجة الى العكس والخلف.

(٥١) وليس لمبدّعى ان يقول: انّ الخلف المورد فى العكس ليس بقياس. وانّ من عرف القياس والخلف عرف انه قياس، إلاّ انّ العكس خلفه يبتنى على قياس استثنائى واقترانى شرطى ايضا. فان مطلوبنا فيه شرطى،[٢٨] وهو قولنا «كلّما كان لا شئ من ج ب، فلا شئ من ب ج». وصورته ان نقول «ان صحّ لا شئ من ج ب وشئ من ب ج، فيصحّ بعض ب ج». فالجملة الاولى هى المقدم، والتالى هو قولنا «فيصحّ

syllogism is formed from two compound conditionals, the middle term is dropped, and the contradictory of the consequent is excepted, as you have learned. Even though the second premise is composed of two particular categorical propositions, it is universal because generality in conditional propositions does not depend on quantification, but on positions and times. Since all this is so, it is clear that the *reductio ad absurdum* used to prove the validity of conversion is not valid in form, for the syllogisms are based on proofs that cannot themselves be carried out without recourse to these syllogisms. Rather, it is correct to say that the validity of the forms of the syllogism can only be established by reflection or inspection. These few comprehensive rules are better than a multitude of rules requiring great efforts and boring explanations.

Section three

Concerning the Illuminationist judgments on certain points

[This section will] also examine certain principles in order to ascertain their truth and thereby also provide examples of particular fallacies. To further our goal, we will preface this with an introduction establishing some technical terms.

Introduction

(52) If something having existence outside the mind is subsistent in something else and completely diffused in it, we call it a "state." If it is not subsistent in it so as to be entirely diffused in it, we call it a "substance." In the definition of the state, we do not need to specify that it is "not as a part of it," for the part is not diffused in the whole. Furthermore, being

بعض ب ج». فنأخذه ونجعله مقدما فى مقدمة اُخرى فنقول «وكلّما يصح بعض ب ج، فيصح بعض ج ب». ونقرنه بالمقدمة الاولى، فينتج «انه ان صحّ لا شئ من ج ب ولم يصحّ لا شئ من ب ج، فيصحّ بعض ج ب». وكان القياس اقترانيا من متصلتين فانحذف الحدّ الاوسط؛ ثم يستثنى بعد هذا نقيض التالى على ما عرفت. والمقدمة الثانية، وان كانت مركبة من بعضيتين حملتين كلية لانّ عموم الشرطيات ليس بالاعداد بل بالاوضاع والاوقات. واذا كان كما ذكرنا، فيكون الخلف فى العكس مذكورا غير تام الصورة، فتبنى القياسات على حجج لا يتمّ كونها حجة إلاّ بها، بل الصواب ان يقال «الاشكال لا تحتاج فى اثبات صحتها إلاّ الى تنبيه او[٢٩] اخطار بالبال». والضوابط القليلة الجامعة خير من الكثيرة المحوجة الى تكلفات واعتذارات واهية.

الفصل الثالث

فى بعض الحكومات فى نكت اشراقية

والنظر فى بعض القواعد ليعرف فيها الحق ويجرى ايضا مجرى الامثلة لبعض المغالطات. ولنقدم على ذلك مقدمة يصطلح فيها على بعض الاشياء ليكون توطئة الى المقصود.

مقدمة

(٥٢) هى انّ كل شئ له وجود فى خارج الذهن، فاما ان يكون حالاّ فى غيره شائعا فيه بالكلية ونسمّيه «الهيئة»؛ او ليس حالاّ فى غيره على سبيل الشيوع بالكلية ونسمّيه «جوهرا»، ولا يحتاج فى تعريف الهيئة بالتقييد بقولنا «لا كجزء منه»، فان الجزء لا يشيع فى الكل. واما اللونية

a color, substantiality, and the like are not parts according to Illuminationist principles, as we will explain, so there is no need to specify or worry about this. Therefore, the notions of substance and state are general meanings.

(53) When a state is in a locus, it needs, by virtue of being a state, to be diffused throughout that locus. That need lasts as long as the state lasts, and it is inconceivable that the state could be self-subsistent or could move to another locus: at the moment of transfer it would be independent in its motion, dimensions, and existence; would have three dimensions; and would thus be a body, not a state. A body is a substance that may be pointed to and that obviously must always have some length, width, and depth. Since a state has none of these, it is different from a body. Since bodies share in corporeality and substantiality but differ in being black or white, these latter are superadded to corporeality and substantiality and are therefore different from them.

(54) A thing may be either necessary or contingent. The contingent is that which is not itself a sufficient reason for itself to exist rather than to be nonexistent, but whose sufficient reason is something else. The sufficient reason for its existence is the presence of its cause, and [the sufficient reason] for its nonexistence is the nonexistence of its cause. It is either impossible or necessary by another, so its existence or its nonexistence is contingent. If its existence made it necessary, as some have imagined, its nonexistence would have made it impossible, and there would never be anything contingent. That which is dependent on something else will not exist when that other is nonexistent. Since that other has an influence on its existence, the thing is contingent in itself.

We mean by "cause" that whose existence immediately and without conceivable delay necessitates the existence of something else. Conditions and the removal of impediments also enter into the cause; for if the impediment is not removed, the existence of the thing is still contingent in relation to what was assumed to be its cause. If [the impediment's] relation to the thing partakes of contingency without reaching the

والجوهرية وامثالهما ليست باجزاء على قاعدة الاشراق، على ما سنذكره. فلا يحتاج الى التقييد به والاحتراز عنه؛ فمفهوم الجوهر والهيئة معنى عام.

(٥٣) واعلم انّ الهيئة لما كانت فى المحل، ففى نفسها افتقار الى الشيوع فيه فيبقى الافتقار ببقائها فلا يتصوّر ان تقوم بنفسها أوّلا ان تنتقل فانها عند النقل تستقل بالحركة والجهات والوجود فيلزمها ابعاد ثلاثة، فهى جسم لا هيئة. والجسم هو جوهر يصحّ ان يكون مقصودا بالاشارة، وظاهر انه لا يخلو عن طول وعرض وعمق مّا، والهيئة ليس فيها شئ من ذلك، فهما متباينان. والاجسام لما تشاركت[٣٠] فى الجسمية والجوهرية[٣١] وفارقت فى السواد والبياض، فهما زائدان على الجسمية والجوهرية، فهما متباينان.

(٥٤) واعلم ان الشئ ينقسم الى واجب وممكن والممكن لا يترجح وجوده على عدمه من نفسه. فالترجح بغيره، فيترجح وجوده بحضور علته وعدمه بعدم علته. فيمتنع ويجب[٣٢] بغيره، وهو فى حالتى وجوده وعدمه ممكن، فلو اخرجه الوجود الى الوجوب كما ظن بعضهم، لاخرجه العدم الى الامتناع، فلا ممكن ابدا وما توقف على غيره، فعند عدم ذلك الغير لا يوجد، فله مدخل فى وجوده فيمكن فى نفسه. ونعنى بالعلة ما يجب وجوده وجود شئ آخر بتّة دون تصور تأخر،[٣٣] ويدخل فيه الشرائط وزوال المانع فان المانع ان لم يزل يبقى الوجود، بالنسبة الى ما يُفرض علته ممكنا. فاذا[٣٤] كانت نسبته اليه امكانية دون ترجح، فلا علية ولا معلولية. وليس هذا مصيرا الى ان العدم يفعل شيئا، بل معنى دخول العدم فى العلية ان العقل اذا لاحظ وجوب المعلول، لم يصادفه حاصلا دون عدم المانع وللعلة على المعلول تقدم

condition of sufficient reason, there can be no relation of cause and effect. This is not to say that nonexistence does something; it only means that nonexistence enters into the causality in the sense that, when the mind considers the necessity of the effect, it cannot do this without considering the nonexistence of the impediment. The cause has an intellectual but not a temporal priority over the effect. They may be simultaneous in time, as in breaking and being broken, but we still say, "He broke it, so it broke," and not the opposite.

There also is a priority that is temporal, as well as a priority of place or position—as in bodies—or of nobility in attributes admitting of being more or less noble. A part of the cause may be temporally prior or intellectually prior.

Here we encounter another subject of which we must take account for our purposes.

(55) Know that any series that has an order—any order whatsoever—and whose individuals are coexistent must be finite. The reason for this is that if there is an infinite number of items between some two members of the series, this infinite number of members must be contained between the two limits in an order—which is absurd. If there are no two members of the series between which there is an infinite number of other members, then there is only a finite number of members between any two members of the series, and the whole must necessarily be finite. We must also examine how this applies to bodies. If we posit a series of differing qualities in bodies, or if we posit a series of bodies, this demonstration also applies. Moreover, suppose that a finite quantity was removed from the middle of a series and the two parts of the series were connected as before. Now consider the series in this way once and then another time as it was before, with the restoration of the quantity that had been assumed not to exist, thinking of [these instances] as though they were two series. Now, if you compare the two in your imagination—or match each number of the one series with the corresponding number of the other in your mind, if they are numbers—they will certainly differ. It would not be in the middle, since we connected those, so it would have to be at the end; one series would come to an end, and the other would exceed it by a finite amount and not exceed the finite series by a finite amount. By this, the finitude of all dimensions, causes and effects, and so on is established.[26]

عقلى لا زمانى؛ وقد يكون فى الزمان معا، كالكسر مع الانكسار، فنقول «كسّر فانكسر» دون العكس. ومن المتقدم، ما هو زمانى، ومن المتقدم، ما هو مكانى او وضعى كما فى الاجرام؛ او شرفى بحسب صفات الاشرف. وجزء العلة قد يتقدم زمانا، وقد يتقدم تقدما عقليا. وهاهنا أمر آخر تُبنى عليه ما نحن بسبيله.

(٥٥) واعلم انّ كل سلسلة فيها ترتيب، ایّ ترتيب كان، وآحادها مجتمعة يجب فيها النهاية. فان كل واحد من السلسلة بينه وبين ایّ واحد كان، ان كان عددا غير متناه، فيلزم ان يكون منحصرا بين حاصرى الترتيب، وهو محال. وان لم يكن فيها اثنان، ليس بينهما لا يتناهى، فما من احد لا بينه ایّ واحد كان مما فى السلسلة اعداد متناهية. والكل يجب فيه النهاية وهذا فى الاجسام ايضا متوجه فنفرض فيها سلسلة من حيثيات مختلفة او اجسام مختلفة فيطّرد فيها البرهان. وايضا لك ان تفرض عدم قدر متناه من وسط السلسلة، تأخذه كأنّه ما كان وطرفاه من السلسلة متصل احدهما بالآخر؛ تأخذ هكذا مرة ومع القدر المفروض عدمه مرة أُخرى كانهما سلسلتان وتطبق احداهما على الأُخرى فى الوهم؛ او يجعل عدد كل واحد مقابلا لعدد الآخر فى العقل، ان كان من الاعداد، فلا بدّ من التفاوت وليس فى الوسط، لانّا اوصلنا. فيجب فى الطرف فيقف الناقص على طرف والزائد يزيد عليه بالمتناهى وما زاد على المتناهى بمتناه، وبه يتبيّن تناهى الابعاد باسرها والعلل والمعلولات وغيرهما.

A judgment [on the beings of reason]

(56) "Existence" is used with a single meaning and as a single concept for blackness and substance, for man and horse. It is an intelligible meaning more general than any one of these, as are the concepts of quiddity taken absolutely, thingness, and reality taken absolutely. We claim that all these predicates are purely intellectual. Consider: If "existence" were just an expression for blackness, it could not apply with the same meaning to blackness, to whiteness, and to substance. If it were considered to be a meaning more general than substantiality, it would be either subsistent in the substance or independent in itself. If it were independent in itself, then the substance could not be described by it, for its relation to the substance would be the same as its relation to everything else. If it were in the substance, it would certainly be actual in it, and the actuality would certainly be the existence. If the existence were actual, it would be existent. If its "being existent" were taken to be an expression for the existence itself, then "existent" would not apply to both existence and other things with the same meaning. This is because the concept of existent with respect to things is that an existent is something *having* existence, while in the case of existence itself it would be that it *is* the existence. We ourselves do not say something of many things except with a single meaning. Next, we argue that if blackness is nonexistent, then its existence is not actual. Therefore, its existence is not existent, since its existence is also nonexistent.[27] If we do intellect existence and judge that it is not existent, then the concept of existence is distinct from the concept of existent. We might say that the blackness, which we had taken as nonexistent, now exists and that its existence was not yet actual, and then its existence became actual. If so, the actuality of the existence would not be the existence itself, and the existence would have existence. This same argument applies to the existence of the existence, and so on to infinity. But a simultaneous ordered infinity of attributes is absurd.

حكومة [فى الاعتبارات العقلية]

(٥٦) الوجود تقع بمعنى واحد ومفهوم واحد على السواد والجوهر والانسان والفرس، فهو معنى معقول اعم من كل واحد. وكذا مفهوم الماهية مطلقا والشيئية والحقيقة على الاطلاق، فندعى ان هذه المحمولات عقلية صرفة. فان الوجود، ان كان عبارة عن مجرد السواد ما كان بمعنى واحد يقع على البياض وعليه وعلى الجوهر فاذا أُخذ معنى اعم من الجوهرية،[٣٥] فاما ان يكون حاصلا فى الجوهر قائما به او مستقلا بنفسه، فان كان مستقلا بنفسه فلا يوصف به الجوهر، اذ نسبته اليه والى غيره سواء. وان كان فى الجوهر، فلا شكّ انه يكون حاصلا له والحصول هو الوجود فالوجود اذا كان حاصلا فهو موجود، فان أُخذ كونه موجودا انه عبارة عن نفس الوجود فلا يكون الموجود على الوجود وغيره[٣٦] معنى واحدا اذ مفهومه فى الاشياء انّه شئ له الوجود وفى نفس الوجود انّه هو الوجود. ونحن لا نطلق على الجميع إلاّ بمعنى واحد. ثم نقول «ان كان السواد معدوما، فوجوده ليس بحاصل، فليس وجوده بموجود اذ وجوده ايضا معدوم». فاذا عقلنا الوجود وحكمنا بانّه ليس بموجود، فمفهوم الوجود غير مفهوم الموجود ثم اذا قلنا «وُجد السواد الّذى كان قد أخذناه معدوما وكان وجوده غير حاصل ثم حصل وجوده فحصول الوجود غيره»، فللوجود وجود ويعود الكلام الى وجود الوجود، فيذهب الى غير النهاية. والصفات المرتبة الغير متناهية اجتماعها محال.

(57) Another consideration is that their opponents, the followers of the Peripatetics, understand existence yet doubt whether it is actual in concrete things, just as they do with the original quiddity.[28] Existence would have another existence, resulting in a regression. It is clear from this that there is nothing in existence which is itself the quiddity of existence; for as soon as we conceive its concept, we may wonder whether or not it has existence. Thus, it would have another existence—and so there would be an infinite regress.

(58) Another consideration is that if the quiddity had existence, the existence would have a relation to it. This relation would then also have an existence that would have a relation to the relation—and so on to infinity.

(59) Yet another consideration is that if existence were actually in concrete things and were not a substance, it would obviously be a state in the thing and so would not actually be independent. Thus, its locus would be actualized, but it would exist before its locus. Its locus could not be actualized simultaneously with it, since its locus would exist *with* the existence, not *by* the existence—which is absurd. It could not become actual after its locus, obviously. Moreover, if existence in concrete things were superadded to the substance, it would subsist by the substance and would be, according to the Peripatetics, a quality—which they define as a stable state whose conception does not require positing a division or a relation to something external. They assert without qualification that the locus is prior to any accident, whether a quality or something else. Thus, the existent would be prior to existence, which is impossible. Moreover, existence would not be the most general of things absolutely: quality and accidentality would be more general in a certain respect. Moreover, if [existence] were an accident, it would subsist in a locus. What is meant by its "subsisting in a locus" is that it is existent in a locus, needing [the locus] for its realization. Since there can be no doubt that the locus is existent by existence, the subsistence is circular—which is absurd.

It is erroneous to try to prove that existence is superadded in concrete things by arguing that if something were not conjoined to the quiddity by a cause, the quiddity would remain in nonexistence. The one who makes this argument posits a quiddity and then joins existence to it, so his opponent can argue that this concrete quiddity is itself from the efficient cause. The argument also can return to the question of whether the added existence itself is given something else by the efficient cause or whether it is left as it was.

(٥٧) وجه آخر: هو ان مخالفى هؤلاء، اتباع المشائين، فهموا الوجود وشكّوا هل[٣٧] هو فى الاعيان حاصل، ام لا، كما كان فى اصل الماهية. فيكون للوجود وجود آخر ويلزم التسلسل. وتبيّن بهذا انّه ليس فى الوجود ماعين ماهية الوجود، فانّه[٣٨] بعد ان نتصوّر مفهومه، قد نشكّ فى انه هل له وجود ام لا؟[٣٩] فيكون له وجود زائد ويتسلسل.

(٥٨) وجه آخر: هو انّه اذا كان الوجود للماهية، فله نسبة اليها، وللنسبة وجود، ولوجود النسبة نسبة اليها، ويتسلسل الى غير النهاية.

(٥٩) وجه آخر: هو انّ الوجود اذا كان حاصلا فى الاعيان وليس بجوهر، فتعين ان يكون هيئة فى الشئ فلا يحصل مستقلا. ثم يحصل محله، فيوجد قبل محله ولا ان يحصل محله معه اذ يوجد مع الوجود لا بالوجود، وهو محال؛ ولا ان يحصل بعد محله، وهو ظاهر؛ وايضا اذا كان الوجود فى الاعيان زائدا على الجوهر فهو قائم بالجوهر؛ فيكون كيفية عند المشائين لانّه هيئة قارة لا تحتاج فى تصورها الى اعتبار تجزء واضافة الى أمر خارج كما ذكروا فى حدّ الكيفية. وقد حكموا مطلقا ان المحل يتقدم على العرض من الكيفيات وغيرها فيتقدم الموجود على الوجود، وذلك ممتنع. ثم لا يكون الوجود اعم الاشياء مطلقا، بل الكيفية والعرضية اعم منه من وجه. وايضا اذا كان عرضا فهو قائم بالمحل؛ ومعنى انّه قائم بالمحل انه موجود بالمحل مفتقر فى تحققه اليه. ولا شك انّ المحل موجود بالوجود، فدار القيام، وهو محال.

ومن احتج فى كون الوجود زائدا فى الاعيان بانّ الماهية ان لم ينضم اليها من العلة أمر فهى على العدم اخطأ فانه يفرض ماهية، ثم يضم اليها وجودا والخصم يقول نفس هذه الماهية العينية من الفاعل، على ان الكلام يعود الى نفس الوجود الزائد فى انه هل افاده الفاعل شيئا آخر ام[٤٠] هو كما كان؟

(60) The followers of the Peripatetics argue that we can think of man without existence, but we cannot think of him without a relation to animality. Yet the relation of animality to humanity means nothing except its being existent in him, either in the mind or in concrete reality. Thus, they posit two existences in the relation of animality to humanity: one belonging to the animality which is in him; and the second, that which becomes existent in humanity by reason of the existence of humanity. Indeed, some of the followers of the Peripatetics base their whole system of metaphysics upon existence.

"Existence" can be said of relations to things, as when one says that something is existent in the house, in the market, in the mind, in concrete reality, in a time, or in a place. Here the word "existence" occurs with the word "in" with the same meaning in all of these. "Existence" may be used as a copula, as when one says, "Zayd exists writing."[29] It may be said of the reality and essence, as when one says, "The essence of the thing and its reality, the existence of the thing, its concreteness, and its self." These are taken as beings of reason and are applied to external quiddities. This is what most people understand by "existence," but the Peripatetics give it another meaning, for they are in the habit of explaining it in their arguments, overlooking the fact that they had also assumed that it is the most evident of things, not definable by anything else.

(61) So, too, unity is not a meaning added to the thing in concrete objects, for unity would be one thing among others and would itself have unity. Moreover, one could say "a one" and "many ones," just as one can say "a thing" and "many things." Moreover, if the quiddity and the unity belonging to the quiddity are taken as two things, they are two—one of them the unity and the other the quiddity to which the unity belongs—so that each one of them would have a unity. From this follow absurdities, for if we say that they are two, the quiddity without the unity would have a unity apart from the unity, and so on to infinity; and the unity would have a unity, and so on, creating an ordered infinity of attributes. If such is the case with unity, number must also be something intellectual,[30] for if number is made up of ones and unity is an intellectual attribute, number must also be so.

(٦٠) واعلم ان اتباع المشائين قالوا «انّا نعقل الانسان دون الوجود ولا نعقله دون نسبة الحيوانية». والعجب ان النسبة الحيوانية الى الانسانية ليس معناها إلاّ كونها موجودة فيه، اما فى الذهن او فى العين. فوضعوا فى نسبة الحيوانية الى الانسانية وجودين: احدهما للحيوانية التى فيه، والثانى ما[٤١] يلزم من وجود الانسانية حتى يوجد فيها شئ. ثم انّ بعض اتباع المشائين بنوا كل أمرهم فى الالهيات على الوجود. والوجود قد يقال على النسب الى الاشياء، كما يقال: الشئ موجود فى البيت، وفى السوق، وفى الذهن، وفى العين، وفى الزمان، وفى المكان؛ فلفظة «الوجود» مع لفظة «فى» فى الكل بمعنى واحد؛ ويطلق بازاء الروابط، كما يقال «زيد يوجد كاتبا». وقد يقال على الحقيقة والذات، كما يقال «ذات الشئ وحقيقته.ووجود الشئ وعينه ونفسه»، فتؤخذ اعتبارات عقلية وتضاف الى الماهيات الخارجية، هذا ما فهم منه الناس. فان كان عند المشائين له معنى آخر فهم ملتزومون ببيانه فى دعاويهم، لاعلى ما يأخذون من انه اظهر الاشياء، فلا يجوز تعريفه بشئ آخر.

(٦١) واعلم انّ الوحدة ايضا ليست هى بمعنى زائد فى الاعيان على الشئ، والا لكانت[٤٢] الوحدة شيئا واحدا من الاشياء، فلها وحدة. وايضا يقال: واحد وآحاد كثيرة، كما يقال: شئ واشياء كثيرة. ثم الماهية والوحدة التى لها اذا أُخذتا شيئين فهما اثنان: احداهما الوحدة، والآخر الماهية التى هى لها؛ فيكون لكل واحد منهما وحدة فيلزم منه محالات، منها انّا اذا قلنا هما «اثنان» يكون للماهية دون الوحدة وحده، ويعود الكلام متسلسلا الى غير النهاية، ومنها ان يكون للوحدة وحدة ويعود الكلام، فتجتمع صفات مترتبة غير متناهية. واذا كان حال الوحدة كذا، فالعدد ايضا أمر عقلى، فان العدد اذا كان من الآحاد والوحدة صفة عقلية فيجب ان يكون العدد كذلك.

(62) Another consideration is that if four, for example, is an accident subsisting in man, either "four-ness" must be complete in each one of the individuals, which is not the case, or else there must be something of four-ness in each one, which can only be the unity. Therefore, either the totality of four-ness must have no locus other than the intellect, or else neither four-ness nor anything of four-ness can be in each one. On this latter supposition, too, four-ness is only in the intellect. It is obvious that if the mind links one in the east to another in the west, it will behold duality. If a man looks at a large group, he can count three or four or five, linking them together as his eye happens to fall upon them, and he can also count numbers like hundreds, scores, and the like.

(63) The contingency of a thing is prior in the intellect to its existence, for the contingents are contingent and then exist. It is not correct to say that they exist and then become contingent. Contingency applies with a single meaning to things of different sorts; so it is accidental to the quiddity, and the quiddity is described by it. Thus, contingency is not something self-subsistent. It is not a necessary existent, since if its existence were necessary in itself, it would be self-subsistent and so would not need a relation to a subject. Therefore, it is contingent, and its contingency is intellected before its contingency, for what is not contingent in the first place never comes to exist. Thus, its contingency is not itself; and so the argument regresses in this way to the contingency of the contingency, and so on to infinity—leading to an infinity that is impossible because of the conjunction of its individuals in an order.

The same is the case with necessity, since necessity is an attribute of existence. If it were added to existence and were not self-subsistent, it would be contingent and have both necessity and contingency. Its individual contingencies and necessities would form an ordered infinity. The necessity of a thing would be prior to it and would not be the thing itself, since the thing was necessary and then existed; it did not exist and then become necessary. Then, also, the existence would have necessity, and the necessity existence. Thus, there would be another regression of repeated existence of necessity and necessity of existence. This, too, is impossible, in the same way as indicated before.

(٦٢) وجه آخر: هو ان الاربعة اذا كانت عرضا قائما بالانسان مثلا فاما ان يكون فى كل واحد من الاشخاص الاربعية تامة، وليس كذا؛ او فى كل واحد شئ من الاربعية، وليس إلاّ الوحدة، فمجموع الاربعية ليس له محل غير العقل او ليس فى كل واحد الاربعية ولا شئ منها افليست على هذا التقدير ايضا فى غير العقل. فظاهر انّ الذهن اذا جمع واحدا فى الشرق الى آخر فى الغرب، فيلاحظ الاثنينية.[٤٣] واذا رأى الانسان جماعة كثيرة، أخذ منهم ثلاثة واربعة وخمسة بحسب ما يقع النظر اليه وفيه بالاجتماع. فيأخذ ايضا فى الاعداد مئة ومئات وعشرة وعشرات ونحوهما.

(٦٣) واعلم ان الامكان للشئ متقدم على وجوده فى العقل فان الممكنات تكون ممكنة، ثم توجد ولا يصح ان يقال انها توجد، ثم تصير ممكنة. والامكان بمفهوم واحد يقع على المختلفات. ثم هو عرضى للماهية وتوصف به الماهية فليس الامكان شيئا قائما بنفسه وليس بواجب الوجود، اذ لو وجب وجوده بذاته لقام بنفسه؛ فما افتقر الى اضافة الى موضوع. فيكون ممكنا اذن، فامكانه يعقل قبل وجوده. فانّه ما لم يمكن أوّلا، لا يوجد فليس امكانه هو، ويعود الكلام هكذا الى امكان امكانه الى غير النهاية فيفضى الى السلسلة الممتنعة لاجتماع آحادها مترتبة.

وكذا الوجوب فان الوجوب صفة للوجود. فاذا زاد عليه ولم يقم بنفسه فهو ممكن؛ فله وجوب وامكان فيذهب اعداد امكاناته ووجودياته مترتبة الى غير النهاية. ووجوب الشئ يكون قبله فلا يكون هو ما اذ «يجب ثم يوجد» ولا «يوجد ثم يجب» ثم للوجود وجوب وللوجوب وجود، وهكذا يلزم سلسلة أُخرى من تكرار الوجود على الوجوب والوجوب على الوجود غير متناهية، وهى ممتنعة لما سبق.

(64) In concrete things, the "color-ness" of blackness[31] is not color-ness and something else, for positing it to be color is the same as positing it to be blackness. Were color-ness to have an existence and the particularization, blackness, to have another existence, color-ness could have any particularization that might by chance attach to it, since no one of the particularizations would be a condition of color-ness. Otherwise, it would not be possible for it to have a particularization opposite to or different from the one it has. It would thus be possible for particularizations to alternate in their connection to it.[32] Moreover, if color-ness had an independent existence, it would be a state: either a state in blackness (in which case the blackness would exist before it, not by it) or a state in the locus (in which case black would have two accidents—color and its differentia—not one).

(65) Relations are also beings of reason; for if brotherhood, for example, were a state in an individual, it would have a relation to another individual and a relation to its locus. One relation would be distinct from the other; and by necessity, neither would be the essence of brotherhood, since its essence—if it is posited as existent—would be one essence and the relation of the two to two individuals would be two distinct things. How, then, could these two [relations] be brotherhood? It is clear that each one of the two relations would be a different existent. Also, this argument would apply to the relation [brotherhood] had to the locus, and an impossible regression would occur. Therefore, all of these are no more than ways of thinking about the thing.

(66) Privations—rest, for example—are also something intellectual. "Rest" is a term for the absence of motion in what may be conceived[33] to be in motion, and absence is not something realized in concrete things but is something intelligible in the mind. Contingency is also something intellectual. It therefore follows that the negative privations[34] are all intellectual things.

(67) Substantiality, too, is not something added to corporeality in concrete things. Rather, to make a thing a body is also to make it a substance, since substantiality—according to us—is just the perfection of the quiddity of the thing such that it subsists independently of a locus. The Peripatetics define it as an existent not in a subject; but the denial of a subject is negative and being existent is accidental.[35] Their defender

(٦٤) واعلم ان لونية السواد ليست لونية وشيئا آخر فى الاعيان فان جعله لونا هو بعينه جعله سوادا ولو كان للونية وجود ولخصوص السواد وجود آخر، جاز لحوق اى خصوصية اتفقت بها اذ ليس واحد من الخصوصيات بعينه شرطا للونية، والا ما امكنت مع ما يضادها او يخالفها، فيجوز تعاقب اقتران الخصوصيات بها وايضا اللونية ان كان لها وجود مستقل فهى هيئة، اما ان تكون هيئة فى السواد، فيوجد السواد قبلها لا بها؛ او فى محله، فللسواد[٤٤] عرضان، لون وفصله لا واحد.

(٦٥) والاضافات ايضا اعتبارات عقلية، فان الاخوّة مثلا، ان كانت هيئة فى شخص فلها اضافة الى شخص آخر واضافة الى محلها. فاحدى الاضافتين غير الأُخرى، فهما غير ذاتها بالضرورة، اذ ذاتها اذا فُرضت موجودة ذات واحدة واضافتهما[٤٥] الى شخصين متغايرتان، فكيف تكونان هى؟ فتعيّن ان يكون كل واحدة من الاضافتين موجودا آخر. ثم الاضافة التى لها المحل يعود هذا الكلام اليها ويتسلسل على الوجه الممتنع فاذن هذه كلها ملاحظات عقلية.

(٦٦) والعدميات، كالسكون أمر عقلى؛ فان السكون اذا كان عبارة عن انتفاء الحركة فيما تتصور فيه الحركة، والانتفاء ليس بأمر محقق فى الاعيان، ولكنه فى الذهن معقول، والامكان ايضا أمر عقلى، فيلزم ان تكون الاعدام المقابلة كلها أمورا عقلية.

(٦٧) واعلم انّ الجوهرية ايضا ليست فى الاعيان أمراً زائدا على الجسمية، بل جعل الشئ جسما بعينه هو جعله جوهرا، اذ الجوهرية عندنا ليست إلاّ كمال ماهية الشئ على وجه يستغنى فى قوامه عن المحل، والمشاؤون عرّفوه بانّه الموجود لا فى موضوع فنفى الموضوع سلبى والموجودية عرضية، فاذا قال الذّابّ عنهم انّ

might say that substantiality is another existent entity, but it would be difficult to explain or to prove this to the skeptic. If it were another existent entity in the body, it would have an existence other than in a subject and would be described by substantiality. Thus, the argument would turn to the substantiality of the substantiality and would regress to infinity.

(68) Therefore, all attributes may be divided into two classes. The first is the concrete attribute, which also has a form in the intellect—such as black, white, and motion. The second is the attribute whose only concrete existence is its existence in the mind and which has no existence at all except in the mind—for example, contingency, substantiality, color-ness, existence, and the other such things we mentioned. Thus, the being that it has in the mind is equivalent to the being something else has in concrete reality. If a thing has existence outside the mind, then what it is in the mind ought to correspond to it. However, that which is solely in the mind has no existence outside the mind to which the mental might correspond. Predicates as predicates are mental; but blackness is concrete. Since "nigritude" is a term for something by which blackness subsists,[36] corporeality and substantiality do not enter into it. But if blackness were to subsist in something other than a body, it would be said that blackness was black. Then, if there is something that enters in some way into nigritude, it would be something intellectual, nothing more, even though blackness has an existence in concrete reality. However, if intellectual attributes are derived from them and become predicated[37]—as when we say, "Every C is contingent"—then both contingentness and contingency[38] are just intellectual [and] nothing more. This is different from nigritude; for although blackness is an intellectual predicate, it is concrete, and blackness as such is not predicated of a substance.[39] If we say, "C is impossible in concrete reality," it does not mean that impossibility occurs in concrete reality but, rather, that it is something intellectual that we attach sometimes to what is in the mind and sometimes to what is concrete. This is also the case with other things of this sort. In such cases, the error arises from considering mental things as occurring independently in concrete reality. Once you know that things

الجوهرية أمر آخر موجود، فيصعب عليه شرحه واثباته على المنازع. ثم اذا كانت أمراً آخر موجودا فى الجسم، فلها وجود لا فى موضوع فتكون موصوفة بالجوهرية ويعود الكلام الى جوهرية الجوهرية، فيتسلسل الى غير النهاية.

(٦٨) فاذن الصفات كلها تنقسم الى قسمين؛ صفة عينية ولها صورة فى العقل، كالسواد والبياض والحركة؛ وصفة وجودها فى العين ليس إلاّ نفس وجودها فى الذهن وليس لها فى غير الذهن وجود، فالكون فى الذهن لها فى مرتبة كون غيرها فى الاعيان، مثل الامكان والجوهرية واللونية والوجود وغيرها مما ذكرنا. واذا كان للشئ وجود فى خارج الذهن، فينبغى ان يكون ما فى الذهن منه يطابقه. واما الّذى فى الذهن فحسب، فليس له فى خارج الذهن وجود حتى يطابقه الذهنى. والمحمولات من حيث انها محمولات ذهنية، والسواد عينى والاسودية لما كانت عبارة عن شئ مّا قام به السواد ولم تدخل فيها[٤٦] الجسمية والجوهرية؛ بل لو كان السواد يقوم بغير الجسم لقيل عليه انّه اسود، فاذا كان شئ مّا له مدخل فى الاسودية، فلا يكون إلاّ أمراً عقليا فحسب، وان كان السواد له وجود فى الاعيان، واما الصفات العقلية اذا اشتق منها وصارت محمولة،[٤٧] كقولنا «كل جيم هو ممكن»، فالممكنية والامكان كلاهما عقليان فحسب بخلاف الاسودية. فانّها وان كانت محمولا عقليا، فالسواد عينى والسواد وحده لا يحمل على الجوهر، واذ قلنا «جيم هو ممتنع فى الاعيان» ليس معناه انّ الامتناع حاصل فى الاعيان بل هو أمر عقلى نضمّه الى ما فى الذهن تارة والى ما فى العين أُخرى، وكذا نحوه. ففى مثل هذه الاشياء الغلط ينشأ من أخذ الأمور الذهنية واقعة مستقلة فى الاعيان. واذا علمت ان مثل هذه الاشياء

like those just mentioned—contingency, color-ness, and substantiality—are intellectual predicates, you will understand why they are not parts of the concrete quiddities. This does not mean that we can take a mental predicate (like a genus predicated of a thing, for example), attach it in the mind to any arbitrary quiddity, and still speak the truth. Rather, the predicate must be applied to that which is specifically appropriate to it. This is also the case for existence and the rest of the beings of reason.

Section [four]

[Showing that accidentality is external to the reality of accidents]

(69) The followers of the Peripatetics say that accidentality is external to the reality of accidents. This is correct, for accidentality is another intellectual attribute. Some of them explain this by saying that man can intellect something yet be unsure about its accidentality. However, they fail to apply this reasoning to substantiality, not thinking that when man is unsure about the accidentality of something, he is unsure about its substantiality as well. That blackness is a quality is also accidental to it, so quality is a being of reason. The argument that we intellect color and then intellect blackness is arbitrary, for one might equally well say that we first intellect that this is blackness and then judge of it that it is color and a quality. However, we have no need for such an argument, for it is rhetorical, and the true basis of the discussion is what came before.

Another judgment [showing that the Peripatetics have made it impossible for anything to be known]

(70) The Peripatetics have made it impossible for anything at all to be known, since substances have unknown differentia. They define substantiality by something negative, while the soul and the separate substances, according to them, have unknown differentia. They define an accident like blackness, for example, as a color that collects vision. Collecting vision is accidental, and you already know about color-ness.

المذكورة من قبل، كالامكان واللونية والجوهرية محمولات عقلية، فلا تكون اجزاء للماهيات العينية. وليس اذا كان الشئ محمولا ذهنيا، كالجنسية المحمولة على الشئ مثلا، كان لنا ان نلحقه فى العقل باى ماهية[٤٨] اتفقت ويصدق، بل لما يصلح له بخصوصه. وكذا الوجود وسائر الاعتبارات.

فصل

[فى بيان انّ العرضية خارجة عن حقيقة الاعراض]

(٦٩) قال اتباع المشائين: والعرضية خارجة عن حقيقة الاعرض، وهو صحيح، فان العرضية ايضا من الصفات العقلية. وعلّل بعضهم بان الانسان قد يعقل شيئا ويشكّ فى عرضيته ولم يحكموا فى الجوهرية هكذا، ولم يتفكروا بانّ الانسان اذا شكّ فى عرضية شئ، يكون قد شكّ فى جوهريته. وكون السواد كيفية ايضا عرضى له، وهو اعتبار عقلى. وما يقال انّه «نعقل اللون ثم نعقل السواد» نحكّم بل لقائل ان يقول «نعقل أوّلا ان هذا سواد ثم نحكم عليه انّه لون وانّه كيفية». ونحن لا نحتاج الى هذا، إنمّا هو قول جدلى وعمدة الكلام ما سبق.

حكومة اُخرى [فى بيان انّ
المشائين اوجبوا ان لا يُعرف شئ من الاشياء]

(٧٠) وهى انّ المشائين اوجبوا ان لا يُعرف شئ من الاشياء اذ الجواهر لها فصول مجهولة. والجوهرية عرفوها بأمر سلبى، والنفس والمفارقات لها فصول مجهولة عندهم. والعرض، كالسواد مثلا، عرّفوه بانّه لون يجمع البصر. فجمع البصر[٤٩] عرضى، واللونية عرفت حالها.

Thus, bodies and accidents would not be conceivable at all. According to them, existence is the most evident of things—about this you already know. Then, if conception is posited to be by concomitants, the concomitants will also have specific properties, about which the same difficulty will recur. This is not permissible, since it would imply that nothing at all in existence could be known. The truth is that blackness is one simple thing. It can be intellected and has no unknown part. It cannot be defined as it is to someone who has not beheld it, but anyone who has beheld it has no need for a definition. Its form in the mind is like its form in sensation. Such things have no definitions. Rather, the compound realities are known from the simple realities: one conceives the simple realities separately and knows the compound by uniting them in a single subject.

(71) Know that the categories they list are all beings of reason with respect to their being categories and predicates. That one from which it is derived—that is, the simple from which the predicate is taken in its particularity—is also an intellectual attribute, like the objects of a relation and the numbers in their particularity (as was explained before) and also all that relation enters into. Some of them are concrete attributes in themselves, but their inclusion in those categories is due to a being of reason—like an odor or black, for example—for their being qualities is something intellectual whose meaning is that they are states fixed as such-and-such, even though they are both in themselves attributes realized in concrete actuality. If the thing's being an accident, a quality, or the like were another existent, the argument would regress in the same way as above.

Another judgment [on denial of prime matter and form][40]

(72) The Peripatetics argue that body admits of connection and division but that connection does not admit of division. Therefore, something must exist in the body that admits of both, and this is prime matter. They further argue that magnitude does not enter into the reality of bodies, since all bodies share in corporeality yet differ in magnitudes—and

فالاجسام والاعراض غير متصوّرة اصلا. وكان الوجود اظهر الاشياء لهم وقد عرفت حاله. ثم ان فُرض التصور باللوازم، فللوازم ايضا خصوصيات يعود مثل هذا الكلام اليها. وهو غير جائز اذ يلزم منه ان لا يعرف فى الوجود شئ مّا والحق ان السواد شئ واحد بسيط، وقد عُقل وليس له جزء آخر مجهول، ولا يمكن تعريفه لمن لا يشاهده كما هو، ومن شاهده استغنى عن التعريف، وصورته فى العقل كصورته فى الحس فمثل هذه الاشياء لا تعريف لها، بل قد يُعرف الحقائق المركبة من الحقائق البسيطة، كمن تصوّر الحقائق البسيطة متفرقة فيعرف المجموع بالاجتماع فى موضع مّا.

(٧١) واعلم ان المقولات التى حرّروها، كلها اعتبارات عقلية من حيث مقوليتها ومحموليتها وبعضها المشتق منه، اى البسيط الّذى منه اتخذ[٥٠] المحمول بخصوصه ايضا صفة عقلية، كالمضاف والاعداد بخصوصها كما سبق؛ وكل ما تدخل فيه الاضافة ايضا. ومنها ما يكون فى نفسه صفة عينية؛ اما دخوله تحت تلك المقولات لاعتبار عقلى، كالرائحة مثلا والسواد، فان كونهما كيفية أمر عقلى معناه انه هيئة ثابتة كذا وكذا، وان كانا فى انفسهما صفتين محققتين[٥١] فى الاعيان. ولو كان كون الشئ عرضا او كيفية ونحوهما موجودا آخر، لعاد الكلام متسلسلا على ما سبق.

حكومة أُخرى [فى ابطال الهيولى والصورة]

(٧٢) قال المشاؤون: الجسم يقبل الاتصال والانفصال. والاتصال لا يقبل الانفصال، فينبغى ان يوجد فى الجسم قابل لهما وهو الهيولى. وقالوا المقدار غير داخل فى حقيقة الاجسام لاشتراكها فى الجسمية

because a single body may become smaller or larger with compression and rarefaction. They are refuted by [the argument] that connection is said of what is between two bodies; it may be judged that one of them is connected to the other. This is what admits of separation. The body has extension in length, width, and depth; yet separation does not admit of extension at all.[41] How can [the Peripatetics] answer someone who claims that body is just magnitude admitting of the three extensions and nothing else?[42]

(73) The argument that these are accidents because of the alteration of length, width, and depth, as in a candle, is a baseless assertion. Even if this magnitude extending in various directions is an accident, it does not follow that magnitude in itself is accidental to the body or is an accident; for to the extent that the length increases, the breadth, for example, decreases. Likewise, if the breadth is increased, the length is decreased; and certain parts, previously unconnected, are now in contact with each other, while other parts, previously connected, are now separated. Its moving alternately in various directions is a concomitant of it, and its particular movements in different directions are accidental alterations. Body is nothing but magnitude, and the three extensions are the extent to which the sides of the body have gone in different directions.

They are right in saying that connection does not admit of separation if they mean the connection between two bodies. However, if by "connection" is meant magnitude, it is impossible for magnitude not to accept separation. Thus, using "connection" in place of "magnitude" leads to error, because the ambiguity of the term leads one to imagine that what is meant is the connection that is destroyed by separation.

(74) It is not correct to argue that since bodies share in corporeality and differ in magnitude, magnitude is thus external to them. Absolute body corresponds to absolute magnitude, and the particular body corresponds to the particular magnitude. It is as though one were to say, "The particular magnitudes differ in being small and large and share in being

وافتراقها فى المقادير ولان جسما واحدا يصغر ويكبر بالتخلخل والتكاثف. ويردّ عليهم ان الاتصال يقال فيما بين جسمين، فيحكم بان احدهما اتصل بالآخر وهو الّذى يقابله الانفصال. وفى الجسم امتداد من الطول والعرض والعمق، والامتداد ليس يقابل[٥٢] الانفصال اصلا؛ فما قولك فيمن يدّعى انّ الجسم مجرد المقدار الّذى يقبل الامتدادات الثلاثة لا غير؟

(٧٣) وقول القائل انّها اعراض، لتبدل الطول والعرض والعمق على شمعة مثلا، ليس إلاّ دعوى؛ انّ جُعل هذا المقدار، ذاهبا فى بعض الجهات عرضا، فلا يلزم منه انّ المقدار نفسه عرضى للجسم او عرض. فان ما يزداد بالطول عند المدّ ينتقص من عرضه وكذا ما يبسط فى العرض ينتقص من طوله فيتصل فى المدّ بعض اجزاء كانت مفترقة ويفترق بعض ما كانت متصلة. فذهابه فى الجهات المختلفة على سبيل البدل لازم له، وآحاد الذهاب فى الجهات عرض متبدل؛ والجسم ليس إلاّ نفس المقدار، والامتدادات الثلاثة هى ما يؤخد بحسب ذهاب جوانب الجسم فى الجهات.

وقولهم[٥٣] «الاتصال لا يقبل الانفصال»، صحيح اذا عنى به الاتصال بين الجسمين؛ وانّ عنى بالاتصال المقدار، فيمنع[٥٤] انّ المقدار لا يقبل الانفصال. واستعمال الاتصال بازاء المقدار يوجب الغلط، لانّه اشتراك فى اللفظ، فيوهم انّ المراد منه الاتصال الّذى يبطله الانفصال.

(٧٤) وقول القائل «انّ الاجسام تشاركت فى الجسمية واختلفت فى المقدار فيكون خارجا عنها» كلام فاسد فان الجسم المطلق بازاء المقدار المطلق والجسم الخاص بازاء المقدار الخاص. وما هو إلاّ كمن يقول: المقادير الخاصة بالكبير والصغير[٥٥] مختلفة وتشاركت فى انّها

magnitude. Therefore, their difference in being small or large can only be due to something other than magnitude—something by which the large magnitude differs from the small, since they both share in magnitude." This is unsound, for if a magnitude exceeds another magnitude, we cannot say that it does so by something besides magnitude. Magnitudes differ only by magnitude. The difference is in respect to their being magnitude and because one is more perfect and the other more deficient. This is like the difference between the more intense and the weaker light or the more intense and the weaker heat. By "more intense light or heat," we merely mean its intensity of resistance, power, and the like. The intensity and weakness of light is not due to the admixture of particles of darkness—darkness being privative—nor due to darkened particles, for our argument concerns what we see from a light and what is reflected from luminous things by something shiny, like a mirror. In fact, its intensity and dimness is a completeness and perfection that it has in its quiddity. Length is also something of this sort; for if one length is greater than another, it is more perfect in its length and magnitude. Its increase, then, is also length. We cannot call this "intensity of length," because it is possible to point to the amount by which it is identical and to the additional length. This is unlike more intense whiteness, for in the case of length the difference is not confined between two limits, as is the case with more intense whiteness. Thus, the inclusive term is "the more perfect," not "the more intense"—but one cannot refute a name.[43]

The result of the argument is that absolute body is absolute magnitude and particular bodies are particular magnitudes. Just as bodies share in absolute magnitude and differ by their particular different magnitudes, so too they share in corporeality and differ in their particular divergent magnitudes.

(75) Rarefaction and compression are just[44] the separation and bringing together of the parts, with the subtle body filling in between them. The assertion that fire does not enter the whistling bottle[45] is correct; but [the bottle's] splitting is not because of the increase in volume, as the Peripatetics have said, but because the heat disperses the parts.

مقدار، فافتراقها بالصغر والكبر ليس إلاّ لشئ غير المقدار، حتى يزيد المقدار الكبير على الصغير بشئ غير المقدار لاشتراكهما فى المقدار، وهو فاسد. فانّ المقدار اذا زاد على المقدار، لا يجوز ان يقال زاد بغير المقدار، اذ لا تفاوت فى المقادير إلاّ بالمقدار؛ فالتفاوت بنفس المقدارية ولانّ احدهما أتمّ والآخر انقص. وهذا كالتفاوت بين النور الأشدّ والاضعف، والحرّ الأشدّ والاضعف ولا نعنى[٥٦] بالنور الأشدّ والحرّ الأشدّ إلاّ شدته فى الممانعة والقدرة وغير ذلك. وليس شدة النور وضعفه لمخالطة اجزاء الظلمة اذ الظلمة عدمية، ولا اجزاء مظلمة؛ فانّ كلامنا فيما يحس من النور وما ينعكس على املس، كالمرآة من نيّر، بل تمامية وكمال له فى الماهية. ففى الطول ايضا هكذا، فانّ هذا الطول اذا كان اعظم من ذلك الطول فانّه أتمّ طولية ومقدارية والزيادة ايضا طول فان لم نسمّ هذا «شدة فى الطول»، بسبب انّ هاهنا يمكن الاشارة الى قدر ما به المماثلة والزائد بخلاف الأتمّ بياضا فانّه لا ينحصر التفاوت فيه بين الطرفين، كالأشدّ بياضا؛ فيجعل الجامع «الاتمية» دون الأشدّية، ولا مشاحة فى الاسم.[٥٧]

فحاصل الكلام انّ الجسم المطلق هو المقدار المطلق، وانّ الاجسام الخاصة هى المقادير الخاصة، وكما تشاركت الاجسام فى المقدار المطلق وافترقت بخصوص المقادير المتفاوتة تشاركت فى الجسمية وافترقت بخصوص المقادير المتفاوتة.

(٧٥) واما التخلخل والتكاثف[٥٨] ليس إلاّ بتبديد الاجزاء واجتماعها وتخلل الجسم اللطيف بينها، واما ما قيل فى القمقمة الصيّاحة «انّ النار لا تداخلها»، فذلك صحيح؛ واما الشق فليس كما ذكره المشاؤون من زيادة المقدار، بل لان الحرارة مبددة للاجزاء. فاذا اشتدت مالت

When the heat becomes intense, its sides have an inclination to go in separate directions, which the body prevents. This inclination has strength; and a vacuum, as the books explain, is impossible. Thus, the inclination to separation and the necessity of there being no vacuum causes the bottle to break, but this is not because the contents acquire a greater magnitude.

When a bottle is sucked and overturned in water, water enters it. Nonetheless, the conclusion drawn by some people is not correct: that since the air remains inside and some water enters, the air is compressed. It may be that when the water enters, some of the air leaves, forced out through pores by the entry of the water. It may also be that the one who is sucking gives something to the air equal in quantity to what he takes, so that rarefaction results after the sucking. It is very difficult for us to ascertain such matters through observation. If their conception of rarefaction as the increase of magnitude is correct, we know intuitively that bodies would have to interpenetrate. Assume that magnitudes increase and that the whole universe is already a plenum. If the increase of the magnitudes of bodies does not necessitate the decrease of the magnitude of other bodies different from them without some cause that necessitates compression, bodies necessarily interpenetrate. This is most obvious in the case of great watery storms. Moreover, if the whistling bottle on which they rely is supposed to be full, does the magnitude in it increase and the bottle then break, or does it break and the magnitude then increase? If the bottle breaks and the magnitude then increases, the breaking is not due to that rarefaction that they have made its cause. If [these events] are simultaneous, then the cause of the breaking must be something else prior to it. If the magnitude increases first, bodies must interpenetrate. If it is argued that the increase in magnitude is essentially prior to the breaking, we would ask the same question about the inclination of the parts to separation, so that what they say does not follow.

Therefore, rarefaction occurs only by the separation of the parts of heat and the interpenetration of a subtle body like air. Then, if the parts are inclined to separate and something hinders them, they push it back if they have the strength. This separation of parts is seen in cases of rarefaction when water and other fluids are heated. If we push together their parts, they will nonetheless return to their original magnitude. By

جوانبها الى الافتراق، ومانعها الجسم، والميل ذو مدد؛ والخلأ كما بيّن فى الكتب ممتنع؛ فبميلها الى الافتراق وضرورة عدم الخلأ ينشق القمقمة لا بحصول مقدار اكبر.

واما ما يقال «انه يمصّ القارورة فتكبّ على الماء، فيدخلها الماء مع بقاء الهواء الّذى كان فيها، فيتكاثف الهواء» غير مسلم. فانّ بعد المصّ لا يمكن الحكم بانّ عند دخول الماء ما خرج شئ من الهواء، بل يخرجه دخول الماء ويبقى له منفذ مّا؛ ولا يمكننا ان نحكم بانّ الماصّ لا يعطى من الهواء بقدر ما يأخذ، حتى يلزم التخلخل بعد المصّ. ومثل هذه الاشياء يعسر علينا ضبطه بالمشاهدة؛ ونحدس انّه لو كان التخلخل متصوّرا، كما يقولون، بزيادة المقدار، لزم منه تداخل الاجسام. فانّ المقادير اذا ازدادت والعالم قبلها كله ملأ، ولا يلزم من زيادة مقدار اجسام نقصان مقدار اجسام اُخرى متباينة عنها من غير سبب يوجب التكاثف، فلزم التداخل بالضرورة؛ وهذا عند الطوفانات العظيمة المائية اظهر. ثم القمقمة الصيّاحة التى عليها اعتمادهم، اذا فرضت ممتلئة، ايزيد المقدار فيها ثم تنشق؟ او تنشق ثم يزيد المقدار؟ فان كان تنشق القمقمة ثم يزيد المقدار، فالشق ليس للتخلخل كما علّلوه به، وكذا ان كانا معا، فان الشق يكون سببه شيئا آخر متقدما عليه. وان زاد المقدار اولا، فيلزم منه التداخل. وان قيل انّه يتقدم على الشق زيادة المقدار بالذات، فكذا نقول فى ميل الاجزاء الى التفريق، فلا يلزم ما قالوا. فاذن ليس التخلخل إلاّ بتفريق اجزاء الحرارة وتخلخل جسم لطيف كالهواء حتى اذا مالت الاجزاء الى الافتراق ومنعها مانع دفعته ان كان لها قوة ويحس هذا التبديد فى المتخلخلات كالماء وغيره من المائعات اذا تسخّنت، ولو ضممنا اجزائها لانضمت ورجعت الى المقدار الأوّل

this it has been shown that body is magnitude and that the magnitudes of the world are neither increased nor decreased in the slightest. A mustard seed's matter has not the capacity to accept all the magnitudes of the world, as the Peripatetics would argue. This was the opinion of the Ancients, the first sages.

(76) Though being extended or having a determinate magnitude are predicated of a body, that is not grounds for arguing that they are superadded to a body. Just because we say that a body has a determinate magnitude, it does not follow that its magnitude is superadded to it. Realities do not depend on turns of phrase, for the latter are often metaphorical. Often a man will think of thingness with magnitude and say, "A body is a thing that has magnitude." If he examines the reality, he will find that the thing is simply magnitude. Even though common usage permits expressions like "a far distance," it does not mean that the farness of distance is something added to it. It is, rather, a turn of phrase, like "fleshy flesh." It is permissible to say, "The body is extended," in the sense that it has an extension peculiar to it in a particular dimension, but what this really means is that its magnitude extends in various directions, or in a particular direction, or the like.

They fall into these fallacies because they confuse connection with extension due to certain inexact expressions and because of their invalid notion that distinction by perfection and deficiency—for example, between a long and short line—is by something added to magnitude.

A judgment [that the prime matter of the elemental world is self-subsistent magnitude]

(77) In the previous chapter you learned that body is just self-subsistent magnitude. Therefore, there is nothing in the world that is simply existent, accepting magnitudes and forms, like that which [the Peripatetics] name "prime matter." According to them, this is not something particular in itself; it is particularized only by forms. The implication is that this is

فتقرر من هذا ان الجسم هو المقدار ومقادير العالم لا تزداد ولا تنقص اصلا، وان ليس للخردلة مادة لها استعداد ان تقبل مقادير العالم كله كما التزم به المشاؤون. وهذا رأى الاولين الاقدمين من الحكماء.

(٧٦) وما يقال «انّ الجسم يحمل عليه انه ممتد او متقدر فيكون زائدا عليه» ليس كلام مستقيم. فانّا اذا قلنا انّ الجسم متقدر لا يلزم ان يكون المقدار زائدا عليه. والحقائق لا تبتنى على الاطلاقات لما يجرى فيها من التجوّزات.[٥٩] فربما يأخذ الانسان فى ذهنه شيئية مع المقدار.[٦٠] فيقول «الجسم شئ له المقدار». فاذا رجع الى الحقيقة، لم يجد الشئ إلاّ نفس المقدار واذا اطلق فى العرف مثل قولهم «بعد بعيد» لا يدّل ان البعدية فى البعد شئ زائد عليه، بل هو تجوّز كما يقال[٦١] «جسم جسيم» ويجوز ان يقال «الجسم ممتد» بمعنى ان له امتدادا خاصا فى جهة متعينة، فيرجع حاصله الى ان المقدار ذاهب فى جهات مختلفة او جهة متعينة، ويجوز ذلك.

فهذه المغالطات لزمتهم من أخذ الاتصال بمعنى الامتداد ومن بعض التجوزات ومن ظنّهم انّ الامتياز بالكمال والنقص، كما بين الخط الطويل والقصير بشئ زائد على المقدار وذلك غير مستقيم.

حكومة [فى انّ هيولى
العالم العنصرى هو المقدار القائم بنفسه]

(٧٧) فاذا تبيّن لك من الفصل السابق، ان الجسم ليس[٦٢] إلاّ المقدار القائم بنفسه فليس شئ فى العالم هو موجود فحسب يقبل المقادير والصور وهو الّذى سموه «الهيولى». وليس فى نفسه شيئا متخصصا عندهم، بل تخصصه بالصور. فحاصله يرجع الى انه موجود مّا

an existent whose substantiality is the denial that it has a subject. Our expression "a certain existent" is something mental, as has been explained. Therefore, that which they name "prime matter" is really nothing at all. According to the principle that we have established, the substantiality of this magnitude, which is the body, is a being of reason. If it is considered in relation to the varying states in it and the various compound species occurring from its states, it is called their prime matter, but it is really just body.

Another judgment [concerning investigations related to prime matter and form]

(78) The Peripatetics explain that the existence of the so-called prime matter that they posit as existent is inconceivable without forms, and that the forms are inconceivable without prime matter. Then they sometimes assert that the form has something to do with the existence of prime matter, often trying to prove that the form can be a cause of the prime matter by citing matter's inconceivability without form. That is not sound, for a thing may have a concomitant without which it never exists, yet the concomitant is not a cause of the thing.

Some of them give another argument as to why the existence of prime matter is inconceivable without form. They explain that otherwise it would either be divided, in which case it would be bodily and not incorporeal, or undivided, in which case it would be so essentially and not admit of division under any circumstances. This is not correct; for if it were undivided, it would not be absurd that it be divided, nor would it be indivisible essentially. Rather, the absurdity would be in denying it the condition of divisibility, which is magnitude.

(79) Among their proofs is the following: If prime matter is posited to be without forms and a form then occurs in it, the form must occur either in all places or in no place. Both are clearly false. Thus, it must occur in a particular place; but there is nothing to particularize it according to the principles well known in the books.

وجوهريته سلب الموضوع عنه. وقولنا «موجود مّا» أمر ذهنى كما سبق، فما سمّوه هيولى ليس بشئ وعلى القاعدة التى قررناها هذا المقدار الّذى هو الجسم جوهريته اعتبار عقلى فاذا أُضيف بالنسبة الى الهيئة المتبدلة عليه والانواع الحاصلة منها المركبة يسمّى «هيولى» لها لا غير وهو جسم، فحسب.

حكومة أُخرى [فى مباحث تتعلّق بالهيولى و الصورة]

(٧٨) وهؤلاء بيّنوا انّ الّذى وضعوه موجودا وسمّوه «هيولى» لا يتصور وجوده دون الصور ولا الصور دونه. ثم ربما يحكمون[٦٣] بانّ للصورة مدخلا فى وجود الهيولى؛ وكثيرا مّا يعوّلون[٦٤] فى كون الصورة علة مّا للهيولى بناء على عدم تصور خلوّها عنها. وذلك ليس بمتين، فانّه يجوز ان يكون للشئ لازم لا يكون دونه ولا يلزم ان يكون ذلك علة.

ثم منهم من يبيّن[٦٥] انّ الهيولى لا يتصور وجودها دون الصورة، لانّها حينئذ اما ان تكون منقسمة، فيلزم جسميتها فلا تكون مجردة، او غير منقسمة، فيكون ذلك لذاتها فيستحيل عليها الانقسام، وهذا غير مستقيم. فانّها اذا كانت غير منقسمة، فلا يلزم ان يستحيل عليها ذلك ويكون ذلك لذاتها، بل يستحيل فرضه فيها لأجل انتفاء شرط القسمة وهو المقدار.

(٧٩) ومن جملة حججهم: انّ الهيولى ان فُرضت مجردة، ثم حصل فيها الصورة، اما ان تحصل فى جميع الامكنة او لا فى مكان، وهما ظاهرا البطلان، او فى مكان مخصص، ولا مخصص على التفصيل المشهور فى الكتب.

One might answer them thus: "Its impossibility in a particular place is due to the lack of something to particularize it, not because it is absurd for it to be without form." The most that follows from this proof is that if the world came into being and prime matter remained without form, it could not thereafter acquire a form, since nothing would make the form peculiar to a place. The absurdity of something under a particular condition does not imply its absurdity in itself. Such errors result from confusing what attaches to the thing in itself with what attaches to it by something else.

(80) Closely related to their previous proof that prime matter cannot be freed from form is their argument that if it were freed from form, it would be either one or many. But multiplicity requires something that distinguishes, and distinction can only be by form. If prime matter were characterized by unity, its unity would be necessitated by its essence, and it could not become multiple under any condition. To this one ought to reply that unity is an intellectual attribute implied by the necessity of indivisibility and that the impossibility of its divisibility is only because of the denial of the condition of division—which is magnitude, as has been explained. Since we have asserted that body is only magnitude, we have no need to investigate prime matter. The only reason we mention these proofs is to explain the errors in them.

(81) The Peripatetics also assert that there are other forms,[46] arguing that the body must be either indivisible or divisible, and in the latter case it must accept division and change in shape either easily or with difficulty. Therefore, they say that it must have other forms that necessitate these things and by which the body becomes particular. To this, one must reply that these things by which it becomes particular are qualities either in the elements—like moisture, dryness, heat, and cold—or in the heavens, so that they too are states.

If they say, "Accidents cannot constitute a substance, and what we are talking about does constitute a substance," I will reply, "You assert that these entities you call 'forms' constitute substance. This cannot be because a body is never without some one of them, for the fact that something is never without some entity does not imply that that thing is constituted by that entity, some concomitants being accidents. If you think that the body is constituted by them because they make the body particular,

فلقائل ان يقول لهم: امتناعها فى مكان خاص لعدم المخصص لا لاستحالة التجرد وغاية ما يلزم من هذه الحجة انّ العالم اذا حصل وبقيت هيولى مجردة، لا يمكن عليها بعد ذلك لبس الصورة لعدم المخصص بمكان، واستحالة الشئ لغيره لا تدل على استحالته فى نفسه وهذه وامثالها لزمت من اهمال الاعتبارات اللاحقة بالشئ لذاته ولغيره.

(٨٠) ويقرب مما سبق من حجتهم قولهم فى اثبات ان الهيولى لا يمكن تجردها عن الصورة، انها ان تجردت عن الصورة[٦٦] اما ان تكون واحدة او كثيرة. فالكثرة تستدعى مميزا، وذلك بالصورة. والوحدة ان اتصفت بها الهيولى، يكون اقتضاء لذاتها ولا يمكن عليها التكثر اصلا. اذ[٦٧] لقائل ان يقول: ان الوحدة صفة عقلية تلزم من ضرورة عدم انقسامها، واستحالة انقسامها إنمّا هى لانتفاء شرط القسمة، وهو المقدار كما سبق. ولما اثبتنا ان ليس الجسم إلاّ المقدار فحسب، استغنينا عن البحث فى الهيولى، إلاّ انّ الغرض فى ايراد هذه الحجج بيان ما فيها من السهو.

(٨١) ثم اثبتوا صورا اُخرى فقالوا الجسم لا يخلوا ممن كونه ممتنعا عليه القسمة او ممكنا، مع ان يقبل ذلك والتشكل[٦٨] وتركه بسهولة، او ان يقبل هذه الاشياء بصعوبة. فلا بد من صور اُخرى تقتضى هذه الاشياء ويتخصص بها الجسم. فلقائل ان يقول بان هذه المخصصات هى كيفيات اما فى العناصر، فمثل الرطوبة واليبوسة والحرارة والبرودة، واما فى الافلاك، فهيئآت اُخرى.

فان قال «ان الاعراض لا يمكن عليها تقويم الجوهر وما ذكرناه مقوّم للجوهر». اجيب: بان كون هذه الأمور التى سمّيتموها صورا، مقوّمة للجوهر ان كان لكون الجسم لا يخلو عن بعضها، فكون الشئ غير خال عن أمر لا يدلّ

it is still not necessarily the case that what makes the body particular is a form and substance. After all, you admit that individuals of a species are distinguished by accidents. If it were not for the things that make them particular, neither species nor other things would exist. You admit that the species' natures exist more completely than the genera, yet these cannot be conceived to exist without what particularizes them. If the entities that make a body particular are thought to be forms and substance because the body cannot be conceived to be without something to particularize it, then the things that particularize species are more worthy of being substances. Since this is not the case, an entity that makes something particular may be an accident, and an accident may be among the conditions of the realization of a substance, just as the entities that particularize the species are accidents, and the species cannot conceivably be realized in concrete things without accidents."

(82) The argument that the reality[47] of the species occurs and the accidents follow is unsound, for if the nature of a species—humanity, for example—occurs first and the accidents then follow, it must occur as universal absolute humanity and then be individualized, which is absurd. Humanity only occurs individually; absolute humanity never occurs among concrete things. If these accidents were not conditions for the realization of the nature of the species and if what this individual is distinguished by were not a concomitant of the reality of humanity, then it would be possible to posit humanity remaining in a state of absoluteness, as it was when it first occurred, and the accidents then attaching to it, without anything to distinguish it. This is because these accidents by which the individuals of the species are distinguished are not among the things that necessitate the reality of the species, nor are they among its concomitants; for otherwise, they would occur in every case. Therefore, they must be from an external agent. If the nature of the species were then able to dispense with them, we would be able to posit its existence without them—that is, without these accidents—which is not the case. From this it follows that an accident may be a condition of the existence of a substance and a constituent of its existence in this sense. Moreover, were it possible for humanity to occur absolutely with the things that particularize and distinguish it coming later, then why could corporeality not occur absolutely with that which particularizes it coming later? Whatever arguments they may advance to defend themselves in this case apply also to species.

على تقوّمه بذلك الأمر، اذ من اللوازم اعراض. وان كان تقوّم الجسم بها لكونها مخصصات الجسم، فليس ايضا من شرط المخصص ان يكون صورة وجوهرا. فانّ اشخاص النوع اعترفتم بانها ميّز بالعوارض؛ ولولا المخصصات، لما وجدت الانواع وغيرها. والطبايع النوعية اعترفتم بانها أتمّ وجودا من الاجناس ولا يتصوّر فرض وجودها دون المخصصات، فان كانت مخصصات الجسم صورا وجوهرا، لأجل انّ الجسم لا يتصوّر دون مخصص فمخصصات الانواع اولى بان تكون جواهر، وليس كذا، فيجوز ان يكون المخصص عرضا والعرض يكون من شرائط تحقق الجوهر، كما ان المخصصات فى الانواع اعراض ولا يتصوّر تحقق النوع فى الاعيان إلاّ مع العوارض.

(٨٢) والّذى يقال «انّ الحقيقة[٦٩] النوعية تحصل، ثم تتبعها العوارض» كلام ضعيف، فان الطبيعة النوعية، كالانسانية مثلا، ان حصلت اولا ثم بعها العوارض، فكان حصولها انسانية مطلقة كلية ثم شخص، وهو محال. اذ لم تحصل إلاّ متشخصة والمطلق لا يقع فى الاعيان اصلا. وان كانت هذه العوارض ليست بشرائط لتحقق الطبيعية، وليس ما يمتاز به هذا الشخص لازما لحقيقة الانسانية، فيجوز فرض انسانيته باقية على الاطلاق، كما حصلت اولا ثم لحقتها العوارض دون مميّز، اذ هذه العوارض التى يتشخّص[٧٠] بها اشخاص النوع، ليست من مقتضيات الحقيقة النوعية ولوازمها والا اتفقت فى الكل، فهى اذا من فاعل خارج فاذا استغنت عنها الطبيعة النوعية، كان لنا فرض وجودها دونها، اى دون هذه العوارض، وليس كذا. فصحّ من هذا جواز ان يكون العرض شرط وجود الجوهر ومقوّما لوجوده بهذا المعنى، ثم ان جاز حصول الانسانية مطلقة، ثم تتبعها المميّزات المخصصات فهلا جاز حصول الجسمية مطلقة، ثم تتبعها المخصصات؟ وكل ما يعتذرون به هنالك مثله واقع فى الانواع.

(83) Strangely, the Peripatetics say that the intellect necessitates body through its intellection of its own contingency, even though its own contingency is necessarily an accident according to the principles of their school. The same is true of intellection of contingency, for intellection of contingency is not intellection of necessity; for if they were the same, one would necessitate the same thing as the other, which is not the case. Thus, if intellection of necessity is not intellection of contingency, then they are two things added to the quiddity of the intellect—both of them accidentals to it and both accidentals in it. Since existence does not enter into the reality of the thing, how much less appropriate is it that contingency and necessity do so, let alone the intellection of them! If their intellection is accidental and [if] by intellecting the two a separate corporeal substance and another separate, noncorporeal substance[48] occur, then it is correct to say that accidents have a role in the existence of substances, either as some sort of cause or as conditions. A constituent of existence is something that has a role in the existence of the thing. Also, is not the capacity requiring the body's soul a result of the bodily constitution, which is an accident? This is a condition of the occurrence of the soul. Are not the souls after separation from the body particularized and distinguished one from another by accidents? Thus, it is correct to say that among that which particularizes substances may be accidents and that being particularized by accidents is a condition of the existence of the realities of species.

(84) It is astonishing that they think that heat destroys the form of water and that its absence is a condition of the existence of the form of water. If it is possible for the absence of an accident to be a condition of the existence of a substance and to be a cause, why will they not admit that an accident can be a cause or condition of its existence? What is a constituent of existence if not something that has some role in the existence of the thing? They admit that heat calls the form of air into being. Thus, it is one of the causes of the occurrence of air, despite its accidentality. Such errors result in part from using terms ambiguously—such as "form" and the like—and in part from making arbitrary exceptions to general principles.

(٨٣) ثم العجب ان العقل إنمّا يقتضى الجسم لتعقله لامكان نفسه على ما قالوا[٧١] وامكان نفسه بالضرورة عرض على سياق مذهبهم؛ وكذا تعقل الامكان، فان تعقل الامكان غير تعقل الوجوب، لانهما ان كانا واحدا، كان اقتضائهما واحدا، وليس كذا. فاذا كان تعقل الوجوب غير تعقل الامكان، فهما زائدان على ماهيته، عرضيان له عرضيان فيه والوجود لما لم يدخل فى حقيقة الشئ، فالاولى ان لا يدخله[٧٢] الامكان والوجوب فضلا عن تعقلهما. فاذا كان تعقلهما عرضيا وباعتبار ذينك حصل جوهر مفارق جسمانى وجوهر مفارق آخر غير جسمانى،[٧٣] فصحّ ان الاعراض لها مدخل فى وجود الجواهر بضرب من العلية او الاشتراط، وليس مقوّم الوجود إلاّ ما له مدخل مّا فى وجود الشئ. ثم الاستعداد المستدعى للنفس الّذى للبدن اليس لأجل المزاج، وهو عرض، وهو من شرائط حصول النفس؟ والنفوس بعد المفارقة اليست خصص وتمتاز بعضها عن بعض بالاعراض؟ فصحّ ان من مخصصات الجواهر الاعراض، والتخصص بها شرط وجود الحقائق النوعية.

(٨٤) والعجب انّهم جوّزوا ان تكون الحرارة مبطلة للصورة المائية وعدمها، شرطا لوجودها، فاذا جاز ان يكون عدم العرض شرطا لوجود الجوهر وعلة، فلم لا يجوز ان يكون وجوده علة او شرطا لوجوده؟ وهل كان مقوّم الوجود إلاّ ما له مدخل مّا فى وجود الشئ؟ وقد اعترفوا بان المستدعى للصورة الهوائية الحرارة، وهى من علل حصولها مع عرضيتها، فمثل هذه الاغاليط لزم بعضه من استعمال الالفاظ على معان مختلفة، كلفظ الصورة وغيرها، وبعضه من الاستثناء عن القاعدة التى نسبة حجة ثبوتها اليها والى ما استثنى عنها سواء.

(85) Some of them argue that water, fire, and the like contain entities that change the answer to the question "What is it?" These, then, would be forms, for accidents do not change the answer to the question "What is it?" This argument is unsound; for if a chair is made from a piece of wood, nothing changes in the wood except states and accidents; yet if you were asked what it was, you would say that it is a chair, not that it is wood. In blood, for example, the forms of the elements are preserved, according to what has been established; yet there is nothing in blood except the states with respect to which it has become blood. If one were to ask concerning particular instances of blood, "What are they?" the reply would not be that they are elements or something of that sort but that they are blood. Likewise, if one were to point at a house and ask, "What is it?" the answer would not be that it is clay or stone but that it is a house. Thus, accidents can change the answer to the question "What is it?" Non-simple realities are named in accordance with their compositions, but nouns and simples have no parts, so the answer to "What is it?" cannot change with one of the parts. The rule in the case of the composite species is to consider the combination of most of the best-known accidents, not considering anything else that might alter the answer to "What is it?"

(86) One of their proofs is that this form is part of the substance, and a part of a substance is a substance. The fallacy of this proof is that each part of that which is predicated to be a substance in a certain respect is not necessarily itself a substance. One may predicate of a chair that it is a substance in a certain respect and that the states by which it is a chair are part of the chair, but it does not follow that these are substance. Only in the case of a substance that is a substance in every respect are all the parts substance. The fact that it is a substance in all respects just means that all its parts are substance, if it has parts. Water and air are considered to be pure substances, yet they are only substances with respect to their corporeality, and their being water and air in particular is by accidents. Water is a substance with accidents that are not themselves substance.

(٨٥) ومنهم من احتج بانّ الماء والنار ونحوهما أمورا تغيّر جواب «ما هو؟» فتكون صورا، فان الاعراض لا تغير جواب «ما هو؟» وهو كلام غير متين. فان الخشب اذا اتخذ منه الكرسى، ما حصل فيه إلاّ هيئآت واعراض، ولا يقال انّه خشب عند السؤال عن انّه «ما هو؟» بل يقال انّه كرسى. والدم مثلا محفوظ فيه صور العناصر على ما قرّر وليس فيه إلاّ الهيئآت التى باعتبارها صار دما. واذا سُئل عن اشخاصه انّها «ما هى؟» لا يجاب بانّها عناصر او نحو ذلك، بل بانّها دم. وكذا البيت المشار اليه اذا سُئل انّه «ما هو؟» لا يُجاب بانّه طين او حجارة، بل انه بيت. فالاعراض مغيّرة جواب «ما هو؟» والحقائق الغير البسيطة إنمّا هى بحسب التركيبات. والاسامى والبسائط لا جزء لها حتى يتغير فيها جواب «ما هو؟» ببعض الاجزاء. والانواع المركبة الضابطة فيها اجتماع معظم اعراض مشهورة لا يلتفت الى ما سواها حتى يغيّرها[٧٤] جواب «ما هو؟»

(٨٦) ومن حججهم انّ هذه الصورة جزء الجوهر، وجزء الجوهر جوهر. وهذا فيه غلط. فانّ جزء ما يحمل عليه انّه جوهر بجهة مّا لا يلزم ان يكون جوهر، فالكرسى يحمل عليه بجهة مّا انّه جوهر والهيئات التى بها الكرسوية جزء الكرسى، ولا يلزم ان تكون جوهرا بل الجوهر الّذى هو من جميع جهاته[٧٥] جوهر يكون جميع اجزائه جوهرا، فانّ نفس كونه جوهرا من جميع الوجوه نفس كون جميع اجزائه جوهرا، ان كان له جزء. والماء والهواء من الّذى سلّم انّها جواهر محضة، بل من حيث جسميتها جواهر، وخصوص المائية الهوائية بالاعراض، فالماء جوهر مع اعراض ليس نفس الجوهر.

(87) They argue, "The form is a constituent of the substance, so it is a substance. But the substantiality of the forms consists in their not being in a subject. Their being not in a subject means that the locus is not independent of them. That the locus is not independent of them means that they are constituents of the locus." Thus, to say, "The form is a constituent of the substance, so it is a substance" is equivalent to saying, "The form is a constituent of the substance, so it is a constituent of the substance." We have shown that accidents may be constituents of substance. By "form," we mean in this book only the simple reality of the species, whether substantial or accidental. There is nothing in the elements but corporeality and states—nothing else! Now that we have proven that there are no non-sensible forms such as they had affirmed, all that remain are qualities that become more or less intense.

(88) It is erroneous to say, "When heat intensifies, it does not change in itself by an accident. Therefore, the intensification of heat is by a differentia."[49] Heat does not change; its locus changes with individual heats. The individual instances of heat are not distinguished by a differentia, for the answer to the question "What is it?" does not change; nor do they differ by an accident. They differ by a third category: perfection and deficiency. The intellectual quiddity encompasses the essences of all the individuals, perfect or deficient, but alteration does not lead to a change in quiddity. The theory of the Peripatetics about what is more or less intense is arbitrary; for according to them, one animal cannot be more intense in its animality than another. However, they define animal as "a body with a soul, sensible and moving at will." That animal whose soul is more able to cause motion and whose senses are keener certainly has more perfect sensation and movement. The fact that common usage does not allow one to say that this animal is more perfectly animal than that one does not imply that it is not so. Their argument that one thing is not said to be more watery than another and their other arguments of that sort are based on inexact common usages. If they are challenged and asked the basis of their assertions, the weakness of their argument becomes apparent. Later, we will mention the states peculiar to each of the elements and show that there is nothing in the elements beyond what

(٨٧) ثم قولهم «الصورة مقومة للجوهر، فتكون جوهرا وجوهرية الصور كونها لا فى موضوع، وكونها لا فى موضوع عدم استغناء المحل عنها وعدم استغناء المحل عنها هوائها مقومة للمحل»؛ فقولنا «الصورة مقومة للجوهر، فتكون جوهرا» كانّا قلنا «الصورة مقومة للجوهر فتكون مقومة للجوهر». فثبت بما ذكرنا انّ الاعراض يجوز ان تقوّم الجوهر والصورة لا نعنى لها إلاّ كل حقيقة بسيطة نوعية، كانت جوهرية او عرضية فى هذا الكتاب. وليس فى العناصر شئ سوى الجسمية والهيئات لا غير واذا اندفعت الصور التى اثبتوها وقالوا انّها غير محسوسة، فبقيت الكيفيات التى تشتدّ وتضعف.

(٨٨) واعلم انّ من قال «انّ الحرارة اذا اشتدت فتغيّرها فى نفسها ليس بعارض فيكون بفصل»، اخطأ. فانّ الحرارة ما تغيّرت بل محلها باشخاصها. واما الفارق بين اشخاصها فليس بفصل؛ فان جواب «ما هو؟» لا يتغيّر فيها ولا[٧٦] هو عارض، بل قسم ثالث هو الكمالية والنقص. والماهية العقلية تعمّ ذوات اشخاصها التامة والناقصة على ان من التغيّر ما يؤدى الى تبدل الماهية وكلام المشائين فى الأشدّ والاضعف مبنى على التحكم، فانّ عندهم لا يكون حيوان أشدّ حيوانية من غيره، وقد حدّوا الحيوان بانّه «جسم ونفس حساس متحرك بالارادة». ثم الّذى نفسه اقوى على التحريك وحواسه اكثر، لا شكّ انّ الحساسية والمتحركية فيه أتمّ فبمجرد ان لا يطلق فى العرف ان هذا أتمّ حيوانية من ذلك لا ينكر انه أتمّ منه. وقولهم انّه لا يقال ان هذا أشدّ مائية فى ذلك،[٧٧] ونحوها، كله بناءا على التجوّزات العرفية فاذا مُنعوا وطولبوا بلميّة دعاويهم، تبيّن وهن هذا الكلام. ونحن سنذكر فيما بعد ما يتخصص به كل واحد من العناصر من الهيئات وان ليس فيها إلاّ ما يحسّ.

can be perceived. The Peripatetics, however, affirm that particular things contain entities that cannot be sensed or intellected in their particularity, thus making realities unknown even after they are known. It is the Ancients who know the truth in this matter.

A principle [on the denial of the individual atom][50]

(89) Among the errors resulting from confusing the potential with the actual is this argument: "A body is divisible into parts indivisible in imagination or intellect. If it could be divided infinitely, the body and its parts would be equal in magnitude, since both would be equal in their infinite divisibility. However, the equality of the part and the whole is absurd." These people do not realize that the division is not actually existent but is only potential. It does not have actual instances that would allow one to say whether they were the same or different. Moreover, there is no reason why the infinite should never be different, especially if it is potential. Thousands may potentially be infinite in the intellect. These thousands include hundreds, which are more numerous than they, in spite of their also being infinite. The absurdity of a body having a part that is indivisible in imagination and mind is clear. If this part exists in space, its extension in one direction is different from its extension in another—so it is divisible. Moreover, if a body did have an indivisible part, then if one of these parts were assumed to be at the meeting point of two others, it could not conceivably be in complete contact with the whole of both, since in that case it would not be indivisible. Nor would it be in contact with only one, for it is at their meeting point. Therefore, it must be in contact with something of each and thus be divisible into three. Furthermore, if the one that is between the other two does separate them, then that which the one side meets is not what the other side meets, so it is divisible. On the other hand, if it does not separate them, its existence and nonexistence would be indistinguishable and there would be no volume in the world, which is an absurd conclusion. Therefore, since a body may not be conceived to have an indivisible part, nothing of the body—such as movement—may be conceived to have indivisible parts. Movement occurs in distance and must be infinitely divisible, as distance is.

والمشاؤون اثبتوا فى الاشياء المتشخصة أمورا لا تُحسّ ولا تُعقل بخصوصها حتى تصير الحقائق، بعد ان عُلمت مجهولة. والحق مع الاقدمين فى هذه المسألة.

قاعدة [فى ابطال الجوهر الفرد]

(٨٩) ومن الغلط الواقع بسبب أخذ ما بالقوة مكان ما بالفعل، قول القائل «الجسم ينقسم الى ما لا ينقسم فى الوهم والعقل، بناءا على انه لو انقسم الى غير النهاية، لكان الجسم وجزء منه متساويين فى المقدار لتساويهما فى قبول القسمة الى غير النهاية، ومساواة الجزء لكله، محال». ولم يعلم هؤلاء ان القسمة غير موجودة بالفعل بل بالقوة، وليس لها اعداد حاصلة حتى يقال انه يساوى شيئا او يتفاوت. ثم ليس من شرط ما لا يتناهى انه لا يتفاوت لا سيّما اذا كان بالقوة؛ فان الالوف فى العقل ممكنة الى غير النهاية وهى تشتمل على مئات اعدادها اكثر من اعداد الالوف، ولا يخل بكونهما غير متناهيين. واستحالة الجزء الّذى لا يتجزء فى العقل والوهم للجسم ظاهر؛ فانّ هذا الجزء، ان كان فى الجهات فما منه الى جهة غير ما منه الى الأُخرى، فينقسم. وايضا لو كان للجسم جزء لا يتجزء، لكان الواحد اذا فرض على ملتقى الاثنين، لما لم يتصوّر ان يماس كل كليهما، اذ لا يكون حينئذ لا يتجزء، ولا مقتصرا على مماسة احدهما فانّه على الملتقى فلا بدّ من التقاء شئ من كل واحد؛ فانقسمت الثلاثة. وايضا الواحد بين الاثنين ان حجب لقى كل من الطرفين غير ما يلقاه الآخر فانقسم؛ او لم يحجب فوجوده وعدمه سواء، فلم يبق فى العالم حجم، وهو محال. واذا لم يتصور للجسم جزء لا يتجزء فلا يتصوّر لكل ما يكون فى الجسم حتى الحركة، فانها واقعة فى المسافة، فيلزم انقسامها الى غير النهاية من انقسام المسافة.

A principle [in refutation of the vacuum]

(90) As you know, body is nothing more than magnitude. Thus, the space between bodies cannot be vacant, since this nonbeing posited to be between bodies has magnitude extended in three dimensions. That which encompasses the body must exceed that which is smaller than it and so have length, width, and depth that can be pointed to. Therefore, it must be a body. Moreover, if a body occurred in a vacuum, the distances would become one distance and interpenetrate so that each would meet every other. This is absurd. How could it not be absurd for two magnitudes to be combined without the total of the two being more than one of them?

A judgment [on proofs of the immortality of the soul]

(91) Among the fallacies resulting from changing the meaning of a technical term to respond to an objection is the following argument: "The soul does not contain the potentiality of nonexistence and the actuality of perdurance, for it is actually existent and unitary. Therefore, it cannot cease to exist." Against this, one may reply, "You have judged that the separate intellects are both contingent and actually existent. However, what contingently is, also contingently is not. Therefore, its existence has the potential not to perdure."

One of the Peripatetics responds, "The meaning of contingency in the separate intellects is that they are dependent on causes; if the cause were supposed to be nonexistent, they would cease to be. This does not mean that they have in themselves the potential to become nonexistent." This is special pleading, for their dependence on a cause and the necessity of their annihilation with the annihilation of their cause follows from their contingency in themselves. When some difficulty is raised, one cannot explain contingency by that which follows from contingency after admitting that that which is necessary by another is contingent in itself. Its contingency in itself is intellectually prior to its necessity by another. All the intellects are contingent, and none are worthy in themselves of existence!

قاعدة [فى ابطال الخلاء]

(٩٠) واذا علمت انّ الجسم ليس فيه ما يزيد على المقدار، فلا يمكن ان يكون ما بين الاجسام خاليا، اذ العدم الّذى يفرض ما بين اجسام له مقدار فى جميع الاقطار. فانّ ما يتسع لجسم يفضل على ما هو اصغر من ذلك، فله طول وعرض وعمق، وهو مقصود بالاشارة، فيكون جسما ثم اذا حصل فى الخلاء جسم، فتصير الابعاد بعدا واحدا وداخل بحيث يلقى كل واحد كل الآخر، وهو محال. وكيف لا يستحيل ان يجتمع مقداران ولا يكون مجموع الاثنين اكثر[٧٨] من احدهما.

حكومة [فيما أُستدلّ به على بقاء النفس]

(٩١) ومن الغلط الواقع بسبب تغيير الاصطلاح عند توجه النقض ما قيل «انّ النفس لا تنعدم اذ ليس فيها قوة ان تنعدم وفعل ان تبقى لانها موجودة بالفعل وهى وحدانية». فأُورد عليهم ان المفارقات حكمتم بكونها ممكنة مع انها بالفعل موجودة وممكن الكون ممكن اللاكون، ففيه قوة ان لا يبقى.

اجاب بعضهم بانّ معنى الامكان فى المفارقات هو انّها متوقفة على عللها، حتى لو فرض عدم العلة انعدمت لا انّ لها قوة العدم فى نفسها. وهذا الاعتذار غير مستقيم؛ فان توقفها على العلة ولزوم انتفائها من انتفاء العلة إنمّا كان تابعا لامكانها فى نفسها؛ فكيف يفسّر الامكان عند توجه الاشكال بما يتبع الامكان، بعد الاعتراف بانّ الواجب بغيره ممكن فى نفسه، وامكانه فى نفسه متقدم على وجوبه بغيره تقدما عقليا، وانّ العقول كلها ممكنة ولا تستحق الوجود بذاتها؟

(92) Thus, it is astonishing that he says, "The corruptible beings, unlike the separate intellects, cease to exist even though their causes continue to exist." He asserts this absurdity without qualification, even though the composite cause of the corruptible beings is like the cause of the separate intellects in that it becomes necessary through the necessity of its cause. Among the causes of the corruptible beings are the capacity of the locus and the absence of that which would make the thing impossible. Thus, a corruptible thing only ceases to exist when part of its cause ceases to exist. It would only have been correct for him to have said this of the emanating cause of the separate intellects, not of the cause absolutely—for beings do cease to exist despite the perdurance of the separate intellects that are their causes. They cease to exist only when some other part of their cause ceases to exist. One ought to explain contingency by the proximate potentiality that is the proximate capacity, not repudiate the basis of contingency or the worthiness to exist of the separate intellects. The object here is not to discuss this at length but only to indicate the basis of the error.

(93) Another of the worthless arguments with which they reply to the objections raised is: "Unity in the Necessary Existent is negative, its meaning being that it is indivisible; but in other things it is affirmative, the basis of number. Since number is existential, so is its basis." To this, one can reply, "The Necessary Existent is also described by this unity that is the basis of number, for we say that the Everlasting is one, and its second is the First Intellect, its third is this, and its fourth is that. Thus, we have described it by the unity that is the basis of number, for we have counted it and the enumerated existences together." Such special pleading and equivocation are of no use. The truth is that unity is an intellectual attribute and nothing more, as we have said.

A judgment [concerning the Platonic Forms]

(94) Among the sophistries arising from taking the image in place of the thing is an argument used by the Peripatetics to deny the Platonic Forms: "Were the forms of man and horse, water and fire self-subsistent, it would be impossible to conceive of anything that shared their realities being incarnated in a locus. If any one of their particulars needed a locus,

(٩٢) ثم من العجب انّه قال «ان الكائنات الفاسدات تنعدم مع بقاء عللها دون المفارقات»، واورد هذا هكذا مطلقا، وذلك محال. فان العلة المركبة للكائنات الفاسدات كالعلة فى المفارقات فيما يرجع الى الوجوب بوجوب العلة. والكائنات الفاسدات من جملة عللها استعداد محلها وانتفاء ما يوجب بطلانها فلا تنعدم إلاّ لانعدام جزء من العلة. والاصلح له ان كان يذكر، بدل العلة مطلقا، العلة الفياضة من المفارقات، فان الكائنات تنعدم مع بقاء عللها[٧٩] المفارقة، ولكن انتفائها إنمّا يكون لانتفاء بعض الاجزاء الأُخرى للعلة. وكان ينبغى ان يؤوّل الامكان بالقوة القريبة التى هى الاستعداد القريب لا ان يجحد اصل الامكان ولا استحقاق الوجود فى المفارقات، وليس هذا موضع التطويل فيه، بل الغرض التنبيه على جهة الغلط.

(٩٣) ومن جملة المراوغات فى دفع الاشكال قولهم «ان الوحدة فى واجب الوجود سلبية معناه انه لا ينقسم، وفى غيره ايجابية وهى مبدأ العدد، والعدد شئ وجودى وكذا مبدأه». ولقائل ان يقول: «ان هذه الوحدة التى هى مبدأ العدد يوصف بها ايضا واجب الوجود، فانّا نقول القيّوم واحد، وثانيه العقل الأوّل، وثالثه كذا، ورابعه كذا. فقد وصفناه بالوحدة التى هى مبدأ العدد، اذا أخذناه مع اعداد الوجود، فانّه واحد منها». فلم ينفع ذلك الاعتذار وتغيير الاصطلاح، بل الحق انّ الوحدة صفة عقلية لا غير كما ذكرنا.

حكومة [فى المُثُل الافلاطونية]

(٩٤) ومن الغلط الواقع بسبب أخذ مثال الشئ مكانه قول المشائين فى ابطال مُثُل افلاطون: «انّ الصورة الانسانية والفرسية والمائية والنارية لو كانت قائمة بذاتها لما تصوّر حلول شئ مما يشاركها فى الحقيقة فى

then the reality itself would need a locus. Thus, none of them could be free of a locus." To this, one may reply, "Do you not acknowledge that the form of a substance occurs in the mind as an accident? After all, you say that the thing has existence among concrete things and existence in minds. If it is permissible for the reality of substantiality to occur in the mind as an accident, then there may also be self-subsistent quiddities in the world of intellect, having images[51] in this world that are not self-subsistent. These are a perfection for another, but they do not have the perfection of the intellectual quiddities, just as the forms of the quiddities of substances external to the mind occur in the mind and are not self-subsistent—being a perfection or attribute of the mind and not having the independence and self-subsistence that the external quiddities have. In this case, that which is true of a thing is not necessarily true of its image.[52]

(95) "Then you assert that existence applies with a single meaning to the Necessary Existent and to everything else. Existence is the Necessary Existent itself, while in others existence is superadded as an accident of the quiddity. Against this, one may argue as follows: If the independence of the existence of the Necessary Existent from a quiddity to which it might be related is due to existence itself, then all would be so. If it is due to something added to the Necessary Existent, then it contradicts your principles and implies a multiplicity of aspects in the Necessary Existent—which has been shown to be absurd. It cannot be because the Necessary Existent is uncaused, for its lack of need for a cause is because it is necessary and not contingent. 'Necessity' cannot be interpreted as negation of a cause, for it is because of its necessity that it has no need for a cause. Moreover, if its necessity were additional to its existence, the Necessary Existent would be multiple, and the argument would turn to the necessity added to the existence—which is an attribute of the existent—asking whether the necessity would be posterior to and a concomitant of the existent as existent. If so, the same would be true for all existents; if not, the necessity would be due to a cause. If the necessity is due to existence itself, the difficulty is obvious

المحل. فاذا افتقر شئ من جزئياتها الى المحل، فللحقيقة نفسها استدعاء المحل، فلا يستغنى شئ منها عن المحل»، فيقول لهم قائل: «ألستم اعترفتم بان صورة الجوهر تحصل فى الذهن وهى عرض حتى قلتم ان الشئ له وجود فى الاعيان ووجود فى الاذهان؟ فاذا جاز ان تحصل حقيقة الجوهرية فى الذهن وهى عرض، جاز ان تكون فى عالم العقل[٨٠] الماهيات القائمة بذاتها، ولها اصنام فى هذا العالم لا تقوم بذاتها، فانها كمال لغيرها، وليس لها كمال الماهيات العقلية كما ان مُثُل الماهيات الخارجة عن الذهن من الجواهر تحصل فى الذهن فلا[٨١] تكون قائمة بذاتها، لانهّا كمال او صفة للذهن وليس لها من الاستقلال ما للماهيات الخارجة حتى تقوم بذاتها. فلا يلزم ان يطّرد حكم الشئ فى مثاله.

(٩٥) «ثم حكمتم بانّ الوجود يقع بمعنى واحد على واجب الوجود وعلى غيره؛ وفى واجب الوجود نفسه وفى غيره زائد عارض للماهية؛»[٨٢] فيقول لكم القائل: استغناء الوجود عن الماهية ينضاف اليها ان كان لنفس الوجود، فليكن الجميع كذا. وان كان لأمر زائد فى واجب الوجود، فهو يخالف قواعدكم ويلزم منه تكثر الجهات فى واجب الوجود، وقد تبيّن[٨٣] انّه محال. وليس لكونه غير معلول، فانّ عدم احتياجه الى علة[٨٤] لكونه واجبا غير ممكن. والوجوب لا يجوز ان يفسّر بسلب العلة فانّه إنمّا استغنى عن العلة لوجوبه. ثم وجوبه ان زاد على وجوده فقد تكثر وعاد الكلام الى انّ وجوبه الزائد على الوجود الّذى هو صفة للموجود، ان كان تابعا للموجود من حيث هو موجود ولازما له، فليكن كذا فى جميع الموجودات والا يكون لعلة؛ وان كان لنفس الوجود، فالاشكال متوجهة. فيقال: انّ استغنائه ان كان لعين

and leads one to say that if its independence is due to existence itself, it would have to be so in the case of all things." He might reply, "Its necessity is the perfection, completeness, and intensity of its existence. Just as one thing is more black than another through an intrinsic perfection in the black itself, not through something added to blackness, so likewise does an intensity and perfection distinguish necessary existence from contingent existence." Here he has admitted that it is possible for the quiddities to have perfection in themselves, making them independent of a locus, or to have deficiency, making them in need of a locus, as is the case with necessary existence and other existence respectively.

A principle [stating that a simple thing may have a composite cause]

(96) A thing may have a cause compounded of parts. The one who denies that the cause of a thing may have two causative parts argues that if the effect is unitary, then either it must be entirely attributed to each part, or one of them must have no influence on the effect at all, or each one must have an influence on the effect. The first alternative is absurd, since what can be attributed to one does not need to be attributed to the other. In the second case, that part would not be part of the cause. If neither had an influence, the cause is not their combination. If each one had an influence, the effect would be composite, not unitary.

This fallacy arises from his imagining that if each part does not have an influence on the effect, then each one is not a part of the cause. This is obviously false, for a part of the cause of a unitary thing does not in itself have an effect that is connected with that thing. Rather, the totality has a single influence, not each part separately. Thus, though each part does not have an influence, what is true of each part is not true of the totality. Rather, the totality has an influence, which is precisely the unitary effect.

Moreover, just as the part of a heterogeneous cause does not necessarily necessitate the effect independently or even necessitate part of the effect, so too is the case with parts from a single species. For example, although a thousand men may move some heavy thing a particular distance

الوجود، ففى الجميع ينبغى ان يكون كذا.» فان قال: انّ وجوبه كمالية وجوده وتماميته وتأكّده، وكما ان كون هذا الشئ أشدّ اسودية من غيره ليس بأمر زائد على الاسودية، بل لكمال فى نفس السواد غير زائد عليه، فكذا الوجود الواجب يمتاز عن الوجود الممكن لتأكّده وتماميته. فقد اعترف هاهنا بجواز ان تكون للماهيات تمامية فى ذاتها مستغنية عن المحل ونقص محوج اليه كما فى الوجود الواجب وغيره.

قاعدة: [فى جوازّ العلة المركبة الشىء البسيط]

(٩٦) يجوز ان يكون للشئ علة مركبة من اجزاء. واخطأ من منع ان يكون لعلة الشئ جزءان معللان بان الحكم اذا كان وحدانيا اما ان ينسب بكليته الى كل واحد، وهو محال، اذ ما ثبت بواحد لا يحتاج الى الاثبات بالآخر، او لا يكون لاحدهما أثر فيه بوجه فليس بجزء للعلة، اذ ليس لكليهما أثر فالعلة غير مجموعهما؛ وان[٨٥] كان لكل واحد منهما فيه أثر فهو مركب لا وحدانى. والغلط فيه إنمّا ينشأ من ظنه انّه اذا لم يكن لكل واحد منهما فيه أثر، فلا يكون كل واحد جزءا وذلك بيّن البطلان فانّ جزء العلة للشئ الوحدانى لا أثر له بنفسه فيما يتعلق بذلك الشئ، بل المجموع له أثر واحد لا ان لكل واحد فيه أثرا، فليس لكل واحد أثر، ولا يلزم حكم كل واحد على المجموع بل المجموع له أثر وهو نفس المعلول الوحدانى. فكما[٨٦] انّ جزء العلة التى هى ذات اجزاء مختلفة الحقيقة، لا يستقل باقتضاء المعلول، ولا يلزم ان يقتضى جزء المعلول، فكذلك الاجزاء التى تكون من نوع واحد. فانّه اذا حرّك الف من الناس شيئا من الاثقال حركة مضبوطة

in a particular time, it does not follow that one man would be able to move that heavy thing a part of that movement. Rather, he might not be able to move it at all.

(97) It is said that if a body possesses no inclination,[53] it cannot be moved by constraint. Suppose that a particular force will move it a particular distance in a particular time and will move something possessing inclination a similar distance. It must then move that first thing in a lesser time. So, let us now posit another thing, whose inclination is less than that of the first thing possessing inclination in the proportion that the time of the motion of the thing possessing no inclination is less than the time of the motion of the body possessing inclination. Thus, it would move by that force for a similar distance. There is no doubt that the time of its movement would be less by the amount that its inclination is less. Thus, its movement would be the same as the thing lacking inclination—which is absurd.

One ought to argue: Why can it not be the case that the weaker inclination—which is a part of the other inclination and has no relation posited to all of it—is unable to resist that which the whole resists? Thus, the thing lacking inclination would be like the previous example of moving the heavy thing. This proof of theirs even implies that the bodies of the spheres and even the outer sphere have an inclination other than what arises from their souls. The positions of a circular thing are equivalent, so that no particular side and no inclination in a particular direction can have a special right.

(98) An individual thing may not have two causes. If each one had some influence on its existence, then each would be a part of the cause and not a complete cause. If one of them did not have an influence, then the cause would be the other. Something general may have different causes. For example, heat may be necessitated by an adjacent hot body, by radiation, or by motion.

The following are judgments concerning certain perceptions and perceptibles. We mention them because they will be useful later.

بزمانها ومسافتها، لا يلزم ان يقدر واحد على تحريك ذلك الثقل جزءا من تلك الحركة، بل قد لا يقدر على تحريكه اصلا.

(٩٧) وما يُقال انّ الجسم اذا كان عديم الميل، لا يقبل الحركة قسرا؛ فانّه ان قبلها ففرض انّ قوة مّا حركته زمانا ومسافة، وحركت ذا ميل فى مثل تلك المسافة فلا بدّ وان يكون تحريكه فى زمان اقصر، فنفرض بقدر ما نقص عن زمان تحريك[٨٧] ذى الميل زمان عديمه جسما آخر ينقص ميله عن ميل ذى الميل المذكور، فتحرك بمثل تلك القوة فى مثل مسافته فلا شك فى[٨٨] انه ينقص زمان حركته بقدر نقصان ميله، فتساوى حركته حركة عديم الميل، وهو محال. فلقائل ان يقول: لم لا يجوز ان يكون الميل الضعيف، الّذى هو جزء لميل آخر ولا نسبة له الى كله معتبرة لا يقدر على ممانعة ما يمانعه الكل؟ فيكون فى حكم عديم الميل على سياق المثال المذكور فى تحريك الثقيل. والعجب انّ هذه الحجة التى ذكروها توجب للافلاك والمحدد ميلا لاجرامها غير ما يحدث من نفوسها؛ والمستدير اوضاعه متساوية؛ فلا يتعيّن استحقاق جانب ولا ميل إلاّ[٨٩] الى صوب معين.

(٩٨) ولا يجوز ان يكون للشئ الشخصى علتان، فانّه ان كان لكل واحد مدخل فى وجوده فكل واحد جزء للعلة لا علة تامة. وان لم يكن لاحدهما مدخل، فالعلة احدهما. والأمر العام يجوز ان يكون له علل، كالحرارة مثلا. فانّها قد توجبها مجاورة جرم[٩٠] حارّ، وقد يوجبها الشعاع والحركة.

وهاهنا حكومات فى بعض الادراكات والمدركات نذكرها لانها يُنتفع بها فيما بعد.

A judgment [denying the corporeality of radiation]

(99) Some men falsely imagine that rays are body. If they were body, they would not vanish when a window is shut suddenly. If it is argued that small dark bodies remain but they are no longer luminous, it would have to be admitted that the rays themselves are not body. Moreover, if they were body, they would be reflected more readily from something solid than from something damp. The bulk of the Sun would be diminished by their emission. They would emerge only at right angles—not in various directions, as is seen to happen—since a single body does not move naturally[54] in various directions. The lights of many lamps would pile up in a thick layer, its thickness increasing with every increase of illumination. All this is not the case. Thus, rays do not move from the Sun or from place to place. They are only states, which do not move. Their cause is a luminous entity mediated by a transparent body like air.

(100) Some imagine that rays are color and that the ray that is upon something black is nothing other than [the thing's] blackness. They say, "Colors do not exist in the dark. The dark does not veil them, for it is privative, as has been explained. Therefore, colors are simply qualities evident to the sense of vision, and rays are the perfection of their being evident, not something added to the color."

One might reply to them, "Even if one admits to you that colors do not exist when the light is extinguished, it still does not follow that they are the rays themselves. The fact that things are concomitant or that one depends on another does not imply the unity of their realities. That rays are not color is shown by the fact that although 'color' may be taken as an expression for being evident in itself or for being evident in a particular sense, 'color' may not be taken as an expression for being evident to vision; for luminosity such as belongs to the Sun is not the same as the color that is evident to vision. Moreover, if the illumination of certain

حكومة [فى ابطال جسمية الشعاع]

(٩٩) ظن بعض الناس انّ الشعاع جسم وذلك باطل. اذ لو كان جسما كان اذا سدّت الكوّة بغتة[٩١] ما كان يغيب. فان قيل: بقيت اجسام صغار مظلمة فزال ضوئها، فسلّم انّ الشعاع نفسه ليس بجسم وايضا لو كان جسما لكان انعكاسه من الصلب اولى من[٩٢] الرطب ولنقص جرم الشمس اذا فارقها، وما حصل إلاّ على زوايا قائمة لا على ما يرى على جهات مختلفة فان جسما واحدا بطبعه لا يتحرك الى جهات مختلفة، ولتراكم اضواء سُرج كثيرة حتى صار غليظا[٩٣] ذا عمق، وكلّما ازداد اعداد المضئ ازداد عمقه، وليس كذا. فليس مما ينتقل من الشمس او من محل الى محل، بل هو هيئة، فلا ينتقل علتها المضئ بواسطة جرم شفاف كالهواء.

(١٠٠) وظن انّ الشعاع هو اللون وليس الشعاع الّذى على الاسود غير سواده. قالوا: الالوان معدومة فى الظلمة وليس انّ الظلمة ساترة فانّها عدمية على ما بيّن؛ وليست الالوان إلاّ الكيفيات الظاهرة لحاسة البصر والشعاع كمالية ظهورها لا أمر زائد على اللونية.

فلقائل ان يقول لهم: اذا سُلم لكم ان الالوان عند انتفاء الضوء ليست موجودة، لا يلزم ان يكون نفس الشعاع، وليس تلازم الاشياء او توقف الاشياء بعضها على بعض يلزم منه اتحاد الحقائق؛ ومما يدل على انّ الشعاع غير اللون؛ انّ اللون اما ان يأخذ عبارة عن نفس الظهور، او عن الظهور على جهة خاصة، ولا يمكن ان يؤخذ اللون عبارة عن نفس الظهور للبصر، فان الضوء، كما للشمس، ليس بنفس اللون وهو ظاهر للبصر. فكذلك الضوء اذا غلب على بعض الاشياء

shiny black things—jet, for example—is sufficiently strong, the color will vanish, yet its being evident is actualized by the illumination. If color is taken not just as being evident per se but as being evident with something to particularize it, then there are two possibilities. First, the relation of being evident to black and white may be like the relation of color to them in the sense that being evident is not added in concrete things to the black itself, as we have said is the case with color. Therefore, only black, white, and so on exist among concrete things; and being evident is an intellectual predicate. The being evident of white in concrete things would be nothing but white itself; and that which is more perfectly white ought to be more perfectly evident, and so also that which is more perfectly black. This is not so. If we place ivory in the light and snow in the shadow, we still perceive the snow as being whiter than the ivory and perceive the ivory in the light as being more brightly lit than the snow in the shadow. Thus, we perceive that whiteness is not brightness and that color is not light. So, also, if we place something blacker in the shadow and something less black in the light, that which is less black is brighter and that which is blacker is less bright. That is not because of the darkness caused by its being in the shadow; for if we were to move the blacker thing into the light and the less black thing into the shadow, that which is more black would be brighter, despite its still being blacker. The other possibility is that being evident in concrete things is something other than black or white, which is what we set out to prove." It is clear from what has been said that rays are not color but that colors are not actualized without them. This is not a topic that we consider to be especially important. Even if it turned out that they were right about it, it would not disturb us.

A judgment [in refutation of what is said about vision]

(101) Some people have imagined that vision occurs by the emission from the eye of a ray that encounters the objects seen.[55] If this ray were an accident, how could it move? If it were a body and moved by the will, one would be able to hold it back in such a way that one would not see while looking; but this is not so. If it moved by nature, it would not go in

السود الصقلية، كالشبح، يغيب لونها والظهور يتحقق بالضوء. فان أُخذ اللون على انه ليس بمجرد الظهور بل مع مخصص،[٩٤] فاما ان تكون نسبة الظهور الى السواد والبياض كنسبة اللونية اليهما، فى انّ الظهور لا يزيد فى الاعيان على نفس السواد، كما ذكرنا فى اللونية، فليس فى الاعيان إلاّ السواد والبياض ونحوهما. والظهور محمول عقلى، فلا يكون ظهور البياض فى الاعيان إلاّ هو، فالأتمّ بياضا ينبغى ان يكون أتمّ ظهورا، وكذا الأتمّ سوادا، وليس كذا. فانّا اذا وضعنا العاج فى الشعاع والثلج فى الظل ندرك مشاهدة انّ الثلج أتمّ بياضا من العاج وانّ العاج الّذى هو فى الشعاع اضوء وانور من الثلج الّذى فى الظل؛ فندرك على انّ الابيضية غير الانورية واللون غير النور وكذا الأتمّ سوادا اذا وضعناه فى الظل والانقص فى الشعاع كان الانقص انور، والأشدّ سوادا انقص نورا. وليس ذلك من الظلمة باعتبار كونه فى الظل، فانّا اذا نقلنا الأتمّ سوادا الى الشعاع والانقص الى الظل، يصير الأتمّ انور مع بقاء أشدّيته. واما ان يكون الظهور فى الاعيان شيئا آخر غير السواد والبياض، فهو المطلوب. فيتضح مما ذكرنا انّ الشعاع غير اللون وان لم يتحقق اللون دونه وليست هذه المسألة من مهماتنا، ولو كان الحق معهم فيها، ما كان يضرّنا.

حكومة [فى تضعيف ما قيل فى الابصار]

(١٠١) ظن بعض الناس انّ الابصار إنمّا هو بخروج الشعاع من العين يلاقى المبصرات. فان كان هذا الشعاع عرضا فكيف ينتقل؟ وان كان جسما، فان كان يتحرك بالارادة كان لنا قبضه الينا على وجه لا يبصر مع التحديق، وليس كذا؛ وان كان يتحرك بالطبع فما تحرك الى

every direction and would penetrate colored fluids more readily than clear glass and would penetrate earthenware, whose pores are more numerous, more readily than glass. The nearer and farther planets would not be seen simultaneously but would be seen in an order relative to their distance. This body would move in an instant to the farthest spheres and pierce them, or this thing that emerges from the eye would spread out over half the orb of the world! All these deductions are absurd, so vision does not occur by a ray.

(102) Other scientists[56] have argued that vision is the imprinting of the thing's form in the crystalline humor,[57] but this theory involves them in difficulties. Among them is the fact that we see the mountain as being large. If vision is by the form and of the form and if the mountain does have the magnitude that it has, how, then, can this great magnitude be contained within the tiny pupil? One of them has responded to this by saying that the crystalline humor is potentially divisible to infinity—as has been shown to be the case with bodies—and the form of the mountain is also potentially divisible to infinity, so that the former may contain the latter. This is not correct, for even though the mountain is potentially infinitely divisible and the eye likewise, the magnitude of the mountain and each of its parts, however it is supposed to be divided, remains incomparably greater than the magnitude of the eye and its parts. How, then, could this huge magnitude be contained within a small magnitude?

(103) One of them argues that even though the form is smaller than what is seen, the soul is able to infer from the magnitude of the form what the magnitude of the original must be. This is not correct, since a large magnitude is seen by direct experience, not by an inference. One of them claims that a single material thing may contain its own small magnitude and another large magnitude that is the image of something else. Yet their adversary can compel them to admit that if the magnitude belonging to a mountain were imprinted in the crystalline humor, the parts that had been posited as belonging to that extension would not be

جهات مختلفة ولكان نفوذه فى المائعات التى لها لون اولى من نفوذه فى الزجاجات الصافية؛ ولكان نفوذه فى الزجاج لانّ مسامّه اكثر؛ ولما شوهد الكواكب القريبة والبعيدة معا، بل كان يختلف على نسبة المسافة؛ ولكان الجرم يتحرك دفعة الى الافلاك، فيخرقها او[٩٥] ينبسط على نصف كرة العالم ما يخرج من العين، وهذه كلها محالات، فالرؤية ليست بالشعاع.

(١٠٢) وقال بعض اهل العلم ان الرؤية إنمّا هى[٩٦] انضباح صورة الشئ فى الرطوبة الجليدية فوقع عليهم اشكالات: منها انّ الجبل اذا رأيناه مع عظمته والرؤية إنمّا هى بالصورة وللصورة، فان كان هذا المقدار لها، فكيف حصل المقدار العظيم فى حدقة صغيرة؟ اجاب البعض عن هذا بانّ الرطوبة الجليدية تقبل القسمة الى غير النهاية، كما بيّن فى الاجسام، والجبل ايضا صورته قابلة للقسمة الى غير النهاية فيجوز ان يحصل فيها، وهذا باطل. فانّ الجبل وان كان قابلا للقسمة الغير المتناهية،[٩٧] وكذا العين، إلاّ انّ مقدار الجبل اكبر من مقدار العين بما لا يتقارب، وكذا كل جزء يفرض فى الجبل فى القسمة على النسبة اكبر من اجزاء العين، فكيف ينطبق المقدار الكبير على الصغير؟

(١٠٣) وقال بعضهم ان النفس تستدل بالصورة وان كانت اصغر من المرئى، على انّ ما مقدار صورته هذا كم يكون اصل مقداره، وهذا باطل، فان رؤية المقدار الكبير إنمّا هو بالمشاهدة لا بالاستدلال. وبعضهم جوّزوا[٩٨] ان يكون فى مادة واحدة مقدار صغير لها وآخر كبير هو مثال للغير. فالزمهم الخصم بانّ المقدار الّذى هو للجبل، اذا انطبع فى الجليدية لا يجتمع مع ما يفرض اجزاء

joined with each other in one locus. Were it otherwise, it would no longer be possible to perceive their arrangement. If the parts posited to belong to that extension were not combined, each thing posited to be a part of that extension would be in another part of the crystalline humor. If the magnitude of the crystalline humor were equal to the magnitude of the extended form of the mountain, its great size could not conceivably be perceived. If the extended form were greater than the magnitude of the crystalline humor and the parts of the crystalline humor were entirely filled with its parts, it would have parts and extension extended beyond the limits of the eye. Thus, the magnitude would not be seen as it is and would not be in a locus. Whosoever judges fairly will understand the difficulty inherent in the theory of the imprinting of forms. This is an extremely important principle in our method.[58]

A principle [on the reality of the forms in mirrors]

(104) Know that the form is not in the mirror, for otherwise your view of the thing would not change with your point of view. Moreover, if with your finger you touch a mirror a cubit's distance from your face, you find that the distance between the form of your finger where it meets the glass and the form of your face is greater than the thickness of the mirror. Were the form actually in the mirror, it would be in its visible surface, since that is its polished part; but this is not so. The form cannot be in the air; nor can it be in the eye, since it is larger than the pupil in accordance with the argument just given. Nor can it be your own form itself, reversed by the reflection of rays from the mirror, as some have imagined, for we have already disproved the existence of rays. It cannot be your own form seen by another path, since you see the image of your face as much smaller than your face, despite its exact resemblance in every feature. In addition, it is facing the opposite direction from your face. Moreover, if it were by the reflection of rays, that which was reflected from a small mirror would be seen in its real size—not as

ذلك الامتداد، بعضها مع بعض فى محل واحد، فانّه لو كان كذا ما بقى مشاهدة الترتيب. واذ لا يجتمع ما يفرض اجزاء ذلك الامتداد، فكل ما يفرض جزءا لذلك الامتداد فهو فى جزء آخر من الجليدية. فان استوى مقدار الجليدية مع مقدار الصورة الامتدادية للجبل، فلا يتصوّر مشاهدة عظمه وان زادت الصورة الامتدادية على مقدار الجليدية وقد استغرقة اجزاء الجليدية باجزائها، فلها اجزاء وامتداد خرج عن حدّ العين، فلا يُرى كما هو ولا يكون فى محل. ومن انصف نقض لصعوبة انطباع الشبح. وهذه قاعدة مهمة جدا فيما نحن بسبيله.

قاعدة: [فى حقيقة صُور المرايا]

(١٠٤) اعلم انّ الصورة ليست فى المرآة، والا ما اختلفت رؤيتك للشئ فيها باختلاف مواضع نظرك اليها. وايضا اذا لمست المرآة باصبعك، وهى بعيدة عن وجهك بذراع، صادفت بين صورة اصبعك وملتقى اصبعك ايضا وبين صورة الوجه مسافة لا يفى بها عمق المرآة على ان الصورة لو كانت فيها لكانت فى سطحها الظاهر، اذ هو المصقول منها، وليس كذا. وليست هى فى الهواء، وليست هى فى البصر، لما سبق من انها اكبر من الحدقة؛ وليست هى صورتك بعينها على ان ينعكس الشعاع من المرآة كما ظنه بعضهم، فانّا قد ابطلنا الشعاع؛ وليست هى نفس صورتك تراها بطريق آخر،[٩٩] فانّك قد ترى مثال وجهك اصغر من وجهك بكثير مع كمال هيئته بجميع الاعضاء؛ وايضا هى متوجهة الى خلاف توجه وجهك. وايضا لو كان بانعكاس شعاع، فكان ما ينعكس من المرآة الصغيرة، ان اتصل بجميع الوجه

smaller—since it would be in contact with the entire face. If it were only in contact with part of the face or part of each feature, the shape of the face would not be seen, nor would all its features be seen correctly. Since it is possible for an observer to see his finger and its form, then if the ray contacts the finger and is united with it, the finger would be seen only once, and its form would not be seen. This is not the case. Moreover, if someone saw a planet in the water, the movement of his ray would go instantly to the star, since the water and the form of the star are seen at the same moment. Since the form is not in the mirror, and [since] the relation of the crystalline humor to the objects of vision is like the relation of the mirror to them, therefore the form that these people assume to be in the crystalline humor must be comparable to the form in the mirror.

If we use the sense of vision to perceive bodies in a particular direction, bodies that are far away and of great size—lofty mountains, one behind another, for example—surely, according to them, their forms would be imprinted, along with the distances to them. How could the crystalline humor and its parts suffice for it? The solution to the problems of vision, forms in mirrors, and the imagination will come later. Our reason for mentioning these questions here is only to ease the attainment of our aim.

A judgment [on objects of hearing—that is, sounds and words]

(105) The notion that air is shaped by the positions of the mouth into phonemes[59] is false, according to what has been said about sound. Air will not hold a shape, being quick to blend. If someone stirs the air around his ears, he ought then to hear nothing, since the vibrations in the air would be disturbed and altered. The response that the sound itself cuts through and penetrates the air by reason of its intensity is incorrect, for if all the air near the ear were disturbed, the part would not retain the power to penetrate and be distinguished from the rest. Actual compression and rarefaction have nothing to do with the reality

لرُأى على مقداره لا اصغر منه، وان اتصل ببعض الوجه او بعض كل عضو منه فما رُأى هيئة الوجه وكل اعضائه تامة. ولما امكن ان يرى الرائى اصبعه وصورتها، فان الشعاع اذا اتصل بالاصبع واتحد فلا يرى إلاّ الاصبع مرة واحدة ولا صورة، وليس كذا. وايضا لو كان[١٠٠] من يرى مثال الكوكب فى الماء وقع حركة شعاعه الى الكوكب دفعة فان رؤية الماء وصورة الكوكب دفعة. واذا تبيّن انّ الصورة ليست فى المرآة، ونسبة الجليدية الى المبصرات كنسبة المرآة، فحال الصورة التى فرض هؤلاء الناس فيها كحالة صورة المرآة.

ثم انّ البصر اذا احسسنا به اجساما على سمت واحد بينها مسافات طويلة وهى عظيمة المقدار، مثل شوامخ جبال بعضها وراء بعض، فلا بدّ من ارتسام صورها، عند هؤلاء، وصور المسافات التى بينها على سمت واحد، فكيف يفى به الجليدية واقطارها؟ فسرُّ الرؤية وصور المرايا والتخيل يأتى من بعد. وغرضنا من ذكر هذه المسائل هاهنا تسهيل السبيل فيما نحن بصدده.

حكومة [فى المسموعات
وهى الاصوات والحروف]

(١٠٥) تشكّل الهواء بمقاطع الحروف باطل على ما ذكر فى الصوت. فان الهواء لا يحفض الشكل وهو سريع الالتئام. ثم من تشوّش الهواء الّذى عند اُذُنه، كان ينبغى ان لا يستمع[١٠١] شيئا لتشوّش المتموّجات واختلافها. والاعتذار بانّ الصوت نفسه يخرق الهواء وينفذ فيه لشدته، باطل. فانّه اذا تشوّش ما عند الأُذُن من الهواء كله، لا يبقى للبعض قوة النفوذ والامتياز عن الباقى. والقرع والقلع بالفعل

of sound, since the sound remains after both of them have ceased. Sound cannot be defined by something else, for none of the simple sensations can be defined. Such definitions would ultimately have to be reduced to objects of knowledge needing no definitions. Otherwise, there would be infinite regression; but there is not. There is nothing more evident than sensations to which the definitions might be reduced, since all our knowledge is abstracted from sensations. Therefore, the simple sensibles are known innately and have no definitions. But [the Peripatetics'] analogy that existence has no need of definition is even more absurd than what they have to say about sensations. The dispute does not arise with sensations insofar as they are sensation, or black, or sound, or odor; but it does arise with regard to other aspects. The simple sensations and experiences are all without parts, and nothing is more evident than they. By them, their compounds are known. The reality of sound cannot be defined at all to someone without the sense of hearing, nor can luminosity be defined to someone without the sense of sight. By whatever definition it might be defined, he would not grasp its reality. Nor are the sensations of one sense of any avail in defining the sensations of another sense in their particularity. Someone with the senses of hearing and sight has no need for definitions of luminosity and sound. Sound is a simple entity whose form in the mind is exactly like its form in sense. Its reality is just that it is sound. However, the argument about its cause is another matter—whether its cause is compression and rarefaction, whether air is its condition, and whether air is a condition in some other way if it is not a condition in the sense that the phonemes occur in it. Such questions belong to a different investigation.[60]

غير راخل فى حقيقة الصوت لبقاء الصوت بعد الفرغ عنهمآ وا لصوت لا يعرف بشئ، والمحسوسات بسائطها لا تُعرّف اصلا. فان التعريفات لا بدّ وان تنتهى الى معلومات لا حاجة فيها الى التعريف، والا تسلسل الى غير النهاية. فاذا انتهى، فليس شئ[١٠٢] اظهر من المحسوسات حتى تنتهى اليه، اذ جميع علومنا منتزعة من المحسوسات، فهى الفطرية التى لا تعريف لها اصلا. واما مثل الوجود الّذى مثّلوا به انّه مستغن عن التعريف، فالتخبيط فيه اكثر مما فى المحسوسات. ولا يقع الخلاف فى المحسوسات من حيث هى[١٠٣] محسوسة او هى سواد او صوت او رائحة، وان كان يقع الخلاف فى جهات اُخرى. فبسائط المحسوسات والمشاهدات بأسرها لا جزء لها ولا شئ اظهر منها، وبها تُعرف مركباتها. فحقيقة الصوت لا تُعرف اصلا لمن ليس له حاسة السمع، وكذا الضوء لمن ليس له حاسة البصر. فانّه باىّ تعريف عُرّف، لا يحصل له حقيقة ذلك. وليس فى محسوسات حاسة واحدة ما يُعرّف به محسوس حاسة اُخرى من حيث خصوصيتها. ومن كان له حاسة السمع والبصر، فهو مستغن عن التعريف، الضوء والصوت؛ بل الصوت أمر بسيط صورته فى العقل كصورته فى الحس لا غير، وحقيقته انّه صوت فقط. واما الكلام فى سببه، فذلك شئ آخر من انه القّلع والقرع؛ وانّ الهواء شرط، وانه اذا لم يكن على سبيل حصول المقاطع فيه، يكون شرطا بطريق آخر، فذلك بحث آخر.

Section [five]

[On unity and multiplicity]

(106) That which is one in all respects is not divisible in any respect, whether into quantitative parts or into parts of a definition or into particulars of a universal. That which is one in some respect is not divisible in that respect. Remember this, and beware of loose expressions like "Zayd and ʿAmr are one in humanity." Its meaning is that they both have a form in the mind with the same relation to each of them. Other expressions are similar.

This is what we intended to say here, and thereby part one is ended.

Unending praise be to the Light of Light![61]

فصل
[فى الوحدة والكثرة]

(١٠٦) الواحد من جميع الوجوه هو الّذى لا ينقسم بوجه من الوجوه، لا الى الاجزاء الكمية ولا الحدّية ولا انقسام الكلى الى جزئياته. والواحد من وجه هو الّذى لا ينقسم من ذلك الوجه. فتحفظ هكذا، وتترك التجوّزات التى هى مثل قولنا «زيد وعمرو واحد فى الانسانية» ويكون معناه انّ لهما صورة فى العقل لنسبتهما اليها سواء، وكذا غيرها.[١٠٤]

هذا ما اردنا هاهنا، وقد انتهى به القسم الأوّل.

ولنور النور[١٠٥] حمد لا يتناهى.

PART TWO

On the Divine Lights, the Light of Lights,[1] *and the Bases and Order of Existence, in Five Discourses*

The First Discourse

On light and its reality, the Light of Lights, and that which first was generated from It, in nine sections and rules.

Section [one]

[Showing that light needs no definition]

(107) Anything in existence that requires no definition or explanation is evident. Since there is nothing more evident than light, there is nothing less in need of definition.[2]

Section [two]

[On the definition of the independent]

(108) If neither the essence nor any perfection of a thing rests upon another, it is "independent." If its essence or any one of its perfections rests upon another, it is "dependent."[3]

القسم الثانى
فى الانوار الالهية ونور الانوار
ومبادى الوجود وترتيبها

وفيه خمس مقالات

المقالة الاولى
فى النور وحقيقته ونور الانوار[1]
وما يصدر منه اولا

وفيه تسعة[2] فصول وضوابط

فصل

[فى انّ النور لا يحتاج الى تعريف]

(١٠٧) ان كان فى الوجود ما لا يحتاج الى تعريفه وشرحه فهو الظاهر ولا شئ اظهر من النور، فلا شئ اغنى منه عن التعريف.

فصل

[فى تعريف الغنىّ]

(١٠٨) الغنى هو ما لا تتوقف ذاته ولا كمال له على غيره؛ والفقير ما يتوقف منه على غير ذاته او كمال له.

Section [three]
[On light and darkness]

(109) A thing either is light and luminosity in its own reality or is not light and luminosity in its own reality. The meanings of "light" and "luminosity" are the same here, for I do not use these in a metaphorical way, as when "light" is used to mean that which is evident to the mind, though even such usages do at the last derive from this light. Light is divided into light that is a state of something else (the accidental light) and light that is not a state of something else (the incorporeal or pure light). That which is not light in its own reality is divided into that which is independent of a locus (the dusky substance) and that which is a state of something else (the dark state). The barrier is the body and may be described as a substance that can be pointed to. Some barriers are seen to be dark when light ceases to shine on them. Darkness is simply an expression for the lack of light, nothing more; and it is not one of the privatives conditioned upon possibility.[4] If the world were posited to be a vacuum or a sphere with no light in it, it would be dark. This would imply the deficiency of darkness without implying the possibility of light in it. Thus, it is established that everything that is neither a light nor illumined is dark. If a barrier is cut off from light, it does not need something else to be dark. Therefore, these bodies are dusky substances. There remain some barriers that never lose their light—the Sun, for example. These are like other barriers that may cease to have light in that they are barriers, yet they differ in having light continually. The light by which these barriers differ from the others is superadded to their being barriers and subsists in them. It is thus accidental light, and its bearer is a dusky substance. Therefore, every barrier is a dusky substance.

(110) Sensible accidental light is not independent in itself, since otherwise it would not depend on the dusky substance. Since [light] subsists in [the dusky substance], it is dependent and contingent. [The light's] existence is not from the dusky substance, since it would otherwise be its concomitant and the dusky substance would never be without it. This is not so; how, indeed, could it be, considering that nothing necessitates

فصل
[فى النور والظلمة]

(١٠٩) الشئ ينقسم الى نور وضوء فى حقيقة نفسه والى ما ليس بنور وضوء الى حقيقة نفسه. والنور والضوء المراد بهما واحد هاهنا، اذ لست اعنى به ما يعدّ مجازيا، كالّذى يُعنى به الواضح عند العقل، وان كان يرجع حاصله فى الاخير الى هذا النور. والنور ينقسم الى ما هو هيئة لغيره، وهو النور العارض، والى نور ليس هو هيئة لغيره، وهو النور المجرد والنور المحض. وما ليس بنور فى حقيقة نفسه ينقسم الى ما هو[٣] مستغن عن المحل، وهو الجوهر الغاسق، والى ما هو هيئة لغيره، وهى الهيئة الظلمانية. والبرزخ هو الجسم، ويرسم بانّه هو الجوهر الّذى يقصد بالاشارة. وقد شوهد من البرازخ ما اذا زال عنه النور، بقى مظلما. وليست الظلمة عبارة إلاّ عن عدم النور فحسب. وليس هذا من الاعدام التى يشترط فيها الامكان، فانّه لو فُرض العالم خلأً وفلكا لا نور فيه، كان مظلما ولازمه نقص الظلمة مع عدم امكان النور.[٤] فثبت انّ كل غير نور ونورانى مظلم. والبرزخ اذا انتفى عنه النور لا يحتاج فى كونه مظلما الى شئ آخر؛ فهذه البرازخ جواهر غاسقة. بقى من البرازخ ما لا يزول عنه النور، كالشمس وغيرها، وشاركت هذه فى البرزخية بما[٥] يزول عنه الضوء وفارقته بالضوء الدائم. فما فارقت به هذه البرازخ تلك من النور زائد على البرزخية وقائم بها، فيكون نورا عارضا، وحامله جوهر غاسق. فكل برزخ[٦] جوهر غاسق.

(١١٠) والنور العارض المحسوس ليس بغنى فى نفسه، والا ما افتقر الى الغاسق. فلما قام به، فهو فاقر ممكن ووجوده ليس من الجوهر الغاسق، والا لازمه واطّرد معه، وليس كذا، كيف والشئ لا يوجب

that which is nobler than its own essence? Thus, that which gives all dusky substances their lights must be something other than their gloomy quiddities and dark states. You will learn that dark states[5] are caused by light, even though the light itself may also be accidental. The dark states, moreover, are hidden: how could they necessitate something less hidden than themselves?[6] Therefore, that which gives lights to the barriers is not a barrier, nor is it a dusky substance. Otherwise, all barriers and dusky substances would cause accidental lights. Thus, that which gives them their lights must be something other than the barriers and dusky substances.

Section [four]

[On the dependence of the body in its existence upon the incorporeal light]

(111) The dusky barriers possess dark aspects—shapes, for example—and particularities of magnitude. Although magnitude is not superadded to the barrier, nevertheless there is a certain particularity, boundary, and limit by which one magnitude is distinguished from another. These things by which barriers differ from each other do not belong to the barriers by essence, since otherwise all barriers would share them. Nor do the boundaries of barriers belong to them by essence, since otherwise all would be equal. Therefore, they have the accidents by virtue of another. Were the shapes and other dark states independent, their existence would not depend on the barrier. Were the reality of the barrier independent by its essence and were it necessary, its existence would not have to be actualized by particular dark states and other such entities. Were the barriers independent of magnitudes and states, they could not be multiple, for there would be no separate states to distinguish them, nor could the essence of each one be particularized. It cannot be argued that the distinguishing states are concomitants of the quiddities of barriers that necessitate them, for were that so, they would not be different in different barriers—yet they do differ.

Intuition affirms that no lifeless dusky substance receives its existence from another, since with respect to the lifeless reality of the barrier no one [substance] would have priority over the others. Through another

اشرف من ذاته؟ فالمعطى لجميع الجواهر الغاسقة انوارها غير ماهياتها المظلمة وهيآتها الظلمانية. وستعلم ان[٧] الهيآت الظلمانية معلولة للنور وان كان عارضا ايضا وهى خفية، كيف توجب ما ليس اخفى منها او مثلها؟ فينبغى ان يكون معطى الانوار للبرازخ غير برزخ ولا جوهر غاسق، والا دخل فى هذا الحكم الّذى هو على الجميع، فهو أمر خارج عن البرازخ والغواسق.

فصل

[فى افتقار الجسم فى وجوده الى النور المجرد]

(١١١) الغواسق البرزخية لها أمور ظلمانية، كالاشكال وغيرها، وخصوصيات للمقدار؛ وان لم يكن المقدار زائدا عن البرزخ إلاّ ان له تخصيصا مّا ومقطعا واحداً ينفرد به مقدار عن مقدار. فهذه الاشياء التى تختلف بها البرازخ، ليست للبرزخ بذاته، والا تشاركت فيه البرازخ؛ ولا حدود المقادير لها بذاتها، والا استوى الكل فيها. فله ذلك من غيره، اذ لو كان الشكل وغيره من الهيئة الظلمانية غنية، ما توقف وجودها على البرزخ. والحقيقة البرزخية لو كانت غنية بذاتها واجبة، ما افتقرت فى تحقيق وجودها الى المخصصات من الهيآت الظلمانية وغيرها. فان البرازخ لو تجرّدت عن المقادير والهيآت، لا يمكن تكثرها لعدم المميّز من الهيئات الفارقة، ولا يمكن تخصص ذات كل واحد. وليس بجائز ان يقال ان الهيئات المميّزة لوازم للماهية البرزخية تقتضيها هى، اذ لو كان كذا، ما[٨] اختلفت فى البرازخ، وقد اختلفت.

والحدس يحكم بان الجواهر الغاسقة الميتة ليس وجود بعضها من[٩] بعض، اذ لا اولوية بحسب الحقيقة البرزخية الميتة. وستعلم من طريق

proof, you will learn that one barrier does not bring another barrier into existence. Moreover, neither the barrier nor its dark and luminous states can receive their existence in a circular manner from something else, for nothing can depend on something that depends on it. Were that the case, it would bring into existence that which brought it into existence and would so be prior to it and to itself—which is an absurdity. Since they are not independent by essence, they are all dependent on something that is neither a dusky substance nor a dark or luminous state—that is to say, an incorporeal light. The substantiality of the dusky substance is intellectual[7] and its duskiness privative. Therefore, it does not exist in virtue of these. It is simply a concrete thing with particular properties.

A rule [stating that incorporeal light cannot be pointed out by sensation]

(112) Since you know that any light that can be pointed to is an accidental light, then if there is a pure light, it cannot be pointed to, nor be located in a body, nor have spatial dimensions.[8]

A rule [that anything that is light in itself is incorporeal light]

(113) Accidental light is not light in itself, since its existence is in another. Thus, it can only be light due to another. The incorporeal pure light is light in itself. Therefore, everything that is light in itself is incorporeal pure light.

[Five] a general section

[Showing that whatever perceives its own essence is an incorporeal light]

(114) Nothing that has an essence of which it is not unconscious is dusky,[9] for its essence is evident to it. It cannot be a dark state in something else, since even the luminous state is not a self-subsistent light, let alone the dark state. Therefore, it is a nonspatial pure incorporeal light.

اُخرى ان البرزخ لا يوجد البرزخ. والبرزخ وهيآته الظلمانية والنورية، لما لم يكن وجود شئ منها عن شئ على سبيل الدور، للإمتناع توقف شئ على ما يتوقف عليه، فيوجد موجده فيتقدم على موجده ونفسه، وهو محال. واذا لم تكن غنية لذاتها، فكلها فاقرة الى غير جوهر غاسق وهيئة نورية وظلمانية، فيكون نورا مجردا. والجوهر الغاسق جوهريته عقلية وغاسقيته عدمية؛ فلا يوجد من حيث هو كذا، بل هو فى الاعيان مع الخصوصيات.

ضابط [فى انّ النور المجرد
لا يكون مشارا اليه بالحس]

(١١٢) لما علمت انّ كل نور مشار اليه فهو نور عارض، فان كان نور محض، فلا يشار اليه ولا يحل جسما، ولا يكون له جهة اصلا.

ضابط [فى انّ كل ما هو نور لنفسه فهو نور مجرد]

(١١٣) النور العارض ليس نورا لنفسه، اذ وجوده لغيره، فلا يكون إلاّ نورا لغيره. فالنور المحض المجرد نور لنفسه، وكل نور لنفسه فهو نور محض مجرد.

فصل اجمالى

[فى انّ مَن يدرك ذاته فهو نور مجرد]

(١١٤) كل من كان له ذات لا يغفل عنها فهو غير غاسق لظهور ذاته عنده؛ وليس هيئة ظلمانية فى الغير، اذ الهيئة النورية ايضا ليست نورا لذاتها فضلا عن الظلمانية، تف فهو نور محض مجرد لا يشار اليه.

A detailed section [on what we have just mentioned]

(115) The self-subsistent, self-conscious thing does not apprehend its essence by an image of its essence in its essence. If its knowledge is by an image and if the image of its ego is not the ego itself, the image of the ego would be an "it" in relation to the ego. In that case, that which was apprehended would be the image. Thus, it follows that while the apprehension of its ego is precisely its apprehension of what it is itself, its apprehension of its essence would also be the apprehension of something else—which is absurd. This is not the case with externals, since the image and its object are each an "it." Moreover, if its apprehension of itself were by an image and it did not know that this was an image of itself, it would not know itself. If it did know that this was an image of itself, it must have already known itself without an image. How could something be conceived to know itself by something superadded to itself—something that would be an attribute of it? If it were to judge that every attribute added to its essence, be it knowledge or something else, belonged to its essence, it would have to have known its essence prior to and apart from any of the attributes. It would therefore not have known its essence by the superadded attributes.

(116) You are never unconscious of your essence or your apprehension of your essence. Since this apprehension cannot be by a form or by something superadded, you need nothing to apprehend your essence save that essence, which is evident in itself and not absent from itself. Therefore, it must apprehend its essence due to what it itself is in itself, and you can never be unconscious of your essence or any part of your essence. That of which your essence can be unconscious—organs such as the heart, liver, and brain, and all the dark and luminous barriers and states—do not belong to that part of you that apprehends. Therefore, that in you which apprehends is not an organ nor anything to do with a barrier, since otherwise you would always be aware of these as you are always and unceasingly aware of your own essence. Substantiality, whether taken as the perfection of its quiddity or as an expression for the denial of a subject or a locus, is not an independent entity that could be your essence itself. If substantiality is taken to be an unknown meaning and if you apprehend your essence continually by some means other than something superadded to your essence, then this substantiality, of which you are unconscious, can be neither the whole of your essence nor any part thereof. If you examine this matter closely, you will find that that by which you are you is only a thing that apprehends its own essence—your "ego."

فصل تفصيلى [فى ما ذكرناه ايضا]

(١١٥) هو انّ الشئ القائم بذاته المدرك لذاته لا يعلم ذاته بمثال لذاته فى ذاته، فانّ علمه ان كان بمثال ومثال الانائية[١٠] ليس هى، فهو بالنسبة اليها هو والمدرَك هو المثال حينئذ، فيلزم ان يكون ادراك الانائية هو بعينه ادراك ما هو هو، وان يكون ادراك ذاتها بعينه ادراك غيرها، وهو محال، بخلاف الخارجيات؛ فانّ المثال وما له ذلك كلاهما هو. وايضا ان كان بمثال ان لم يعلم انّه مثال لنفسه، فلم يعلم نفسه؛ وان علم انّه مثال نفسه، فقد علم نفسه لا بالمثال. وكيف ما كان، لا يتصوّر ان يعلم الشئ نفسه بأمر زائد على نفسه، فانّه يكون صفة له. فاذا حكم انّ كل صفة زائدة على ذاته، كانت علما او غيره، فهى لذاته، فيكون قد علم ذاته قبل جميع الصفات ودونها، فلا يكون قد علم ذاته بالصفات الزائدة.

(١١٦) وانت لا تغيب عن ذاتك وعن ادراكك لها، واذ ليس يمكن ان يكون الادراك بصورة او زائد، فلا تحتاج فى ادراكك لذاتك الى غير ذاتك الظاهرة لنفسها او الغير الغائبة عن نفسها. فيجب ان يكون ادراكها لها لنفسها كما هى، وانّه لا تغيب قط عن ذاتك وجزء ذاتك. وما تغيب ذاتك عنه، كالاعضاء من القلب والكبد والدماغ وجميع البرازخ والهيآت الظلمانية والنورية، ليست من المدرِك منك، فليس المدرِك منك بعضو ولا أمر برزخى والا ما غابت عنه حيث كان لك شعور بذاتك مستمر لا يزول. والجوهرية اذا كانت كمال ماهيتها او تؤخذ عبارة عن سلب الموضوع او المحل، ليست بأمر مستقل تكون ذاتك نفسها هى. وان اخذت الجوهرية معنى مجهولا وادركت ذاتك لا بأمر زائد ادراكا مستمرا، فليست الجوهرية الغائبة عنك كل ذاتك. ولا جزء ذاتك، فاذا تفحصت، فلا تجد ما ان به انت إلاّ شيئا مدرِكا لذاته

All else that apprehends its own essence and ego shares with you in this. Apprehension, therefore, occurs neither by an attribute nor by something superadded, of whatever sort. It is not a part of your ego, since the other part would still remain unknown. Were there something beyond consciousness and awareness, it would be unknown and would not belong to your essence, whose awareness is not superadded to it. It is thereby apparent too that thingness is not superadded to awareness, for it is evident in itself and to itself. There is no other property with it of which being evident could be a state. It is simply the evident itself—nothing more. Therefore, it is light in itself, and it is thus pure light. Your apprehension is not something else posterior to your essence, nor is the capacity for apprehension accidental to your essence. If your essence were assumed to be an identity that apprehends its essence, it would itself be prior to its apprehension and therefore be unknown—which is absurd. Thus, the matter is as we have said.

A rule

(117) If you wish to have a rule regarding light, let it be that light is that which is evident in its own reality and by essence makes another evident. It is, thus, more evident in itself than anything to whose reality being evident is superadded. Moreover, that the accidental lights are evident is not due to something superadded to them, since if that were the case they would be hidden in themselves. Rather their being evident is simply due to their own reality. Nor is it the case that the light occurs and its being evident is a concomitant of it, since then it would not be light in its own definition and would be made evident by something else. Rather, light is evident, and its being evident is its being light. Some incorrectly argue that our vision makes evident the light of the Sun, whereas in reality its being evident is its being light. Were there no men and nothing at all possessed of senses, it would not cease to be light.

(118) Here is another way to express this: You ought not to say, "My ego is a thing whose concomitant is being evident, but that thing is hidden in itself." Rather, it is nothing but being evident and being light. You already know that thingness is one of the intellectual predicates and

وهو «انائيتك». وفيه شاركك كل من ادرك ذاته وانائيته. فالمدركية اذن ليست بصفة ولا أمر زائد، كيف ما كان. وليست جزءا لانائيتك، فيبقى الجزء الآخر مجهولا حينئذ اذا كان وراء المدركية والشاعرية، فيكون مجهولا، ولا يكون من ذاتك التى شعورها لم يزد عليها. فتبيّن من هذا الطريق ان الشيئية ليست بزائدة ايضا على الشاعرية؛[١١] فهو الظاهر لنفسه بنفسه ولا خصوص معه حتى يكون الظهور حالا له، بل هو نفس الظاهر لا غير، فهو نور لنفسه، فيكون نورا محضا. ومدركيتك لا شئ آخر تابع لذاتك، واستعداد المدركية عرضى لذاتك، وان فرضت ذاتك إنيّة تدرك نفسها، فيتقدم نفسها على الادراك، فتكون مجهولة، وهو محال؛ فليس إلاّ ما قلنا. واذا اردت ان يكون للنور عندك، [فههنا]:

ضابط

(١١٧) فليكن انّ النور هو الظاهر فى حقيقة نفسه المظهر لغيره بذاته، وهو أظهر فى نفسه من كل ما يكون الظهور زائدا على حقيقته. والانوار العارضة ايضا ظهورها لأمر زائد عليها، فتكون فى نفسها خفية، بل ظهورها إنمّا هو لحقيقة نفسها. وليس انّ النور يحصل ثم يلزمه الظهور، فيكون فى حدّ نفسه ليس بنور، فيُظهره شئ آخر، بل هو ظاهر وظهوره نوريته. وليس كما يتوّهم فيقال «نور الشمس تظهره ابصارنا»، بل ظهوره هو نوريته، ولو عدم الناس كلهم وجميع ذوات الحس، لم تبطل نوريته.

(١١٨) عبارة أُخرى: ليس لك ان تقول «أنيتى شئ يلزمه الظهور فيكون ذلك الشئ خفيا فى نفسه»، بل هى نفس الظهور والنورية وقد علمت انّ الشيئية من المحمولات والصفات العقلية وكذا كون

attributes, as are a thing's being a reality and a quiddity. Lack of unawareness is something negative and cannot be your quiddity. Nothing, then, remains but being evident and being light. Thus, anything that apprehends its own essence is a pure light, and every pure light is evident to itself and apprehends its own essence. This is one of the methods of proof.

A judgment [that a thing's apprehending itself is its being evident to itself]

(119) In addition, we argue that were we to posit a flavor abstracted from barriers and matter, we would only have shown that it was a flavor in itself—nothing more. If we assume a light to be incorporeal, it is light in itself; and it then follows that it is evident to itself, which is apprehension. It does not follow that an incorporeal flavor is evident to itself, only that it is a flavor in itself. Were the fact that a thing is free from prime matter and barriers sufficient to make it aware of itself, as is the opinion of the Peripatetics, then that prime matter whose existence they assert would also be aware of itself, since it is not a state in something else but has its own quiddity and is free from any other prime matter—there being no matter of prime matter. Thus, it would not be unconscious of itself, if by "unconsciousness" is meant distance from itself. If by "lack of unconsciousness" they mean awareness, then the awareness of the separate intellects cannot be attributed to lack of unconsciousness. Indeed, lack of unconsciousness is an allusion to and symbol for awareness, in this sense. According to the Peripatetics, a thing's apprehension is the fact that it is incorporeal and is not unconscious of its essence. The particularity of the matter itself, as they argue, only occurs through states. So, granting that the states are hindered from apprehending their own essences by the matter, what, then, is it that hinders the matter? They admit that prime matter has particularity only through the states that they call "forms." If these forms occur in us, we perceive them. If prime matter in itself is just something unconditioned, or a certain substance considered apart from magnitudes and all other states, as they claim, then there is nothing that is more perfectly simple in its own definition

الشئ حقيقة وماهية وعدم الغيبة أمر سلبى لا يكون ماهيتك؛ فلم يبق إلاّ الظهور والنورية. فكل من ادرك ذاته فهو نور محض، وكل نور محض ظاهر لذاته ومدرك لذاته، هذا احدى الطرائق.

حكومة [فى انّ ادراك الشئ نفسه هو ظهوره لذاته]

(١١٩) ونزيد فنقول: لو فرضنا الطعم مجردا عن البرازخ والمواد، لم يلزم إلاّ ان يكون طعما لنفسه لا غير. والنور اذا فُرض تجرده يكون نورا لنفسه؛ فيلزم ان يكون ظاهرا لنفسه وهو الادراك، ولا يلزم ان يكون الطعم عند التجرد ظاهرا لنفسه بل طعما لنفسه فحسب. ولو كفى فى كون الشئ شاعرا بنفسه تجرده عن الهيولى والبرازخ، كما هو مذهب المشائين، لكانت الهيولى التى اثبتوها شاعرة بنفسها، اذ ليست هى هيئة لغيرها بل ماهيتها لها، وهى مجردة عن هيولى اُخرى، اذ لا هيولى للهيولى، ولا تغيب عن نفسها، اذ عُنى بالغيبة بُعدها عن نفسها؛ وان عُنى بعدم الغيبة الشعور، فلم يرجع الشعور فى المفارقات الى عدم الغيبة، بل عدم الغيبة كناية وتجوّز عن الشعور على هذا التقدير. وكان عند المشائين كون الشئ مجردا عن المادة غير غائب عن ذاته هو ادراكه. والمادة نفسها كما قالوا خصوصها إنمّا يحصل بالهيآت، فهب انّ الهيآت منعتها المادة، فالمادة ما الّذى منعها. واعترفوا بانّ الهيولى ليس لها تخصص إلاّ بالهيآت التى سمّوها «صورا». والصور اذا حصلت فينا، ادركناها، وليست الهيولى فى نفسها إلاّ شيئا مّا مطلقا او جوهرا مّا عند قطع النظر عن المقادير وجميع الهيآت كما زعموا. فلا شئ فى حدّ نفسه أتمّ بساطة من الهيولى سيّما انّ جوهريتها هو

than prime matter—especially since its substantiality is the denial of its having a subject, as they admit. Why, then, does it not apprehend its essence by reason of this freedom from substrata and parts? And why does it not apprehend the forms that are in it? But we have explained this substantiality and thingness and have shown that these and their likes are beings of reason.

(120) Then these people argue that the Creator of everything is nothing but pure existence. But if we examine the prime matter posited by their school, it turns out that it is simply existence, since its particularity is by means of forms and substantiality, as has been explained. There is nothing that is quiddity absolutely; but rather, when some particularity is established, it is said that it is a quiddity or an existent. Prime matter, then, must either be some quiddity or some existent. If its need for forms is due to its being some existent, then the same is true of the Necessary Existent—exalted is He above that! If the Necessary Existent intellects His essence and the things because of such simplicity, then this must also be the case with prime matter, since it too is an existent and nothing more. The falsity of such doctrines is plain. Thus, it is established that whatever apprehends its own essence is a light in itself, and vice versa. If an accidental light were assumed to be incorporeal, it would be evident in itself and to itself. That whose reality is evident in itself to itself has the reality of the light posited to be incorporeal. The one is the other; they are one and the same.

Section [six]

[On the lights and their classes]

(121) Light is divided into light of itself and in itself and light of itself but in another.[10] You know that accidental light is light in another. Thus, it is not a light *in* itself although it is a light *of* itself, since its existence is in another.[11] The dusky substance is not evident of itself or to itself, according to what you know. Life is a thing's being evident to itself, and a living thing is percipient and active. You know about perception; and the

سلب الموضوع عنها كما اعترفوا به. فلِمَ ما ادركت ذاتها بهذا التجرد عن الحوامل والاجزاء ولمِ ما ادركت الصور التى فيها على انّا بيّنا حال الجوهرية والشيئية وان امثالهما اعتبارات عقلية.

(١٢٠) ثم قال هؤلاء انّ مبدع الكل ليس إلاّ مجرد الوجود. واذا بُحث عن الهيولى على مذهبهم رجع[١٢] حاصلها الى نفس الوجود، اذ التخصص إنمّا هو بالهيآت الجوهرية كما سبق، فليس شىء هو نفس الماهية مطلقا، بل اذا ثبت خصوص،[١٣] فيقال له انه ماهية او موجود. والهيولى لا تبقى إلاّ ماهية مّا او وجود مّا؛ فافتقارها الى الصور ان كان لنفس كونها موجودا مّا، فكان واجب الوجود كذا، تعالى ان يكون هكذا![١٤] واذا كان واجب الوجود يعقل ذاته والاشياء لمثل هذه البساطة، فكان يجب ايضا فى الهيولى، لانها موجود فحسب؛ وبطلان هذه الاقاويل ظاهر. فثبت انّ الّذى يدرك ذاته هو نور لنفسه وبالعكس. واذا فُرض النور العارض مجردا، كان ظاهرا فى نفسه لنفسه. فما حقيقته انه الظاهر فى نفسه لنفسه حقيقته[١٥] حقيقة النور المفروض مجردا، فان «الهُو هُو» ينعكس رأسا برأس.

فصل

[فى الانوار واقسامها]

(١٢١) النور ينقسم الى نور فى نفسه لنفسه، والى نور فى نفسه وهو لغيره. والنور العارض عرفت انّه نور لغيره، فلا يكون نورا لنفسه وان كان نورا فى نفسه، لان وجوده لغيره. والجوهر الغاسق ليس بظاهر فى نفسه ولا لنفسه على ما عرفة. والحياة هى ان يكون الشئ ظاهرا لنفسه، والحىّ هو الدرّاك الفعّال، فالادراك عرفته، والفعل ايضا للنور

attribution of activity to light is clear, since light emanates by essence. Thus, pure light is alive, and every living thing is a pure light. If a dusky thing perceived its own essence, it would be light in itself and not a dusky substance. If the barrier or some dusky substance as such necessitated life and knowledge, that would have to be the case for all other things that were also barriers or dusky substances, which is not true. If the dusky substance were posited to have life and knowledge through an added state, the same argument would apply. Moreover, a state certainly cannot be evident to itself, as we already know. Nor would it be evident to the barrier, since the barrier is dusky in itself. How could something be evident to it, when something to which something else is evident must certainly be evident to itself of itself? That which has no awareness of itself cannot be aware of another. Since neither the barrier nor the state is evident to itself, nor are they evident to each other, then nothing evident to itself may result from either of them. Since the state has existence only in another, then nothing self-subsistent may result from it and the barrier. Of those two, only the barrier is self-subsistent. If one of those two perceives its own essence, it could only be that which has its own essence: the barrier. For the barrier and the state are two things, not one—but you know that the barrier is not evident in itself.

(122) Here is another proof: We say that a thing may make something evident to something else—as accidental light does for the locus—but its being evident to another does not imply its being evident to its own essence. If a thing makes something evident to another, then that other thing ought to be evident to itself so that something else could be evident to it. Once this is established, we say that there cannot be an entity that makes a thing evident to that same thing in such a way that that thing becomes evident to itself. This is because there is nothing closer to itself than itself. It was hidden from itself, and its self being hidden from itself is of itself. Therefore, nothing else could ever make it evident to itself. How could it be otherwise, when the fact that something else made its self evident to itself implies the absurdity that its self was already evident to itself? The barrier is thus in itself hidden from itself, and nothing can make it evident to itself.

ظاهر، وهو فيّاض لذاته.[١٦] فالنور المحض حيّ وكل حيّ فهو نور محض. والغاسق انّ ادرك ذاته كان نورا لذاته، فلم يكن جوهرا غاسقا. وان اقتضى البرزخ او غاسق مّا من حيث هو كذا الحياة والعلم، لكان يجب على مشاركه ذلك، وليس كذا. وان فُرض للجوهر الغاسق حياة وعلم لهيئة زائدة كان على ما سبق؛ وايضا لا شك انّ الهيئة ليست ظاهرة لنفسها لما سبق. وليست ظاهرة للبرزخ، فانّه غاسق فى نفسه؛ كيف يظهر له شئ اذ لا بد لمن يظهر له شئ ان يكون لنفسه ظهور فى نفسه؟ فانّه لا يشعر بغيره من لا شعور له بذاته. فلما لم يكن البرزخ ظاهرا لنفسه ولا الهيئة ولا البرزخ للهيئة ولا الهيئة للبرزخ، فلا يحصل منهما ظاهر لنفسه. والهيئة لما لم يكن وجودها إلاّ لغيرها، لم يحصل منها ومن البرزخ شئ قائم بنفسه، بل القائم منهما هو البرزخ. فانّ كان شئ مّا مدركا منهما لذاته، فلا يكون إلاّ ما له ذاته منهما، وهو البرزخ. فان البرزخ والهيئة شيئان لا شئ واحد، ودريت انّه غير ظاهر فى نفسه.

(١٢٢) ايضاح آخر: نقول يجوز ان يكون شئ يُظهر الشئ لغيره، كالنور العارض للمحل، وليس يلزم من ظهوره لغيره ظهوره لذاته. واذا كان الشئ اظهر أمراً لغيره ينبغى ان يكون ذلك الغير ظاهرا لنفسه حتى يظهر عنده أمر مّا. واذا تقرّر هذا، فنقول: لا يجوز ان يكون أمر يُظهر الشئ لنفس ذلك الشئ على ان يصير به الشئ ظاهرا عند نفسه، اذ لا اقرب من نفسه الى نفسه وقد خفى نفسه عن نفسه وخفاء نفسه على نفسه لنفسه، فلا يُظهر نفسه لنفسه شئ مّا ابدا. كيف ويستدعى اظهار غيره نفسه لنفسه ان تكون نفسه ظاهرة لنفسه قبل ذلك، وهو محال.[١٧] والبرزخ خفى لنفسه على نفسه، فلا يظهره عند نفسه شئ.

(123) There is still another way of proving this. If anything were to make the barrier evident to itself, it would be light. Every illumined body would be evident to itself and so would be alive, which is not so. No particularity that the dark states give to the barrier can make it necessary for light to make the barrier evident to itself. It has been shown by another proof that if something is evident to itself, its being evident to itself is not by any state nor by any dusky substance.

A principle [stating that a body cannot bring another body into existence]

(124) You know that you are in yourself an incorporeal light and that you are incapable of giving existence to a barrier. If an active, living, substantial light can be incapable of giving existence to a barrier, a lifeless barrier will certainly be unable to do so.

Section [seven]

[Showing that the intellectual, incorporeal lights differ by perfection and deficiency, not by species]

(125) Light in itself varies in its reality only by perfection and deficiency and by entities external to it. If it had two parts, neither of which was light in itself, each would be either a dusky substance or a dark state, and the whole would not be a light in itself. Were one of them light and the other not light, the latter would not participate in the luminous reality, though it was one of the parts. You will learn in detail how the lights are distinguished.

(١٢٣) وايضا من طريق آخر: لو اظهره عند نفسه شئ لاظهره النور وكان كل برزخ استنار ظاهرا لنفسه، فكان حيا، وليس كذا. وايّ خصوص يوجد للبرزخ بهيئات ظلمانية لا يوجب ان يظهره نور عند نفسه. فيقرر[١٨] من جهة أُخرى ان ما ظهر نفسه لنفسه، ظهوره لنفسه ليس بهيئة مّا ولا جوهر غاسق مّا.

قاعدة [فى انّ الجسم لا يوجد جسما]

(١٢٤) واذا دريت أنّك فى نفسك نور مجرد ولست تقوى على ايجاد برزخ، فاذا كان من النور الجوهرى الحىّ الفاعل ما يقصر عن ايجاد البرزخ، فالاولى ان يقصر البرزخ الميت عن ايجاد البرزخ.[١٩]

فصل

[فى انّ اختلاف الانوار المجردة العقلية هو بالكمال والنقص لا بالنوع]

(١٢٥) النور كله فى نفسه لا تختلف حقيقته إلاّ بالكمال والنقصان وبأمور خارجة عنه،[٢٠] فانّه ان كان له جزءان وكل واحد غير نور فى نفسه، كان جوهرا غاسقا او هيئة ظلمانية، فالمجموع لا يكون نورا فى نفسه. وان كان احدهما نورا والآخر غير نور، فليس له مدخل فى الحقيقة النورية، وهى احدهما. وستعرف الفارق بين الانوار على التفصيل.

Section [eight]

Also on the differences among the incorporeal lights

(126) We claim that the incorporeal lights do not differ in reality. Were their realities to differ, there would be luminosity and something else in each incorporeal light. Either that other would be a state in the incorporeal light, or the incorporeal light would be a state in it, or each would be self-subsistent. If it were a state in the incorporeal light, it would be external to its reality, since a state of a thing occurs in it only after its realization as an independent quiddity in the mind. Thus, the reality does not differ by the state. Were the incorporeal light a state in that other, it would not be an incorporeal light. Instead, there would be a dusky substance with an accidental light in it. Since it was posited to be an incorporeal light—this is absurd. Were each of them self-subsistent, neither could be the locus of the other or share in a locus with the other. Not being barriers, they could not intermingle or touch, so neither would have any attachment to the other. Therefore, the incorporeal lights do not differ in their realities.

(127) Here is another proof: It has been shown that your ego is an incorporeal light, that it is self-conscious, and that the incorporeal lights do not differ in their realities. Thus, all the incorporeal lights must apprehend their own essences, since that which is necessarily true of a thing must also be true of that which has the same reality. This is another method—though if you have understood what came before, you will have no need of these proofs.

A principle [stating that that which gives existence to the barriers must apprehend its own essence]

(128) Since an incorporeal light gives all the barriers their lights and existence, that light must be alive and self-conscious, since it is a light in itself.

فصل

[ايضا فى اجتلاف الانوار المجردة]

(١٢٦) ومن طريق آخر نقول: الانوار المجردة لا تختلف بالحقيقة،[٢١] والا ان اختلفت حقائقها، كان كل نور مجرد فيه النورية وغيرها. وذلك الغير اما ان يكون هيئة فى النور المجرد، او النور المجرد هيئة فيه، او كل منهما قائم بذاته. فان كان[٢٢] هيئة فى النور المجرد، فهو خارج عن حقيقته، اذ هيئة الشئ لا تحصل فيه إلاّ بعد تحققه ماهية مستقلة فى العقل، فالحقيقة لا تختلف به؛ وان كان النور المجرد هيئة فيه، فليس بنور مجرد، بل هو جوهر غاسق فيه نور عارض، وقد فُرض نورا مجردا، وهو محال. وان كان كل واحد منهما قائما بنفسه،[٢٣] فليس احدهما محل الآخر ولا الشريك فى المحل، وليسا ببرزخين ليمتزجا وليتصلا فلا تعلق لاحدهما بالآخر، فالانوار المجردة غير مختلفة الحقائق.

(١٢٧) ايضاح آخر: اذا تبين انّ انائيتك نور مجرد ومدرك لنفسه والانوار المجردة غير مختلفة الحقائق، فيجب ان يكون الكل مدركا لذاته، اذ ما يجب على شئ يجب على مشاركه فى الحقيقة. هذا طريق آخر. واذ علمت ما سبق اولا، استغنيت عن هذه الوجوه.

قاعدة [فى انّ موجد البرازخ مدرِك لذاته]

(١٢٨) فلما كان واهب جميع البرازخ انوارها ووجودها نور مجرد فهو حيّ مدرِك لذاته، لانّه نور لنفسه.

Section [nine]

[Proving that there is a Being necessary by essence]

(129) If an incorporeal light is dependent in its quiddity, its need is not directed toward the lifeless dusky substance, which is not worthy to give existence in any respect to that which is nobler and more perfect than it. How could the dusky emanate light? Thus, though the actualization of the incorporeal light depends on a self-subsistent light, these lights ordered in ranks cannot form an infinite series, since you know by demonstration that an ordered simultaneous series must be finite. Therefore, the self-subsistent and accidental lights, the barriers, and the states of each must end in a light beyond which there is no light. This is the Light of Lights, the All-Encompassing Light, the Eternal Light, the Holy Light, the All-Highest Almighty Light, the Dominating Light. It is absolutely independent, since there is nothing beyond It. The existence of two independent incorporeal lights is inconceivable. They would not differ in reality, as has been shown. One would not be distinguished from the other by something they have in common; nor would they be distinguished by something assumed to be a concomitant of their reality, since they share in this as well. They would not differ by a foreign accident, dark or luminous, since there is nothing beyond them that would cause them to become particularized. If one of them particularizes itself or the other, both would be individual before their particularization without something to particularize them—though individuality and duality are inconceivable without a particularizer. Therefore, the independent incorporeal light is one. It is the Light of Lights. Everything other than It is in need of It and has its existence from It. It has no equal, nor any peer. It rules over all things, and nothing rules it or opposes it; for all sovereignty, all power, all perfection derives from It. Nonbeing cannot overtake the Light of Lights; for were it contingently nonexistent, it would be a contingent existent and there would not be sufficient reason in itself for it to come into reality, as you know, but it would require some sufficient reason. Thus, it would not be independent in truth and would need something absolutely independent—which would be the Light of Lights, since this series must end.

فصل

[فى اثبات الواحبب بالذات]

(١٢٩) النور المجرد اذا كان فاقرا فى ماهيته، فاحتياجه لا يكون الى الجوهر الغاسق الميت، اذ لا يصلح هو لان يوجد اشرف وأتمّ منه لا فى جهة، وانّى يفيد الغاسق النور؛ فان كان النور المجرد فاقرا فى تحققه الى نور قائم. ثم لا تذهب الانوار القائمة المترتبة سلسلتها الى غير النهاية، لما عرفت من البرهان الموجب للنهاية فى المترتبات المجتمعة فيجب ان تنتهى الانوار القائمة والعارضة والبرازخ وهيآتها الى نور ليس ورائه نور، وهو نور الانوار، والنور المحيط، والنور القيوم، والنور المقدس، والنور الاعظم الاعلى، وهو النور القهار، وهو الغنى المطلق، اذ ليس ورائه شئ آخر. ولا يتصور وجود نورين مجردين غنيين، فانّهما لا يختلفان فى الحقيقة لما مضى؛ ولا يمتاز احدهما عن الآخر بنفس ما اشتركا فيه ولا بأمر يفرض انّه لازم بالحقيقة اذ يشتركان فيه، ولا بعارض غريب كان ظلمانيا او نوريا، فانّه ليس ورائهما مخصص. وان خصص احدهما نفسه او صاحبه، فيكونان قبل التخصص متعينين لا بالمخصص، ولا بالتصور العين ولا تنبيه إلاّ بمخصص، فالنور المجرد الغنى واحد وهو نور الانوار، وما دونه يحتاج اليه ومنه وجوده، فلا ندّ له ولا مثل له. وهو القاهر لكل شئ ولا يقهره ولا يقاومه شئ اذ كل قهر وقوة وكمال مستفاد منه. ولا يمكن على نور الانوار العدم، فانّه لو كان ممكن العدم لكان ممكن الوجود، ولم يترجح تحققه من نفسه على ما دريت، بل بمرجح، فلم يكن بغنى حقا، فيحتاج الى غنى مطلق هو نور الانوار لوجوب تناهى السلسلة.

(130) Moreover, there is another proof: A thing does not imply its own nonbeing, or else it would never enter reality. The Light of Lights is unitary, having by Its own essence no condition, and everything else follows from It. If It has no condition and no opposite, nothing can nullify It, so It is eternal and everlasting. No state, be it luminous or dark, adheres to the Light of Lights, and It may have no attribute in any respect.

(131) The general proof is that if a dark state were in It, It would necessarily have a dark aspect, in Its own reality, necessitating It. Thus, It would be composite and not a pure light. A luminous accident may only belong to that in which light is increased. Were the Light of Lights made more luminous by a state, Its independent essence would be illuminated by an accidental dependent light that It Itself necessitated. This is because there is nothing above It to necessitate a luminous accident. Thus, this is absurd.

(132) Another general proof is this: That which illumines is more luminous than that which is illuminated in that respect in which the former gives the latter its light. Thus, its essence is more luminous than the other essence—which is, in this case, impossible.

(133) Here is a detailed proof: Were the Light of Lights of Itself to necessitate a state, It would act and receive. The aspect of activity would be different than the aspect of receptivity; for were the aspect of activity itself the aspect of receptivity, every recipient would be active when it received, and every agent would be a recipient by the activity itself when it acted—but this is not so. Then it would follow that in the Light of Lights there would be two aspects: an aspect that necessitated activity and an aspect that necessitated receptivity. Since this could not regress infinitely, the series would end in two aspects in Its essence.

(134) Of course, neither of the two aspects would be an independent light, since there are not two independent lights, as you know. Nor could one of them be an independent light and the other a dependent light, since if the dependent light were a state in the other, the argument would regress. If it were not a state, it would be independent and would not be in the independent light; but this is impossible, since the dependent light was posited to be a state in the essence of the independent light. Nor could one of them be a light and the other a dark state, since this argument, too, is regressive. Nor could one of them be a dusky substance and the other an incorporeal light. In that case, neither would be connected

(١٣٠) وايضا من طريق آخر: الشئ لا يقتضى عدم نفسه، والا ما تحقّق. ونور الانوار وحدانى لا شرط له فى ذاته، وما سواه تابع له. واذ لا شرط له ولا مضاد له، فلا مبطل له، فهو قيّوم دائم. ولا يلحق نور الانوار هيئة مّا نورية كانت او ظلمانية، ولا يمكن له صفة بوجه من الوجوه.

(١٣١) اما اجمالا: فلان الهيئة الظلمانية لو كانت فيه، للزم ان يكون له فى حقيقة نفسه جهة ظلمانية توجبها، فيتركب، فليس بنور محض. والهيئة النورية لا تكون إلاّ فيما يزداد بها نورا؛ فنور الانوار ان استنار بهيئة، فكان ذاته الغنية مستنيرة بالنور الفاقر العارض الّذى ياوجبه هو بنفسه، اذ ليس فوقه ما يوجب فيه هيئة نورية، وهو محال.

(١٣٢) اجمال آخر: هو انّ المنير أنور من المستنير من جهة اعطاء ذلك النور، فتكون ذاته أنور من ذاته، وذلك ممتنع.

(١٣٣) طريق[٢٤] تفصيلى: هو انّ نور الانوار لو اوجب بنفسه هيئة، لفعل وقبل. وجهة الفعل غير جهة القبول، فلو[٢٥] كان جهة الفعل بعينها جهة القبول لكان كل قابل لما قبل فاعلا وكل فاعل لما فعل قابلا بنفس الفعل؛ وليس كذا. فيلزم ان يكون فيه جهتان: جهة تقتضى الفعل واُخرى القبول؛ ولا سلسل الى غير نهاية فتنتهى الى جهتين فى ذاته.

(١٣٤) ثم الجهتان ليس كل واحد منهما نورا غنيا اذ لا نورين غنيين، لما عرفت، ولا احدهما نور غنى والآخر نور فقير، فان[٢٦] الفقير ان كان هيئة فيه يعود الكلام اليه؛ وان لم يكن هيئة، فهو مستقل، فلا يكون فيه، وقد فُرض جهة فى ذاته وذلك ممتنع. ولا ان يكون احدهما نورا والآخر هيئة ظلمانية لعود هذا[٢٧] الكلام بعينه.[٢٨] ولا ان يكون احدهما جوهرا غاسقا والآخر نورا مجردا، فيكون كل واحد منها[٢٩] غير متعلق بالآخر فلا يكون فى ذات نور الانوار ايضا. فثبت انّ نور الانوار

to the other, and the one, moreover, would not be in the essence of the Light of Lights. Thus, it is established that the Light of Lights is abstracted from all else and nothing is part of It. Nothing is conceivably more splendorous than It! Since a thing's knowledge of itself amounts to its being evident to its essence, and since the Light of Lights is pure luminosity whose being evident is not by another, the life and self-consciousness of the Light of Lights are essential, not additional to Its essence. You have already seen the proof of this for every incorporeal light.

مجرد عمّا سواه، ولا ينضمّ اليه شئ مّا، فلا[٣٠] يتصور ان يكون أبهى منه. ولما رجع حاصل علم الشئ بنفسه الى كون ذاته ظاهرة لذاته، وهو النورية المحضة التى لا يكون ظهورها بغيرها، فنور الانوار حياته وعلمه بذاته لا يزيد على ذاته. وقد سبق بيانه لك فى كل نور مجرد.

The Second Discourse

On the order of existence,
in [fourteen] sections

Section [one]

[Showing that from the Truly One,
in that respect in which It is one,
only one effect is generated]

(135) A light and a darkness, whether dusky substance or dark state, cannot both occur[1] from the Light of Lights; for causing a light is not the same as causing a darkness. If this could occur, the essence of the Light of Lights would be compounded from that which necessitated the light and that which necessitated the darkness. The absurdity of this has been made plain to you. Indeed, darknesses can only be engendered by It through an intermediary. Moreover, the Light as light engenders only light. Nor may two lights occur from It, for the one would not be the other and that which engendered one would not be that which engendered the other. Thus, there would be two aspects in the Light of Lights—the impossibility of which we have already made clear. This is indeed sufficient proof of the impossibility of any two things occurring from It, whatsoever they might be. In further explanation, we say that there must be something that distinguishes between two things. Thus, we must explain that which they share and that by which they are distinguished. This would imply two aspects in its essence—which is absurd.

المقالة الثانية

فى ترتيب الوجود

وفيها فصول

فصل

[فى انّ الواحد الحقيقى لا يصدر عنه
من حيث هو كذلك اكثر من معلول واحد]

(١٣٥) لا يجوز ان يحصل من نور الانوار نور وغير نور من المظلمات كان جوهرها او هيئتها، فيكون اقتضاء النور غير اقتضاء الظلمة، فذاته تصير مركبة مما يوجب النور ويوجب الظلمة، وقد تبيّن لك استحالته، بل الظلمة لا تحصل منه بغير واسطة، وايضا النور من حيث هو نور ان اقتضى، فلا يقتضى غير النور، ولا يحصل منه نوران فانّ احدهما غير الآخر، فاقتضاء احدهما ليس اقتضاء الآخر ففيه جهتان وقد بيّنا امتناعهما. وهذا يكفى فى حصول كل شيئين منه، كيف كانا. وفى التفصيل نقول لا بدّ من فارق بين الاثنين. ثم يعود الكلام الى ما به الافتراق والاشتراك بينهما، فيلزم جهتان فى ذاته، وهو محال.

Section [two]

[Showing that what is first generated from the Light of Lights is a single incorporeal light]

(136) If we posit the existence of a darkness [occurring directly from the Light of Lights], then no light in addition to it would come about from the Light of Lights, for otherwise the aspects of the Light of Lights would have to be multiple, as was explained before. Yet, it is obvious that there are many self-conscious incorporeal lights and accidental lights. Were a darkness to be generated from the Light of Lights, it would be alone and nothing else would exist, whether lights or darknesses. Existence itself testifies to the falsity of this. Multiplicity cannot conceivably result from the Light of Lights in Its unity, nor can any darkness be conceived to result from a dusky substance or state, nor yet two lights result from the Light of Lights in Its unity. Therefore, that which first results from the Light of Lights must be a single incorporeal light. This, then, cannot be distinguished from the Light of Lights by any dark state acquired from the Light of Lights. This would imply the multiplicity of aspects in the Light of Lights in contradiction to the demonstration that the lights, particularly the incorporeal lights, do not differ in their realities. Therefore, the Light of Lights and the first light that results from It are only to be distinguished by perfection and deficiency. Just as among the objects of sensation the acquired light is not like the radiating light in its perfection, so, too, is the case with the incorporeal lights. The accidental lights may differ in their perfection and weakness by reason of the light that illumines them, though the recipient and its capacity remain the same. A single wall may accept the light of the Sun or of a lamp or the light of the Sun's rays reflected from a glass onto the clay; but it is plain that the light the clay receives from the Sun is more perfect than that which is reflected from a glass or which comes from a lamp. The difference in perfection and deficiency between them is due only to the two givers of light. The agent may also be the same; but the perfection or deficiency of the ray may differ by reason of the recipient, as is the case with the rays of the Sun that fall upon crystal, jet, or earth. That which crystal or jet accepts, for example, is more perfect. The incorporeal light, however, has no recipient, so that all such lights other than the Light of Lights have their perfection and deficiency by reason of the rank of their agent. The perfection of the Light of Lights has no cause; rather, It is the pure light which has no admixture of dependence or deficiency.

فصل

[فى انّ أوّل صادر من نور الانوار نور مجرد واحد]

(١٣٦) وان فُرض وجود ظلمة، فلا يحصل منه معها نور، والا تعددت جهاته على ما سبق. والانوار المجردة المدركة والعارضة كثرتها ظاهرة؛ فلو صدر منه ظلمة لكانت واحدة، وما وجد غيرها من الانوار والظلمات[1] والوجود يشهد ببطلانه. فنور الانوار لما لم يتصور ان يحصل به على وحدته كثرة ولا امكان لحصول ظلمة من غاسق او هيئة ولا نورين، فأوّل ما يحصل منه نور مجرد واحد. ثم لا يمتاز من نور الانوار بهيئة ظلمانية مستفادة عن نور الانوار، فتعدد جهات نور الانوار مع ما بُرهن من انّ الانوار سيّما المجردة غير مختلفة الحقائق. فاذا التمييز بين نور الانوار وبين نور الأوّل الّذى حصل منه، ليس إلاّ بالكمال والنقص، وكما انّ فى المحسوسات النور المستفاد لا تكون كالنور المفيد فى الكمال، فالانوار المجردة حكمها كذا. والانوار العارضة قد يختلف كمالها وضعفها بسبب المفيد وان اتحد القابل واستعداده، كحائط واحد يقبل النور من الشمس ومن السراج او ما ينعكس من الزجاج على الارض من شعاع الشمس، وبيّن انّ الارض تقبل من الشمس أتمّ مما انعكس عليها من الزجاج او ما يقبل من السراج، ولا يخفى انّ التفاوت فى الكمال والنقص بينهما ليس إلاّ لتفاوت المفيدين هاهنا. وقد يكون الفاعل واحدا ويختلف كمال الشعاع ونقصانه بسبب القابل، كما يقع من شعاع الشمس على البلور والسبح او الارض[2] فان الّذى يقبل البلور او السبح مثلا أتمّ. فالنور[3] المجرد لا قابل له؛ فما وراء نور الانوار كماله ونقصه يكون بسبب رتبة فاعله. وكمال نور الانوار لا علة له، بل هو النور المحض الّذى لا يشوبه فقر ولا نقص.

(137) Question: Insofar as the quiddity of luminosity does not necessitate perfection, would not its particularization as the Light of Light [*sic*] be a contingent effect?[2]

Answer: The quiddity of luminosity is a mental universal, not in itself particularized in the external world. That which is concrete is a single thing, neither a basis nor a perfection. The mental thing has beings of reason inconceivable in the concrete thing.

(138) Allusion has already been made to the arbitrary assertion that the self-subsistent thing does not admit of perfection and deficiency. Indeed, the difference between the accidental lights and the incorporeal lights, to which reference has already been made, consists in two aspects: the ranks of the agent and of the recipient. It has been shown that the first emanation of the Light of Lights is single—the Proximate Light, the Mighty Light, that which some of the Pahlawīs aforetime called "Bahman."[3] The Proximate Light is dependent in itself but independent by virtue of the first. The existence of a light from the Light of Lights does not happen by the separation of something from It, for you know that separation and connection are specific properties of bodies. Far exalted is the Light of Lights above that! Nor can it be by something moving from It, since states do not move, and you know the absurdity of there being states in the Light of Lights. We have written for you a chapter in which it is shown that the rays of the Sun simply exist by reason of it, nothing more. So you must also understand that this is so for every accidental shining light or incorporeal light. It must not be imagined that an accident is transferred or that a body is separated from it.

Section [three]

Concerning the determinations of these barriers

(139) Know that in any direction you may point, there are limits. If there were no impenetrable barrier surrounding all other barriers, then movement and pointing would go on into nothingness once they passed this last sphere—though it has been clearly explained to you that ordered simultaneous classes, whether bodily or otherwise, are finite. Nonbeing cannot conceivably be pointed to. It would be the same if this all-encompassing barrier admitted of division or if it were composed of

(١٣٧) سؤال: الماهية النورية من حيث هى لا تقتضى الكمال، فتخصصها بنور النور ممكن معلول؟

جواب: هى كلية ذهنية لا خصص نفسها بخارج، وما فى العين شئ واحد ليس اصل وكمال، وللذهنى اعتبارات لا صور على العينى.

(١٣٨) وما قيل «ان القائم بذاته لا يقبل الكمال والنقص» تحكّم قد سبقت الاشارة اليه. بلى الانوار العارضة على الانوار المجردة، التى سنشير اليها، يكون التفاوت بينها من وجهين: رتبة الفاعل والقابل. فثبة ان أوّل حاصل بنور الانوار واحد وهو النور الاقرب والنور العظيم وربما سمّاه بعض الفهلوية «بَهمَن». فالنور الاقرب فقير فى نفسه غنىّ بالأوّل. ووجود نور من نور الانوار ليس بان ينفصل منه شئ، فقد علمت ان الانفصال والاتصال من خواص الاجرام، وتعالى نور الانوار عن ذلك، ولا بان ينتقل عنه شئ اذ الهيآت لا تنتقل وعلمت استحالة الهيآت على نور الانوار. وقد ذكرنا لك فصلا يتضمن ان الشعاع من الشمس ليس إلاّ على انّه موجود به فحسب. فهكذا ينبغى ان تعرف فى كل نور شارق عارض او مجرد، ولا وهم فيه نقل عرض او انفصال جسم.

فصل

فى احكام هذه[٤] البرازخ

(١٣٩) اعلم ان الاشارات فى جميع الجوانب غايات، وانّه ان لم يكن برزخ محيط بجميع البرازخ غير قابل للانفكاك، وقد تبيّن لك تناهى المترتبات المجتمعة الجرمية وغيرها، لكانت الحركة والاشارة عند عبورها وخروجها عن جميع الاجسام واقعة الى لا شئ، والعدم لا يتصور الاشارة اليه. وسواء كان محيطا بالكل قابلا للانفصال او برازخ

many barriers. In the latter case, each one of these barriers—even if it was assumed to be indivisible—would necessarily be composite and so would be subject to compounding and division. Thus, movement could occur toward nothing and in no particular direction—which is absurd. Also, heterogeneous things must necessarily occur individually first and then be compounded. The simple substance must first be made as a single body and then be divided, if it admits of that. Thus, it must necessarily be a homogeneous, single, indivisible, all-encompassing barrier in which parts cannot even be imagined to exist. Two different directions cannot occur from it alone, for it is single and homogeneous, from which in itself only one direction can occur—namely, height. All that is near to it is high. Therefore, the low is simply the extremity of distance from it—that is, the center. This, then, is the encompassing barrier.

(140) There is evidence showing the indivisibility of that entity from which direction is derived and which was posited to be unique. If that which moves upwards were to divide it, then either it moves upwards after penetrating the nearer of the two parts (in which case "up" refers only to the farther part) or it moves away from up (in which case "up" refers only to the nearer part). In either case, all of that which was assumed to be the direction of a part is the direction [of the whole], and the other part would have no role in it. While we said that that which has no role in direction is not to be considered together with that from which the direction is, the same arguments do not apply to the "down" determined by the center of the celestial sphere.[4] When the moving thing reaches its limit, it becomes, by virtue of its portion of bulk, part of that which has essentially the extreme of lowness. Each thing is related to a place by being in it, its place being different from it and different from its parts. It is possible for its parts to move in relation to the parts of that which is posited to be its place, whether the transfer cannot be complete (as is the case with the spheres) or can be complete (as is the case with other things). Therefore, place is the interior of its proximate container, and that which is not contained has no place.

كثيرة متألفة، فان كل واحد من هذه البرازخ، وان فُرض انّه غير ممكن ان تنفصل، فلا بدّ من ان تكون مؤتلفة، فيمكن تأليفها وانقسامها، فتقع الحركة الى لا شئ ولا صوب، وهو محال. والمختلفات لا بدّ من حصول افرادها اولا حتى ركب، والبسيط يجعل جسما واحدا دفعة، ثم يتجزى ان كان مما يقبل ذلك؛ فلا بدّ من المحيط الغير منفصل الواحد المتشابه ما يفرض له اجزاء فى الوهم. ولا يحصل من نفسه جهتان مختلفتان، فانّه واحد متشابه لا يحصل من نفسه إلاّ جهة واحدة وهى العلو، وكل ما قرب منه فهو العالى. فاذا لا يكون الاسفل إلاّ فى غاية البعد عنه وهو المركز، وهذا هو البرزخ المحيط.

(١٤٠) ومما يدل على انّ ما منه الجهة، المفروض انّه هو لا غير لا ينقسم؛ انّ المتحرك الى فوق لو قسمه، فاما ان يتحرك بعد عبور اقرب جزئيه الى فوق، وحينئذ لا يكون الفوق إلاّ الجزء الابعد؛ او يتحرك من الفوق،[٥] فلا تكون جهة الفوق إلاّ من الجزء الاقرب. فعلى التقديرين يصير جملة ما يفرض جهة جزؤه هو الجهة، فيكون الجزء الآخر لا مدخل له. وكلامنا فى عين ما منه الجهة التى لا نأخذ معه ما لا مدخل له فى الجهة. وليس هذا كالسفل المتعين بمركزية المحدد، اذا وصل المتحرك الى غايته، صار بحصة حجمه من الكل له السفلية القصوى بذاته. وكل شئ نسب الى مكان بانه فيه، يكون مكانه غيره وغير اجزائه، ويصح تبدل اجزائه بالنسبة الى اجزاء ما فُرض مكانا له، ان لم يمكن الانتقال بالكلية كما فى الافلاك، او النقل بالكلية كما فى غيرها. فاذن المكان هو باطن حاوية الاقرب، وما لا حاوى له لا مكان له.

Section [four]

[Showing that the movements of the spheres are voluntary and how the many are generated from the Light of Lights]

(141) The lifeless barrier does not revolve of itself; for no lifeless thing can have a goal that it seeks, reaches, and then separates itself from. If an inanimate thing does tend, of itself and by nature, toward something, it does not then leave its goal; for it would then tend by nature toward something from which it was also repelled—which is absurd. Every point that the celestial barriers seek they also leave without anything compelling them, for the lower has no power over the higher. Nor do they vie with each other, since there is no mutual resistance between the encompassing and the encompassed, neither one of which leaves its place. How, indeed, could they, when they have differing movements while sharing the daily movement? The daily movement is not compelled, for the compelled movement would not result from another movement,[5] and the body cannot at the same time have two different movements by essence in one state. There can be no doubt that some of the movements of the spheres are accidental and some essential, as when a man walks on board a ship in a direction different from its movement so that he accepts one motion essentially and the other by virtue of what he is in. Thus, the daily motion in which all the celestial barriers participate can only be from the encompassing sphere, while each one of the spheres has another motion. The mover of each one of these barriers is alive by essence and is therefore an incorporeal light. Thus, it is also plain to you that the barriers are ruled by the lights. Because the spheres are preserved from corruption, desires, and anger and the movement cannot be for the sake of some desire related to barriers, it must be for some luminous goal. The seven planets are known to have many movements, so they must have many barriers. None of these are independent; rather, each is in need of an incorporeal light for its realization and perfections.

فصل

[فى بيان انّ حركات الافلاك ارادية
وفى كيفية صدور الكثرة عن نور النوار]

(١٤١) البرزخ الميت لا يدور بنفسه؛ فان كل ما له مقصد يقصده ويصل اليه ويفارقه بنفسه، فليس بميت. اذ الموات اذا قصد بنفسه طبعا الى شئ لا يفارق مطلوبه، فانه يلزم منه ان يكون طالبا بالطبع لما يهرب عنه طبعا، وهو محال. والبرازخ العلوية كل نقطة تقصدها تفارقها قاسر لها اذ لا سلطة[٦] للسافل على العالى. وليس بعضها مزاحما للبعض، اذ لا مدافعة بين المحيط والمحاط اللّذين كل[٧] منهما لا يفارق موضعه، كيف ولها حركات مختلفة ويشارك الكل فى حركة يومية؟ وليست الحركة اليومية قسرية، فان القسرية لا تتمكن[٨] من حركة اُخرى ولا يتحرك الجسم فى حالة واحدة بحركتين مختلفتين بذاته، فلا بدّ وان يكون شئ من حركات الافلاك بالعرض وشيئ منها بالذات، كالمارّ فى السفينة على خلاف حركتها، فيقبل احدهما بذاته، والآخر بتوسط ما هو فيه. فلا تكون الحركة اليومية التى اشترك فيها جميع البرازخ السماوية، إلاّ من محيط، ولكل واحد حركة اُخرى. ومحرّك كل واحد من هذه البرازخ حيّ بذاته، فيكون نورا مجردا. ويلوح لك من هذا ايضا انّ البرازخ مقهورة للانوار، والافلاك آمنة من الفساد والشهوات والغضب، فليست الحركة لمراد برزخى، فتكون لمقصد نورى. والكواكب السبعة عهد لها حركات كثيرة فلا بدّ لها من برازخ كثيرة، وكل هذه غير غنية بل مفتقرة فى تحققها وكمالاتها الى نور مجرد.

(142) Now, only the Proximate Light comes to be from the Light of Lights. The Proximate Light does not contain multiple aspects, since any multiplicity in it would imply multiplicity in that which necessitated it and thus imply the absurdity of multiplicity in the Light of Lights. However, there is multiplicity in the barriers. If only a single barrier and no light came to be from the Proximate Light, existence would cease with it. But this is not so, since barriers do have multiplicity, as do their managing lights. Then, if an incorporeal light came to be from the Proximate Light, and from this light came another incorporeal light without ever leading to barriers, everything would be lights. Thus, although the Proximate Light cannot bring into being a dusky substance with respect to its own luminosity, yet still a barrier and an incorporeal light must result from it, since it contains dependence in itself and independence by virtue of the First. Its intellection of its dependence is a dark state; but it beholds the Light of Lights and beholds its own essence, since there is no veil between it and the Light of Lights. There are only veils among barriers, dusky substances, and dimensions. The Light of Lights and the incorporeal lights have no direction or dimension at all. Thus, by that whereby [an incorporeal light] beholds the Light of Lights, it shadows and darkens itself in comparison to It, since the more perfect light rules the more deficient. By the manifestation to itself of its dependence and the darkening of its own essence in its contemplation of the glory of the Light of Lights in relation to itself, a shadow results from [the incorporeal light]. This is the loftiest barrier, greatest of the barriers, the all-encompassing barrier of which we made mention. But with respect to its independence and its necessity by the Light of Lights and its contemplation of its glory and might, it brings into being another incorporeal light. The barrier is its shadow, and the self-subsistent light is illumination from it. Its shadow is only due to the darkness of its dependence. By "darkness" here, we merely mean that which is not light in its own essence.

A principle [explaining how multiplicity comes to be]

(143) Since there is no veil between the lower and the higher light, the lower light beholds the higher and the higher shines upon the lower. Thus, a ray[6] from the Light of Lights shines upon the Proximate Light. If it is argued that the aspects of the Light of Lights must become multiple by

(١٤٢) ولما لم يصدر من نور الانوار غير النور الاقرب وليس فى النور الاقرب ايضا جهات كثيرة، فانّه ترجع الكثرة فيه الى كثرة جهات ما يقتضيه فيفضى الى تكثر نور الانوار، وهو محال. وفى البرازخ كثرة، فان حصل به برزخ واحد ولم يحصل منه نور، توقف الوجود عنده، وليس كذا. اذ فى البرازخ كثرة وفى الانوار المدبّرة كثرة.[٩] وان حصل من النور الاقرب ايضا نور مجرد وهكذا من هذا النور نور مجرد آخر فلم يتأد الى البرازخ. ثم ما دام كل واحد نورا، فمن حيث نوريته لا يحصل منه الجوهر الغاسق فلا بدّ وان يكون النور الاقرب يحصل به برزخ نور مجرد. فان له فقرا فى نفسه وغنى بالأوّل. فله تعقل فقره، وهو هيئة ظلمانية له. وهو يشاهد نور الانوار ويشاهد ذاته لعدم الحجاب بينه وبين نور الانوار، اذ الحجب[١٠] إنمّا تكون فى البرازخ والغواسق والابعاد، ولا جهة ولا بعد لنور الانوار ولا للانوار المجردة بالكلية. فبما يشاهد من نور النور، ليستغسق ويستظلم نفسه بالقياس اليه، فان النور الأتمّ يقهر النور الانقص. فبظهور فقره له واستغساق ذاته عند مشاهدة جلال نور الانوار بالنسبة اليه، يحصل منه ظل هو البرزخ الاعلى الّذى لا برزخ اعظم منه، وهو المحيط المذكور. وباعتبار غناه ووجوبه بنور الانوار ومشاهدة جلاله وعظمته، يحصل منه نور مجرد آخر. فالبرزخ ظله والنور القائم ضوء منه، وظله إنمّا هو لظلمة فقره. ولسنا نعنى بالظلمة إلاّ ما ليس بنور فى ذاته هاهنا.

قاعدة [فى كيفية التكثر]

(١٤٣) النور السافل اذا لم يكن بينه وبين العالى حجاب، يشاهد العالى ويشرق نور العالى عليه، فالنور الاقرب يشرق عليه شعاع من نور الانوار. فان قيل: يلزم ان تتكثر جهة الانوار باعطاء الوجود والاشراق،

Its giving existence and illuminating, one may reply that that which is impossible because it leads to multiplicity is that the Light of Lights should give existence to two things simply by virtue of Its essence. That is not the case here. The existence of the Proximate Light is solely from the essence of the Light of Lights, but the Light of Lights shines Its light upon the Proximate Light simply by virtue of the suitability of the recipient, its love for the Light of Lights, and the absence of any veil. There are a multiplicity of aspects here, a receptive cause, and conditions. Many different things may indeed result from the one thing by virtue of differing and multiple states of receptivity.

Section[7] [five]

[Concerning the generosity of the Light of Lights]

(144) Generosity is giving that which is appropriate without any recompense. The one who seeks praise or reward works for a wage, as does the one who seeks to be free of blame and the like. But there is nothing more generous than that which is light in its own reality. By its essence, it reveals itself to and emanates upon every receptive one. The True King is He who possesses the essence of everything but whose essence is possessed by none. He is the Light of Lights.

A principle [governing beholding]

(145) Since you know that vision is not by the imprinting of the form of its object in the eye nor by something emerging from the eye, it can only be by the illuminated object being opposite a sound eye—nothing more. Imagination and images in mirrors will be explained later, for they have great importance. Being opposite amounts to the absence of a veil between that which sees and that which is seen. Extreme nearness hinders vision only because illumination or luminosity is a condition of being seen. There must be two lights: the seeing light and the light seen. When the eyelid is covered, there can be no question of its being illuminated by external lights, nor does the light of vision have the power of luminosity to illuminate it. Thus, one cannot see due to the lack of illumination. This is the case with all excessive nearness. Extreme distance acts as a veil because of the small degree to which they face each other. Thus, the nearer the illuminated object or light, the more easily it is beheld, so long as it remains a light or illuminated.

فيقال:[١١] الممتنع الموجب للتكثر إنمّا هو ان يوجد عنه شيئان عن مجرد ذاته وليس هاهنا كذا. اما وجود النور الاقرب، فلذاته فحسب. واما شروق نوره عليه فلصلوح القابل وعشقه اليه وعدم الحجاب، فهاهنا جهات كثيرة وعلة قابلية وشرائط. والشئ الواحد يجوز ان يحصل منه لاختلاف احوال القوابل وتعددها اشياء متعددة مختلفة.

فصل[١٢]

[فى جود نور الانوار]

(١٤٤) الجود افادة ما ينبغى لا لعوض، فالطالب لحمدة او ثواب[١٣] معامل وكذا المتخلّص عن مذّمة ونحوها. فلا شئ أشدّ جودا ممن هو نور فى حقيقة نفسه، وهو متجل وفياض لذاته على كل قابل، والملك الحق[١٤] هو من له ذات كل شئ وليست ذاته لشئ وهو نور الانوار.

قاعدة [فى المشاهدة]

(١٤٥) لما علمت انّ الابصار ليس بانطباع صورة المرئى فى العين، وليس بخروج شئ من البصر، فليس إلاّ بمقابلة المستنير للعين السليمة لا غير. واما الخيال والمثل فى المرايا، وسيأتى[١٥] حالها، فانّ لها خطبا آخر. وحاصل المقابلة يرجع الى عدم الحجاب بين الباصر والمبصَر. فانّ القرب المفرط إنمّا يمنع الرؤية، لانّ الاستنارة او النورية شرط للمرئى فلا بدّ من النورين: نور باصر ونور مبصَر. والجفن لدى الغموض لا تتصور استنارته بالانوار الخارجة، وليس لنور البصر من القوة النورية ما ينوّره فلا يرى لعدم الاستنارة. وكذا كل قرب مفرط. والبعد المفرط فى حكم الحجاب لقلة المقابلة. فالمستنير او النور كلّما كان اقرب، كان اولى بالمشاهدة ما بقى نورا او مستنيرا.

Another Illuminationist principle [explaining that beholding the light is not the same as the shining of a ray of that light upon that which beholds it]

(146) Know that your eye both beholds and is shone upon by a ray. The shining of the ray is not beholding; for the ray falls upon the eye wherever it is, but the seeing eye can only behold the Sun when it faces the Sun from a great distance, as was indicated before. Were the eyelid luminous or the Sun as near as the eyelid, both the ray and the beholding would be increased accordingly.

Section [six]

[Showing that every higher light has dominance in relation to the lower light and that the lower light has love in relation to the higher light]

(147) The lower light cannot comprehend the higher light, for the higher light dominates it; but the lower light nevertheless beholds the higher. When the lights become many, the higher light possesses a dominance over the lower light, and the lower has a desire and passion for the higher. The Light of Lights has a dominance in relation to what is other than It. It does not Itself have a passion for another, but It does have a passion for Itself, because Its perfection is evident to It. It is the most beautiful of things, the most perfect of things. It is more evident to Itself than anything else; for nothing else is so evident, either to that thing itself or to another. Pleasure occurs only by the apprehension of the actual perfection in respect to its being perfection and actual. He who is unconscious of the acquisition of a perfection does not experience pleasure. The pleasure experienced by the one who experiences pleasure is in the measure of his perfection and his apprehension of his perfection. Since there is nothing more perfect, nothing more beautiful than the Light of Lights—nothing more evident to Itself and to another—then there is nothing more pleasurable to Itself and to another than the Light of Lights. It has a passion for Its own essence and is the object of the passion of its own essence and of everything else.

At the root of the deficient light is passion for the higher light. At the root of the higher light is dominance over the lower light. Just as the fact that the Light of Lights is evident to its essence is not something added

قاعدة أُخرى اشراقية [فى انّ مُشاهدة النور
غير اشراق شعاع ذلك النور على مَن يشاهده]

(١٤٦) اعلم ان لعينك مشاهدة وشروق شعاع. وشروق الشعاع[١٦] غير المشاهدة، فان الشعاع يقع عليها حيث هى والمشاهدة للشمس لا تكون إلاّ مباينة للبصر على مسافة بعيدة حيث كانت الشمس، كما سلفت[١٧] الاشارة اليه. ولو كان الجفن نوريا او كانت الشمس فى القرب مثل الجفن، لزاد الشعاع والمشاهدة ايضا.

فصل

[فى انّ لكل نور عال قهرا بالنسبة الى النور
السافل، وللسافل محبة بالنسبة الى العالى]

(١٤٧) النور السافل لا يحيط بالنور العالى، فان النور العالى يقهره، اما ليس لا يشاهده. والانوار اذا تكثرت، فللعالى على السافل قهر وللسافل الى العالى شوق وعشق. فنور الانوار له قهر بالنسبة الى ما سواه، ولا يعشق هو غيره ويعشق[١٨] نفسه، لانّ كماله ظاهر له وهو اجمل الاشياء واكملها، وظهوره لنفسه أشدّ من كل ظهور لشئ بالقياس الى غيره ونفسه. وليست اللذة إلاّ بالشعور بالكمال الحاصل من حيث انّه كمال وحاصل. فالغافل عن حصول الكمال لا يلتذ. وكل لذة للاذ إنمّا هى بقدر كماله وادراكه لكماله، ولا اكمل ولا اجمل من نور الانوار، ولا اظهر منه لذاته ولغيره، فلا الذّ منه لذاته وغيره. وهو عاشق لذاته فحسب، ومعشوق لذاته وغيره.

وفى سنخ النور الناقص عشق الى النور العالى، وفى سنخ النور العالى قهر للنور السافل. وكما لا يزيد ظهور نور الانوار لذاته على ذاته، فلا

to its essence, so, too, its pleasure and passion are not additional to its essence. Just as the luminosity of another cannot be compared to it, the pleasure and passion of another cannot be compared to its pleasure in its own essence or to its passion for its own essence—nor can the passion of other things for another be compared to their passion for and pleasure in it. Thus, all existence is ordered on the basis of love and dominance. The rest of this will be explained to you. Since the incorporeal lights are multiple, they necessarily have the most perfect order.

Section [seven]

[Showing that the love of each lower light for itself is dominated by its love for the higher light]

(148) The Proximate Light beholds and is illuminated by the Light of Lights. It loves the Light of Lights and itself, but its love for itself is dominated by its love for the Light of Lights.

Section [eight]

[Showing that the incorporeal light does not shine by something being separated from it]

(149) The illumination of the Light of Lights upon the incorporeal lights is not by something being separated from it, as has already been made clear to you. Rather, the illumination is a radiated light that occurs due to it in the incorporeal light. It is like the illumination caused by the Sun in that which admits of such illumination. Beholding is another matter, to which we have made an analogy for you. The light that occurs in the incorporeal lights from the Light of Lights is that which we distinguish by the name "propitious[8] light." It is an accidental light, for accidental light is divided into that which occurs in bodies and that which occurs in the incorporeal lights.

تزداد لذته وعشقه على ذاته. وكما لا يقاس نورية غيره اليه، فلا يقاس لذة غيره وعشق غيره الى لذته بذاته وعشقه لذاته، ولا عشق الاشياء وتلذذها بغيره الى عشقها وتلذذها به. فانتظم الوجود كله من المحبة والقهر، وسيأتيك تتمّة هذا. والانوار المجردة اذا تكثّرت، يلزمما النظام الأتمّ.

فصل

[فى انّ محبة كل نور سافل
مقهورة فى محبته للنور العال]

(١٤٨) فللنور الاقرب مشاهدة لنور الانوار وشروق منه عليه، ومحبة له ولنفسه، ومحبة لنفسه مقهورة فى قهر محبة نور الانوار.

فصل

[فى ان اشراق النور المجرد
ليس بانفصال شئ منه]

(١٤٩) اشراق نور الانوار[19] على الانوار المجردة ليس بانفصال شئ منه كما تبيّن لك، بل هو نور شعاعى يحصل منه فى النور المجرد على مثال ما مرّ فى الشمس على ما يقبل منها، والمشاهدة أمر آخر كما ضربنا لك المثال. فالنور الحاصل فى النور المجرد من نور الانوار هو الّذى نخصصه باسم «النور السانح» وهو نور عارض. والنور العارض ينقسم الى: ما يكون فى الاجسام، والى ما يكون[20] فى الانوار المجردة.

Section [nine]

[On how and in what order the many are generated from the truly one]

(150) From the Proximate Light a barrier and an incorporeal light result, and from this light result another incorporeal light and barrier. This continues until there are the nine spheres and the elemental world. You know that the succession of ordered lights must be finite, so the series ceases with a light from which no other incorporeal light results. Since we meet with a star in each of the ethereal barriers—and, in the sphere of fixed stars, with such stars as are beyond the power of man to number—to these must correspond individuals and aspects beyond our reckoning. Thus, it is known that the sphere of fixed stars does not result from the Proximate Light, since the causal aspects thereof do not suffice for the fixed stars. If it is from one of the higher lights, that light cannot have many aspects, especially in the view of those who consider each intellect to have only the aspects of necessity and contingency. If it is from the lower lights, how, then, may this sphere be conceived to be greater and higher than the barriers of the higher intellects when its stars are more numerous than theirs? This leads to absurdities. Let us not, then, linger over this series that the Peripatetics talk of. Each star in the sphere of fixed stars has a particularity, requiring it to be necessitated and requiring something to necessitate it, by which it is particularized.

(151) Therefore, the dominating lights—that is, the incorporeal lights free of connections with barriers—are more in number than ten, or twenty, or one hundred, or two hundred, or a thousand, or two thousand, or a hundred thousand. Some among them cause no independent barrier, for the individual independent barriers are fewer in number than the stars and are ordered in rank. So a second light results from the Proximate Light, and from the second a third, and likewise a fourth and fifth, up to a great number. Each of these beholds the Light of Lights and is shone upon by Its rays. Moreover, light is reflected from one to another

فصل

[فى كيفية صدور الكثرة عن الواحد الأحد، و ترتيبها]

(١٥٠) النور الاقرب لما حصل منه برزخ ونور مجرد، ومن هذا نور مجرد آخر وبرزخ، فاذا أخذ هكذا الى ان يحصل تسعة افلاك والعالم العنصرى، وتعلم ان الانوار المترتبة سلسلتها واجبة النهاية، فينتهى الترتيب[٢١] الى نور لا يحصل منه نور آخر مجرد. واذا صادفنا فى كل برزخ من الاثيريات كوكبا وفى كثرة الثوابت من الكواكب ما ليس للبشر حصرها، فلا بدّ لهذه الاشياء من اعداد وجهات لا تنحصر عندنا. فتعلم[٢٢] انّ كثرة الثوابت لا تحصل من النور الاقرب اذ لا تفى جهات الاقتضاء فيه بالكواكب الثابتة. فهو ان كان من احد من العوالى، فليس فيه جهات كثيرة سيّما على رأى من يجعل[٢٣] فى كل عقل جهة وجوب وامكان لا غير. وان كان من السوافل، فكيف يتصور ان يكون اكبر من برازخ العوالى وفوقها، وكواكبه اكثر من كواكبها؟ ويؤدى الى المحالات، فلا يستمر على هذا الترتيب الّذى ذكره المشاؤون وكل كوكب فى كثرة الثوابت له تخصص لا بدّ له من اقتضاء ومقتض يتخصص به.

(١٥١) فاذن الانوار القاهرة، وهى المجردات عن البرازخ وعلائقها، اكثر من عشرة وعشرين ومائة ومائتين والف والفين ومائة الف[٢٤] ومنها ما لا يحصل منه برزخ مستقل، فانّ البرازخ المستقلة اعدادها اقلّ من عدد الكواكب وهى مترتبة؛ فيحصل من النور الاقرب ثان، ومن الثانى ثالث، وهكذا رابع وخامس الى مبلغ كثير. وكل واحد يشاهد نور الانوار ويقع عليه شعاعه. والانوار القاهرة ينعكس النور من

of the dominating lights. Each higher light shines upon those which are below it in rank, and the lower light receives rays from the Light of Lights by the mediacy of those which are above it, rank on rank. Thus, the second dominating light receives the propitious light from the Light of Lights twice: once from it, without intermediary, and another time with respect to the Proximate Light. The third light receives it four times: the two reflections from its master,[9] from the Light of Lights without mediacy, and from the Proximate Light. The fourth receives it eight times: the four reflections from its master, the two reflections from the second, once from the Proximate Light, and from the Light of Lights without intermediary. In this way they are doubled and redoubled to a very great number; for in the case of the higher incorporeal lights, the lower light is not veiled from the Light of Lights, veiling being a peculiarity of the dimensions and distractions of the barriers. Moreover, each dominating light beholds the Light of Lights, and beholding is not the same as being shone upon and the emanation of rays, as you know. If the propitious lights have redoubled from the Light of Lights in this way, how, then, must be the doubling by reflection of each higher light by its beholding and by its shining its light upon each lower light with, and without intermediaries!

(152) If the rays of physical light fall upon a barrier, the light on it is increased in accordance with their numbers. These may be united in a single locus in such a way that the individual rays may not be distinguished except through their causes. When the rays of several lamps fall upon a wall, for example, though one of them may be shaded, another will remain. This is not like something that becomes more intense from one or two sources with the intensity remaining after them, nor is it like the parts of a cause of one thing, however it may be. Many illuminations may be combined in a single locus, like two desires for two things in a single locus. The barrier has no knowledge of the increase caused by each illumination, but the essence of a living thing is itself conscious of what illuminates it and of the increase in illumination from each. Thus, a great number of dominating lights result, rank on rank, one from another, in accordance with the particular beholdings and the magnitude of the complete rays. These are the fundamental and highest dominating lights. Then other

بعضها على بعض، فكل عال يشرق على ما تحته بالمرتبة، وكل سافل يقبل الشعاع من نور الانوار بتوسط ما فوقه رتبة رتبة، حتى انّ القاهر الثانى يقبل من نور السانح من نور الانوار مرتين: مرة منه بغير واسطة، وباعتبار النور الاقرب مرة أُخرى. والثالث اربع مرات: ينعكس مرتان صاحبه عليه، وما يقبل من نور الانوار بغير واسطة، ومن النور الاقرب. والرابع ثمانى مرات: اربع مرات من انعكاس صاحبه، ومرتا الثانى، ومرة من النور الاقرب من نور الانوار بغير واسطة. وهكذا تتضاعف الى مبلغ كثير، فان الانوار المجردة العالية لا تحجب بين السافلة وبين نور الانوار اذ الحجاب من خاصية الابعاد وشواغل البرازخ، مع ان كل نور قاهر يشاهد نور الانوار، والمشاهدة غير الشروق وفيض الشعاع على ما علمت. فاذا تضاعفت الانوار السانحة هكذا من نور الانوار، فكيف مشاهدة كل عال واشراق نوره على سافل من غير واسطة وبواسطة متضاعف الانعكاس.

(١٥٢) واعلم ان الاشعة البرزخية اذا وقعت على برزخ، يشتد النور فيه لاعداد. وقد يجتمع فى محل واحد ما لا مايز اعداده إلاّ بتمايز العلل كأشعة سُرُج فى حائط، فيقع الظن عن بعضها مع بقاء بعض، وليس هذا كشئ يشتد من مبدأ واحد او عن مبدأين، ويبقى بعدهما الشدة؛ ولا كاجزاء علة لواحد كيف كان. وقد تجتمع اشراقات مّا كثيرة فى محل واحد مثل شوقين الى شيئين فى محل واحد،[٢٥] ولكن لا علم للبرزخ بزيادة من كل اشراق، بخلاف ما اذا كانت الاشراقات المتعددة على حىّ لا تغيب عنه ذاته ولا ما يشرق عليه ولا ما يزداد من كل واحد. فيحصل عدد من القواهر المترتبة كثير بعضها من بعض باعتبار آحاد المشاهدات وعظمتة الاشعة التامة، وهى القواهر الاصول الاعلين. ثم

individual lights result from these fundamental lights by reason of the combinations of aspects, interactions, and correspondences. For example, there is the interaction of the aspect of dependence with the rays, or the interactions of the aspects of independence, dominance, or love with them. There is the interaction of the rays of one dominating light with another, or the rays of dominating lights with the aspects of beholding each other. There is the interaction of their substantial essences, or the interaction of one of the rays of some one of them with one of the rays of another. The fixed stars and their sphere result from the interaction of the rays of all of them, especially the lower, weak lights with the aspect of dependence. The constellations of the fixed stars correspond to the interaction of the rays of some with others. By the interaction of the rays with the aspects of independence, dominance, and love, and the extraordinary correspondences between the perfect, intense rays and the others, the dominating lights bring into being the celestial archetypes[10] of species and the talismans of the simples, the elemental compounds, and all that is beneath the sphere of the stars.

(153) The origin of each of these talismans is a dominating light that is the "archetype of the talisman" and the luminous self-subsistent species. Insofar as the archetypes of the talismans fall under the classes of love, dominance, and moderation in accordance with their origins, the planets and other things differ in being fortunate, sinister, or intermediate. The dominating luminous species are prior to their individuals—that is, prior intellectually. The most noble contingency[11] necessitates the existence of these incorporeal luminous species. The species do not occur in our world simply by chance, for there is no man save man, nor wheat save wheat. The species preserved among us are not by chance. They are not due solely to the conception of the souls moving the spheres, nor are they ends. Because the conceptions of these souls are from above them, they must have causes. We shall prove the nonexistence of that which they name "providence." There are no such things as species forms corresponding to what is below them engraved in the dominating incorporeal lights, for

يحصل من هذه الاصول بسبب تراكيب الجهات ومشاركاتها ومناسباتها، كما بمشاركة جهة الفقر مع الشعاعات، وكذا بمشاركة جهة الاستغناء معها، وكذا بمشاركة جهة القهر معها، وكذا بمشاركة جهة المحبة معها، وبمشاركات اشعة قاهرة[٢٦] بعضها مع بعض، وبمشاركات اشعة انوار قاهرة ومشاهداتها بعضها مع بعض[٢٧] وبمشاركات ذواتها الجوهرية، وبمشاركات بعض اشعة بعض مع بعض اشعة غيره عددا عددا.[٢٨] فبمشاركات[٢٩] اشعة الجميع سيّما الضعيفة النازلة فى الجميع مع جهة الفقر يحصل الثوابت وكرتها وصور الثوابت المتناسبة باعتبار مشاركة اشعة بعض مع بعض؛ وبمشاركات الاشعة مع جهة الاستغناء والقهر والمحبة والمناسبات العجيبة بين الاشعة الشديدة الكاملة والبواقى تحصل الانوار القاهرة ارباب الاصنام النوعية الفلكية وطلمسات البسائط والمركبات العنصرية وكل ما تحب كرة الثوابت.

(١٥٣) فمبدأ كل من هذه الطلمسات هو نور قاهر هو «صاحب الطلسم» والنوع القائم النورى. وبحسب ما يقع ارباب الطلسمات تحت اقسام المحبة والقهر والاعتدال لمباديها تختلف فى الكواكب وغيرها ما يوجد سعدية ونحسية واعتدالا. والانواع النورية القاهرة اقدم من اشخاصها اى متقدمة عقلا. والامكان الاشرف يقتضى وجود هذه الانواع النورية المجردة. والانواع ليست فى عالمنا عن مجرد الاتفاقات، فانّه لا يكون من الانسان غير الانسان، ومن البُرّ غير البرّ. فالانواع المحفوظة عندنا ليست عن مجرد الاتفاق ولا عن مجرد تصور نفوس محركة للفلك وغايات، لأن تصوراتها من فوقها اذ لا بدّ من علل لها. وما سمّوه «عناية» سنبطله. والصور النوعية المنتقشة فى المجردات

these lights are not affected by what is below them. Nor do the forms occurring accidentally in some of them result from the forms occurring in another, for this would imply multiplicity in the Light of Lights. Thus, their species must be self-subsistent and fixed in the World of Light.

(154) It is inconceivable that dominating lights of equal rank come into existence simultaneously from the Light of Lights, for multiplicity is inconceivable from It. Thus, there must be intermediate lights ranked vertically. Nor can the higher-ranked dominating lights be archetypes and of equal rank. Therefore, the archetypes of equal rank must be caused by the exalted lights and their multiplicity be from the interactions of rays in the higher lights. If some excellence and some deficiency is conceivable in the archetypes of talismans due to the perfection and deficiency of the rays that necessitate them, the like must occur in the talismans,[12] so that one species rules over another species in some respect, but not in all. Were the ranks of volume among the spheres caused by the exalted ranked lights, Mars would be unconditionally more noble than the Sun and Venus. This is not so, since some have larger planets and some larger spheres while being equal in other respects. Thus, the same must also must be true of their lords—which is to say, the archetypes. The fixed and everlasting excellences are not based on chance, but on the archetypes of the ranks of their sphere.[13]

(155) The incorporeal lights are divided into two classes. The first are the dominating lights, those with no connection to barriers, either of imprinting or control. The dominating lights include exalted dominating lights and formal dominating lights: the archetypes. Second are the lights managing barriers. Though they are not imprinted in the barriers, they occur from each master of an idol in its barrier shadow with respect to some exalted luminous aspect. If its barrier admits of being controlled by a managing light, the barrier itself is from an aspect of dependence. The incorporeal light does not admit of connection or division; for division,

القاهرة المطابقة لما تحتها غير صحيحة، اذ هى لا تنفصل عما تحتها، ولا تكون الصور العارضة فى بعضها حاصلة عن صور عارضة فى بعض، فانه ينتهى الى تكثر نور الانوار. فلا بدّ ان يكون نوعها قائما بذاته فى عالم النور ثابتا.

(١٥٤) ولا يتصور ان توجد الانوار القاهرة المتكافئة عن نور الانوار معا، اذ لا تصور للكثرة عنه، فلا بدّ من متوسطات مترتبة طولية. وليست القواهر العالية المترتبة اصحاب اصنام متكافئة، فيجب ان يكون اصحاب الاصنام المتكافئة عن الاعلين، وتكثرها بمناسبات اشعة فى الاعلين. وان كان يتصور فضيلة مّا فى اصحاب الطلسمات ونقص مّا لأجل كمال الاشعة المقتضية بها ونقصها، فيقع فى اصحاب الطلسمات[٣٠] مثلها، حتى يكون متسلطا على نوع من وجه لا من جميع الوجوه. ولو كانت الترتيبات الحجمية فى الافلاك للاعلين[٣١] المترتبين، لكان المريخ أشرف من الشمس مطلقا ومن الزهرة، وليس كذا. بل بعضها اعظم كوكبا وبعضها اعظم فلكا وبينها تكافؤ من وجوه أُخرى. فبين اربابها، اى اصحاب الاصنام، ايضا كذا. والفضائل الدائمة الثابتة ونحوها لا تبتنى على الاتفاقات، بل على مثل[٣٢] مراتب الفلك.[٣٣]

(١٥٥) فالانوار المجردة تنقسم الى انوار قاهرة، وهى التى لا علاقة لها مع البرازخ لا بالانطباع ولا بالتصرف؛[٣٤] وفى الانوار القاهرة انوار قاهرة اعلون وانوار قاهرة صورية ارباب الاصنام؛ والى انوار مدبرة للبرازخ، وان لم تكن منطبعة فيها يحصل من كل صاحب صنم فى ظله البرزخى باعتبار جهة عالية نورية، والبرزخ إنمّا هو من جهة فقرية، اذا كان برزخه قابلا لتصرف نور مدبر. والنور المجرد لا يقبل الاتصال

though it is but the lack of connection, is only said of that in which there might be connection. The aspects of dependence in the exalted lights is made evident in the common barrier.[14] These aspects of dependence are also made evident in the talismanic archetypes as an aspect of dependence by which their luminosity is diminished. Dependence in the lower lights is greater than in the exalted lights. Since ranks must be finite, there cannot be a dominating light from every dominating light, nor multiplicity from every multiplicity, nor a ray from every ray. Deficiency ends in that which necessitates nothing at all, even though multiplicity may only be conceived to be caused by multiplicity and a dominating light by another dominating light.

(156) Since the spheres are alive and have managing lights, their managing lights are not their causes, since the luminous cause is not perfected by the dusky substance, and the dusky substance does not dominate the luminous cause by this connection. On the other hand, the managing light is dominated in a certain respect by its connection. That which manages it is an incorporeal light that we might name "the commanding light." From this fact, you will know that by virtue of the First it necessarily has the aspects of dominance and love; and in the dominating lights there are the two aspects of the duskiness of dependence and luminosity. Thus, the classes of effects must be ordered as follows: a light in which dominance is predominant; a light in which love is predominant; a dusky substance in which dominance is predominant, as some of the luminous planets; another dusky substance in which love is predominant, as other luminous planets; nonluminous dusky substances in which dominance is predominant—the ethereals immune from induced corruption; and the dusky substances in which love and lowliness are predominant—the elementals obedient to and loving their vile lights when they are veiled from them. Since fire is near to the ethereals, it also necessarily has dominance over what is below it. We will explain that, if God the Exalted be willing.

(157) Know that in relation to its effect every luminous cause possesses love and dominance, and that its effect possesses a love whose concomitant is humility. Therefore, all existence occurs in pairs, being divided into luminous and dusky; love and dominance; might—the concomitant

والانفصال، فان الانفصال وان كان عدم الاتصال، لا يقال إلاّ فيما يمكن فيه الاتصال. والاعلون جهات فقرهم تظهر فى البرزخ المشترك، وتظهر ايضا فى اصحاب الطلسمات جهات فقر الاعلين بجهة فقرية تنقص من نوريته. والفقر فى السافلين اكثر منه فى الاعلين. والنهاية فى المترتبات واجبة، فلا يلزم من كل قاهر قاهر، ولا عن كل كثرة كثرة، ولا عن كل شعاع شعاع، وينتهى النقص الى ما لا يقتضى شيئا اصلا، وان كان لزوم الكثرة إنمّا يتصور عن كثرة ولزوم القاهر عن قاهر.

(١٥٦) واذا كانت الافلاك حيّة ولها مدبرات، فلا تكون مدبراتها عللها، اذ لا تستكمل العلة النورية بالجوهر الغاسق. ولا يقهرها الغاسق بالعلاقة، فانّ النور المدبر مقهور من وجه بالعلاقة. فيكون مدبرها نورا مجردا قد نسمّيه «النور الاسفهبد». وهذا يرشدك الى انه لما كان من لدن الأوّل ضروريا[٣٥] جهات قهر ومحبة، وفى القواهر جهتا استغساق فقرى واستنارة، فتركبت الاقسام فى المعلولات، فصارت هكذا نور الغالب عليه القهر؛ ونور الغالب عليه المحبة، وغاسق فيه القهر من المستنيرات الكوكبية، وغاسق الغالب فيه المحبة ايضا من المستنيرات الكوكبية،[٣٦] وغواسق غير مستنيرة الغالب فيها القهر وهى الاثيريات المتأبية عن الفساد المؤثرة، وغواسق الغالب عليها المحبة والذل وهى العنصرياة المطيعة لها العاشقة لاضوائها القبيحة عند احتجابها عنها. ثم النار لما قربت من الاثيريات، لزمها ايضا قهر على ما تحتها، وسنذكر شرح ذلك ان شاء الله تعالى.

(١٥٧) واعلم انّ لكل علة نورية بالنسبة الى المعلول محبة وقهر، والمعلول بالنسبة اليه[٣٧] محبة يلزمها ذلّ. ولأجل ذلك صار الوجود بحسب تقاسيم النورية والغاسقية، والمحبة والقهر، والعزّ[٣٨]

of dominance in relation to the lower—and humility—the concomitant of love in relation to the higher. As it is written, "All things have We created in pairs, that perchance ye might take heed" [Qurʾān 51:49].

Section [ten]
[Completing the discussion of the fixed stars and the other planets]

(158) Since the arrangement of the fixed stars is not haphazard, it is the shadow of some intelligible order; but this order—nay, even the pattern of the planets among the fixed stars—is beyond the knowledge of any man. The wonders of the ethereal world, the relations among the spheres, their precise and certain enumeration—all these are very difficult. And there is nothing to prevent there being other wonders imperceptible to us in and beyond the fixed stars.[15]

(159) There is nothing lifeless in the ethereal world. The sovereignty and power of the higher managing lights reach the spheres through the mediacy of the planets. From them their faculties go forth, and the planet is like the absolute and supreme organ. "Hūrakhsh," who is the talisman of "Shahrīr,"[16] is a light of great brilliance, the maker of the day, lord of the sky, to be venerated, according to the custom of the Illuminationists. It does not exceed the planets by magnitude and nearness—rather, by intensity—for the magnitude of all that which is seen from the fixed stars at night and from the rest of the planets is incomparably greater than the Sun and yet does not make the day.

Section [eleven]
[In explanation of His knowledge—exalted be He!—according to the Illuminationist principle]

(160) It is clear that vision is not conditioned on the imprinting of an image or on the emission of something: it is sufficient for there to be no veil between the seer and the object of vision. The Light of Lights is

اللازم للقهر بالنسبة الى السافل والذل اللازم للمحبة بالنسبة الى العالى واقعا على ازواج،[39] كما قال تعالى «ومن كل شئ خلقنا زوجين لعلكم تذكرون».[40]

فصل

[فى تتمّة الكلام على الثوابت وبعض الكواكب]

(١٥٨) ولما لم يكن ترتيب الثوابت واقعا على جزاف، فيكون ظلا لترتيب عقلى. ومن الترتيبات، بل ومن الكواكب فى الثوابت، ما لا يحيط البشر به علما وعجائب عالم الاثير ونسب الافلاك وحصرها فى عدد بحيث يتيقن أمر صعب، ولا مانع عن ان يكون وراء[41] الثوابت عجائب أُخرى وكذا فى فلك الثوابت ولا يدركها.[42]

(١٥٩) واعلم انه لا ميت فى عالم الاثير. وسلطان الانوار المدبرة العلوية وقوتها تصل الى الافلاك بتوسط الكواكب، ومنها ينبعث القوى والكواكب كالعضو الرئيس المطلق. و«هورَخش» الّذى هو طلسم «شهرير» نور شديد الضوء، فاعل النهار، ورئيس السماء، واجب تعظيمه فى سنة الاشراق. وما ازداد على الكواكب بمجرد المقدار والقرب بل بالشدة، فان ما يتراءى من الثوابت بالليل وباقى السيارات مقدار مجموعها اكثر من الشمس بما لا يتقايس ولا يفعل النهار.

فصل

[فى بيان علمه تعالى على ما هو قاعدة الاشراق]

(١٦٠) لما تبيّن ان الإبصار ليس من شرطه انطباع شبح او خروج شئ، بل كفى عدم الحجاب بين الباصر والمبصَر، فنور الانوار ظاهر

evident to Itself, as was shown before, and all else is evident to It. "Not the weight of an atom in the heavens or in the earth escapes Him" [Qurʾān 34:3], since nothing veils It from anything. Thus, Its knowledge and vision are one, as are Its luminosity and power, since light emanates by Its essence.

(161) The Peripatetics and their followers say: "The Necessary Existent's knowledge is not something superadded to It but is only its lack of absence from Its incorporeal essence." They also say: "The existence of things is from Its knowledge of them." Against them, it may be argued that if [the Necessary Existent] knows and then the thing follows from Its knowledge, the knowledge is prior to the things and to the lack of absence from them; for lack of absence of things is posterior to their actualization. Just as [the Necessary Existent's] effect is not Its essence, so, too, Its knowledge of Its effect is not Its knowledge of Itself. Their argument that Its knowledge of Its concomitant is bound up in Its knowledge of Itself is without force, since according to this Its knowledge is negative. How can the knowledge of things be contained in a negation? Incorporeality is negative, as is lack of absence; for "presence" cannot be taken to mean "lack of absence," since the thing is not present to itself. That which is present is not him to whom it is present. Thus, "presence" may only be said of two things, or "lack of absence" is yet more general. How, then, may knowledge of another be encompassed in a negation? Moreover, risibility[17] is something other than humanity, and knowledge of it is not knowledge of humanity. For us, the knowledge of risibility is not bound up in humanity,[18] for humanity does not indicate it by correspondence or inclusion, but only externally. Even if we know risibility, we also need another form[19] known to us potentially, apart from that form. They make analogies to explain the differences among the detailed knowledge of subjects, the potential knowledge of them, and the kind of knowledge man finds in himself as soon as the question is asked, but these analogies are worthless. When men find knowledge potentially in themselves when they are presented with questions, they have found in themselves an ability and power to answer such questions. This power is nearer than before the question [was asked], for potentiality has degrees.

لذاته على ما سبق، وغيره ظاهر له «فلا يعزب عنه مثقال ذرة فى السموات ولا فى الارض»[٤٣] اذ لا يحجبه شئ عن شئ؛ فعلمه وبصره واحد ونوريته قدرته، اذ النور فياض لذاته.

(١٦١) والمشاؤون واتباعهم قالوا: علم واجب الوجود ليس زائدا عليه، بل هو عدم غيبته عن ذاته المجردة عن المادة. وقالوا: وجود الاشياء عن علمه بها. فيقال لهم: انّ علم ثم لزم من العلم شئ، فيتقدم العلم على الاشياء وعلى عدم الغيبة عن الاشياء، فانّ عدم الغيبة عن الاشياء يكون بعد تحققها. وكما انّ معلوله غير ذاته، فالعلم[٤٤] بمعلوله غير علمه[٤٥] بذاته. واما ما يقال «ان علمه بلازمه منطو فى علمه بذاته» كلام لا طائل تحته، فان علمه سلبى عنده، فكيف يندرج العلم بالاشياء فى السلب؟ والتجرد عن المادة سلبى، وعدم الغيبة ايضا سلبى، فان عدم الغيبة لا يجوز ان يعنى به الحضور، اذ الشئ لا يحضر عند ذاته، فان الّذى حضر غير من يكون عنده الحضور فلا يقال إلاّ فى شيئين، بل اعم؛ فكيف يندرج العلم بالغير فى السلب؟ ثم الضاحكية شئ غير الانسانية، فالعلم بها غير العلم بالانسانية. والضاحكية علمها عندنا ما انطوى فى الانسانية،[٤٦] فانّها ما دلّت مطابقة او تضمنا عليها، بل دلالة خارجية. فاذا علمنا الضاحكية احتجنا الى صورة اُخرى، ودون تلك الصورة معلومة لنا بالقوة. واما ما ضربوا من المثال فى الفرق بين العلم التفصيلى بمسائل وبين العلم بالقوة بها وبين مسائل ذكرت فوجد الانسان من نفسه علما لجوابها لا ينفع. فانّ ما يجده[٤٧] الانسان من نفسه عند عرض المسائل علم بالقوة يجد من نفسه ملكة وقدرة على الجواب لهذه المسائل المذكورة. وهذه القوة اقرب مما كانت قبل السؤال، فان للقوة مراتب، ولا يكون عالما بجواب كل واحد على الخصوص ما لم يكن

[A man] does not know the answer to each one in particular so long as he does not possess the form of each one. [But] the Necessary Existent is exalted above these things. Moreover, if C is not B, how can such a negation be knowledge of both and be the providence that knows the order best for both? And if Its knowledge of things occurs from the things, then how can you seek prior providence toward the things or prior knowledge of them?

(162) Therefore, the truth about the Necessary Existent's knowledge is given in the Illuminationist principle—that is, Its knowledge of Its essence is Its being a light in Its essence and evident to Its essence. Its knowledge of things is their being evident to It, either in themselves or in their connections, which are the locations where the higher managing lights continuously perceive them.[20] That is a relation, and the lack of veil is negative. That this in itself is sufficient is indicated by the fact that vision occurs simply by the relation of the thing's being evident to vision, along with the lack of any veil. Thus, the relation of the Necessary Existent to anything evident to It is Its vision and perception of that thing. The multiplication of intellectual relations does not imply multiplicity in Its essence. Though there is no such thing as providence, the order of the world is a concomitant of the wonderful arrangement and relations necessitated by the incorporeal lights and their reflected illuminations, as was explained before. This "providence" is part of what they use to refute the principles of those upholding the luminous realities and the talismanic archetypes—but there is no truth to it. Once this is refuted, it follows that the order of the barriers is based on the order among the pure lights and their illuminations in the descending order of causal rank, such causality being impossible for barriers.[21]

(163) If there is black and white in a certain surface, the white will appear nearer, since it is closer to being evident in the way that near things are. The black will appear more distant for the opposite reason. Thus, in the world of pure light, which is without the dimension of distance, all that is higher in degree of cause is closer to that which is lowest because of the intensity of its being evident. Exalted be the Farthest and the Nearest, the Loftiest and the Lowest! If it is nearer, it is more worthy to influence and perfect each essence. Light is the very lodestone of nearness!

عنده صورة كل واحد واحد. وواجب الوجود منزّه عن هذه الاشياء، ثم اذا كان جيم غير باء، فسلب مّا كيف يكون علما بهما وعناية بكيفية ما يجب ان يكونا عليه من النظام؟ وان كان علمه بالاشياء حاصلا من الاشياء، فليطلب العناية المتقدمة على الاشياء والعلم المتقدم.

(١٦٢) فاذن الحق فى العلم هو قاعدة الاشراق، وهو انّ علمه بذاته هو كونه نورا لذاته وظاهرا لذاته، وعلمه بالاشياء كونها ظاهرة له اما بانفسها او متعلقاتها التى هى مواضع الشعور المستمر للمدبرات العلوية. وذلك اضافة، وعدم الحجاب سلبى، والّذى يدل على ان هذا القدر كاف، هو انّ الابصار إنمّا كان لمجرد اضافة ظهور الشئ للبصر مع عدم الحجاب. فاضافته الى كل ظاهر له ابصار وادراك له. وتعدد الاضافات العقلية لا يوجب تكثرا فى ذاته. واما العناية، فلا حاصل لها. واما النظام، فلزم من عجيب الترتيب والنسب اللازمة عن المفارقات واضوائها المنعكسة كما مضى. وهذه العناية كما كانوا يبطلون بها قواعد اصحاب الحقائق النورية ذوات الطلسمات، وهى فى نفسها غير صحيحة. واذا بطلت، تعين ان يكون ترتيب البرازخ عن ترتيب الانوار المحضة واشراقاتها المندرجة فى النزول العلى الممتنع فى البرازخ.

(١٦٣) واعلم انه اذا كان فى سطح مّا سواد وبياض، يتراءى البياض اقرب لانه اشبه بالظاهر الاشبه بالقريب، والسواد ابعد لمقابل ما قلنا. ففى عالم النور المحض المنزه عن بعد المسافة كل ما كان اعلى فى مراتب العلل، فهو ادنى الى الادون لشدة ظهوره. فسبحان الابعد الاقرب الارفع الادنى! واذا كان هو اقرب، فهو اولى[٤٨] بالتأثير فى كل ذات وكمالها، والنور هو مغناطيس القرب.

Section [twelve]

[On the principle of the most noble contingency]

(164) One of the Illuminationist principles is that if a baser contingent exists, a nobler contingent must already have existed. Thus, if the Light of Lights had necessitated the basest darkness through Its unitary aspect, no aspect would have remained to necessitate that which was more noble. If it were supposed to exist, it would require the absurdity of an aspect more noble than the Light of Lights to necessitate it. We have demonstrated the existence of the incorporeal managing lights in man. The dominating light—that which is entirely incorporeal—is nobler than the managing light; being further from connections with darkness, it is thus nobler. Thus, its existence must be prior. Therefore, in all things except contingency, you must believe that which is noblest and best of the Proximate Light, the dominating lights, the spheres, and the managing lights. These are beyond the world of chance, so nothing prevents them from being as perfect as they may be.

(165) There is a wondrous order occurring in the world of darknesses and barriers, but the relations among the noble lights are nobler than the relations of darkness and so must be prior to them. The followers of the Peripatetics admit that there is such a wondrous order among the barriers, yet they confine the intellects to ten. Thus, according to their principles, the world of barriers would have to be more wondrous than the world of lights, more subtle and generous in its order, and the wisdom therein greater. This is not true, since a sound mind will judge that the wisdom of the world of light and the subtle order and astonishing correspondences occurring therein are greater than that of the world of darkness, which is but a shadow of the world of light. That there are dominating lights, that the Creator of all is a light, that the archetypes are among the dominating lights—the pure souls have often beheld this to be so when they have detached themselves from their bodily temples. They then seek proof of it for others. All those possessing insight and detachment bear witness to this. Most of the allusions of the prophets and the great philosophers point to this. Plato, Socrates before him, and those before Socrates—like Hermes, Agathadæmon, and Empedocles—

فصل
[فى قاعدة امكان الاشرف]

(١٦٤) ومن القواعد الاشراقية ان الممكن الاخس اذا وُجد، فيلزم ان يكون الممكن الاشرف قد وُجد. فانّ نور الانوار اذا اقتضى الاخس الظلمانى بجهته الوحدانية لم يبق جهة اقتضاء الاشرف. فاذا فُرض موجودا، يستدعى جهة تقتضيه اشرف مما عليه نور الانوار، وهو محال. والانوار المجردة المدبرة فى الانسان برهنا على وجودها؛ والنور القاهر، اعنى المجرد بالكلية، اشرف من المدبر وابعد عن علائق الظلمات، فهو اشرف. فيجب ان يكون وجوده او لا. فيجب ان تعتقد فى النور الاقرب والقواهر والافلاك والمدبرات ما هو اشرف واكرم بعد امكانه، وهى خارجة عن عالم الاتفاقات، فلا مانع لها عما هو اكمل لها.

(١٦٥) ثم عجائب الترتيب واقعة فى عالم الطلسمات والبرازخ، والنسب بين الانوار الشريفة اشرف من النسب الظلمانية، فتجب قبلها. واتباع المشائين اعترفوا بعجائب الترتيب فى البرازخ وحصروا العقول فى عشرة. فعالم البرازخ يلزم ان يكون اعجب واطرف واجود ترتيبا، والحكمة فيه اكثر على قواعدهم، وليس هذا بصحيح. فان العقل الصريح يحكم بان الحكمة فى عالم النور ولطائف الترتيب وعجائب النسب واقعة اكثر مما هى فى عالم الظلمات، بل هذه ظل لها. والانوار القاهرة وكون مبدع الكل نورا وذوات الاصنام من الانوار القاهرة شاهدها المجردون بانسلاخهم عن هياكلهم مرارا كثيرة. ثم طلبوا الحجة عليها لغيرهم، ولم يمكن ذو مشاهدة مجرد إلاّ اعتراف بهذا الأمر. واكثر اشارات الانبياء واساطين الحكمة الى هذا، وافلاطون ومن قبله مثل سقراط ومن سبقه مثل هرمس واغاثاذيمون وانباذقلس، كلهم

all held this view. Most said plainly that they had beheld it in the world of light. Plato related that he himself had stripped off the darkness and beheld it. The sages of Persia and India without exception agreed upon this. If the observations of one or two individuals are to be given weight in astronomy, how, then, may we ignore the testimony of the pillars of philosophy and prophecy as to that which they beheld in their spiritual observations?

(166) The author of these lines was once zealous in defense of the Peripatetic path in denying these things.[22] He was indeed nearly resolved upon that view, "until he saw his Lord's demonstration" [Qurʾān 12:24]. Whoso questions the truth of this—whoever is unconvinced by the proof—let him engage in mystical disciplines and service to those visionaries, that perchance he will, as one dazzled by the thunderbolt, see the light blazing in the Kingdom of Power and will witness the heavenly essences and lights that Hermes and Plato beheld. He will see the spiritual luminaries, the wellsprings of kingly splendor[23] and wisdom that Zoroaster told of, and that which the good and blessed king Kay-Khusraw unexpectedly beheld in a flash. All the sages of Persia were agreed thereon. For them, even water possessed an archetype in the heavenly kingdom, which they named "Khordad." That of trees they named "Mordad," and that of fire "Ordibehesht."[24] These are the lights to which Empedocles and others alluded.

(167) Do not imagine that these great men, mighty and possessed of insight, held that humanity had an intellect that was its universal form and that was existent, one and the same, in many. How could they allow there to be something unconnected to matter, yet in matter? How could one thing be in many and uncounted material individuals? It is not that they considered the human archetype, for example, to be given existence as a copy of that which is below it. No men hold more firmly that the higher does not occur because of the lower. Were this not their view, the form would have another form, and so to infinity.

يروون هذا الرأى. واكثرهم صرّح بانّه شاهدها فى عالم النور. وحكى افلاطون عن نفسه انّه خلع الظلمات وشاهدها، وحكماء الهند والفرس قاطبة على هذا واذا اعتبر رصد شخص او شخصين فى أمور فلكية، فكيف لا يعتبر قول اساطين الحكمة والنبوة على شئ شاهدوه فى ارصادهم الروحانية؟

(١٦٦) وصاحب هذه الاسطر كان شديد الذب عن طريقة المشائين فى انكار هذه الاشياء عظيم الميل اليها، وكان مصرا على ذلك «لولا ان رأى برهان ربه».[٤٩] ومن لم يصدق بهذا ولم تقنعه الحجة فعليه بالرياضات وخدمة اصحاب المشاهدة. فعسى تقع له خطفة يرى النور الساطع فى عالم الجبروت، ويرى الذوات الملكوتية والانوار التى شاهدها هرمس وافلاطون والاضواء الميناوية[٥٠] ينابيع الخرّه والرأى التى عنها اخبر زرادشت. ووقع خلسة الملك الصديق كيخسرو المبارك اليها فشاهدها. وحكماء الفرس كلهم كانوا متفقين[٥١] على هذا، حتى ان الماء كان عندهم صاحب صنم من الملكوت وسمّوه «خُرداد»، وما للاشجار سمّوه «مُرداد» وما للنار سموه «أُرديبهشت»، وهى الانوار التى اشار اليها انباذقلس وغيره.

(١٦٧) ولا تظن ان هؤلاء الكبار اولى الايدى والابصار ذهبوا الى ان الانسانية لها عقل هو صورتها الكلية وهو موجود بعينه فى الكثيرين. فكيف يجوّزون ان يكون شئ ليس متعلقا بالمادة ويكون فى المادة؟ ثم يكون شئ واحد بعينه فى مواد كثيرة واشخاص لا تحصى؟ ولا انّهم حكموا بانّ صاحب الصنم الانسانى مثلا إنمّا اوجد لأجل ما تحته حتى يكون قالبا له، فانهم أشدّ الناس مبالغة فى ان العالى لا يحصل لأجل السافل؛ فانّه لو كان كذا مذهبهم، للزمهم ان يكون للمثال مثال آخر الى غير النهاية.

(168) Nor should you imagine that they held [universal forms] to be composite, for that would have implied that they would disintegrate some day. Instead, these are luminous simple essences, though their idols[25] are only conceivable as composite. The form need not have a resemblance [to concrete things] in every respect, for even the Peripatetics admit that humanity in the mind corresponds to the many and is a form of the concrete things, though it is incorporeal and they are not, and that it is without magnitude or substance and the concrete things are otherwise. Thus, being a form is not conditioned on resemblance [to concrete things] in every respect. Moreover, they need not hold that animality has a form, and bipedality as well. Rather, each thing whose existence is independent has something holy that corresponds to it. The scent of musk does not have a form and the musk another; rather, there is a dominating light in the world of pure light with luminous states—rays and states of love, pleasure, and dominance—whose shadow falling in this world has as its idol musk with its scent, or sugar with its taste, or the human form with its various organs, according to the interaction mentioned above.

(169) There are metaphors in the words of the Ancients. They did not deny that predicates are mental and that universals are in the mind; but when they said, "There is a universal man in the world of intellect," they meant that there is a dominating light containing different interacting rays and whose shadow among magnitudes is the form of man. It is a universal—not in the sense that it is a predicate, but in the sense that it has the same relation of emanation to these individuals. It is as though it were the totality and the principle. This universal is not that universal whose conception does not preclude being shared; for they believe that it has a particularized essence and that it knows its essence. How, then, could it be a universal idea? When they called one of the spheres a universal orb and another particular, they did not mean "universal" in the sense used in logic. Know this well!

(170) Some men adduce in proof of the forms the argument that humanity per se is not many, and so it is one. This is not valid, for humanity

(١٦٨) ولا تظن انّهم يحكمون بانّها مركبة حتى يقال انّ يلزم ان ينحل وقتا مّا، بل هى ذوات بسيطة نورية، وان لم يتصور اصنامها إلاّ مركبة. وليس من شرط المثال المماثلة من جميع الوجوه. فان المشائين سلموا ان الانسانية فى الذهن مطابقة للكثيرين، وهى مثال ما فى الاعيان مع انّها مجردة وما فى الاعيان غير مجردة، وهى غير متقدرة ولا متجوهرة بخلاف ما فى الاعيان. فليس من شرط المثال المماثلة بالكلية. ولا يلزمهم ايضا ان يكون للحيوانية مثال وكذا كون الشئ ذا رجلين، بل كل شئ يستقل بوجوده له أمر يناسبه من القدس. فلا يكون لرائحة المسك مثال وللمسك آخر، بل يكون نور قاهر فى عالم النور المحض له هيئة نورية من الاشعة وهيئات من المحبة واللذة والقهر، واذا وقع ظله فى هذا العالم يكون صنمها المسك مع الرائحة او السكر مع الطعم او الصورة الانسانية مع اختلاف اعضائها على المناسبة المذكورة من قبل.

(١٦٩) وفى كلام المتقدمين تجوزات، وهم لا ينكرون ان المحمولات ذهنية وان الكليات فى الذهن. ومعنى قولهم «انّ فى عالم العقل انسانا كليا»، اى نورا قاهرا فيه اختلاف اشعة متناسبة يكون ظله فى المقادير صورة الانسان؛ وهو كلى لا بمعنى انه محمول، بل بمعنى انه متساوى نسبة الفيض على هذه الاعداد، وكأنّه الكل وهو الاصل. وليس هذا الكلى ما نفس تصور معناه لا يمنع وقوع الشركة، فانهم معترفون بان له ذاتا متخصصة وهو عالم بذاته، فكيف يكون معنى عاما؟ واذا سمّوا فى الافلاك كرة كلية واُخرى جزئية، لا يعنون به الكلى المشهور فى المنطق، فتعلم هكذا.

(١٧٠) واما الّذى احتج به بعض الناس فى اثبات المُثُل من «انّ الانسانية بما هى انسانية ليست بكثيرة فهى واحدة» كلام غير مستقيم.

as such implies neither unity nor multiplicity but may be said of both. Were unity a condition of the notion of humanity, humanity could not be said of many. To say that humanity does not imply multiplicity does not mean that its not implying multiplicity then implies unity. Though the contradictory of multiplicity is nonmultiplicity, its not implying multiplicity is not an implication of nonmultiplicity, and the contradictory of implying multiplicity is nothing more than not implying multiplicity. This latter may be so without implying unity. Therefore, the unitary humanity said of all is only in the mind, and its use as a predicate does not require another form. The argument that the individuals perish but the species endures does not necessitate that there be something universal and self-subsistent. One might well answer that what endures is a form in the mind and with the origins.[26] All such arguments are rhetorical.

(171) The faith of Plato and the master visionaries is not built upon such rhetorical arguments, but upon something else. Plato said: "When freed from my body I beheld luminous spheres." These that he mentioned are the very same highest heavens that some men will behold at their resurrection "on the day when the earth will be changed for another earth and heavens, and will appear before God, the One, the 'Triumphant'" [Qurʾān 14:48]. Plato and his companions showed plainly that they believed the Maker of the universe and the world of intellect to be light when they said that the pure light is the world of intellect. Of himself, Plato said that in certain of his spiritual conditions he would shed his body and become free from matter. Then he would see light and splendor within his essence. He would ascend to that all-encompassing divine cause and would seem to be located and suspended in it, beholding a mighty light in that lofty and divine place. The passage of which this is a summary ended with the words "but thought veiled that light from me."[27]

فان الانسانية بما هى الانسانية لا تقتضى الوحدة والكثرة، بل هى مقولة عليهما جميعا. ولو كان من شرط مفهوم الانسانية الوحدة، فما كانت الانسانية مقولة على كثيرين.[٥٢] واذا لم تقتض الانسانية الكثرة يكون لاقتضاء كثرتها اقتضاء الوحدة، بل نقيض الكثرة اللاكثرة، وعدم اقتضاء الكثرة ليس اقتضاء اللاكثرة، ونقيض اقتضاء الكثرة إنمّا هو لا اقتضاء الكثرة، فيجوز صدقه مع الاقتضاء الوحدة. ثم الانسانية الواحدة المقولة على الكل إنمّا هى فى الذهن، لا تحتاج لأجل الحمل الى صورة اُخرى. وما قيل «انّ الاشخاص فاسده والنوع باق» لا يوجب ان يكون أمراً كليا قائما بذاته، بل للخصم ان يقول: انّ الباقى صورة فى العقل وعند المبادئ. ومثل هذه الاشياء اقناعية.

(١٧١) وليس اعتقاد افلاطون واصحاب المشاهدات بناء على هذه الاقناعيات، بل على أمر آخر. وقال افلاطون «انى رأيت عند التجرد افلاكا نورانية». وهذه التى ذكرها بعينها السموات العلى التى يشاهدها بعض الناس فى قيامتهم «يوم تبدل الارض غير الارض والسموات وبرزوا لله الواحد القهار».[٥٣] ومما يدل على انهم يعتقدون ان مبدع الكل نور وكذا عالم العقل ما صرّح به افلاطون واصحابه: ان النور المحض هو عالم العقل. وحكى عن نفسه انه يصير فى بعض احواله بحيث يخلع بدنه ويصير مجردا عن الهيولى، فيرى فى ذاته النور والبهاء ثم يرتقى الى العلة الالهية المحيطة بالكل. فيصير كأنّه موضوع فيها معلق بها، ويرى النور العظيم فى الموضع الشاهق الالهى. ما هذا مختصره الى قوله «حجبت الفكرة عنى ذلك النور».

And thus spoke he who gave the Law to Arab and Persian: "God hath seven and seventy veils of light. Were these to be stripped from His face, the majesty of His countenance would consume all that He beheld." And God, "the Light of the heavens and the earth" [Qur'ān 24:35], revealed unto him, "The throne is of My light."

In the prophetic prayers we find: "O Light of Light! Thou wouldst be veiled without Thy creation and no light would behold Thy light. O Light of all light! The people of the heavens are illumined by Thy light, and the people of earth are brightened by Thy light. O Light of all light! O Thou Who dost extinguish every light by Thy light." And among the traditional prayers is this: "I ask Thee by the light of Thy countenance, which fills the pillars of Thy throne." I do not adduce these things as proofs; I only point them out. The testimonies in the holy books and the words of the ancient sages are beyond count.

A principle [showing how the simple is generated from the many]

(172) By virtue of its rays, something may result from the dominating light that does not resemble it. This thing may come to be from the essence of one of the other higher lights by virtue of the many lights present in it as rays. These are like parts of the cause, thereby allowing an effect that differs from it by being different from the whole of the cause. The effect then accepts the rays that its cause had accepted, as well as an additional ray from its cause. Thus, many differences arise in the dominating lights. Entities may occur from the whole that are different from any of the parts, and the simple may occur from differing things.

A principle [in explanation of the classes of the archetypes]

(173) Some of the lower dominating lights are not far removed from souls. Some souls require the mediacy of the spirit of the soul,[28] while others, such as the vegetative soul, are so greatly deficient as to dispense with that. Some minerals, like coral, closely approach the station of plants; and some plants, like the date-palm, closely approach the station of animals. Some animals, such as the ape, approach the condition of man in the perfection of their inner faculties and in other respects. In general, the lowest ranks of the higher degree are close to the lower degree, while the highest ranks of the lower degree of all existents nearly

وقال شارع العرب والعجم «انّ لله سبعا وسبعين حجابا من نور لو كُشفت عن وجهه لاحرقت سُبُحات وجهه ما ادرك بصره». واوحى اليه: «الله نور السموات والارض»[٥٤] وقال «انّ العرش من نورى».

ومن الملتقط عن الادعية النبوية: «يا نور النور! احتجبت دون خلقك، فلا يدرك نورك نور. يا نور النور! قد استنار بنورك اهل السموات واستضاء بنورك اهل الارض. يا نور كل نور! خامد بنورك كل نور». ومن الدعوات المأثورة «اسألك بنور وجهك الّذى ملأ اركان عرشك». ولست اورد هذه الاشياء لتكون حجة، بل نبّهت بها تنبيها، والشواهد من الصحف وكلام الحكماء الاقدمين مما لا يحصى.

قاعدة [فى بيان جواز صدور البسيط عن المركب]

(١٧٢) النور القاهر يجوز ان يحصل منه باعتبار اشعته أمر لا يماثله، بل يصدر ما يصدر عن بعض الاعلين من ذاته وباعتبار انوار كثيرة شعاعية فيه، فتصير كجزء للعلة، فيحصل من المجموع المعلول مخالفا له. ثم المعلول يقبل من اشعة اُخرى مما يقبل[٥٥] علته وزيادة شعاع من علته، فيقع اختلافات كثيرة فى القواهر. ويجوز ان يحصل من مجموع أمور غير ما يحصل من افرادها، ويجوز ان يكون البسيط حاصلا من اشياء مختلفة.

قاعدة [فى بيان اقسام ارباب الاصنام]

(١٧٣) ومن القواهر النازلة ما يقرب من النفوس، وكما انّ من النفوس ما احتاج الى توسط الروح النفسانى، ومنها ما يكون من شدة نقصه لا يحتاج الى ذلك، كالنفس النباتية، ومن المعادن ما قرب من هيئة النبات، كالمرجان، ومن النبات ما قرب من الحيوان، كالنمل؛ ومن

approach the higher degree. Some of the human managing lights are nearly intellect, while the lower of them are nearly like those of the beasts. Thus, some of the lower dominating lights are nearly managing lights, and there can be no other incorporeal light beneath them as a managing light due to the deficiency of their substance.[29] Though the aspects of illumination are doubled and redoubled in the lower dominating lights, the weakness of their substance is not mended by borrowed light, especially if that light is from one of the higher lights. The dominating lights that necessitate the elements have a solicitude for them—which is to say that there is no intermediary between them and their idols, such as the managing light, because of the deficiency of these lights and their inability to bring into being another incorporeal light, as well as due to the lack of capacity of the idol. This is also the case for the composite inanimate beings.

Section [thirteen]

[In explanation of the infinity of the effects of intellects and the finitude of the effects of souls]

(174) You should not imagine that the incorporeal lights, whether dominating or managing, have magnitude—their existence being spiritual[30]—for everything having magnitude is of a barrier, and such a thing cannot apprehend its essence, as has been said. Rather, these are simple lights in which there is no composition in any respect. All share in the luminous reality, as you know. They differ only in perfection and deficiency. Deficiency in the luminous reality ends in that which is not self-subsistent but is only a state in another. One ought not to follow the critic who says, "Light is a quality and accident here, so how could it be self-subsistent? If any light were without need for a locus, all would be." This is without foundation, however, since independence for light is due to its perfection, and its perfection is by its substance. The final end of its deficiency is accidentality and relation to a locus. The deficiency of

الحيوان ما قرب من الانسان فى كمال القوة الباطنة وغيرها، كالقرد وغيره. فالطبقة العالية نازلها يقرب من السافلة والطبقة السافلة، عاليها فى جميع الموجودات يكاد يقرب من الطبقة العالية. ومن الانوار المتصرفة البشرية ما كاد يكون عقلا وفى النزول منها ما كاد يكون، كبعض البهايم؛ فمن القواهر النازلة ما كاد يكون نورا متصرفا، فلا يستحق ان يكون دونه نور مجرد آخر يتصرف هو فيه لنقصها فى جوهره. والانوار القاهرة وان كان سافلها يتضاعف فيه جهات الاشراق، إلاّ انّ الضعف الّذى فى الجوهر لا ينجبر بالنور المستفار، لا سيّما اذا كان ذلك النور من العوالى. فالانوار القاهرة التى توجب العناصر لها عناية بها، اى ليس بينها وبين صنمها واسطة أُخرى مثل النور المتصرف لنقصها وقصورها عن افادة نور مجرد، ولعدم استعداد الصنم ايضا. وكذا غيرها من مركبات الجمادات.

فصل

[فى بيان عدم تناهى آثار العقول وتناهى آثار النفوس]

(١٧٤) ولا تظننّ ان الانوار المجردة من القواهر والمدبرات لها مقدار، ووجودها وجود معنوى اذ كل مقدّر برزخى[٥٦] فلا يدرك ذاته لما سبق، بل هى انوار بسيطة لا تركيب فيها بوجه من الوجوه. وكلها متشاركة[٥٧] فى الحقيقة النورية، كما عرفت. والتفاوت بينها بالكمال والنقص، وينتهى النقص فى الحقيقة النورية الى ما لا يقوم بنفسه، بل تكون هيئه[٥٨] فى غيره، وليس بصحيح تشنيع من يقول: ان النور كيفية وعرض هاهنا، فكيف يقوم بنفسه؟ ولو استغنى بشئ[٥٩] من النور عن

something does not imply the deficiency of that which is like it in some respect. Therefore, the difference could be by magnitude, by number, or by intensity and perfection. The magnitude of the bearer of a lamp's light may be smaller than the magnitude of the bearer of its ray, and the bearers of its rays may be greater in number than it,[31] so the fact that it necessitates the ray in whatever way posited and the difference in luminosity are only due to its greater intensity and perfection. Thus, the intensity of the Light of Lights and the perfections of Its luminosity are infinite, and nothing else can rule over It by encompassing It. We ourselves are only veiled from It by the perfection of Its light and the deficiency of our faculties—not because It is hidden. Its intensity cannot be particularized by any limit beyond which some other light could be imagined, since this would imply that It had a limit and a particularity requiring something to particularize and dominate It. By Its light and Its power, It dominates all things. Its knowledge is Its luminosity, and Its power and dominance over all things are Its luminosity, as well. Activity is a property of light. The proximate dominating lights are finite, if by "finitude" is meant that beyond the thing is something more perfect than it; but they are infinite in intensity, if by this is meant that effects may result from them infinitely. We shall demonstrate that the barriers and the circular motions are perpetual and that these movements are infinite in number. The effects of the managing light must be finite; for if its power were infinite, it could not be imprisoned by the connections of darknesses, whose essences and the attractions of whose powers and natural desire are finite, nor could it be distracted by the attractions of barriers from the luminous horizon. These unending movements resulting from the controlling lights occur only through the aid of the dominating lights and their infinite power, which is the perfection of their luminosity. Since that is so, the Light of Lights must be infinitely beyond the infinite; for the infinite, as we have explained before, admits of differences. Each of the managing lights in barriers is aided by its master, which is the dominating light that is the archetype; but it does not take new aid from the Light of Lights, for we will demonstrate that there is no conceivable renewal in the world of dominating lights.

المحل، لاستغنى الجميع. فانّه لا اصل له، اذ الاستغناء للنور إنمّا هو لكماله، وكماله لجوهره وغاية نقصه بالعرضية والاضافة الى المحل. فلا يلزم من نقص شئ نقص ما يشاركه فى وجه. فاذن التفاوت قد يكون بالمقدار، وقد يكون بالعدد، وقد يكون بالشدة والكمال. والنور المصباحى لما كان مقدار حامله اصغر من مقدار حامل شعاعه، وحوامل الشعاع قد تكون اكثر عددا منه، فكونه موجبا للشعاع على اى وجه يُفرض، وتفاوت النورية ليست إلاّ بالشدة والكمال. فنور الانوار شدته وكمال نوريته لا تتناهى، فلا يتسلط عليه بالاحاطة شئ؛ واحتجابه عنا إنمّا هو لكمال نوره وضعف قوانا لا لخفائه. ولا خصص شدته عند حد يمكن ان يتوهم ورائه نور، فيكون له حد وتخصص مستدع لمخصص وقاهر له، بل هو القاهر بنوره وقدرته[٦١] لجميع الاشياء. فعلمه نوريته. وقدرته ايضا نوريته وقهره للاشياء، والفاعلية من خاصية النور. واما الانوار القاهرة من المقربين، فانوار متناهية، ان عُنى بالنهاية ان يكون الشئ ورائه ما هو أتمّ منه؛ وهى غير متناهية الشدة ان عُنى ان لها صلوح ان يحصل منها آثار غير متناهية. فانّا سنبرهن على دوام البرازخ والحركات الدورية وان هذه الحركات غير متناهية العدد. والنور المدبر يجب نهاية آثاره، فانّه ان كان غير متناهى القوة، ما انحبس فى علائق الظلمات المتناهية الذوات ومتناهية جواذب القوى والشوق الطبيعى، وما جذبها شواغل البرازخ عن الافق النورى. فهذه الحركات الدائمة التى هى من الانوار المتصرفة، إنمّا تكون بمدد من الانوار القاهرة، ولها القوة الغير المتناهية، وهو كمال نوريتها. فاذا كان كذا، فنور الانوار وراء ما لا يتناهى بما لا يتناهى، وغير المتناهى قد يتطرق اليه التفاوت كما بيّنا

(175) Know that there must be redoubling of the illuminations and the relations among them. I do not presume to claim that all the relations are included within those which I have mentioned. There are indeed wonders that the minds of men cannot encompass so long as they remain dabbling in the darknesses. All such wonders as have been described are less subtle, less astonishing than other wonders there. That we know even this amount is one of the proofs showing that things yet more wonderful will be found there. If what we know were all that there is, we would have encompassed with our syllogisms and deductions—we, who are in the darkness!—the plan of the Light of Lights. How absurd this is! The mere fact that we are in darkness prevents us from beholding or seeing these wonders. What we have mentioned is but an example.

(176) The deficient light cannot be conceived to be independent in its effects as it beholds a light that dominates it but, rather, is dominated in its effects by that light more perfect than it. Therefore, the Light of Lights is the ruling Agent despite all intermediaries, the Cause of their activity, the Origin of every emanation, the absolute Creator, with or without intermediary. There is no effect that does not contain Its effect, although It may allow the relation of activity to be shared with another [Qurʾān 55:29].

من قبل. وكل واحد من الانوار المدبرة فى البرازخ يمده صاحبه، وهو النور القاهر الّذى هو صاحب الصنم، وهو لا يأخذ المدد الجديد من نور الانوار، كما سنبرهن عليه ان فى عالم القواهر لا يتصور التجدد.

(١٧٥) واعلم انّ تضاعف الاشراقات لا بد منه ونسبها. ولست ادعى انّ جميع النسب محصورة فيما ذكرته، بل هناك عجائب لا يحيط بها عقول البشر ما داموا متصرفين فى الظلمات. وكل ما فُرض من العجائب، فان هناك الطف واعجب من ذلك. ومن الادلة على ان هناك اعجب من ذلك هو انا عرفنا هذا القدر؛ فلو كان هناك هذا فحسب، لكنا قد احطنا، ونحن فى الظلمات، بتدبير نور الانوار بقياساتنا واستنباطاتنا، وهو محال. بل كوننا فى الظلمات مانع عن المشاهدة ورؤية العجائب وما ذكرناه انموذج.

(١٧٦) واعلم انّه لما لم يتصور استقلال النور الناقص بتأثير فى مشهد نور يقهره دون غلبة النور التام عليه فى نفس ذلك التأثير، فنور الانوار هو الفاعل الغالب مع كل واسطة، والمحصل منها فعلها، والقائم على كل فيض فهو الخلاّق المطلق مع الواسطة، ودون الواسطة، ليس شأن ليس فيه شأنه على انه قد يتسامح فى نسبة الفعل الى غيره.

The Third Discourse

Explaining the activity of the Light of Lights and the dominating lights and the rest of the discussion of the celestial movements, in four sections

Section [one]

[Showing that the activity of the Light of Lights is eternal]

(177) Nothing results from the Light of Lights and the dominating lights after it was not, except in the way we will explain; for anything that depends on only one other thing exists necessarily if that latter thing exists. Otherwise, its existence would be either inconceivable or would depend on something else, not on that which it was supposed to depend on. Since it was assumed to depend on that one other thing, the conclusion is absurd. Since everything other than the Light of Lights is from It, they do not depend on another in the way that some one of our actions depends on a time or the removal of an obstacle or the existence of a condition, each of which has a role in our actions. There is no time for the Light of Lights prior to everything other than the Light of Lights, for time itself is also one of the things other than the Light of Lights. Because the Light of Lights and all that the "people of attributes"[1] posit to be attributes are perpetual, these must endure as long as that from which they come to be endures, for they do not depend on something that comes later. Pure nonbeing cannot be supposed to be renewed, considering that the same argument applies to everything renewed.[2] Thus, the shadows and incorporeal illuminations of the Light of Lights

لمقالة الثالثة
فى كيفية فعل نور الانوار والانوار القاهرة ونحوهم وتتميم القول فى الحركات العلوية

وفيه فصول

فصل

[فى بيان انّ فعل الانوار ازلى]

(١٧٧) نور الانوار والانوار القاهرة لا يحصل منهم شئ بعد ان لم يحصل، إلاّ على ما سنذكره. فانّ كل ما لا يتوقف على غير شئ اذا وُجد ذلك الشئ وجب ان يوجد، وإلاّ فهو مما لا يتصور وجوده او يتوقف على غيره، فما كان هو الّذى يتوقف عليه، وقد فُرض ان التوقف عليه، فهو[1] محال. وكل ما سوى نور الانوار لما كان منه فلا يتوقف على غيره كما يتوقف شئ من افعالنا على وقت او زوال مانع او وجود شرط. فانّ لهذه مدخلا فى افعالنا، ولا وقت مع نور الانوار متقدما على جميع ما عدا نور الانوار، فان نفس الوقت ايضا من الاشياء التى هى غير نور الانوار. فلما كان نور الانوار، وجميع ما يفرضه «الصفاتية» صفة دائمة، فيدوم بدوامه ما منه لعدم توقفه على أمر منتظر؛ ولا يمكن فى العدم البحت فرض تجدد مع ان كل ما يتجدد يعود الكلام اليه. فنور الانوار

and the dominating lights are perpetual. You know that the sensible ray is from the luminous body, not the luminous body from the ray. So long as the most great luminary endures, its ray will endure even though it comes to be from it.

Section [two]

[Explaining that the world had no beginning in time and that the motions of the spheres are completely circular]

(178) Any state that cannot be conceived to be fixed is motion. Anything that was not at one time and then occurs is a temporal. Any temporal that comes to be depends in part upon a temporal, since a temporal cannot necessitate its own existence. This is because every contingent must have a sufficient reason. If everything having a part in the sufficient reason is perpetual, then the thing would be perpetual and would not be temporal. Since it is temporal, something of that upon which it is dependent must be temporal. The same argument applies as well to that thing. Therefore, there is a series; and an infinite series whose parts exist together is absurd. Thus, this must be an infinite series whose parts do not exist together and which has no breaks. Otherwise, the argument would end in a first temporal after the break. Therefore, there must be in existence an ever-renewed, uninterrupted temporal, but that [temporal] whose quiddity is such as to be renewed is motion. Rectilinear motion is limited, since an actual infinity of barriers is inconceivable. You know that barriers only move naturally because of the absence of something suitable, but when they reach what is suitable, they stop. Therefore, if a barrier had everything suitable for it and everything whose existence was preferable for it, it would not move, since it would not seek that whose existence was indifferent to it. Constrained motions are either by nature or by volition. You will discover that nothing in the sublunar world capable of voluntary motion admits of perpetual motion, nor can its barrier last forever; for these compounds must dissolve. Thus, each motion beneath

والانوار القاهرة ظلالها واضوائها المجردة دائمة. وقد علمت ان الشعاع المحسوس هو من النيّر لا النير من الشعاع وكلّما يدوم النير الاعظم يدوم الشعاع مع انه منه.

فصل

[فى بيان ان العالم قديم، وان حركات الافلاك دورية تامّة]

(١٧٨) كل هيئة لا يتصور ثباتها، هى الحركة. وكل ما لم يكن زمانا ثم حصل، فهو حادث. وكل حادث اذا حدث فشئ مما توقف عليه هو حادث، اذ لا يقتضى الحادث وجود نفسه، اذ لا بد من مرجح فى جميع الممكنات. ثم مرجحه ان دام مع جميع ما له مدخل فى الترجيح، لدام الشئ، فلم يكن حادثا. ولما كان حادثا، فشئ مما يتوقف[٢] عليه هذا الحادث حادث؛ ويعود الكلام الى ذلك الشئ، فلا بد من التسلسل، والسلسلة الغير المتناهية مجتمعة وجودها محال. فلا بدّ من سلسلة غير متناهية لا يجتمع آحادها ولا تنقطع، ولا يعود الكلام الى أوّل حادث بعد الانقطاع. فينبغى ان يكون فى الوجود حادث متجدد لا ينقطع. وما يجب فيه لماهيته التجدد، إنمّا هو الحركة. وللحركات المستقيمة حد، اذ البرازخ الغير متناهية غير متصور تحققها. وتعلم انّ البرزخ لا يتحرك بطبعه إلاّ لفقد ملائم؛ فاذا وصل اليه وقف، حتى لو كان البرزخ معه جميع ما يلائمه ويترجح وجوده له، فلا يتحرك، اذ لا يطلب ما لا يترجح له وجوده. والقسريات من الحركات اما من الطبع او الارادة. وستعلم ان ما تحت فلك القمر مما يمكن ان يكون له حركة ارادية لا يحتمل الحركة الدائمة ولا بقاء لبرزخه دائما، لوجوب تحلل هذه التراكيب؛ فلجميع

the spheres must come to an end. Since there must be a perpetual motion continuing without end, this motion must belong to the spheres and be circular. This explains the perpetuity of what bears them. By virtue of the presumed origin of their movements, the end of their movements, and their relations, the spheres may have right, left, and other directions, and the points determining these directions may also be determined.

(179) Remark: When the Sun sets, it returns to its rising point by a complete circular motion. If it returned before completing a circular motion, it would rise from its setting point. You will know that the day occurs only by its rising, so the day would be doubled; but this is not so. You know of the existence of the encompassing sphere and that down is determined by the center and that the earth is there. If it were to depart from the center in any direction, it would be tending upwards, which is not suitable for it. There will be an explanation of how this is. All the temporal things that we see are the result of the effects of the movements of the spheres, which are the cause of the occurrence of temporals. But the spheres do not fall within the sway of generation and corruption or composition from simples, since otherwise they would dissolve, their movements would not be perpetual, and they would possess the temporality that necessitates prior movements and being encompassed by other, perpetual barriers.

(180) The spheres in their movements and the interrelations, correspondences, and so forth of their movements also resemble the relations of the holy entities[3] and the rays of the dominating lights. Since all of these positions cannot be combined and since some of the planets veil others from each other, there cannot be an exact, unveiled correspondence among all, such as exists in the world of dominating lights. This is because the barriers have distances and veils. They preserve it [the exact correspondence] in different times so that they express all the correspondences successively, and [this succession is] renewed through ages and cycles.[4]

حركات ما تحت الافلاك مقطع. ولما وجب استمرار حركة دائمة لا تنقطع، فهى للافلاك وتكون دورية، ويتبين من ذلك دوام حواملها. وقد تكون للافلاك بحسب مبدأ حركتها المفروض ومنتهى حركتها واضا فاتها يمين ويسار وغير ذلك من الجهات، ويتعين فيه نقط الاضافات.

(١٧٩) اعلم انّ الشمس اذا غربت لم ترجع الى مشرقها إلاّ بتمام حركة دورية. ولو رجعت قبل تمام حركة دورية لطلعت من مغربها؛ واعلم انّ النهار ليس إلاّ من طلوعها فيتثنى النهار، وليس كذا. وعلمت وجود المحدد، وان السفل بالمركز والارض عنده؛ ولو جاوزت المركز من اى جانب فُرض كانت قاصدة الى العلو ولا يلائمها، وسيأتيك كيفية أمره وجميع الحوادث التى عندنا هى من آثار حركات الافلاك، وهى علة حدوث الحوادث، ولا تقع الافلاك تحت الكون والفساد والتركيب من بسائط، وإلاّ لزم التحلل وعدم دوام الحركات والحدوث الموجب لتقدم حركات وبرازخ أُخرى عليها محيطة دائمة.

(١٨٠) واعلم ان الافلاك فى حركاتها ومناسباته حركاتها ومقابلاتها وغير ذلك ايضا متشبهة بمناسبات الأمور القدسية واشعة الانوار القاهرة. ولما لم يمكن لها الجمع بين جميع الاوضاع والكواكب كل منها يحجب بعضها عن بعض، فلم يكن يمكن[٣] مقابلة بين الكل وعدم حجاب ومناسبة بين الجميع، كما فى عالم القواهر، اذ فى البرازخ ابعاد وحجب، فحفظت ذلك على سبيل البدل حتى تصير آتية فى الاكوار والادوار على جميع المناسبات على طريق التعاقب والاستئناف.

(181) It is not true, as the followers of the Peripatetics have supposed it to be, that each of the spheres in its many movements resembles a single incorporeal intellect in all respects, for the spheres are many and their movements diverse.[5] As they explain it, the goal [of the movement of the spheres] is the movements of the planets. But a planet's motion is sometimes retrograde and sometimes rectilinear. Sometimes the planet is at the apex and sometimes at the perigee. How can the planet resemble a single entity if we accept the Peripatetic rejection of the illuminations caused by the multiplicity of luminous correspondences? Therefore, their movements with their diversity of states are due to the correspondence of the rays and intelligible lights in their beloveds. Their relations to each other are patterned on the relations of their beloveds to each other—relations of dominance that can be imitated and repeated through the ages and cycles. In these doubtful matters[6] the Peripatetics actually accepted a variety of the form that they had rejected from the Ancients. Among the evidence pointing to the multiplicity of beloveds is that if the beloved of the spheres in their movements were one, the movements would be uniform. You know that if one of the celestial barriers was the cause of another, the movements of those that were the effects would resemble those of the causes out of love for them—but this is not so.

Section [three]

[Completing the discussion of the horizontal and vertical dominating lights and explaining that time is without beginning or end]

(182) Because the dominating lights find joy in that One Light which is the Light of Lights, a single barrier results from them due to the common dependence. The dominating lights that necessitate the elemental bodies are lower in rank than the higher dominating lights that are the masters of the celestial barriers, so from them result barriers submissive to and, by nature, influenced by the celestial barriers. These have a common matter that accepts varying forms; so the motion is also circular due

(١٨١) وليس على ما يفرضه اتباع المشائين من ان كل فلك فى حركاته الكثيرة متشبه بواحد من جميع الوجوه. فان الافلاك كثيرة، وحركاتها مختلفة، والغرض على ما صرحوا به حركة الكواكب، فالكواكب تارة راجعة وتارة مستقيمة[٤] وتارة فى الاوج، وتارة فى الحضيض. وكيف يكون[٥] تشبها لشئ واحد، وهم لا يقولون بالاشراقات لكثر المناسبات النورية؟ فليس اذن حركاتها على اختلاف احوالها إلاّ لمناسبات اشعة وانوار فى المعشوقات وليس نسب بعضها الى بعض إلاّ تابعا لمناسبات المعشوقاة بعضها الى بعض، حتى تأتى فى الاكوار والادوار على النسب القاهرة التى يمكن التشبه بها ثم تستأنف. والمشاؤون فى هذه الشبهات[٦] اعترفوا بضرب المثال الّذى ردوا فيه على المتقدمين. مما يدل على كثرة المعشوقاة، هو ان معشوق الافلاك فى حركاتها لو كان واحدا، لتشابهت الحركات، وتعلم انه ان[٧] كانت البرازخ العلوية بعضها علة للبعض، لكانت المعلولات متشبهة فى حركاتها بالعلل عاشقة لها وليس كذا.

فصل

[فى تتمة القول فى القواهر الكلية الطولية والعرضية، وفى أزلية الزمان وأبديته]

(١٨٢) ولما كان للانوار القاهرة ابتهاج بنور واحد هو نور الانوار، حصل[٨] منها برزخ واحد لفقر مشترك. والقواهر التى اقتضت العنصريات نازلة فى الرتبة عن القواهر العالية اصحاب البرازخ العلوية، وحصل منها برازخ خاضعة للبرازخ العالية متأثرة عنها طبعا، ولها مادة مشتركة تقبل الصور المختلفة، فالحركة ايضا مشتركة فى الدورية لتشبه

to its imitation of one beloved, which is the Highest Light. However, these differ in aspects due to the difference of their beloveds, which are the dominating lights. The correspondences correspond to the correspondences in the heavens and earth, and the differences correspond to the differences, and the differing things to the differing things. Thus, the aspects of emanation become many and corresponding.

(183) The priority of some dominating lights to others is intellectual, not temporal; but no man can reckon their number or determine their ranks. They are not ordered only vertically, for some are equal to others. Because the higher lights possess many luminous aspects or interact with each other, the existence of other equal dominating lights may occur from them. Were this not so, equal species could not occur. Those dominating lights that come into being from the higher dominating lights, by virtue of their beholding the Light of Lights and every other higher light, are nobler than those which occur from the aspect of rays. Among the rays there are also ranks and levels. Thus, among the dominating lights are mother-lights—the fundamental vertical lights with few radiant and substantial intermediaries—while others are lights horizontal in their ranks from intermediate rays.

(184) Time is the magnitude of motion when the magnitude of its earlier and later are brought together in the mind. It is ascertained by the daily motion, that most evident of motions. If you do something later and something that was included in the earlier time ceases to be, you know intuitively that something has escaped from you. This is time. You know that it is the magnitude of motion because of the change and lack of fixity that you see. Time is not discontinuous so that there could be a beginning of time, for there would be a "before" not united with an "after." That "before" would not simply be nonbeing, for the nonbeing of a thing can come afterwards. Nor could it be something fixed and combined with it.[7] It would, therefore, also be a temporal priority. Therefore, there would be a time before all time—which would be absurd. Therefore, there is no beginning to time.

بمعشوق واحد هو النور الاعلى، وهى مفترقة فى الجهات لاختلاف معشوقاتها التى هى الانوار القاهرة؛ الاشتراكات بازاء الاشتراكات فى السموات والارض، والافتراقات بازاء الافتراقات، والمفترقات بازاء المفترقات؛ فحصلت جهات الفيض كثيرة متناسبة.

(١٨٣) ولتعلم انّ تقدم القواهر بعضها على بعض تقدم عقلى لا زمانى. والقواهر لا يقدر البشر على احصائها وضبط ترتيبها. وليست هى ذاهبة فى الطول فحسب، بل منها متكافئة. فان الاعلين بجهاتها الكثيرة النورية او مشاركة بعضها مع بعض يجوز ان يصدر[٩] عنها وجود انوار قاهرة متكافئة. ولولا ذلك، ما حصلت انواع متكافئة، وما يحصل من انوار القواهر عن القواهر الاعلين باعتبار مشاهدتها لنور الانوار ولكل عال، اشرف مما يحصل من جهة الاشعة. وفى الاشعة مراتب وطبقات. ففى القواهر اصول طولية قليلة الوسائط الشعاعية والجوهرية، هى الامهات؛ ومنها عرضية من اشعة وساطئة على طبقات.

(١٨٤) واعلم انّ الزمان هو مقدار الحركة اذا جمع فى العقل مقدار مقدمها ومتأخرها. وضُبط بالحركة اليومية، فانها اظهر الحركات. وتحدس من تأخيرك لأمر، اذا أَدّى الى فوات ما يتضمن تقدمه، ان أمراً مّا قد فاتك، وهو الزمان. وتعرف انه مقدار الحركة لما ترى من التفاوت وعدم الثبات. والزمان لا ينقطع بحيث يكون له مبدأ زمانى، فيكون له قبل لا يجتمع مع بعده. فلا يكون نفس العدم، فان العدم للشئ قد يكون بعد، ولا أمراً ثابتا يجتمع معه، فهو ايضا قبلية زمانية، فيكون قبل جميع الزمان زمان، وهو محال. فالزمان لا مبدأ له.

(185) By another method: You know that temporal beings require infinite causes not present together and thus require perpetual motion. Without doubt, that motion belongs to the encompassing sphere, and this motion you know from another proof to be perpetual. Time also has no end, since this end would have an "after." Its "after" is not its nonbeing, since the nonbeing could be before and not something fixed, as was said before. Therefore, there must be time after all time—which is absurd. "Before" and "after" are so considered in relation to the instantaneous moment of imagination, and time is that which is around it. The nearer parts of the past are "after," and the farther "before." The future is the opposite of this. Otherwise, one would encounter the difficulty of homogeneity.[8]

(186) Emanation is pre-eternal, for its Agent does not change or perish. Therefore, the universe is eternal, as He is eternal. It is argued that if the emanation were everlasting, it would be the equal of its Creator; but this does not follow. You know that the luminary is prior to its rays; but even though you may infer its prior existence or nonexistence—if it admits of them—from the existence or nonexistence of the rays, yet that which is caused is not in itself the equal of that which is the cause, but, rather, is from it and by it.

(187) It is unsound to argue that motions are simultaneously existent because when each one has become existent, all are existent.[9] It is absurd to imagine that the successive motions are simultaneous and that for this reason their infinity is possible. They are not simultaneous; for just as they come to be, they also cease to be. You know that the demonstration of the necessity of finitude only applies where it is possible for the individuals to be present simultaneously and to have order. This is not the case with motions. You know that it is invalid to posit an absurdity in order to draw a conclusion from it in that sense in which it is absurd. The causes that are necessarily finite in number are the fixed and emanating essences.

(188) It is argued that if the motions are infinite, no temporal motion can occur, since each of them necessarily depends upon the occurrence of an infinity, which will not occur. This is erroneous, because that which cannot rest upon an infinity is only that for which the ordered infinity

(١٨٥) ومن طريق آخر: عرفت انّ الحوادث تستدعى عللا غير متناهية لا تجتمع، فاستدعت حركة دائمة، ولا بدّ وان تكون لمحيط، وقد عرفت دوامه من طريق آخر. والزمان ايضا لا مقطع له، اذ يلزم ان يكون له بعد؛ وبعده ليس عدمه، اذ قد يكون العدم قبلا، ولا شيئا ثابتا، كما سبق. فيلزم ان يكون بعد جميع الزمان زمان، وهو محال. وتعتبر القبلية والبعدية بالنسبة الى الآن الوهمى الدفعى، والزمان الّذى حواليه؛ فالاقرب من اجزاء الماضى اليه بعد، والابعد قبل، والمستقبل بخلاف هذا؛ وإلاّ يتجه اشكال التشابه.

(١٨٦) والفيض ابدى، اذ الفاعل لا يتغير ولا ينعدم، فيدوم العالم بدوامه. وما يقال «ان الفيض لو دام، لساوى مُبدعه» لا يلزم، لما دريت ان النير يتقدم على الشعاع. وان كان قد استدل[10] بوجود الشعاع وعدمه على وجود النير قبله وعدمه قبل عدمه فيما يمكن ذلك، اما الموجب فى نفسه لا يساوى ما يوجبه بل هو منه وبه.

(١٨٧) واما ما يقال «انّ الحركات مجتمعة فى الوجود لان كل واحد صار موجودا، فيكون الكل قد صار موجودا» ففاسد، اذا الحركات المتعاقبة مستحيلة الاجتماع، ولهذا قد صح عدم النهاية فيها. ولا مجموع لها،[11] فانها كما وجدت عدمت. وبرهان وجوب النهاية دريت انه إنمّا ينساق فيما يمكن اجتماع آحاده وله ترتيب، ولا كذلك الحركات. وفرض المحال ليبتنى على جهة استحالته شئ، عرفت بطلانه. والعلل التى وجب فيها النهاية هى الذوات الثابتة الفياضة.

(١٨٨) وما يقال «انّ الحركات ان كانت عديمة النهاية، يلزم منه ان يكون كل حادث منها متوقفا على حصول ما لا يتناهى فلا يحصل»، فهو غلط. لانّ المتوقف على الغير المتناهى الّذى هو ممتنع إنمّا يكون

has not already occurred. In this case, that which depended upon it would never occur. However, if the infinity is in the past and the temporal must necessarily occur thereafter, the point of disagreement is the same.[10]

(189) It is argued that since the present is the end of the past, the past is finite. If what is meant thereby is that it is the end after which is no end, the argument is not valid. If what is meant is that it is the end and after it are other ages, each of which is the end of that which was before, the usage is correct; for the present is the end of this past and the beginning of what will come, if it is posited to be the beginning. All of time in both directions—I mean the past and the future—is infinite. How often have these people affirmed of the whole what is true of each individual—as, for example: "Each movement is preceded by nonbeing; therefore, all movement must be so." But you know that this does not follow, for you may reply: "Each instance of black must occur in one specific time, but you may not say that the same is true of the class." Thus, what is true of each instance is not necessarily true of the class.

Section [four]

[Showing that the spheres move to attain something holy and pleasurable]

(190) It has been shown that the spheres have motions and that these motions are from managing incorporeal lights. We have pointed out that these managing incorporeal lights are not those dominating lights that are exalted above connections with the darknesses. So, since the lowest light is that which is near the darknesses, then the one nearest to the darknesses is the one furthest from the luminous perfections. It is also known that the motion of the celestial barriers is not because of what is beneath them nor to attain something all at once nor to attain nothing at all, for surely in either of the latter cases the movements would have ceased, either because their end was attained or out of despair. Therefore, these movements are for the sake of the managing lights' attainment of some luminous end from the dominating lights.

اذا كان الغير المتناهى المترتب لم يحصل بعد؛ فما يتوقف عليه لا يحصل ابدا. اما اذا كان الغير المتناهى ماضيا ويكون الحادث ضرورى الوقوع بعده، فهو نفس محل النزاع.

(١٨٩) والّذى يقال «ان الآن هو آخر الماضى فيتناهى» فان عُنى به انه آخر لا آخر بعده، فهو كلام فاسد. وان عُنى به انه آخر ويكون بعده ادوار أُخرى كل منها آخر ما قبله، فهو صحيح.[١٢] فانّه آخر هذا الماضى وهو[١٣] أوّل ما سيأتى اذا جعل مبدأ، وكل واحد من الزمان فى جانبيه، اعنى الماضى والمستقبل، لا يتناهى. وكثيرا ما يثبتون هؤلاء حكم الجميع بناءا على الحكم على كل واحد كما يقال: كل واحد من الحركات مسبوق العدم، فالكل كذا.[١٤] وقد دريت انه لا يلزم، فان لك ان تقول: كل واحد من اعداد السواد على هذا المحل ممكن الحصول فى زمان واحد محدود. ولا يمكنك ان تقول: الجميع كذا، فلا يلزم من الحكم على كل واحد الحكم على الجميع.

فصل

[فى بيان انّ حركات الافلاك لنَيل أمر قدسى لذيذ]

(١٩٠) ولما ثبتت الحركات الفلكية دون الحركات من انوار مجردة مدبرة، واشرنا الى انّ نور الانوار المجردة المدبرة دون الانوار القاهرة المقدسة عن علائق الظلمات، فلما كان النور الاخس ما عنده الظلمات، فالاقرب الى الظلمات ابعد عن الكمالات النورية. وعُرف ايضا[١٥] ان حركة[١٦] البرازخ العلوية ليست لما تحتها وليست لما تناله هى دفعة او لا تناله اصلا، لان الحالين يقضيان الى انصرام الحركات للنيل او اليأس. فهى لنيل مقصد نورى تنالها الانوار المدبرة من الانوار القاهرة

This is, then, a propitious light and a holy ray. Were there not something perpetually renewed in the light managing the celestial barriers, perpetually renewed movements could not result from it, since that which is fixed in itself does not necessitate change. That which is renewed in the celestial controlling lights is not something from the darknesses, as was shown before. Therefore, it must be something luminous renewed from the dominating lights. It would not be formal knowledge, for their knowledge of what is below—of the effects of their movements—is actual, as is also their knowledge of what is above them. As you will learn, the determinations of temporal existents are finite in number and they necessarily recur, and the relations of the dominating ordered existents are also finite. Thus, though they may be many, the causes and effects are finite in number. Since the motions of the spheres are infinite, they must be due to something infinitely renewed—which is to say, the pleasurable and holy ray that we mentioned.

(191) These motions prepare the capacity for illuminations, while at another time the illuminations necessitate the motions. The motion resulting from an illumination is not numerically the same as the motion preparing the capacity for that illumination. There is no impossible circularity here. The motion continues to be the condition of the illumination, and the illumination at another time necessitates the motion that is after it, and so on perpetually. All the individual motions and illuminations are determined by a continuing love and perpetual desire. The succession of motions is in one sequence in the spheres due to the succession of propitious lights in one sequence in the managing lights.

(192) Since both the sphere and its agent are homogeneous, the shape of the sphere is homogeneous. But there is no homogeneity of position in that which is posited to have nonspherical parts. The same is true of any simple barrier. Since the managers of the celestial barriers do not have any connections of desire or anger or anything else keeping them from the world of light, they accept many illuminations. Their movements share in circularity by virtue of that which they accept from the Light of Lights and share with the other managing lights, but their movements differ by virtue of the difference of the illuminations due to

وهو نور سانح وشعاع قدسى؛ ولو لم يكن فى النور المدبر فى البرازخ العلوية أمر دائم التجدد، ما كانت منها الحركة المتجددة دائما، اذ الثابت لنفسه لا يقتضى التغير، ثم ما يتجدد من الانوار المتصرفة العلوية ليس أمراً من الظلمات لما سبق، فيكون أمراً نوريا من القواهر متجددا، وليست صورا علمية، فانها بالفعل من جهة المعلوم بما تحتها من المعلولات حركاتها وكذا بما فوقها. وعلى ما ستعلمه، انّ الضوابط كلها للموجودات الحادثة متناهية واجبة التكرار، والنسب الموجودات المترتبة القاهرية ايضا متناهية، وان كثرت، لتناهى العلل والمعلولات. وحركات الافلاك غير متناهية، فليست إلاّ لأمر غير متناهى التجدد مما ذكرناه من الشعاع القدسى اللذيذ.

(١٩١) فالتحريكات تكون متعددة للاشراقات، والاشراقات تارة أُخرى موجبة للحركات، والحركة المنبعثة عن اشراق غير الحركة التى كانت معدة لذلك الاشراق بالعدد، فلا دور ممتنعا فلا زالت الحركة شرط الاشراق، والاشراق تارة أُخرى يوجب الحركة التى بعده وهكذا دائما. وجميع اعداد الحركات والاشراقات مضبوطة بعشق مستمر وشوق دائم. وتوالى الحركات على نسق واحد فى الافلاك لتوالى الانوار السانحة على نسق واحد فى الانوار المدبرة.

(١٩٢) ولما كان الفلك وفاعله متشابهى الاحوال، فكان شكل الفلك متشابها. ولا متشابه فى وضع ما يفرض له اجزاء غير الكرى، وكذا كل برزخ بسيط. ولما لم تكن لمدبرات البرازخ العلوية العلائق الشهوانية والغضبية وما يمنعها عن عوالم النور، فقبلت الاشراقات الكثيرة، فبما قبلت من نور الانوار وبما[١٧] اشتركت المدبرات فيه، اشتركت تحريكاتها فى الدورية وبما اختلفت من الاشراقات لاختلاف

their different causes. Even though the managing light comes from one of the exalted dominating lights and accepts many illuminations, it is not like a dominating light in the perfection of its substance. The dominating light brings into being the managing incorporeal light only due to perfections of the barrier acquired from the mighty lords[11] and in order to manage it in the way appropriate for controlling barriers of finite power. By this, it strengthens its connection with the barrier.

A principle [showing that that which is made is the quiddity, not its existence]

(193) Since existence is a being of reason, what the thing receives from its emanating cause is its identity. A contingent thing cannot dispense with a sufficient cause for its existence. Otherwise, it would be transformed from being contingent in itself to being necessary by essence. A corruptible being may be destroyed even though its emanating cause remains because it depends upon other causes that have ceased to be. A thing—a statue, for example—may have a cause for its temporal occurrence and a different cause for its continued existence. The cause of the temporal occurrence of a statue is its maker, and the cause of its continuation is the dryness of the element [of which it is made]. The cause of the continued existence and of the temporal occurrence may be the same, such as the shape given by a mold to water. The Light of Lights is the cause of the existence and the cause of the continuation of all existents, and so also are the dominating lights. Since the celestial barriers are neither generated nor corrupted, their managing lights never depart from them, but, rather, control them perpetually.

عللها، اختلفت تحريكاتها. والنور المدبر، وان كان عن قاهر من الاعلين وكان كثير قبول الاشراقات، لا يكون فى كمال الجوهر، كنور قاهر. فانّ القاهر إنمّا يفيض النور المجرد المدبر لكمال البرزخ من الارباب العظيمة وتدبيره على ما يليق بتصرف البرازخ متناهى القوة، ليستحكم مع البرازخ علاقته.

قاعدة [فى بيان انّ المجعول هو الماهية لا وجودها]

(١٩٣) ولما كان الوجود اعتبارا عقليا فللشئ من علته الفياضة هويته.[١٨] ولا يستغنى الممكن عن المرجح لوجوده، وإلاّ ينقلب بعد امكانه فى نفسه واجبا لذاته. وقد يبطل الشئ من الكائنات الفاسدات مع بقاء علته الفياضة لتوقفه على علل أُخرى زائلة. وقد يكون للشئ علة حدوث وعلة ثبات مختلفتين، كالصنم، فان علة حدوثه فاعله مثلا وعلة ثباته يبس العنصر. وقد تكون علة الثبات والحدوث واحدا، كالقالب المشكّل للماء. ونور الانوار علة وجود جميع الموجودات وعلة ثباتها، وكذا القواهر من الانوار. والبرازخ العلوية لما كانت غير كائنة ولا فاسدة لا تفارقها انوارها المدبرة بل هى دائمة التصرف فيها.

The Fourth Discourse

On the classification of barriers, their states, their combinations, and some of their powers, in [eight] sections

Section [one]
[On the classification of barriers]

(194) Each body is either single and not composed of two differing barriers, or dual and composed of two bodies. Each single body is either opaque and blocks light entirely, or is transparent and does not block light at all, or is translucent and blocks light incompletely and in various degrees. The opaque bodies in the heavens are luminous, and all others are transparent. These are the dominating barriers—neither corrupted nor destroyed—in accordance with that which I have explained to you concerning the perpetual movements and their subjects. The enkindled barrier[1] is that which is below them. The enkindled single body belongs to one of three classes: enkindled and opaque, like earth; translucent, like water; or transparent, like space.[2] There is nothing opaque or translucent between us and the heavens, since the celestial lights are not veiled from us. Thus, there is only space. The clouds and the like that you see are only vapors that are translucent to a certain degree. Water, by its nature, is translucent, but it is clouded by that which is mixed with it.

المقالة الرابعة

فى تقسيم البرازخ وهيآتها وتركيباتها وبعض قواها

وفيها فصول

فصل

[فى تقسيم البرازخ]

(١٩٤) كل جسم، فاما[1] ان يكون فاردا، وهو ما لا تركب فيه من برزخين مختلفين؛ واما ان يكون مزدوجا، وهو ما يتركب منهما. وكل فارد، فاما ان يكون حاجزا، وهو الّذى يمنع النور بالكلية؛ واما لطيفا، وهو الّذى لا يمنعه اصلا؛ واما مقتصدا، وهو الّذى يمنعه منعا غير تام، وله فى المنع مراتب. والافلاك حاجزها مستنير، وغيره لطيف؛ وهى برازخ قاهرة لا تفسد ولا تبطل لما بيّنا لك من دوام الحركات وموضوعاتها.[2] والبرزخ القابس هو ما تحتها، ولم يخرج الفارد القابس عن الاقسام الثلاثة: اما ان يكون قابسا حاجزا، كالارض؛ او مقتصدا كالماء؛ او لطيفا كالفضاء. وليس بيننا وبين البرازخ العلوية حاجز ولا مقتصد، والا حجب عنا الانوار العالية، فليس إلاّ الفضاء. وما ترى من السحب وغيرها فانما هى من ابخرة، وهى مقتصدة اقتصادا مّا. والماء طبعه الاقتصاد إلاّ ان يمازجه شئ

A compound is related to one of these by virtue of that which is predominant. If the enkindled compounds are translucent, like crystal, their translucency is due to the predominance of the translucent single body, which is water.

(195) Some[3] say that there are four fundamental enkindled bodies: the cold and dry, which is earth; the cold and moist, which is water; the hot and moist, which is air; and the hot and dry, which is fire. The sign of moisture, according to them, is ease of changing shape and dividing; and the sign of dryness is difficulty in doing so. Reality refutes this in the case of fire, whether they take it in the ordinary sense, with light as a part of its notion, or in some other technical sense. Their proof that it exists adjacent to the sphere—that fire here tends to go upwards—is weak. This fire turns into air in a moment, and its barrier becomes so subtle that light can no longer be made evident in it. Once heat is no longer predominant in it, only air remains. One of the properties of heat is that it makes things more subtle. If fire did remain fire or retained the heat that had been in it, anything that it encountered in a straight line would be burnt—but this is not so. If they argue that the motion of the sphere must heat whatever is adjacent to that sphere, this would only show that there was heated air, but it would not follow that it was fire. If they try to prove that smoke burns when it reaches the vicinity of the sphere, resulting in comet meteors,[4] one must reply that burning is not a property peculiar to fire. Hot iron burns, and hot air burns severely. Nor is it sufficient to cite in proof the thing like a hole that we see in the flame of the lamp. It is only air; for the stronger fieriness is, the more readily it may be transformed into air by becoming more subtle. If it is too weak to be so transformed, the smoke becomes thicker. Things like the part of the flame closest to the wick are more subtle and become air due to the strength of the fire, but the heat remains with this air.

آخر يكدّره. وكل مركب فبحسب الغلبة ينسب الى احد هذه. والمركبات القابسية اذا كانت مقتصدة، كالبلور، فانما اقتصادها لغلبة الفارد المقتصد وهو الماء.

(١٩٥) وقال جماعة ان اصول القوابس اربعة: بارد يابس، وهو[٣] الارض؛ وبارد رطب، وهو الماء؛ وحار رطب، وهو الهواء؛ وحار يابس، وهو النار. وضابط الرطوبة عندهم قبول التشكل عندهم وتركه والانفصال بسهولة، وضابط اليبوسة قبول هذه بصعوبة؛ والحق يأبى هذا. فان النار اما ان يأخذونها كما عند العامة وعند العامة النور داخل فى مفهوم النار، واما ان يأخذوها على اصطلاح آخر. فان كانت حجتهم فى اثباتها عند الفلك هو «ان التى عندنا قاصدة للعلو» فهو ضعيف، لان هذه النار تنقلب هواءً فى الحال، وبرزخه لا يبقى عند شدة تلطفه مستعدا الظهور النور فيه، فتنقطع عنه سلطنت الحرارة ايضا وبقى هواءً، ومن خاصية الحرارة التلطيف. ولو كانت باقية نارا او على الحرارة التى كانت فيه لاحرقت ما قابلها على خط مستقيم، وليس كذا. وان استدلوا بحركة الفلك انها تسخن ما يجاور الفلك فيكون هواءً متسخنا، فلا يلزم ان يكون نارا. وان استدلوا باحتراق الدخان عند الوصول الى قريب من الفلك، فيحصل منه ذوات الاذناب من الشهب[٤] فهذا خطأ لان الحرق ليس من خاصية النار؛ فان الحديدة الحامية تحرق والهواء الحار شديد الحرق. والاستدلال بما نرى فى المصباح من شبه ثقبة من صنوبرتها إنمّا هو هواء، فان النارية كلّما كانت اقوى فهى اقدر على الاحالة الى الهواء بالتلطيف، وانضعفت عن الاحالة فيقوى الدخان؛ فما قرب من الفتيلة ونحوها تلطف فصار هواءً لقوة النار وبقيت معه حرارة.

(196) These people believe that the dry is that which does not easily accept or lose shapes. However, the flame above the wick is not like that, but accepts shapes easily, as is the case with that which is close to the sphere. These only differ from air by intensity and deficiency of heat. Therefore, they are hot air. The argument that fire is dry because it desiccates things is not valid, because desiccation is simply due to the elimination of humidity; and humidity is eliminated by making it subtle and sending it up, not by the thing becoming dry. It is not that fire destroys humidity; indeed, according to his principle[5] it would make it more moist because it would become smoke or air and become more liquid. Therefore, the elements are three: opaque, translucent, and subtle.

(197) The subtle is not conditioned on complete heat, for the heat may be independent of the subtlety. Some water may be sensibly hotter than some air. Forms are only evident states, as we have mentioned. If air that has become intensely hot is called "fire," that is acceptable—in which case the subtle may be divided into two classes in accordance with the intensity of a quality in one and its weakness in the other.

(198) It is also unsound to argue that if fire were hot and moist, it would be air and would not seek a higher place but would instead remain where it was. To this, an opponent may reply that the hotter air becomes, the more it tends to rise—not because it then has another reality, but because it then has another degree of subtlety. It has a greater tendency to rise because it has become more subtle, not because it has become fire. Moreover, who has ever seen fire ascend in reality? An opponent may say that what is adjacent to the sphere is heated by the motion of the sphere. How strange that they should claim that there is a fieriness in compounds! You know that the fire which they imagine to be adjacent to the sphere cannot be brought down by something compelling it; the sphere would not force it. Someone has suggested that some fire will descend because of cold, but it would no longer be fire. The fire which is with us soon becomes subtle and is destroyed. The only thing that occurs in compounds is more or less perfect heat.

(١٩٦) ثم ان هؤلاء اعترفوا بان اليابس هو الّذى لم يقبل التشكل وتركه بسهولة، وليس ما عند الفتيلة كذا بل تقبل بسهولة، وكذا ما يقرب من الفلك، فلا يفارق الهواء إلاّ فى حرارة مختلفة فى الشدة والنقص، فهو هواء حار. وما يقال «ان النار يابسة لتجفيفها الاشياء» ليس بحسن فان التجفيف إنمّا هو لازالة الرطوبة، وازالة الرطوبة إنمّا هو للتلطيف والتصعيد لا بان تكون هى يابسة. وليس انها تفنى الرطوبة، بل على قاعدته تجعلها ارطب لانها تصير بخارا او هواءً فتصير اشد ميعانا. فالاصول ثلاثة: حاجز، ومقتصد، ولطيف.

(١٩٧) واعلم ان اللطيف ليس من شرطه كمال الحرارة، فانّه بعد اللطف قد تقلّ فيه فمن الماء ما هو اشد حرارة من الهواء محسوسة. وليست الصور إلاّ الهيئات القاهرة كما ذكرنا. وان سمى ما اشتد من الهواء حرارته نارا، فذلك مسلم جوازه فيكون اللطيف منقسما الى قسمين باعتبار شدة كيفية واحدة وضعفها.

(١٩٨) وقول القائل «لو كانت النار حارة رطبة لكانة هواءً، فما طلبت موضعا اعلى بل وقفت عنده»، كلام غير مستقيم. فان للخصم ان يقول «ان الهواء كلّما اشتدت حرارته اشتد ارتقائه لا لان له حينئذ حقيقة اخرى، بل لان له حينئذ لطافة اخرى، فزيادة الارتقاء لصيرورته الطف لا لصيرورته نارا». ثم من الّذى شاهد نارا ارتقت حقيقة؟ وما عند الفلك يقول الخصم انه يتسخن بحركة الفلك. ثم العجب انهم فى الممتزجات ادعوا نارية؛ واذا علمت ان النار التى توهموها عند الفلك لا يستنزلها الينا قاسر، اذ الفلك لا يدافعها وما يفرضه فارض انه ينزل لبرد لا يكون نارا، وهذه التى عندنا تلطف وتحلل، فلم يقع فى الممتزجات إلاّ حرارة تامة او ناقصة.

(199) The fluidity of water is due to heat, but it solidifies if it becomes rigid from its own cold or from the cold acquired from air. It is more prone to fluidity than earth is, though heat is still foreign to it and is acquired from light or from movement caused by light. Total cold is not caused by the elemental barrier alone, but by it and the lack of some heat. Were coldness caused by the quiddity of water alone, it would be inconceivable for anything to remove it from water. Thus, the coldness is caused by the barrier and by the lack of some heat, or the causes of heat, to remove it. Nonetheless, cold is existential, since a cold thing—such as ice—chills that which is above or adjacent to it. Translucency is a concomitant of water in all its states, whether heated or frozen, unless something else is mixed with it.

(200) Air may be transmuted into water, as you see when drops form on cups inverted over ice. Since this cannot be from leaks, it must be air becoming water due to the intensity of the cold. One may not argue that small particles of water distributed in the air are attracted to it, since, if that were so, they would be more attracted to great basins, which is not the case. Even if the cup is inverted over ice by basins or swamps, the moisture forms just as it does elsewhere. It is the same whether it is in a place where the vapors are assumed to be many or few. Water may be seen to become air when dense vapors are dispelled, their translucency vanishing so completely that they become totally subtle. The transmutation of water into earth may be seen in the petrifaction of waters in a well.[6] The transmutation of air into luminous fire may be seen when you strike sparks or blow on fires, in both cases making air into luminous fire. Since one element may be transmuted into another, the other may be transmuted into it, since otherwise none of that first element would have remained untransmuted to the other throughout all the unending ages. Moreover, if transmutation is real, the substrata must have the same relation of contingency to each.

(١٩٩) والماء ميعانه للحرارة، وهو اذا تمكن من برده او تمكن فيه برد الهواء المستفاد منه ينجمد، إلاّ انه اقرب الى الميعان من الارض. فالحر غريب وانما هو من النور او الحركة المعللة بالنور. والبرد التام ليس معللا بمجرد البرزخ العنصرى بل به وبعدم حرارة مّا، فان البرودة لو كانت معلولة بالماء لماهيته وحدها، لما تصور لمزيل ان يزيلها عنه. فهى معللة به وبعدم المزيل من الحرارة وموجباتها، إلاّ ان البرد وجودى، اذ البارد، كالجمد، يبرد ما فوقه وما يجاوره. واللازم للماء فى الاحوال كلها، تسخن وتجمد للاقتصاد إلاّ ان يخالطها شئ.

(٢٠٠) والهواء ينقلب ماءً كما ترى مما يركب الطاسات المكبوبة على الجمد من القطرات؛ ولا يتصور ان تكون للرشح، فيتعين ان يكون هواء صار لشدة البرد ماءً. وليس لقائل ان يقول «الاجزاء المائية المتبددة فى الهواء انجذبت اليه»، اذ لو كان كذا لكان انجذابها الى حياض كبيرة اولى وليس كذا حتى ان الطاس، وان كان مكبوبا على الجمد عند احياض ومستنقعات تركيبها من النداوة مثل ما كان دونها، وذلك فى جميع المواضع سواء فرضت فيه الابخرة كثيرة وقليلة، والماء صيرورته هواءً تشاهده من تحلل الابخرة شديدا حتى يزول اقتصادها اصلا بحيث يتلطف بالكلية. وانقلاب الماء عرضا يُرى من استحجار المياه فى الحال. وانقلاب الهواء نارا ذات نورية يُرى فى القدح والنفاخات العظيمة التى تجعل الهواء نارا ذات نورية. واذا صحّ انقلاب احد العنصرين الى الآخر يجب انقلاب الآخر اليه والا كان فى الادوار الغير متناهية لم يبق شئ من ذلك إلاّ انقلب الى هذا، فلا يبقى منه شئ وايضا اذا صحّ الانقلاب، فنسبة الحامل اليهما سواء فى الامكان.

(201) The fire that possesses light is noble because of its luminosity. The Persians all hold that it is the talisman of Ordibehesht[7]—that is, the dominating light emanating upon it. These things are transformed into each other and so have a common prime matter. The prime matter is the barrier. As it is in itself, we give it the name "barrier"; as it is in relation to states, the "bearer" and "locus"; and as it is in relation to the combination of it and the states—that is, the composite species—"prime matter." This is according to our own terminology. The prime matter of the spheres is not shared—that is, the fixed states of their barriers are never separated from them and the composite is not altered.

Section [two]

[Showing that all motions go back to the substantial or accidental lights]

(202) You should know that the first cause—that is, the luminous, highest cause—of all movements is either a managing incorporeal light such as belongs to the celestial bodies, man, and others, or a ray necessitating the heat that gives motion to what is around us, such as is seen with smokes and vapors.

(203) The downward motion of a rock does not occur by its nature alone—were it in its own proper place, it would not move—but also requires constraint. That which constrains it must either go back to a managing incorporeal light or to something caused by heat that necessitates it. The descent of rain also occurs for this reason. Those dry things in our world that become subtle and ascend are smoke, while what is humid and becomes subtle is vapor. The cause in each case is heat, resulting either from light or from heat caused by an incorporeal or an accidental light. If cold becomes predominant in the vapor, it comes down as water. Its descent is due solely to motion imparted by heat, as is seen in baths where heat makes drops go up and cold makes them

(٢٠١) والنار ذات النور شريفة لنوريتها، وهى التى اتفقت الفرس على انها طلسم «اردیبهشت» وهو نور قاهر فيّاض لها. فهذه الاشياء ينقلب بعضها الى بعض، فلها هيولى مشتركة. والهيولى هو البرزخ نقول له فى نفسه «برزخا» وبالقياس الى الهيئات «حاملا» و «محلا» وبالقياس الى المجموع منه ومن الهيئات وهو النوع المركب «هيولى». هذا على اصطلاحنا نحن. وهيولى الافلاك غير مشتركة، اى هيآت ببرازخها الثابتة لا يفارقها ومجموعها لا يتبدل.

فصل

[فى بيان ان انتهاء الحركات كلها
الى الانوار الجوهرية او العرضية]

(٢٠٢) ولك ان تعلم ان الحركات كلها سببها الاول، اى الاعلى النورى، اما نور مجرد مدبر كما للبرازخ العلوية والانسان وغيره؛ واما الشعاع الموجب للحرارة المحركة لما عندنا كما يشاهد من الادخنة والابخرة.

(٢٠٣) واعلم ان حركة الحجر الى اسفل ليست بمجرد طبعه، اذ لو كان فى حيّزه الطبيعى ما تحرك، بل يبتنى على القسر. والقاسر إنمّا ان ينتهى الى نور مدبر مجرد او أمر مّا معلل بحرارة توجبه، ونزول الامطار ايضا لهذا. فان ما يتلطف من الاشياء اليابسة عندنا ويتصاعد هو الدخان؛ وما يتصاعد من الرطب المتلطف هو البخار، وسبب ذلك الحرارة؛ فيرجع الى النور او الى حركة معللة بنور مجرد او عارض. ثم اذا غلب البرد على البخار فينحدر ماءً. وليس انحداره إلاّ بناء على تحريك حرارة على ما يشاهد فى الحمامات° صعود قطرات بالحرارة

congeal. If the vapors congeal in the air and become clouds and if smoke becomes trapped in them and tries to escape, the shuddering and crashing that occurs in resistance to its attempt to escape is called "thunder." This is based on heat. The smoke may escape as fire, resulting in thunderbolts and the like. If the smoke meets with cold, it becomes heavy and falls. It may return when it encounters the enkindled barriers adjacent to the rotating sphere. It presses down upon the air and scatters it. The winds are from this. The first cause of these things is heat, and there is no heat with us except from the rays of the luminaries or from that which occurs from fires resulting from our striking sparks. This is elementary. Now, the striking of sparks results from the controlling lights that are in us. The movements of waters toward their natural places and their eruption from springs result from compressed vapors, as do earthquakes. The cause of the vapors has already been explained. Therefore, all movements are caused by lights.

(204) Although the movements in the celestial barriers are preparatory for the illuminations, the illumination is nonetheless from the dominating lights and the direct cause of the motion is the managing light. The cause here is the incorporeal light, along with the propitious light. Movement is closer than rest to the nature of life and luminosity, for movement demands a luminous existential cause, whereas a privation—the lack of a cause of movement—is sufficient cause for rest. Since rest is privative, it corresponds to inanimate darknesses. In this world, were it not for light—whether self-subsistent or accidental—no movement at all would occur. Thus, the lights become the cause of movements and heats, and light is evident in both movement and heat—not because they are its cause, but because they prepare the receptivity for a light to occur therein from the dominating light that emanates by its substance upon those recipients that are properly prepared to receive it.

(205) The light, however, gives being to both movement and heat and, by its root nature, causes them to occur. The light emanates by essence and is active by its quiddity, not by something making it so. The rays of the planets are caused by the planets. The perfect light is such that in itself it is the cause of the deficient light. Just as the triangle

وتكاثفها ببرد. وما يتكاثف على الجو من الابخرة ويصير سحابا، وينحبس فيه الدخان واراد التخلص، تغلغل فيه عند شدة التقاوم والمصاكة ليتخلص يُسمّى «الرعد» وقد ابتنى على الحرارة. وقد ينفصل الدخان نارا، وكان منه الصواعق وغيرها. والدخان اذا ضربه البرد يثقل فيهبط او رجع لدفع مجاور للفلك الدائر بموافقة من القوابس وتحامل على الهواء متبددا، كان منه الرياح. وكان السبب الأوّل فى هذه الاشياء ايضا الحرارة، ولا حرارة عندنا إلاّ من شعاع النيرات او ما يقع من نيران حاصلة بقدحنا، وهذا يسير. ثم القدح صادر عن الانوار المتصرفة التى لنا. وحركة المياه الى مكانها الطبيعى وانفجارها من العيون إنمّا هو لابخرة محتقنة؛ وكذا الزلازل، وسبب الابخرة ما سبق. فالحركة كلها سببها النور.

(٢٠٤) والحركات فى البرازخ العلوية وان كانت معدّة للاشراقات، إلاّ ان الاشراق من الانوار القاهرة، والمباشر للحركة النور المدبر فالعلة هناك النور المجرد مع النور السانح. والحركة اقرب الى طبيعة الحياة والنورية اذ هى مستدعية للعلة الوجودية النورية بخلاف السكون فانّه عدمى، فيكفيه عدم علة الحركة فالسكون لما كان عدميا، فهو مناسب للظلمات الميتة. فلولا نور، قائم او عارض، لهذا[6] العالم، ما وقعت حركة اصلا. فصارت الانوار علة الحركات والحرارات، والحركة والحرارة كل منهما مظهر للنور، لا انهما علتاه بل تُعدّان القابل لان يحصل فيه من النور القاهر الفائض بجوهره على القوابل المستعدة ما يليق باستعدادها.

(٢٠٥) واما النور فيوجدهما ويحصلهما بسنخه. والنور فيّاض لذاته فعّال لماهيته لا بجعل جاعل. واما اشعة الكواكب، فعلتها الكواكب. والنور التام له فى نفسه ان يكون علة للنور الناقص. ولما

necessarily has three angles, though this is but a state, so, too, it is not unlikely that an accidental light will necessitate another accidental light, given certain conditions. Heat or motion may each bring about the other in that which is suitable for it. The diversity and multiplicity of their effects are due to the diversity and capacities of recipients. There is a companionship between movement and light in the celestial barriers—a companionship more perfect than that between either one of them and heat.

(206) If you investigate things, you will find nothing that has an effect both near and far save light. Since love and dominance are from light—and movement and heat are also its effects—heat, therefore, has a part in striving, passions, and anger. For us, all of these are completed by motion. Desires also necessitate motions. Part of the nobility of fire is that it has the highest motion and the most perfect heat and is nearest to the nature of life. To it one turns for aid in darkness. It has the most perfect dominance, and it most resembles the principles[8] due to its luminosity. It is the brother to the human commanding light. By these two, the lesser and greater caliphates are perfected.[9] Thus it was that in the past the Persians commanded that prayer be performed facing fire. All the lights ought to be praised, according to the Law commanded by God, the Light of Lights.

Section [three]

[In explanation of qualitative change]

(207) Contrary to what is imagined, the heat caused by motion is not hidden and then made evident by the motion. Consider water that is agitated: Both its outside and inside are heated, though both were previously cold. If the heat had emerged from within, the inside would have become cold. There is someone who thinks that water is not heated by fire, but that fiery particles bearing heat are diffused within it. This view is false; for if the heating did occur by diffusion, water contained in

وجب بالمثلث زواياه الثلاثة[٧] مع كونه هيئة، لا يستبعد ان يكون نور عارض يوجب نورا عارضا على شرايط. والحرارة والحركة تستدعى احدهما صاحبتها فيما له صلاحية القبول. والنور اختلاف آثارها وتعددها لاختلاف القوابل واستعداداتها. وبين الحركة والنور مصاحبة فى البرازخ العلوية، وصحبتهما اتم من صحبة احدهما مع الحرارة.

(٢٠٦) واذا فتّشت الاشياء لم تجد ما يؤثر فى القريب والبعيد غير النور. ولما كانت المحبة والقهر من النور والحركة والحرارة ايضا معلولية، فصارت الحرارة لها مدخل فى النزوع والشهوات والغضب، ويتم جميعها عندنا بالحركة وصارت الاشواق ايضا موجبة للحركات. ومن شرف النار كونها اعلا حركة واتم حرارة واقرب الى طبيعة الحياة وبه يستعان فى الظلمات وهو اتم قهرا واشبه؛ لمبادى لنوريته؛ وهو أخ[٨] «النور الاسفهبد» الانسى وبهما تتم الخلافتان الصغرى والكبرى. فلذلك أمر الفرس بالتوجه اليه[٩] فيما مضى من الزمان. والانوار كلها واجبة التعظيم شرعا من الله، نور الانوار.

فصل

[فى بيان الاستحالة فى الكيف التى هى تغيّر فى الكيفيات لا فى الصور الجوهرية]

(٢٠٧) الحرارة التى توجبها الحركة ليست، كما يظن انها كانت كامنة، واظهرها الحركة.[١٠] واعتبر بالماء المتخضخض، فان ظاهره وباطنه يتسخنان، وكان قبل ذلك باردين. ولو كانت خارجة من الباطن ابرد الباطن. وظن بعض الناس ان الماء لا يتسخن بالنار بل يفشوا فيه اجزاء نارية معها الحرارة، وذلك باطل. فانّه لو كان بالفشوّ لكان الماء

earthenware would be heated faster than that in iron or copper kettles due to their relative composition and degree of resistance to diffusion, which is not the case. Moreover, how could the fiery particles be forced into a vessel that was too full to allow diffusion? If these enkindled things are mixed, the generated things result thereby. The constitution is the intermediate quality resulting from the opposing qualities in combined interacting bodies that are homogeneous in all their parts.

(208) Since you know that the forms they posit are not real, there can be nothing in the constitution except the intermediacy of qualities. Briefly, the difference between the constitution and corruption is that corruption is the total alteration of qualities, whereas the constitution is the intermediate of things combined. From this result the compounds: animals, plants, and minerals. Souls take loving delight in any mineral—gold or ruby, for example—which has a luminous barrier and stability, by which it resembles the celestial barriers and their lights. It is dear to them by virtue of the perfection of its stability, and love for it is similar to the love for the luminous star.

(209) Since the earthy substance is predominant in these things because of their need to preserve shape and powers, Esfandarmodh, the dominating light whose talisman is earth, has great solicitude for them. Since its idol[10] is affected by everything else due to the lowliness of its degree, its portion is womanliness—which is to say, Esfandarmodh, in relation to every other lord of an idol, has the portion of females.[11] If the nature of anything is taken without its qualities, it is the light for which that thing is the idol, as has been explained before.

(210) The most perfect constitution belongs to man, so it invokes a perfection from the Giver. You know the impossibility of the dominating lights altering, for their alteration could only be due to an alteration in their agent, the Light of Lights—which is impossible. Thus, neither It nor they ever change. However, from one of the dominating lights, things can come to be, in accordance with a renewed capacity due to the renewal of the perpetual movements. The agent may be perfect, even though the act depends on the capacity of the recipient. Thus, in proportion to its

الّذى فى الخزف اسرع تسخنا من الّذى فى بعض القماقم الحديدية والنحاسية على نسبة قماقمها ومنع الفشوّ، وليس كذا. ثم النارية كيف تدخل فى الظرف المملوء الّذى لم يبق فيه مكان لفاش؟ وهذه القوابس اذا امتزجت، حصل منها المواليد. والمزاج هو الكيفية المتوسطة الحاصلة من كيفيات متضادة لاجسام مجتمعة متفاعلة بتشابه فى جميع الاجزاء.

(٢٠٨) واذا علمت ان الصور التى فرضوها غير متحققة، ففى المزاج لا يكون إلاّ توسط الكيفيات. وحاصل الفرق بين المزاج والفساد ان الفساد تبدل بالكلية، والمزاج توسط المجتمعات ويحصل من هذه المركبات: حيوان، ونبات، ومعادن. ومن المعادن كلّما حصل فيه برزخ نورى والثبات تشبه[١١] بالبرازخ العلوية وانوارها، كالذهب والياقوت، كان محبوبا للنفوس مفرحا، فيه عز من جهة كمال ثباته وامر يناسب المحبة للبصيص النورى.

(٢٠٩) ولما كان الغالب على هذه الاشياء الجوهر العرضى، لحاجتها الى حفظ الاشكال والقوى، كان «اسفندارمذ»، وهو النور القاهر الّذى طلسمه الارض، كثير العناية بها. ولما كان صنمه منفعلا عن الجميع لنزول رتبته كان حصة «كدبانوئيته»، اى اسفندارمذ، عن كل صاحب صنم حصة الاناث.[١٢] وطبيعة كل شئ اذا أخذ غير كيفياته، فهو النور الّذى يكون ذلك الشئ صنمه على ما سبق.

(٢١٠) والمزاج الاتم ما للانسان فاستدعى من الواهب كمالا. والانوار القاهرة علمت استحالة تغييراتها فان تغيرهم لا يكون إلاّ التغير الفاعل، وهو نور الانوار. ويستحيل عليه، فلا تغيير له ولا لها. وانما يحصل من بعضها الاشياء لاستعداد متجدد لتجدد الحركات الدائمة. ويجوز ان يكون الفاعل تاما ويتوقف الفعل على استعداد القابل، فبقدر

moderateness, it accepts the appropriate states and forms that we mentioned in connection with the intellectual relations among the dominating lights and the relations of position among the fixed stars. From one of the dominating lights, the incorporeal light that is the controlling light in the human fortresses[12] is brought into being for the human—the most perfect—constitution. That dominating light is the lord of the talisman of the rational species. It is Gabriel—upon him be peace![13]—the proximate father among the mighty lords of the Kingdom of dominance. It is "Ravān-Bakhsh,"[14] the Holy Spirit, the bestower of knowledge and confirmation, the giver of life and virtue. This emanated light is the managing light, the "commander of humanity," that which calls itself "I."

(211) This light was not existent before the body, for each individual has an essence that knows itself and those of its states that are hidden from others. Thus, the human managing lights are not one, since otherwise that which was known to one would be known to all, which is not the case. Now, if these lights were existent before the body, they could not conceivably be one, since they could not be divided thereafter. This is because they do not have magnitude and are not barriers that could be divided. However, they could not conceivably be multiple either. Before the fortresses come to be, these incorporeal lights are not distinguished by intensity and weakness, since every degree of intensity and weakness would belong to an immeasurable number.[15] Nor could they be distinguished by a foreign accident, since they are not in the world of the movements that cause distinctions. Since they can neither be many nor one before controlling the fortresses, they cannot exist.

(212) Another method: If [the human managing lights] were existent before the fortresses, they could not be veiled or distracted from the world of pure light, nor could they be subject to chance or change. They would thus already be perfect, and their control of the fortresses would be pointless.[16] Moreover, there is no priority with respect to quiddity by which one might be specially associated with a fortress. Chance happenings—by which I mean necessity by the motions—exist only in the world of fortresses. The fortress is made ready to receive a light by motions, but there is nothing in the world of pure light that happens to distinguish that moment. It is not correct to argue that something happens to

الاعتدال يقبل من الهيآت والصور التى ذكرناها فى النسب العقلية فى الانوار القاهرة والوضعية التى للثوابت، ما يليق. ويحصل من بعض الانوار القاهرة، وهو صاحب طلسم النوع الناطق، يعنى جبراييل عليه السلام،[١٣] وهو الاب القريب من عظماء رؤساء الملكوت القاهرة «روانبخش»، روح القدس، واهب العلم والتأييد، معطى الحياة والفضيلة، على المزاج الاتم الانسانى نور مجرد هو النور المتصرف فى صياصى الانسية، وهو النور المدبر الّذى هو «اسفهبد الناسوت»، وهو المشير الى نفسه بالانائية.

(٢١١) وليس هذا النور موجود قبل البدن فان لكل شخص ذاتا يعلم نفسها واحوالها الخفية على غيرها. فليست الانوار المدبرة الانسية واحدة، والا ما علم واحد كان معلوما للجميع، وليس كذا. فقبل البدن ان كانت هذه الانوار موجودة لا يتصور وحدتها، فانها لا تنقسم بعد ذلك، اذ هى غير متقدرة ولا برزخية حتى يمكن عليها بالانقسام ولا تكثيرها، فان هذه الانوار المجردة قبل الصياصى لا تمتاز بشدة وضعف، اذ كل رتبة من الشدة والضعف ما لا يحصى، ولا عارض غريب. فانها ليست فى عالم الحركات المخصصة حينئذ. فلما لم يمكن[١٤] كثرتها ولا وحدتها قبل تصرف الصياصى فلا يمكن وجودها.

(٢١٢) طريق آخر: ان كانت موجودة قبل الصياصى، فلم يمنعها حجاب ولا شاغل من عالم النور المحض، ولا اتفاق ولا تغير فيه، فتكون كاملة، فتصرفها فى الصيصية يقع ضايعا. ثم لا اولوية بحسب الماهية لتخصص بعضها بصيصية، والاتفاقات، اعنى الوجوب بالحركات، إنمّا هو فى عالم الصياصى، فيستعد الصيصية لنور مّا بالحركات، وليس فى عالم النور المحض اتفاق تخصص ذلك الطرف. وما يقال «ان

the controlling lights to make them fall from their stations, for there is no renewal outside of the world of movements and changes, as you know.

(213) Another proof: If the managing lights were prior to the body, we could argue that some of them would not ever control a body. These would not be managing lights, and their existence would be pointless. If there were not such lights among them, there would necessarily come a time in which all would have descended and no managing lights would remain. This time would have occurred in the infinite past ages. Thus, no managing lights would now remain in the world—which is absurd.

(214) Another method: You know that events are infinite in number and that it is impossible for a soul to transmigrate into the world of humanity. Now, if the souls were not temporal, they would be infinite and would imply the existence of an infinite number of aspects in the incorporeal lights—which is absurd.

Section [four]

[On the five outer senses]

(215) Five outer senses have been created in man and the other perfect animals: touch, taste, smell, hearing, and sight. The objects of vision are noblest, for they are the lights of the planets and the like. The objects of touch are more important to animals, for that which is most important is not necessarily that which is noblest. The objects of hearing are subtler in another respect.

Section [five]

[Showing that there is a counterpart in the body to each attribute of the soul]

(216) You know that light emanates by essence and that it has in its substance a love for its origin and a dominance over that which is below it. It thus follows that the commanding light in the dusky fortresses must

المتصرفات يسنح لها حال موجب لسقوطها عن مراتبها» كلام باطل، اذ لا تجدد فيما ليس فى عالم الحركات والتغيرات على ما علمت.

(٢١٣) حجة اخرى: هى ان الانوار المدبرة ان كانت قبل البدن، فنقول: ان كان منها ما لا يتصرف اصلا، فليس بمدبر، ووجوده معطل؛ فان[١٥] لم يكن فيها[١٦] ما لا يتصرف، كان ضروريا وقوع وقت وقع فيه الكل وما بقى نورا مدبرا؛[١٧] وكان الوقت قد وقع فى الازل،[١٨] فكان ما بقى فى العالم نور مدبر، وهو محال.

(٢١٤) طريق آخر: واذا علمت انه لا نهاية للحوادث[١٩] واستحالة النقل الى الناسوت، ولو[٢٠] كانت النفوس غير حادثة، لكانت غير متناهية؛ فاستدعت جهات غير متناهية فى المفارقات، وهو محال.

فصل
[فى الحواس الخمس الظاهرة]

(٢١٥) الانسان وغيره من الحيوانات الكاملة خُلق له حواس خمسة: اللمس والذوق والشم والسمع والبصر. ومحسوسات البصر اشرف، فانها هى الانوار من الكواكب وغيرها، ولكن اللمس اهم للحيوان، والاهم غير الاشرف. والمسموعات الطف من وجه آخر.

فصل
[فى بيان ان لكل صفة
من صفات النفس نظيرا فى البدن]

(٢١٦) واذا علمت ان النور فياض لذاته، وان له فى جوهره محبة لسنخه وقهرا على ما تحته، فيلزم من النور الاسفهبد فى الصياصى

have a faculty of anger by reason of its dominance and a faculty of desire by mediacy of its love. The commanding light beholds bodily forms. It then intellects them and makes them luminous universal forms appropriate to its substance, as when someone beholds Zayd and ᶜAmr and takes from them a universal form of humanity that it predicates of them and of others. Thus, there must be a faculty of digestion in its fortress which transforms all the various foods into something similar to the substance of that which is nourished. Were that not the case, the body of man would be corrupted, would not be replaced, and would cease to exist. Just as it is in the nature of the perfect light to be the basis of another light, so, too, a faculty occurs in the fortress that necessitates another fortress possessing light. This is the reproductive faculty that ensures the preservation of the species, even though its individual cannot continue forever. This faculty separates a portion of matter to be the basis of another individual. It is also in the nature of light to be increased by propitious lights and to be completed by luminous states and thus to move from potentiality to actuality. Accordingly, a faculty occurs in the fortress necessitating increase in proper proportion in all dimensions. This is the faculty of growth. The faculty of nutrition is served by an attractive faculty, which brings it aid; by the retentive, which preserves it to be used by its user; by the digestive, which forms it and prepares it for use; and by the excretory, which expels that which does not accept similarity.

(217) These faculties are divisions of the commanding light in its fortress, and the fortress is an idol of the commanding light. These faculties result from aspects in it and from cooperation with states of the barriers. That they are different is shown by their existence before or after each other, by their differing effects, and by the fact that one can be defective while another is not. Man has the full share of the faculties of animals and plants.

الغاسقة بسبب قهره قوة غضبية، وبتوسط محبته قوة شهوانية. وكما ان النور الاسفهبد يشاهد صورا برزخية، فيعقلها ويجعلها صورا عامة نورية تليق بجوهره، كمن شاهد زيدا وعمرا واخذ منهما للانسانية صورة عامة تحمل عليهما وعلى غيرهما، يلزمه[٢١] فى صيصيته قوة غاذية تحيل الاغذية المختلفة كلها الى شبيه جوهر المغتذى؛ ولولا هذه لتحلل بدن الانسان ولم يجد بدلا فما استمر وجوده. وكما ان فى سنخ النور التام ان يكون مبدأ لنور آخر، فيحصل منه فى صيصيته قوة توجبه صيصية اُخرى ذات نور، وهى المولّدة التى بها بقاء نوع ما لم يتصور بقاء شخصه دايما فتقطع قدرا من الماء ليكون مبدأ لشخص آخر. وكما من سنخ النور ان يزداد بالانوار السانحة ويستكمل بالهيآت النورية ويخرج من القوة الى الفعل، فيحصل منه للصيصية قوة توجب الزيادة فى الاقطار على نسبة لايقة وهى النامية. ثم تخدم الغاذية جاذبة ثانيها بالمدد، وماسكة تحفظه ليتصرف المتصرف، وهاضمة تهيّئه وتعدّه للتصرف، ودافعة لما لا يقبل المشابهة.

(٢١٧) وهذه القوى فروع النور الاسفهبد فى صيصيته، والصيصية صنم للنور الاسفهبد، فتحصل هذه القوى منه باعتبارات فيه وشركة احوال البرازخ. ويدل على تغايرها وجود بعضها قبل بعض او بعد بعض، واختلاف الآثار واختلال بعضها عند كمال بعض. والانسان يستوفى[٢٢] قوى الحيوان والنبات.

Section [six]

[Showing the correspondence between the rational soul and the animal spirit]

(218) The commanding light controls a barrier only by the mediacy of a certain correspondence, that which it has with the subtle substance called the "spirit." Its source is the left cavity of the heart, since it has a moderation and distance from extremes resembling that of the celestial barriers. It has a translucency such that images appear in it, for the pure translucent thing has this property. Other elementals become loci in which the image is made evident by its mediacy. It has an opacity such that it accepts and preserves light and preserves shapes and forms. It also possesses a subtlety and heat corresponding to light. It has a motion corresponding to the accidental light. There is no stability in the instances of the species of spirit because of its rapid dissolution due to its subtlety and the predominance of heat in it. Therefore, its species is preserved by aid.[17] Among elemental things, only spirit corresponds to light in all respects. Air does not accept rays, but it does correspond to light in its heat and its quickly accepting motion. Therefore, it seeks the world of barrial light, which is in perpetual motion, [and] approaches it and loves it. The opaque accepts radiated light and preserves it, so it corresponds to light in this respect. The translucent preserves rays and becomes the locus in which the form of the luminary and the illumined is made evident, but it fails to correspond to light in such aspects as its coldness.

(219) There are many correspondences in this spirit. It is dispersed throughout the entire body and is the bearer of the luminous faculties. The commanding light controls the body by its mediacy and gives it light. The propitious light that the commanding light takes from the dominating lights is reflected from it upon this spirit. Sense and motion occur by that which ascends to the brain and is moderate. It accepts the luminous sovereignty and returns to all the organs. Because there is a correspondence between happiness and light, everything that is generated—that is, from every kind of food—becomes joyful, luminous spirit. Because of

فصل

[فى بيان المناسبة بين النفس الناطقة
والروح الحيوانى]

(٢١٨) النور الاسفهبذ لا يتصرف فى البرزخ إلاّ بتوسط مناسبة مّا، وهى ما له مع الجوهر اللطيف الّذى سمّوه «الروح»، ومنبعه التجويف الايسر من القلب، اذ فيه من الاعتدال والبعد عن التضاد ما يشابه البرازخ العلوية، وفيه من الاقتصاد ما يظهر عنده المثال، فان المقتصد الصافى له ذلك، وغيره من العنصريات يصير مظهرا للمثال بتوسطه. وفيه من الحاجزية ما يقبل النور ويحفظه ويحفظ الاشكال والصور. وفيه[٢٣] اللطافة والحرارة المناسبة للنور. وفيه الحركة ايضا المناسبة للنور العارض. واذا لم يكن فى اعداد نوعه الثبات لسرعة تحلله باعتبار اللطف وغلبة الحرارة، فثبت نوعه بالمداد. فقد أتى على جميع مناسبات النور. فان الفضاء لم[٢٤] يقبل الشعاع ولكن يناسب النور بحرارته وسرعة قبول حركته. ولهذا قصد الى عالم النور البرزخى الّذى دامت حركته وقرب منه وعشقه. والحاجز قبل النور الشعاعى وحفظه، فناسب من هذا الوجه. والمقتصد حفظ الشعاع وصار مظهرا لمثال النيّر والمستنير، ولكن خالف مناسبة النور بالبرد ونحوه.

(٢١٩) وهذا الروح فيه المناسبات الكثيرة، وهو متبدد فى جميع البدن، وهو حامل القوى النورية ويتصرف النور الاسفهبذ فى البدن بتوسطه ويعطيه النور. وما يأخذ من النور السانح من القواهر ينعكس منه على هذا الروح. وما به الحس والحركة هو الّذى يصعد الى الدماغ ويعتدل، ويقبل السلطان النورى، ويرجع الى جميع الاعضاء. ولمناسبة السرور مع النور صار كل ما تولد روحا نورانيا، مفرحا، اعنى من جملة

the correspondence of souls with light, souls flinch from darknesses and are happy in beholding lights. Animals, all of them, seek light in darkness and love the light. Thus, even though the commanding light is not spatial and has no position, the darknesses in its fortress are subservient to it.

[Section seven]

[Showing that the inner senses are not limited to five]

(220) A man may sometimes forget something and find great difficulty in remembering it. Try though he might, he is unable to remember it. Then, it sometimes happens that he remembers that very same thing easily. That which he remembers is not itself present in one of the faculties of his body, since it would not then have been hidden from the managing light after its diligent search. Nor, as is sometimes thought, is it preserved in one of the faculties of his body with something keeping the light from it, for the seeker is the controlling light—not something to do with a barrier that some obstacle could keep from getting at what is preserved in one of the faculties of its fortress. At the moment of his forgetfulness, the man would be unaware of something that is perceived in his essence and in his fortress. Thus, that which is remembered is only in the world of memory, one of the places belonging to the lord of celestial commanding lights. These forget nothing.

(221) The imaginative forms supposed to be preserved in the imagination cannot be real for similar reasons. If they were, they would be present to the managing light, and it would perceive them. But a man finds nothing at all perceptible in himself when the image of Zayd is absent. Indeed, if a man senses something corresponding to Zayd or thinks of him for some reason, his thought moves to him and he acquires a capacity to summon the form of Zayd from the world of memory. That which recalls [the form] from the world of memory is the managing light.

الاغذية ولمناسبة النفوس مع النور متنفرة عن الظلماة منبسطة عند مشاهدة الانوار. والحيوانات كلها تقصد النور فى الظلم وتعشق النور. فان النور[٢٥] الاسفهبذ وان لم يكن مكانيا ولا ذا جهة، إلاّ ان الظلمات التى فى صيصيته مطيعة له.

[**فصل**][٢٦]

[فى ان الحواس الباطنة غير منحصرة فى الخمس]

(٢٢٠) واعلم ان الانسان اذا نسى شيئا ربما يصعب عليه ذكره حتى انه يجتهد عظيما ولا يتيسر له، ثم يتفق انه احيانا ان يتذكر ذلك بعينه، فليس هذا الّذى يذكره بعينه فى بعض قوى بدنه والا ما غاب عن النور المدبر بعد السعى البالغ فى طلبه، وليس على ما يُفرض انه محفوظ فى بعض قوى ومنع عنه مانع، فان الطالب إنمّا هو النور المتصرف، وليس برزخى يمنعه مانع عن أمر محفوظ فى بعض قوى صيصيته، ولا يشعر الانسان فى حال غفلته عن أمر بشئ مدرك فى ذاته وصيصيته له. فليس التذكر إلاّ من عالم الذكر، وهو من موانع سلطان الانوار الاسفهبذية الفلكية فانها لا تنسى شيئا.

(٢٢١) والصور الخيالية على ما فُرضت مخزونة فى الخيال باطلة مثل هذا؛ فانها لو كانت فيها لكانت حاضرة له وهو مدرك لها. فلا[٢٧] يجد الانسان فى نفسه عند غيبته عن تخيل زيد شيئا مدركا له اصلا؛ بل اذا احس الانسان بشئ مّا يناسبه، او تفكر فيه بسبب من الاسباب، ينتقل فكره الى زيد فيحصل له استعداد استعادة صورته من عالم الذكر. والمعيد من عالم الذكر إنمّا هو النور المدبر.

(222) There is someone[18] who asserts that man has an estimative faculty that judges concerning particulars, and another—the imaginative faculty—that separates and combines images. Both are located in the central cavity of the brain. To him, one might reply: "Estimation is the same as the imaginative faculty, for both judge, separate, and combine. The proof [you offer] that the faculties are separate might be that one is corrupted while the other remains, but no one can claim that the imaginative faculty remains sound while there is nothing judging the particulars—that which you call estimation." A difference of locations is known by the corruption of one faculty as a concomitant of the corruption of its location, but it is admitted that these are both in the central cavity.[19] Since it is not the case that one of them is corrupted while the other remains sound, the same must be true of their locations. As for the argument from the multiplicity of effects, one cannot judge that the faculties are multiple just because the effects are, since one faculty may necessitate two effects by virtue of two aspects. Does not he admit that the common sense, which is a unity, perceives all the sensibles, despite their origins in five senses? It combines within itself the images of all the sensibles and perceives them all together. Were that not so, we could not judge that this white is that sweetness when both are present. External sense beholds them separately, but to judge them requires the presence of both forms. Since it is possible for one faculty to have many perceptions, so, too, is it possible to have many separate effects from it. However, the estimative judgment is not in conflict with the actions of the imaginative faculty.

(223) It is strange that some of them say, "The imaginative faculty acts and does not perceive," even though it has the perception of the form. If it does not possess a form and does not perceive, what then can it combine and separate? How can it combine and separate a form that belongs to another faculty? If it is impossible for the imaginative faculty to be sound or to make its judgments without forms, then it cannot be said that the imagination or its location can be corrupted while the imaginative faculty remains sound and active.

(٢٢٢) واثبت بعض الناس فى الانسان قوة وهمية هى الحاكمة فى الجزئيات، واخرى هى متخيلة لها التفصيل والتركيب، واوجب ان محلهما التجويف الاوسط. ولقائل ان يقول: ان الوهم بعينه هو المتخيلة وهى الحاكمة والمفصلة والمركبة. ودليلك على تغيير القوى اما اختلال بعضها مع بقاء البعض، ولا يمكن لاحد دعوى بقاء المتخيلة سليمة وليس ثم شئ حاكم فى الجزئيات الّذى هو الوهم عندك، واختلاف المواضع عُرف بلزوم اختلال بعض القوى لاختلال مواضعها، وقد اعترف بانهما فى التجويف الاوسط، واذ لا يختل احد منهما مع سلامة صاحبه، فمواضعهما ايضا كذا؛ واما تعدد الافاعيل ولا[٢٨] يمكن الحكم بتعدد القوى لتعدد الافاعيل، اذ يجوز ان يكون قوة واحدة بجهتين تقتضى فعلين. أليس الحس المشترك باعترافه مع وحدته يدرك جميع المحسوسات التى ما يأتى[٢٩] ادراكها إلاّ بخمس حواس؟ وهو يجتمع عنده مثل جميع المحسوسات فيدركها مشاهدة. ولولا ذلك ما كان لنا ان نحكم ان هذا الابيض هو هذا الحلو للحاضرين، فان الحس الظاهر منفرد باحدهما، والحاكم يحتاج الى حضور الصورتين ليحكم عليهما. فاذا جاز[٣٠] لقوة واحدة ادراكات كثيرة، فجاز منها افاعيل متعددة كثيرة على ان الحكم الوهمى لا يخالف افاعيل المتخيلة.

(٢٢٣) ثم العجب ان منهم من قال «ان المتخيلة تفعل ولا تدرك» وعنده الادراك بالصورة. فاذا لم يكن عندها صورة ولا تُدرك، فاى شئ تركبه وتفصله؟ والصورة التى عند قوة اُخرى كيف تُركّبها هذه القوة وتُفصّلها؟ واذا لم يكن سلامة المتخيلة وتمكنها من احكامها دون الصور، فلا يمكن ان يقال: يختل الخيال او موضعه والمتخيلة سليمة وهى على افعالها.

(224) The truth is that these three[20] are a single thing and a single faculty, named differently depending on how they are considered. The evidence that they are not the managing light is that when we firmly resolve to do something, we find something in ourselves that resists.[21] We know by introspection that that which tries to be firm in its resolve is other than that which has resisted it and that that which is resolved on something is other than that which opposes it. Since we find that which opposes us in our bodies, it must be something other than that by which we have our identities. Therefore, it is a faculty necessitated in the fortress from the commanding light. Because it is dark and imprinted in the barrier, it denies the incorporeal lights and believes in nothing except the sensibles. Sometimes it even denies itself. It assists in acquiring premises; but when it reaches the conclusion, it returns to its denial, rejecting the consequence of the premises it had accepted. Even though memory is from the world of the spheres, there may nonetheless be a faculty to which is attached a capacity for memory.

[Section eight]

[On the reality of the forms in mirrors and the imagination]

(225) You know that forms cannot be imprinted in the eye and that, for similar reasons, they cannot be imprinted somewhere in the brain. The truth is that the forms in mirrors and the imaginative forms are not imprinted. Instead, they are suspended fortresses—fortresses not in a locus at all. Though they may have loci in which they are made evident, they are not in them. The mirror is the locus in which the form in the mirror is made evident. These forms are suspended and are in neither a place nor a locus. The imaginative faculty is the locus in which the forms of the imagination are made evident and are suspended. Since there can be such a thing as an incorporeal image in a mirror—in a plane and without depth or back, self-subsistent, and not an accident of the mirror—there can also exist a substantial quiddity having an accidental image. The deficient light is like an image of the perfect light—understand this!

(٢٢٤) فالحق ان هذه الثلاثة شئ واحد وقوة واحدة باعتبارات يعبر عنها بعبارات. والذى يدل على ان هذه غير النور المدبر، انّا اذا حاولنا تثبتا[٣١] على شئ نجد[٣٢] من انفسنا شيئا ينتقل[٣٣] عنه، ونعلم منا ان الّذى يجتهد فى التثبيت غير الّذى يروم النقل وان الّذى يثبت[٣٤] بعض الاشياء غير الّذى ينكرها. واذا كنا نجد فى بدننا[٣٥] ما يخالفها هكذا، فهو غير ما به أنائيتنا. فهو اذن قوة لزمت عن النور الاسفهبد فى الصيصية، ولاجل انها ظلمانية منطبعة فى البرزخ تنكر الانوار المجردة ولا تعترف إلاّ بالمحسوسات؛ ولربما تنكر نفسها وتساعد فى المقدمات، فاذا وصلت الى النتيجة عادت منكرة فتجد موجب ما سلمت من الموجب. والتذكر وان كان من عالم الافلاك، إلاّ انه يجوز ان يكون قوة يتعلق بها استعداد مّا للتذكر.

[فصل][٣٦]

[فى حقيقة صور المرايا و التخيل]

(٢٢٥) وقد علمت ان انطباع الصور فى العين ممتنع، وبمثل ذلك يمتنع فى موضع من الدماغ. والحق فى صور المرايا والصور الخيالية انها ليست منطبعة، بل هى صياصى[٣٧] معلقة ليس لها محل اصلا.[٣٨] وقد تكون لها مظاهر، ولا تكون فيها. فصورة[٣٩] المرآة مظهرها المرآة، وهى معلقة لا فى مكان ولا فى محل. وصور الخيال مظهرها التخيل وهى معلقة. واذا ثبت مثال مجرد سطحى لا عمق له ولا ظهور،[٤٠] كما للمرايا، قائم بنفسه وما هو منه عرض، فصح وجود ماهية جوهرية لها مثال عرضى، والنور الناقص كمثال نور التام، فافهم.

(226) Just as all the senses reduce to a single sense—the common sense—so, too, all of the faculties reduce to a single faculty in the managing light—its luminous essence, emanating by essence. Though vision is conditioned both on being opposite and [on possessing] an eye, that which sees is in fact the commanding light. It may not see things before separation,[22] because something can occur to the thing to keep it from seeing that which it is able to see. The hindrance is a sort of veil. Those who have ascended in the soul and cut themselves off from their bodies have at that moment experienced a clear contemplation more perfect than that which the eye possesses. At that moment, they know with certainty that these entities which they behold are not engravings in one of the bodily faculties and that visual contemplation endures as long as the managing light does. Whoso strives in the path of God as he ought and subdues the shadows beholds the lights of the all-highest world more perfectly than he beholds the objects of vision here below. The Light of Lights and the dominating lights are seen by the vision of the commanding light and by their seeing each other. All the incorporeal lights see, and their vision does not reduce to their knowledge; rather, their knowledge reduces to their vision.

(227) Each of these faculties in the body is a shadow of what is in the commanding light, and the temple is only its talisman, so that even the imaginative faculty is the idol of the faculty of judgment in the commanding light. Were it not that the managing light has determinations by its essence, one could not judge that it had a particular body or imagination or that it had a particular imaginative faculty. Thus, none of these things are absent from it but rather are evident to it in a certain way. The imaginative faculty does not deal with its own form, for it judges the sensibles and what follows from them. The commanding light encompasses and judges that it has a particular faculty. It has this judgment by its essence and is thus the sense of all the senses. That which is dispersed throughout the body returns finally in the commanding light to a single thing. The commanding light shines upon the images of the imagination and the like, and it shines upon the vision without need of a form.

(٢٢٦) وكما ان الحواس كلها ترجع الى حاسة واحدة وهى الحس المشترك فجميع ذلك يرجع فى النور المدبر الى قوة واحدة هى ذاته النورية الفياضة لذاتها. والابصار وان كان مشروطا فيه المقابلة مع البصر، إلاّ ان الباصر فيه النور الاسفهبذ؛ وانما لا يرى اشياء قبل المفارقة، لان الشئ قد يعرض له ما يشغله عن ابصار ما من شأنه ان يبصره، والشاغل فى حكم الحجاب. وقد جرّب اصحاب العروج للنفس مشاهدة صريحة اتم مما للبصر فى حالة انسلاخ شديد عن البدن وهم متيقنون حينئذ بان ما يشاهدون من الامور ليست نقوشا فى بعض القوى البدنية، والمشاهدة البصرية باقية مع النور المدبر. ومن جاهد فى الله حق جهاده وقهر الظلمات رأى انوار العالم الاعلى مشاهدة اتم من مشاهدات[٤١] المبصرات ههنا. فنور الانوار والانوار القاهرة مرئية برؤية النور الاسفهبذ ومرئية برؤية بعضها بعضا، والانوار المجردة كلها باصرة وليس بصرها يرجع الى علمها، بل علمها يرجع الى بصرها.

(٢٢٧) فهذه القوى فى البدن كلها ظل ما فى النور الاسفهبذ، والهيكل إنمّا هو طلسمه حتى ان المتخيلة ايضا صنم لقوة النور الاسفهبذ الحاكم. ولولا ان النور المدبر له احكام بذاته، ما حكم بان له بدنا او تخيلا جزئيا او له قوة متخيلة جزئية. فهذه الاشياء غير غايبة عنها، بل ظاهرة لها ظهورا مّا. والتخيل لا يأخذ صورة نفسه، فانّه حاكم على المحسوسات وما يتبعها. والنور الاسفهبذ محيط وحاكم بان له قوة جزئية، فله الحكم بذاته وهو حس جميع الحواس. وما تفرق فى جميع البدن يرجع فى النور الاسفهبذ حاصله الى شئ واحد وللنور الاسفهبذ اشراق على مُثُل[٤٢] الخيال ونحوه، واشراق على الابصار المستغنى عن الصورة.

(228) In general, we must say here that the illumination upon the imagination is like the illumination upon vision. If it were just the image in imagination that was perceived to be the image of the external, it would perceive the external absent thing without an image and thus would be without need of it. This is impossible, because the external imagined thing might not exist at the moment of imagination. Perception through vision occurs by its being a luminous sense and by there being no veil between it and the illumined thing. This luminosity and absence of veils is more perfect in incorporeals, for they are evident by essence. Therefore, they see and are seen.[23]

(٢٢٨) وله ذكر اجمالى: ان هذا الاشراق على الخيال مثل الاشراق على الابصار، والا ان كان مجرد مثال الخيال، ان ادرك انه مثال الخارج، يكون ادراك الخارج الغائب دون مثال واستغنى عنه، وهو ممتنع على ان الخارج المتخيل قد يكون انعدم فى حالة التخيل. والبصر لما كان ادراكه بكونه حاسة نورية وعدم الحجاب بينه وبين المستنير، فالنورية مع عدم الحجاب فى المجردات اتم، وهى ظاهرة لذاتها، فهى باصرة مبصرة.[٤٣]

The Fifth Discourse

On the resurrection, prophecy, and dreams, in [nine] sections

Section [one]

[In explanation of reincarnation[1]]

(229) The constitution of the barrier invokes the commanding light by virtue of its capacity to call that light into existence. The commanding light has a friendship with its fortress because that fortress has called it into existence. Its connection with its body is due to its dependence in itself, and its contemplation of that which is above it is due to its luminosity. The fortress is the locus in which its acts are made evident, the pouch for its lights, the container for its effects, the encampment of its faculties. Since the dark faculties love the commanding light, they cling to it out of love and draw it to their world from the world of pure light, that world where there is no taint of the darkness of barriers. Thus, its desire for the world of pure light is transferred from the world of pure light to the darknesses. The human fortress was created perfect, and all the acts arise from it. In the opinion of the sages of the East, it is the first station of the commanding light in the world of barriers. Since the dusky substance by its nature desires the accidental light to make it evident and the incorporeal light to control it and give it life, the dusky substance must be from the aspect of dependence in the dominating lights. And just as the poor man is desirous of freedom from want,[2] so, too, is the dusky substance desirous of light.

المقالة الخامسة
فى المعاد والنبوات والمنامات
وفيها فصول

فصل
[فى بيان التناسخ]

(٢٢٩) النور الاسفهبذ استدعاه المزاج البرزخى باستعداده المستدعى لوجوده، فله اِلف مع صيصيته لانها استدعت وجوده. وكان علاقته مع البدن لفقره فى نفسه ونظره الى ما فوقه لنوريته؛ وهى مظهر لافعاله وحقيبة[1] لانواره ووعاء لآثاره ومعسكر لقواه. والقوى الظلمانية لما عشقته تشبثت به تشبثا عشقيا، وجذبته الى عالمها عن عالم النور البحت الّذى لا يشوبه ظلمة برزخية اصلا؛ فانقطع شوقه عن عالم النور البحت الى الظلمات. والصيصية الانسية خلقت تامة يتأتى بها جميع الافاعيل، وهى أوّل منزل للنور الاسفهبذ على رأى حكماء المشرق فى عالم البرازخ. ولما كان الجوهر الغاسق مشتاقا بطبعه الى نور عارض ليظهره ونور مجرد ليدبره ويحيى به، فان الغاسق إنمّا هو من جهة الفقر فى القواهر. وكما ان الفقير يشتاق الى الاستغناء فكذا الغاسق يشتاق[2] الى النور.

(230) Buddha and the Eastern sages[3] before him said that the Gate of Gates for the life of all elemental fortresses is the human fortress. Whatever moral habit captures the commanding light, whatever dark state becomes established in it and becomes its support, the commanding light must transfer its attachment after the corruption of its fortress to a fortress corresponding to that dark state: a fortress of one of the brute animals. When the commanding light departs from the human fortress, it is darkened and desirous of darknesses. It does not know its source or the world of light. Wicked states have become fixed in it, and it is drawn to the brute fortresses of other animals, and the darknesses beckon to it.

(231) They said that the most noble constitution belongs to the human fortress. It is thus the constitution most worthy to receive the new commanding emanation from the dominating light. But no commanding light can move to it from another source, since it summons a managing light from the Giver. If a transmigrated soul were to become attached to it, a single man could have two perceptive identities—which is absurd.

(232) They said that though, by virtue of its noble constitution, the human fortress calls into being a commanding light from the dominating light, it does not follow that the brute fortress[4] calls into being a commanding light from the dominating light. If the human fortress is corrupted and the commanding light is clouded by the darknesses,[5] not knowing what is beyond it,[6] it is drawn by its desire to the lowest of the low. The brute fortresses and the world of barriers also thirst for managing lights. Thus, the commanding light is drawn by necessity to another fortress. The wisdom, for the sake of which the commanding light acquired the attachments of the body, has an eternal dimension. But light is perfected only by light, so nothing ascends from the nonrational fortresses to man. Rather, they descend from the human fortresses to the nonrational fortresses by reason of states. To each moral quality correspond fortresses: "To every class thereof an appointed portion" [Qur'ān 15:44].

(٢٣٠) قال بوذاسف ومن قبله من الحكماء[٣] المشرقيين: ان باب الابواب لحياة جميع الصياصى العنصرية الصيصية الانسية. فاى خلق يغلب على النور الاسفهبذ واى هيئة ظلمانية تتمكن فيه ويركن اليها هو، يوجب ان يكون بعد فساد صيصيته منتقلا علاقته الى صيصية مناسبة لتلك الهيئة الظلمانية من الحيوانات المنتكسة. فانّ النور الاسفهبذ اذا فارق الصيصية الانسية، وهو مظلم مشتاق الى الظلمات ولم يعلم سنخه وعالم النور وتمكنت فيه الهيآت الرديئة، فتنجذب الى صياصى منتكسة لحيوانات أُخرى وجذبته الظلمات.

(٢٣١) قالوا: والمزاج الاشرف ما للصيصية الانسية، وهى اولى بقبول الفيض الجديد الاسفهبذى من النور القاهر، فلا ينتقل اليها من غيرها نور اسفهبدى،[٤] اذ يستدعى من الواهب نورا مدبرا وتقارنها مستنسخ، فتحصل فى انسان واحد انائيتان مدركتان، وهو محال.

(٢٣٢) قالوا: ولا يلزم من استدعاء الصيصية الانسية لمزاجها الاشرف[٥] النور الاسفهبذ من النور القاهر استدعاء الصيصية الصامتة النور الاسفهبذ من النور القاهر. فاذا انفسدت الصيصية الانسية، والنور الاسفهبذ غاسق الظلمات،[٦] لا يعلم ما ورائه.[٧] فهو بشوقه منجذب[٨] الى اسفل السافلين. والصياصى المنتكسة وعالم البرازخ ايضا متعطش، فينجذب بالضرورة الى صيصية أُخرى. فانّ الحكمة التى لاجلها اقترن النور الاسفهبذ بعلائق البدن من حاجته الى الاستكمال بعد باقية. والنور لا يتم بغير نور، ولا يرتقى من الصياصى الصامتة الى الانسان شئ، بل ينحدر من الصياصى الانسية الى الصوامت للهيآت. ولكل خلق صياصى و«لكل باب منها جزء مقسوم».[٩]

(233) It is not valid to argue that the number of things generated would fail to correspond to the number corrupted, for a great number of managing lights have been darkened through the long ages. These lights are ordered in descending rank. The greedy will not attach themselves to the fortresses of ants until after separation from the fortresses of many species differing in magnitude and attachments. Since none of them ascend to man, difficulties will not arise in the correspondence of the small number of long-lived fortresses with the very great number of short-lived fortresses.[7] The attachment is destroyed through the pangs of death and torments. Each degree has large individuals and middling and small. Each group of craftsmen has a nation of dumb beasts corresponding to it in morals and manner of life.[8] They transmigrate first to the largest, then to the intermediate in the many degrees, and finally to the smallest at the end of long ages.

(234) According to the Easterners, the statement that every constitution invokes a controlling light from the dominating light is not necessarily correct, since it is not necessarily so for other than the human fortress.[9] There is also no reason to accept the argument that the moment of the corruption of a human body does not necessarily correspond to the moment of the generation of a dumb body. These matters are regulated by celestial states hidden from us. Just as one man's expense is another man's gain, the money not remaining idle between them, so, too, the death of one fortress is the life of another. This is the view of the Easterners. Sometimes they admit the possibility of transmigration from one individual to its peer below the level of man, since this does not imply the duplication of souls that would take place in man due to his capacity to receive emanation.

(235) The Peripatetics say: "Through their individual characteristics, all constitutions invoke controlling souls; so what you said about man must also be true of the constitutions of animals." This is the view of the Peripatetics.

(٢٣٣) وما يقال «انّ عدد الكاينات لا ينطبق على عدد الفاسدات»، فباطل. لان الانوار المدبرة المستظلمة[١٠] فى الازمنة الطويلة كثيرة، وهى مندرجة فى النزول. واصحاب الحرص لا يلحقون الصياصى النملية إلاّ بعد مفارقة صياصى انواع كثيرة متفاوتة المقدار والعلائق. ولا يرتقى منها الى الانسان شئ ليلزم صعوبات فى انطباق العدد الكثير على الصياصى القليلة الطويلة الاعمار من صياصى[١١] قليلة الاعمار كثيرة العدد جدا. وتنتقض العلائق بالسكرات وشدة الموت والبلايا. ولكل مرتبة كبار واوساط وصغار، فلكل قوم من ارباب الصناعات امة من الصوامت تشبههم خلقا وعيشة؛ فتنتقل الى الاكبر ثم الى الاوسط على المراتب الكثيرة، ثم الى الاصغر فى ازمنة متطاولة.

(٢٣٤) وعند هؤلاء ما يقال «ان كل مزاج يستدعى من النور القاهر نورا متصرفا» فكلام غير واجب الصحة، اذ لا يلزم فى غير الصياصى الانسية[١٢] وما يقال «انّه لا يلزم ان يتصل وقت فساد الصيصية الانسانية بوقت كون الصيصية الصامتة»[١٣] ليس بمتوجه ايضا؛ فان الأمور مضبوطة بهيآت فلكية غائبة عنا، كما يوجب فى خسارة بعض الناس ربح بعض بحيث لا يبقى المال بينهما معطلا، فكذا فى موت بعض الصياصى حياة بعض منها. هذا مذهب المشرقيين. وربما يجوزون النقل فيما وراء الانسان من شخص مشاكله ما لم يلزم المزاحمة التى القى الانسان لاستعداد الفيض.

(٢٣٥) وقال المشاؤون «جميع الامزجة مستدعية بخواص مزاجها نفوسا متصرفة، فيلزم فيها ما ذكرتم فى الانسان». هذا مذهب المشائين .

Plato and the sages before him held the doctrine of transference,[10] even though there was disagreement among them about its details.

Some within Islam held this view on the basis of certain revealed verses. It is written, "Whenever their skins scorched, We gave them back different skins" [Qurʾān 4:56]; "Whenever they desired to escape therefrom, We cast them back therein" [Qurʾān 32:20]; and "Every creature crawling on the earth, every bird soaring on its wings belongs to nations like unto yours" [Qurʾān 6:38]. There are verses of metamorphosis and traditions handed down concerning men being resurrected in forms differing in accordance with their differing moral qualities. The words of the damned have been recorded in revelation: "Our Lord, Thou hast twice brought us death and twice life" [Qurʾān 40:11]. Of the blessed it is written: "They shall taste no death therein save the first death" [Qurʾān 44:56]. There are others of this sort. Most of the sages inclined toward this doctrine, and all agreed that the purified managing lights escape to the world of light without transference. We will mention hereafter that which is implied by the mystical experience of the philosophy of illumination.

(236) Know that it would be inconceivable for the incorporeal managing light to become nonbeing after the annihilation of the fortress. If the incorporeal light necessitated its own nonbeing, it would never have existed at all. That which makes it necessary—the dominating light—does not destroy it, for the dominating light never alters; and, in any case, how could a thing destroy by its own essence the concomitant of its essence? How could a light destroy of itself its own ray and luminosity? The incorporeal lights do not jostle each other for locus or place; their holiness is such as to make that impossible. They do not reside in the dusky substances so as to be conditioned on presence or capacity in a locus. The origin of the managing lights is unalterable; they are not like those things that are suspended and result from the conditions of the managing light alone or with something else, like reflections. These latter are conditioned on being seen by a living being possessing vision. The relation of things other than the active soul to that which they possess is like that of the locus to the drawing, whether from it or from another. When the state in the cause ceases, [that which it causes] ceases. But the cause of the incorporeal light is everlasting, so it is everlasting. If the managing lights did admit of nonbeing, their nonbeing would result

وافلاطون ومن قبله من الحكماء قائلون بالنقل، وان كانت جهات النقل قد يقع فيها خلاف.

وتمسك بعض الاسلاميين بآيات من الوحى مثل قوله تعالى «كلّما نضجت جلودهم بدلناهم جلودا غيرها».[١٤] وقوله تعالى «كلّما ارادوا ان يخرجوا منها اعيدوا فيها».[١٥] وقوله «وما من دابة فى الارض ولا طاير يطير بجناحيه إلاّ امم امثالكم».[١٦] وآيات المسخ والاحاديث الواردة فى ان الناس يبعثون على صور مختلفة بحسب اخلاقهم كثيرة. وكما ورد فى الوحى حكاية عن الاشقياء «ربنا امتنا اثنتين واحييتنا اثنتين».[١٧] وكقوله تعالى فى السعداء «لا يذوقون فيها الموت إلاّ الموتة الاولى»،[١٨] وغير ذلك. وصغى اكثر الحكماء الى هذا، إلاّ ان الجميع متفقون على خلاص الانوار المدبرة الطاهرة الى عالم النور دون النقل، ونحن نذكر بعد هذا ما يقتضيه ذوق حكمة الاشراق.

(٢٣٦) واعلم انّ النور المجرد المدبر لا يتصور عليه العدم بعد فناء الصيصية،[١٩] فانّ النور المجرد لا يقتضى عدم نفسه، وإلاّ ما وُجد. ولا يبطله موجبه وهو النور القاهر، فانّه لا يتغير. ثم انّ الشئ كيف يبطل لازم ذاته بذاته؟ ثم ان النور كيف يبطل شعاعه وضوئه بنفسه؟ والانوار المجردة ليس بينها مزاحمة على محل او مكان لتقدسها عنهما. وليست حالة فى الغواسق يشترط فيها مقابلة واستعداد محل. وليس مبدأ المدبرات بمتغير، فلا تكون هى كمتعلقات[٢٠] حصلت من احوال المدبر وحده، او مع غيره كالصقاليات، فانّها مشروطة بشهود الحىّ الباصر. ونسبة غير النفس الفاعلية الى ما لها، كالمحل للنقوش، كانت منه او من غيره، فاذا بطل حال المبدأ بطلت. فالنور المجرد موجبه دائم، فيدوم. ولو كانت الانوار المدبرة قابلة للعدم، لكان انعدامها للهيآت الظلمانية؛

from dark states; and in the condition of connection to the attachments of the body, they would be worthier of nonbeing—not after separation. Once the incorporeal light escapes from the darknesses, it continues as long as the dominating light that is its cause. The death of the barrier is simply due to the destruction of its constitution, the basis of its worthiness to receive the commands of the managing light.

Section [two]

[Explaining how the pure lights escape to the world of light]

(237) If the distractions of the barriers do not dominate the managing light, it will desire the world of holy light more than the dusky substances. The more it increases in light and brightness, the greater will be its passion and love for the dominating light, and the greater will be its independence and its nearness to the Light of Lights. Were the controlling lights infinite in their power to influence, they would not be veiled from the luminous horizon by being drawn to the distractions of the barriers. When the commanding lights rule the dusky substances and their passion and desire for the world of light is strengthened, they are illumined by the dominating lights and acquire the habit of connection with the world of pure light. Then, when their fortresses are corrupted, they are not drawn to other fortresses because of the perfection of their power and the intensity of their attraction to the springs of light. The light that has been strengthened by mighty rays and that loves its source is drawn to the spring of life. The light is not drawn to such fortresses as these, nor has it any wish for them. Thus, it is freed to go to the world of pure light and becomes holy by the holiness of the Light of Lights and the sanctified dominating lights. Since it is fundamental that this nearness is by attributes, not by place, the more that men are abstracted from the darknesses, the nearer they are to them.

(238) Desire bears the perceptive essences to the Light of Lights; that which is greater in its desire is more attracted and climbs higher toward the world of the All-Highest Light. Now, you know that pleasure

ففى حالة مقارنة علائق البدن كانت اولى بالعدم، لا بعد المفارقة. واذا تخلص النور المجرد عن الظلمات، فيبقى ببقاء النور القاهر الّذى هو علته وموت البرزخ إنمّا هو لبطلان مزاجه الّذى كان به صلاحية قبول تصرفات النور المدبر.

فصل

[فى بيان خلاص الانوار الطاهرة الى عالم النور]

(٢٣٧) النور المدبر اذا لم تقهره شواغل البرازخ، يكون شوقه الى عالم النور القدسى اكثر منه الى الغواسق. وكلّما[21] ازداد نورا وضوءً ازداد عشقا ومحبة الى النور القاهر، وازداد غنى وقربا من نور الانوار. ولو كانت الانوار المتصرفة غير متناهية قوة التأثير، ما حجبها جذب شواغل البرزخ عن الافق النورى. والانوار الاسفهبذية اذا قهرت الجواهر الغاسقة، وقوى شوقها وعشقها الى عالم النور واستضائت بالانوار القاهرة، وحصل لها ملكة الاتصال بعالم النور المحض، فاذا انفسدت صياصيها لا تنجذب الى صياص اُخرى لكمال قوتها وشدة انجذابها الى ينابيع النور. والنور المتقوى بالشوارق العظيمة العاشقة لسنخه ينجذب الى ينبوع الحياة. والنور لا ينجذب الى مثل هذه الصياصى، ولا يكون له نزوع اليها. فيتخلص الى عالم النور المحض ويصير قديسا بقداس[22] نور الانوار والقواهر القديسين. ولما كان من المبادى لا يتصور القرب بالمكان بل بالصفات، كان اكثر الناس تجردا عن الظلمات اقرب منها.

(٢٣٨) والشوق حامل الذوات الدرّاكة الى نور الانوار، فالأتمّ شوقا أتمّ انجذابا وارتفاعا الى عالم[23] النور الاعلى. ولما علمت انّ اللذة

is the attainment of that which is agreeable to the thing and its perception of its attaining it. Pain is the perception of the attainment of that which is not agreeable to the thing in that respect in which it is not agreeable. All perceptions are from the incorporeal light, and nothing is more perceptive than it. Therefore, nothing is mightier or more pleasurable than its perfection and those things that are suitable to it—especially, as you know, because the pleasures in the talismans of incorporeal lights trickle down from them, for the talismans are their shadows. Those things that are not suitable for the incorporeal lights are dark states and dusky shadows attaching to them from association with and desire for the dark barriers. So long as the commanding lights have their attachment to the fortresses and the many distractions of barriers, they do not take pleasure in their perfections, nor are they tormented by their infirmities. They are like the drunkard who attains his desire or who is afflicted by a disease while he is staggering in his drunkenness, unaware of what happens to him. He who does not take pleasure in the illuminations of the dominating lights and denies true pleasure is like the impotent man who denies the pleasure of sexual intercourse.

(239) Each of the senses, as well as desire and anger, has a pleasure and pain not shared by any other sense in accordance with its particular perceptions and perfections. The perfection of the commanding light consists in giving each of the twin faculties of dominance and love its due, for light in itself possesses both dominance over and love for that which is below it. Thus, its dominance must rule over the dark fortress, and its love must be directed toward the world of light. If misery is decreed for it, its love and passion are directed toward the dusky substances, and the darknesses will rule it. Its love will only be properly directed toward the world of light if it knows its own essence and knows the world of light, the order of being, the resurrection, and the like, insofar as lies within the capacity of man. Since its management of and solicitude for the body are also necessary, the most excellent of virtues is to be moderate in matters of desire and anger and in thought for the concerns of the body.

(240) No one finds salvation unless his greatest desire is for the afterlife and most of his thought is directed toward the world of light. If the commanding light shines by knowledge of realities and loves the Wellspring of light and life, if it is purified from the filth of barriers, then it will be freed from its fortress when it beholds the world of pure light

وصول ملائم الشئ وادراكه لوصول ذلك، والالم ادراك حصول ما هو غير ملائم للشئ من حيث هو كذا، وجميع الادراكات من النور المجرد ولا شئ ادرك منه، فلا شئ[٢٤] اعظم والذّ من كماله وملائماته، سيّما وقد عرفت انّ اللذات فى طلسمات الانوار المجردة منها ترشحت وهى ظلالها. والغير الملائم لها هيئات ظلمانية وظلال غاسقة تلحقها من صحبة البرازخ المظلمة وشوقها الى ذلك. والانوار الاسفهبذية ما دامت معها علاقة الصياصى والشواغل البرزخية الكثيرة، لا تلتذ بكمالاتها ولا ألم بعاهاتها، كشديد السكر اذا وصل اليه مشتهاه او ارهقته[٢٥] عاهة وهو متخبط فى سكره، غير مدرك لما اصابه. ومن لم يلتذّ باشراقات القواهر النورية وانكر اللذة الحقّة، فهو كالعنين اذا انكر لذة الوقاع.

(٢٣٩) وكمّا ان لكل من الحواس لذة وألما ليس لحاسة اُخرى على حسب اختلاف ادراكاتها وكمالاتها، وكذا ما للشهوة والغضب، وكمال النور الاسفهبذ اعطاء قوّتى قهره ومحبته حقهما، فان القهر للنور على ما تحته فى سنخه، وكذا المحبة فينبغى ان يسلّط قهره على الصيصية الظلمانية ومحبته الى عالم النور. واذا كان كُتب عليه الشقاوة، فتقع محبته وعشقه على الغواسق، فتقهره الظلمات. وإنمّا تقع محبته الى عالم النور كما ينبغى، اذا عرف ذاته وعرف عالم النور وترتيب الوجود والمعاد ونحو هذا[٢٦] على حسب الطاقة البشرية. ولما كان تدبير الصيصية والعناية بها ايضا ضروريا، فاجود الاخلاق الاعتدال فى الأمور الشهوانية والغضبية وفى صرف الفكر الى المهمات البدنية.

(٢٤٠) ولا خلاص لمن لم يكن اكثر همه الآخرة واكثر فكره فى عالم النور واذا تجلى النور الاسفهبذى بالاطلاع على الحقائق وعشق ينبوع النور والحياة وتطهر من رجس البرازخ، فاذا شاهد عالم النور

after the death of the body. The unending illuminations of the Light of Lights will be reflected upon it with and without intermediaries, as has been indicated before. The illuminations of the dominating lights will also be reflected upon it in that way, and so will be the illuminations of the infinite number of pure souls since the beginning that has no beginning—from each and every one its light, and each reflected time and again without end. Thus, will it experience infinite pleasure. Every later one takes pleasure in those before, and those before take pleasure in it. Lights without end shine upon it from others and upon others from it. These are illuminations and luminous intelligible rings of light, but they are surpassed in their splendor by the illumination and contemplation of the glory of the Light of Lights.

(241) Just as the perceptive incorporeal light, its perception, and its object of perception are not to be compared to these three in dark things, so, too, its pleasure is not to be compared to their pleasure, nor can it be comprehended in this world. How could it be otherwise, when every pleasure of the barriers results only from something luminous sprinkled upon the barriers? Even the pleasure of sexual intercourse is only a drop of the true pleasure; for he who desires sexual relations does not desire to possess something lifeless, but rather a barrier and beauty wherein is a trace of light. His pleasure is made complete by that heat which is one of the lovers and effects of the light, and by that motion which is one of the effects and lovers of the light. The two faculties of love and dominance are stirred so that the male desires to dominate the female. From the world of light, a love mixed with dominance occurs in the male and a love mixed with abasement occurs in the female in the proportion of cause and effect, as has been explained before. Each desires to be united with his mate so as to lift the veil of barriers. This is, indeed, the search of the commanding light for the unveiled pleasures of the world of light.

(242) The unity among the incorporeal lights is an intellectual, not a bodily, unity. When the commanding light has a connection to the barrier and to the fortress which is the locus in which it is made evident, it imagines itself to be in the fortress, even though it really is not. When the

المحض بعد موت البدن، تخلص عن صيصيته؛[٢٧] وانعكست عليه اشراقات لا تتناهى من نور الانوار من غير واسطة ومع الواسطة على ما سبقت الاشارة اليه. ومن القواهر ايضا كذا، ومن الاسفهبذية الطاهرة الغير المتناهية فى الآزال، من كل واحد واحد نوره وما اشرق عليه من كل واحد مرارا لا يتناهى، فيلتذ لذة لا تتناهى. وكل لاحق يلتذ بالسوابق، وتلتذ به السوابق، ويقع منه على غيره ومن غيره عليه انوار لا تتناهى، وهى اشراقات ودوائر عقلية نورية تزيد فى رونقها اشراق جلال نور الانوار ومشاهدته.

(٢٤١) وكما ان مدرك النور المجرد وادراكه ومدركه لا يقاس الى ثلاثية[٢٨] الظلمانيات، فلذته لا تقاس الى لذتها، ولا يحاط بها فى هذا العالم؛ كيف وكل لذة برزخية ايضا إنمّا حصلت بأمر نورى رشّ على البرازخ، حتى انّ لذة الوقاع ايضا رشح عن اللذات الحقة؟ فانّ الّذى يواقع لا يشتهى اتيان الميت، بل لا يشتهى إلاّ برزخا وجمالا فيه شوب نورى؛ وتتم لذته بالحرارة التى هى احد عشاق النور ومعلولاته، وبالحركة التى هى احد معلولات النور وعشاقه. وتتحرك قوتا محبته وقهره حتى يريد الذكر ان يقهر الانثى، فوقع من عالم النور محبة مع قهر على الذكر، ومحبة مع الذل على الانثى على نسبة ما فى العلة والمعلول على ما سبق. وكل يريد ان يتحد بصاحبه بحيث يرتفع الحجاب البرزخى. وإنمّا ذلك طلب للنور الاسفهبذى لذّات عالم النور الّذى لا حجاب فيه.

(٢٤٢) والاتحاد الّذى بين الانوار المجردة إنمّا هو الاتحاد العقلى لا الجرمى. وكما ان النور الاسفهبذى لما كان له تعلق بالبرزخ وكانت الصيصية مظهره فتوهم انّه فيها وان لم يكن فيها؛ فالانوار المدبرة اذا

managing lights are separated from the body, they imagine that they themselves are the masterful[11] dominating lights and the Light of Lights, because of their extreme nearness to them and their relations of love with them. Thus, the masterful dominating lights become the loci in which the managing lights are made evident, just as the bodies were the loci in which they were made evident. In the proportion that the love mixed with mastery increases, pleasure and affection increase in our world, as does the mutual love of animals. If that is the case here, then what have you to say about the world of true and perfect love and of the pure, perfect dominance that is entirely light and luster and life?

(243) Do not imagine that the incorporeal lights become a single thing after separation from the body, for two things do not become one. If both remained, there would be no unity; if both ceased to be, there would be no unity; if one remained and the other ceased to be, there would be no unity. Only in bodies is there connection and mixture. The incorporeals do not cease to be, for they are distinguished intelligibly through their cognizance of themselves, through their cognizance of their lights and the illuminations of their lights, and through a particularity based on their control of the fortresses. Indeed, the perfect lights become the loci in which they are made evident, just as, analogously, mirrors become the loci in which the images become evident. The king of the dominating lights descends upon the managing lights, and they achieve a pleasure and love, a dominance and contemplation to which no pleasure can be compared. The dominance of the all-highest world is incorruptible, since there is no nature there admitting of nonbeing. Rather, it brings the pleasure to perfection. These pure managing lights, which resemble the dominating lights, are holy by the holiness of God, the All-Highest. "Blessed are they, happy their end" [Qurʾān 13:29].

Section [three]

[On the states of human souls after separation from the body]

(244) Those who have attained an intermediate bliss and the ascetics whose worship is pure may escape to the world of suspended images, whose locus is some one of the celestial barriers. There they can and do

فارقت من شدة قربها من الانوار القاهرة الغالبة ونور الانوار وكثرة علاقتها العشقية معها، وهم انها هى. فتصير الانوار القاهرة الغالبة[٢٩] مظاهر للمدبرات كما كانت الابدان مظاهر لها. وبحسب ما تزداد المحبة المشوبة بالغلبة، ازداد اللذة والانس فى عالمنا، وكذا تعاشق الحيوانات. هذا هاهنا، فما قولك فى عالم المحبة الحقة التامة والقهر التام الخالصين، الّذى كله نور وبصيص وحياة؟

(٢٤٣) ولا تظنن ان الانوار المجردة تصير بعد المفارقة شيئا واحدا، فان شيئين لا يصيران واحدا، لانه ان بقى كلاهما، فلا اتحاد وان انعدما فلا اتحاد؛ وان بقى احدهما وانعدم الآخر فلا اتحاد. وليس فى غير الاجسام اتصال وامتزاج. والمجردات لا تنعدم فهى ممتازة امتيازا عقليا لشعورها بذاتها وشعورها بانوارها واشراقاتها وتخصص يتنى على تصرفات الصياصى؛ بل تصير مظاهرها الانوار التامة، كما صارت المرايا مظاهر المُثُل، ضربا للمثل. فيقع على المدبرات سلطان الانوار القاهرة فتقع فى لذة وعشق وقهر ومشاهدة ولا تقاس بذلك لذة مّا. وقهر العالم الاعلى غير مفسد، اذ الطبيعة القابلة للعدم منتفية هنالك، بل تكمل اللذة، والمدبرات الطاهرة الشبيهة بالقواهر مقدسة بقدس الله[٣٠] «طوبى لهم وحسن مآب».[٣١]

فصل

[فى بيان احوال النفوس الانسانية

بعد المفارقة البدنية]

(٢٤٤) والسعداء من المتوسطين والزهّاد من المتنزهين قد يتخلصون الى عالم المُثُل المعلقة التى مظهرها بعض البرازخ العلوية،

bring images into being. They can call forth such tastes, forms, pleasant sounds, and the like as they desire. These forms are more perfect than those that we have; for the loci in which these of ours are made evident and their bearers are deficient, while those of the former are perfect. There they may abide forever; for their connection with the barriers and the darknesses is unending, and there is no corruption among the celestial barriers.

(245) But as for the damned—those "kneeling about Gehenna" [Qurʾān 19:68], "who met the morn cowering in their homes" [Qurʾān 11:94]—it is the same whether transference[12] is true or false, for the proofs on each side of the contradictory are weak. Once they have escaped from the barrier fortresses, they will possess shadows of suspended forms in accordance with their moral qualities.

(246) The suspended forms are not the Forms of Plato, for the Forms of Plato are luminous,[13] while some of the suspended forms are dark and others illumined. Those possessed by the blessed, by which they find pleasure, are white and fair, while those of the damned are blue-black. Since the suspended fortresses are not in the mirrors or elsewhere and since they do not have a locus, they may have a locus in this world by which they are made evident. They may also change and become evident in other loci. From them result a kind of jinn and devils. A very great number of the people of Darband and innumerable people of a town called Mīyānaj[14] have testified that they have often beheld these forms. So many people gathered there in a great company beheld them at one time that there can be no question of doubting them. This was not just once or twice! They appear at every moment, but the hands of men cannot reach them. Another phenomenon experienced is bodies clad in armor that cannot be touched. The locus in which they were made evident was not the common sense, but they seemed to armor the whole body, and they resisted the body and wrestled with men.

(247) I myself have had trustworthy experiences indicating that there are four worlds: the worlds of the dominating lights, of the managing lights, of the barriers, and of the dark and illumined suspended images. The damned are tormented in the last of these. The jinn and

ولها ايجاد المُثُل والقوة على ذلك. فيستحضر من الاطعمة والصور والسماع الطيب وغير ذلك على ما يشتهى. وتلك الصور أتمّ مما عندنا، فانّ مظاهر هذه وحواملها ناقصة، وهى كاملة. ويخلّدون فيها لبقاء علاقتهم مع البرازخ والظلمات وعدم فساد البرازخ العلوية.

(٢٤٥) واما اصحاب الشقاوة الذين كانوا «حول جهنم جثيا»[٣٢] «واصبحوا فى ديارهم جاثمين»،[٣٣] سواء كان النقل حقا او باطلا. فان الحجج على طرفى النقيض فيه ضعيفة اذا تخلصوا عن الصياصى البرزخية يكون لها ظلال من الصور المعلقة على حسب اخلاقها.

(٢٤٦) والصور المعلقة ليست مُثُل افلاطون، فان مُثُل افلاطون نورية،[٣٤] وهذه مُثُل معلقة: ظلمانية ومستنيرة، للسعداء على ما يلتذون به بيض مُرد، وللاشقياء سود زرق. ولما كان الصياصى المعلقة ليست فى المرايا وغيرها وليس لها محل فيجوز ان يكون لها مظهر من هذا العالم، وربما تنتقل فى مظاهرها، ومنها يحصل ضرب من الجن والشياطين. وقد شهد جمع لا يحصى عددهم من اهل «دَربَند»، وقوم لا يعدون من اهل مدينة تسمّى «ميانَج» انّهم[٣٥] شاهدوا هذه الصور كثيرا بحيث ان اكثر المدينة كانوا يرونهم دفعة فى مجمع عظيم على وجه ما امكننى دفعهم. وليس ذلك مرة او مرتين، بل فى كل وقت يظهرون؛ ولا تصل اليهم ايدى الناس. وقد جرب من أمور أُخرى صياصى متدرعة غير ملموسة ليس مظهرها الحس المشترك بل تكاد درع لجميع البدن وتقاوم البدن وتصارع الناس.

(٢٤٧) ولى فى نفسى تجارب صحيحة تدل على ان العوالم اربعة: انوار قاهرة، وانوار مدبرة، وبرزخيان، وصور معلقة ظلمانية ومستنيرة فيها العذاب للاشقياء. ومن هذه النفوس والمُثُل المعلقة يحصل الجن

devils result from these souls and suspended images. The estimative happiness is also there. These suspended images may be renewed and destroyed like the images in mirrors and the imaginative faculty. The managing lights of the spheres may create them to serve as the loci in which they are made evident in barriers to the chosen ones. Those created by the managing souls[15] are luminous and are accompanied by a spiritual munificence. The fact that these images have been witnessed and cannot be attributed to the common sense indicates that being opposite is not an absolute condition of beholding; vision alone is dependent on it because being opposite is one sort of removal of veils.

(248) This above-mentioned world we call "the world of incorporeal figures."[16] The resurrection of images,[17] the lordly forms, and all the promises of prophecies find their reality through it. Certain intermediate souls possess illumined suspended figures whose loci are the spheres. These are the numberless angels in their classes—rank upon rank in accordance with the levels of the spheres. But the sanctified godly sages may rise higher than the world of the angels.

Section [four]

[On evil and misery]

(249) Misery and evil in the world of darknesses are concomitants of motion, and darkness and motion are concomitants of the aspect of dependence in the dominating and managing lights. Evil is a concomitant through intermediaries. It would be absurd for the Light of Lights to have dark states and aspects, so evil cannot be generated from it. Need and darknesses are necessary concomitants of effects, just like other inseparable concomitants of quiddities. Existence cannot be conceived to be other than it is, and evil is much less in this world than good.

والشياطين؛ وفيها السعادات الوهمية. وقد تحصل هذه المُثُل المعلقة حاصلة جديدة وتبطل كما للمرايا والتخيلات. وقد تخلقها الانوار المدبرة الفلكية لتصير مظاهر لها فى البرازخ[٣٦] عند المصطفين. وما يخلقها المدبرات تكون نورية وتصحبها اريحية روحانية. ولما شوهدت هذه المُثُل وما نسب الى الحس المشترك، فدل على ان المقابلة ليست بشرط للمشاهدة مطلقا؛ بل إنمّا توقف عليها الابصار، لانّ فيها ضرب من ارتفاع الحجب.

(٢٤٨) وهذا العالم المذكور نسمّيه «عالم الاشباح المجردة» وبه تحقق بعث الامثال[٣٧] والاشباح الربانية وجميع مواعيد النبوة، وقد يحصل من بعض نفوس المتوسطين ذوات الاشباح المعلقة المستنيرة التى مظاهرها الافلاك طبقات من الملائكة لا يحصى عددها على حسب طبقات الافلاك مرتبة مرتبة، ومرتقى المتقدسين[٣٨] والمتألهين اعلى من عالم الملائكة.

فصل
[فى الشر والشقاوة]

(٢٤٩) الشقاوة والشر إنمّا لزما فى عالم الظلمات من الحركات، والظلمة والحركة لزمتا من جهة الفقر فى الانوار القاهرة والمدبرة، والشر لزم بالوسائط. ونور الانوار يستحيل عليه هيآت وجهات ظلمانية، ولا[٣٩] يصدر منه شر. والفقر والظلمات لوازم ضرورية للمعلولات كسائر لوازم الماهيات الممتنعة السلب. ولا يتصور الوجود إلاّ كما هو عليه، والشر فى هذا العالم اقلّ من الخير بكثير.

A principle [explaining how the infinite generated things come to be from the celestials]

(250) The power of the dominating lights is infinite in its activity, and matter is infinitely receptive to that power. The motions that prepare receptivity are infinite. Thus, the door is open to the occurrence of the blessings and outpouring of the Light of Lights without end, age after age. After their separation from the body, the perfect managing lights attach themselves to the dominating lights, the victors in the race.[18] Thus, the number of holy ones among the lights increases without end.

Section [five]

[On the cause of premonitions and cognizance of hidden mysteries]

(251) If the distractions of man's external senses are reduced, he will be freed from the distraction of imagination and will become cognizant of hidden matters and thereby see veridical dreams. Since the incorporeal light has no volume and is not bodily, there is no conceivable veil between it and the celestial managing lights save the distractions of barriers. The veils of the commanding light are the distractions of the external and internal senses. Thus, once it is freed from the external senses and the inner sense is weakened, the soul is freed to join the commanding lights attached to the celestial barriers and becomes cognizant of the inscriptions of beings preserved in the celestial barriers. Thus, these lights know the particulars[19] and the concomitants of their movements. If a trace of them remains clearly in the memory as it was beheld in the celestial tablets, it requires no interpretation or explication. However, its trace may not so remain but may have been taken by the imaginative faculty and transformed into other things resembling it, or opposite to it, or corresponding to it in some respect. In that case, if the imaginative faculty has transformed it in any respect, it does require some explanation and investigation.

قاعدة [فى كيفية صدور
المواليد الغير المتناهية عن العلويات]

(٢٥٠) لما كانت قوة القواهر غير متناهية فى الفعل والمادة قابلة لها قوة ذلك الى غير النهاية، والمعدات من الحركات غير المتناهية، فانفتح[٤٠] باب حصول البركات وفيض الانوار المدبرة الى غير النهاية[٤١] قرنا بعد قرن. والكامل من المدبرات بعد المفارقة يلحق بالقواهر السابقين،[٤٢] فيزداد عدد المقدسين من الانوار الى غير النهاية.

فصل
[فى بيان سبب الانذارات
والاطلاع على المغيبات]

(٢٥١) الانسان اذا قلّت شواغل حواسه الظاهرة، فقد[٤٣] يتخلص عن شغل التخيل، فيطلع على أمور مغيبة وشهدت[٤٤] بذلك المنامات الصادقة. فانّ النور المجرد اذا لم يكن متحجما وجرميا، فلا يتصور ان يكون بينه وبين الانوار المدبرة الفلكية حجاب سوى شواغل البرازخ. والنور الاسفهبذى حجابه شواغل الحواس الظاهرة والحواس الباطنة. فاذا تخلّص عن الحواس الظاهرة وضعف الحس الباطن، تخلصت النفس الى الانوار الاسفهبذية للبرازخ العلوية واطلعت على النقوش التى فى البرازخ العلوية للكائنات. فانّ هذه الانوار عالمة بجزئياتها[٤٥] ولوازم حركاتها. فاذا بقى أثرها فى الذكر كما شاهد فى الالواح العالية صريحا، فلا يحتاج الى تأويل وتعبير. فان[٤٦] لم يبق أثرها بل أخذت المتخيلة فى الانتقالات عنه الى اشياء أُخرى متشابهة او متضادة او مناسبة بوجه آخر، فذلك يحتاج الى تفسير مّا واستنباط انّ المتخيلة من اى شئ انتقلت اليه.

(252) The inscriptions of beings have been recorded as forms in the celestial barrier from the beginning that had no beginning; they will remain forever, and they are inevitably repeated. Were there an ordered infinity of temporal events inscribed in the celestial barriers, one of them not occurring until after some other, these would themselves be ordered and contemporaneous chains, in contradiction to what has already been demonstrated about them. Thus, this is absurd. Then, if they contained an infinity of inscribed ordered events in the future, every single one of them would necessarily have already occurred at some moment, and a time would come when all that is in them would have come to pass, and the chain would end. But they have been assumed to be infinite, so this is absurd. However, were there no future time when all would have come to pass, then some of them would never come to pass and would thus not be future beings. Since they were posited to be future beings, this is absurd. This does not follow for future contingents, however they may be, for they are without detailed intelligible forms and have no totality.

(253) Do not imagine that the celestial managing lights know none of the past or future beings; for dreams, oracles, and the ability of the prophets to tell what has and will happen, as well as the memory of past states, show that they do. It has already been demonstrated that memory also occurs by means of the celestial barriers and their managing lights. He who has premonitions—whether from prophecy, oracles, or veridical dreams—does not obtain his in his own essence by something from his own essence corresponding to what will occur, for his inability to do so and the inability of his species to do so are evident. The person sleeping has no power to do so in his faculties or in his soul, for otherwise he would be able to do it more easily while awake. Moreover, if he devised his knowledge of what will happen from his own soul, he would then have to know it before he knew it, in order to produce certainty as to its correspondence with reality—which is absurd. Also, man knows in general that his prediction is necessarily from something else higher, for the celestial entities comprehend present, past, and future. If it is assumed that the masters of the celestial barriers acquire knowledge from something else

(٢٥٢) واعلم ان نقوش الكائنات ازلا وابدا مضبوطة[٤٧] فى البرازخ العلوية مصورة، وهى واجبة التكرار. فانّه ان كان فى البرازخ العلوية نقوش غير متناهية لحوادث مترتبة لا يكون شئ منها إلاّ بعد شئ، فتلك النقوش هى[٤٨] من السلاسل المجتمعة المترتبة، فيناقض ما برهن عليه، وهو محال. ثم ان كان فيها نقوش غير متناهية الحوادث فى المستقبل مترتبة، فان كان كل واحد منها لا بد وان يقع وقتا مّا، فيأتى وقت مّا يكون الكل قد وقع فيه، فتناهى السلسلة، وقد فرضت غير متناهية، وهو محال. وان لم يكن حصول وقت قد فرغ فيه الكل عن الوقوع ففيها ما لا يقع ابدا فليس من الكائنات فى المستقبل، وقد فُرض منها، هذا محال. ولا يلزم هذا فى الممكنات المستقبلة، كيف كانت، فانّها دون الصور المفصلة المعقولة لا كل لها.

(٢٥٣) ولا ينبغى ان يتوهم ان يكون شئ من الكائنات الماضية او المستقبلة لا تعلمها هى، فتكذبه المنامات والكهانات واخبار النبوات عما[٤٩] وقع بما سيقع وتذكر الاحوال الماضية. فانّ البرهان قد سبق على انّ الذكر إنمّا هو من البرازخ العلوية ايضا والانوار المدبرة لها. فصاحب الانذار بالنبوة او الكهانة او المنام الصادق لا يوجد علمه بالاشياء فى ذاته لذاته موافقا لما يقع فان عجزه ظاهر وعجز نوعه. والنائم ليس فى قواه قدرة ذلك ولا لنفسه، وإلاّ لكان فى اليقظة اقدر على ابداعه ثم ان كان يخترع علمه بنفسه بما سيقع، فينبغى ان يعلمه قبل ان يعلمه ليخترع جَزماً على وفاقه، وهذا محال. وايضا يعرف الانسان بالضرورة فى الجملة انّ الاعلام من شئ آخر فوقها؛[٥٠] فالأمور العالية عندها حيطة بالواقع والماضى والمستقبل. وان فُرض انّ اصحاب البرازخ العلوية تستفيد العلم من شئ آخر

above them by which they are aided, the difficulty is repeated for that thing from which they acquire it and by which they are aided. Therefore, there can be no doubt that these determinations must recur.

(254) By the necessity of the recurrence of determinations, we do not mean that what has ceased to exist returns, for that which separates the states of a single species is the locus, or the time if the locus is the same. Since time is part of that which separates two similar things in a single locus and which particularizes the essences in a single locus of a single species, that which has ceased to exist does not recur, due to the impossibility of the repetition of its time. If the accident and its time were supposed to recur, then this accident and its time would be before themselves and would be two existents. Thus they would possess temporal priority, and time would have time—which is absurd. Moreover, if the repeated accident and its repeated time possessed priority to that [accident] which was repeated and had a particularity thereby, this accident could not be repeated. That which was repeated and was assumed to be time would not be time.

(255) Since you know that beings must be repeated, there can be nothing everlasting among the composites of the three kingdoms since otherwise its like would be multiplied without end through the infinite cycles. This would result in an infinite number of individual bodies existing simultaneously—which is absurd. Neither matter nor the finite bodies would suffice for them. Infinity is conceivable in the case of the incorporeal figures, though not in that sense which the demonstration makes impossible, for they cannot be combined in an infinite extended dimension.

Section [six]

[On the classes of hidden things that the perfected are informed of]

(256) The prophets, saints, and others may learn of the unseen when written lines descend upon their souls or they hear a sound, whether pleasant or terrible. They may behold the forms of a being. They may

فوقها وتستمد منه، فيعود الكلام الى الشئ الّذى منه الاستفادة والاستمداد. فلا بد وان تكون هذه الضوابط واجبة التكرار.

(٢٥٤) ولا نعنى بوجوب تكرار الضوابط ان المعدوم يُعاد فان الفارق بين الهيآت من نوع واحد: المحل والزمان ان اتحد المحل. فاذا كان من الفارق بين المثلين فى محل واحد الزمان، وبه يتخصص ذواته محل واحد من نوع واحد فلا يُعاد لامتناع عود زمانه؛ وان فُرض ان يعود العرض وزمانه، فهذا العرض وزمانه قبل ذلك كانا موجودين، فلهما قبل زمانى، فيكون للزمان زمان، وهو محال. وايضا اذا كان له ولزمانه المستعاد قبلية، ما اعيدت وتخصصه بها، فلا يمكن عوده، والمستعاد المفروض زمانا ما كان[٥١] زمانا.

(٢٥٥) واذا عرفت انّ الكائنات واجبة التكرار، فلا يبقى من المركبات من المواليد الثلاثة أمراً دائما، وإلاّ عاد امثاله فى الادوار الغير المتناهية باقية. فصارت اعداد من الاجسام الغير المتناهية موجودة معا، وهو محال. ثم لا تفى بها المادة والاجسام المتناهية. والاشباح المجردة، يتصور فيها اللانهاية لا كما التى يمنعها البرهان، اذ لا يمكن منها ائتلاف بُعد واحد لا يتناهى ممتد.

فصل[٥٢]

[فى اقسام ما يتلقّى الكاملون من المغيبات]

(٢٥٦) وما يتلقى الانبياء والاولياء وغيرهم من المغيبات[٥٣] قد ترد عليهم فى اسطر مكتوبة وقد تُرد بسماع صوت قد يكون لذيذا وقد يكون هائلا وقد يشاهدون صور الكائن، وقد يرون صورا حسنة انسانية تخاطبهم فى غاية الحسن، فتناجيهم بالغيب.[٥٤] وقد تُرى الصور التى

behold beautiful human forms that address them with fairest speech and speak to them of the unseen in secret. They may see forms like graven statues addressing them with utmost subtlety. These things may descend upon their souls in a thought, or they may see suspended forms. All that is experienced in dreams are self-subsistent images—mountains, seas, lands, loud sounds, and individuals, as well as scents and the like. The mountain or sea that is beheld in the veridical or false dream—how can the brain or one of its cavities encompass it? Just as when the sleeper or the like is awakened, he departs the world of image without motion and without finding it to be in a particular direction, so, too, he who dies from this world beholds the world of light and is there without any motion.

(257) Luminosity is the cause of the images in mirrors. Images occur only with smooth bodies, since the parts of rough bodies have dark pits, with only small areas being free of these pits.

(258) The spheres have sounds not caused by the same causes as our sounds. We have explained that sound is not the vibration of the air; the most that one can say is that sound here is conditioned on it. However, it does not follow that if something is conditioned on a thing in one place, its like is necessarily so conditioned. A thing as a universal may have different causes in different instances, and so it may also have different conditions in different instances. Just as the colors of the planets are not conditioned on that on which colors with us are conditioned, so, too, is the case of their sounds. The awful sounds heard by the mystics cannot be said to be the vibration of air in the brain, for it is inconceivable that the vibration of air by that power is due to a ringing in the brain. Instead, it is an image of sound—which is a sound. Thus, there may be sounds and music in the spheres not conditioned on air or ringing. There is no conceivable music more pleasurable than their music, just as no desire is conceivable like unto their desire. Peace be upon a folk gone dazed and drunk in desire for the world of light and in passion for the glory of the Light of Lights, whose existents are become like unto the mighty seven![20] Therein is "a lesson for those possessed of hearts" [Qurʾān 12:111]. The heavens possess hearing not conditioned on ears, sight not conditioned on eyes, olfaction not conditioned on nostrils. This is the most noble contingency, and it is necessary therein.

تخاطب، كالتماثيل الصناعية فى غاية اللطف، وقد ترد عليهم فى حظرة، وقد يرون مُثُلا معلقة. وجميع ما يُرى فى المنام من الجبال والبحور والارضين والاصوات العظيمة والاشخاص كلها مُثُل قائمة، وكذا الروايح وغيرها. وما يرى من الجبل والبحر صريحا فى المنام الصادق او الكاذب، كيف يسعها الدماغ او بعض تجاويفه؟ وكما انّ النائم ونحوه اذا انتبه فارق العالم المثالى دون حركة ولم يجده على جهة منه، فكذا من مات عن هذا العالم يشاهد عالم النور دون حركة، وهو هناك.

(٢٥٧) ومُثُل المرآة علتها الضوء والاجسام التى لا ملاسة فيها إنمّا لا يحصل معها المثال للاجزاء الغائرة المظلمة، وما ليس فيه غائرة، فهو صغير.

(٢٥٨) وللافلاك اصوات غير معللة بما عندنا، فانا بينّا انّ الصوت غير تموج الهواء غاية ما فى الباب انّ يقال انّ الصوت ههنا مشروط بهذا، فلا يلزم من اشتراط شئ لأمر فى موضع ان يكون شرط لمثله، وكما انّ الأمر الكلى يجوز ان يكون له علل كثيرة على سبيل البدل، جاز ان يكون له شرائط على سبيل البدل. وكما ان الوان الكواكب لا تشترط بما يشترط به الالوان عندنا، فكذا اصواتها. وما يسمع المكاشفون من الاصوات الهائلة لا يجوز ان يقال انّه لتموج هواء فى دماغ، انّ الهواء تموجه بتلك القوة لمصاكّة فى الدماغ لا يتصور، بل هو مثال الصوت وهو صوت. فيجوز فى الافلاك اصوات ونغمات غير مشروطة بالهواء والمصاكّة. ولا يتصور ان تكون نغمة الذ من نغماتها، كما لا يتصور ان يكون شوق مثل شوقها. فسلام على قوم صاروا حيارى سكارى فى شوق عالم النور وعشق جلال نور الانوار، وتشبّهوا بالمواجيد[٥٥] بالسبع الشداد، وفى ذلك «عبرة لاولى الالباب».[٥٦] وللافلاك سمع غير مشروط بالأُذن، وبصر غير مشروط بالعين وشم غير مشروط بالانف، وهو الامكان الاشرف فيجب فيها.

(259) The brethren of incorporeality have a special station in which they are able to bring into existence self-subsistent images in whatever form they desire. This is called "the station of 'Be.'" Whoever sees that station knows with certainty the existence of a world other than that of barriers. In it are self-subsistent images and managing angels, taking for themselves talismans and self-subsistent forms by which they speak and are evident. From there flow violent attacks and overwhelming seizures by astonishing images and sounds of which the imagination can in no wise tell. How very strange that a man hears that sound in a certain incorporeality and attends to it, finding at that moment that his imagination also listens to it, though that sound is from a suspended image! Whoever has experienced this in his divine trances as he ascends will not return until he has ascended from level to level of the agreeable forms. The more perfect is his ascent, the purer and more delightful will be his contemplation of forms. Thereafter, he will penetrate the world of light and finally reach the Light of Lights.

(260) The form of everything in the elemental world is to be found in the sphere exactly as it exists here, in all its states. Every man, all his states and motions and rests as they are and as they will be, are there inscribed: "Everything that they do is in books; all matters great and small are there inscribed" [Qurʾān 54:52–53]. One of the demonstrations of the existence of the soul and of its incorporeality is that the locus in which it is made evident may either be the barrier or a suspended image and that it perceives itself in either case. Thus, it is neither of the two.

Let us mention here and ponder what can be perceived from the Memory, in which is the true metaphor.[21] This is one of the inspirations; seek the mysteries thereof from one who holds the authority to teach the Book.

(٢٥٩) ولاخوان التجريد مقام خاص فيه يقدرون على ايجاد مُثُل قائمة على اى صورة ارادوا، وذلك هو ما يسمّى مقام «كُن» ومن رأى ذلك المقام تيقن وجود عالم آخر غير[٥٧] البرازخ فيه المُثُل المعلقة والملائكة المدبرة يتخذ لها طلسمات ومُثُل قائمة تنطق بها وتظهر بها. وقد جرت منها بطشات صعبة وقبضة ظاهرة بالمُثُل واصوات عجيبة لا يقدر الخيال على محاكاتها. ثم العجب انّ الانسان عند تجرد ما يسمع ذلك الصوت، وهو يصغى اليه ويجد خياله ايضا حينئذ مستمعا اليه، فذلك صوت من المثال المعلق. وكل من احتنك فى السباتات الالهية اذا صعد، لم يرجع حتى يصعد من طبقة الى طبقة من الصور المليحة. فكلّما كان صعوده أتمّ، كانت مشاهدته للصور اصفى والذ، فيبرز بعد ذلك الى عالم النور ثم[٥٨] الى نور الانوار.

(٢٦٠) واعلم ان كل شئ مما فى العالم العنصرى مصور فى الفلك على نحو ما وجدا ههنا بجميع هيأته، وكل انسان منقوش مع جميع احواله وحركاته وسكناته ما وُجد وما سيوجد «وكل شئ فعلوه فى الزبر وكل صغير وكبير مستطر».[٥٩] ومن البرهان على وجود النفس وانها غير جسمانية انها قد يكون مظهرها البرزخ، وقد يكون مظهرها المثال المعلق وهى تدرك ذاتها فى الحالتين. وليست[٦٠] من احدهما.

ولنذكر هاهنا ما يدرك[٦١] به من الذكر به المُثُل الحق ويستبصر به، وهو من الواردات؛ وليطلب وتطلق اسرارها من الشخص القائم بالكتاب.

Section [seven]

Written in the plain tablet of memory

(261) The wayfarers who hammer upon the doors of the chambers of light—they who are sincere and patient—will be met by shining angels of God, who will give them the greetings of the heavenly kingdom and will purify them with water flowing from the spring of glory, for the Lord of Loftiness loves the purity of the traveler. The brethren of insight, those who are devoted to glorification—are they not cloistered, submissive unto God? They persevere in submission, making mention of the Devisor of the planes of the worlds. Standing within the temples of nearness, they shun the sons of shadows. They hold private converse with the companions of glory, pleading for the ransom of the prisoner, enkindled with its evident light. It is these who have followed those arrayed in ranks nearest unto God. They glorify God, who has made the Sun a means, the twin luminaries a caliph, the planets wending through space bearers in the nearness of God. They live in bliss and convey bliss. The folk of brightness in the levels of motion benefit from the light of God; so do they give benefit to those below.

(262) God casts sanctity into the hearts of those who have sought refuge in the mihrabs, reciting prayers[22] and calling upon their Lord: "Our God, wipe us clean from the gloom of denial, for the gloom of denial is the robe of the ignorant. Our God, we have come to Thee obedient. The spirits have pointed to Thee by their glorifications in their search for ascent to the seats of glory before Thine ample throne, the spot bright with Thy guiding light. Sanctify them by Thy firm hand. The souls of those possessed of vision hasten their wanderings when they gaze upon the courts of Thy bounteous luminosity, for Thy generous luminosity is the succor of those who seek refuge."

(263) The guidance of God has reached a people standing in ranks with hands outstretched in expectation of heavenly sustenance. When their eyes were opened, they found God clothed in glory, His name above the circle of the heaven of glory, and beneath His rays a people gazing

فصل

مسطور فى لوح الذكر المبين

(٢٦١) انّ السائرين الذين يقرعون ابواب غُرفات النور مخلصين صابرين لقاهم ملائكة الله، مشرقين يحيّونهم بتحايا الملكوت، ويصبون عليهم ماء نبع من ينبوع البهاء ليتطهروا؛ فانّ رب الطول يحب طهر الوافدين. إلاّ انّ اخوان البصيرة الذين التئموا على التسبيح[٦٢] عاكفين يخشعون لله وهم قيام قانتون يذكرون ناظم الطبقات فى العالمين، وهم عن ابناء الظلمات يجتنبون، قاموا فى هياكل القربات، يناجون مع اصحاب حجرات العزة، يلتمسون فك الاسير ويقتبسون النور من مظهره. اولئك الذين اقتدوا بالصافين عند الله الاقربين سبحوا الله الّذى جعل الشمس وسيلة والنهرين خليفة والجوارى حملة فى قربة الله؛ يتنعمون فينعمون. واشخاص الضوء فى مدارج الحراك بنور الله ينتفعون فينفعون النازلين.

(٢٦٢) القى الله التقديس على قلوب الذين أووا الى المحاريب، يقرأون الاذكار وينادون ربهم، فيقولون «الهنا اطمس عنا غيهب النكر. ان غيهب النكر دثار الجاهلين. الهنا! اتيناك طائعين واشارت اليك الارواح بالتقاديس طالبات الرقى الى مقاعد الجلال من كرسيك الفسيح مطلع[٦٣] نورك الرشيد، فقدّسها[٦٤] بايدك المتين. ركضت نفوس اولى البصاير فى جولتها[٦٥] اذا رمقت نحو عرصات ضوئك الكريم، ان ضوئك الكريم غياث المستجيرين».

(٢٦٣) هداية الله ادركت قوما اصطفوا باسطى ايديهم ينتظرون الرزق السماوى. ولما انفتحت ابصارهم، وجدوا الله مرتديا بالكبرياء اسمه فوق نطاق الجبروت وتحت شعاعه قوم اليه ينظرون. ولولا اولوا

toward Him. Were it not for those possessed of resolve upon the earth purifying all the rest for the presence of God—for they are the friends of God who loathe wicked things—the heavens would have been cast down as a curse upon earth convulsed, and the wicked doers would have been destroyed.

(264) God sent the prophets to men that they might worship Him. Some men worshipped him in piety and drew nigh. Others swerved far from the truth as heretics. God will raise those who have worshipped Him humbly to a plane of light, and they will enter into the ranks of glory and venerate God in His purity. There will they abide in bliss with God forever. But those who turned aside will be cast into abasement, and their heads will be bent down beneath a veil of darkness. Praised be He who has brought forth before Himself the virtuous essences and granted abundance unto them. They have returned unto their people in honor!

(265) The All-Merciful pledges that He will snatch away the people wandering in desire for that meadow of glory—the refuge of the people of eternity around the everlasting pavilion—and will deliver them to the court of the Absolute. They will dwell forever at the spring of life, glorifying the greatness of the station of a people who have stood bowed low in prayer. In the dark of night have they wept in fear of their Lord, tears raining from their eyes. In the scrolls of mercy God hath written that no dust shall remain upon their faces when they meet Him, and He shall make them to attain unto His presence. A thunderbolt of the light of the All-Merciful shall fall upon the one who is obedient unto Him. Is not God's star the best of night visitors?

[Section eight]

Containing Another Inspiration

(266) God has covenanted with every generation that they might answer the one who calls to them[23] and flee the lies that the parties have invented against God ere the veil of the time of Resurrection weighs heavy upon them. How many generations have opposed the revelations of their Lord! But His might has seized them and obliterated their issue. They

عزيمة فى الارض يطهرون الباقيات لجوار الله، هم احباب الرب يبغضون السيئات، لقذفت السموات وبالا على الارض، فترتجتة فتطحن الظالمين.

(٢٦٤) بعث الله النبيين الى الناس ليعبدوه، ففريق عبدوا الله على نسك وتقربوا، وفريق زاغوا عن الحق مبعدين. فاما الذين عبدوه خاضعين، فسيرفعهم الله الى مشهد الضياء. فيدخلون فى صفوف العزة ويقدسهم الله بطهارته، فاذا هم عند الله فى النعيم دائمون. واما الزائغون فيُلقى عليهم الذل وهم على الرؤوس تحت حجاب الظلمات ناكسون. فسبحان الله الّذى برزت له الذوات الصالحات فوهب لها البسطة. فآبوا الى فوقهم مكرمين.

(٢٦٥) وضمان الرحمن ان قوما تاهوا فى شوق مرتع الجلال، الّذى هو مآوى احياء السرمد حول قبة الديهور يقبضهم الى جناب الحق، فهم فى عين الحيوان على الآباد يسبحون عظم موقع قوم وقفوا يركعون وفى دجا الليل تمطر اعينهم من خشية ربهم ويبكون. كتب الله فى زبور الرحمة ان لا يذر على وجوههم غبرة حين يلقونه ويجعلهم بلقائه فائزين. ان مطيع الرحمان يغشاه بارق من نوره، إلاّ ان نجم الله خير الطارقين.

[فصل]

وارد آخر[٦٦]

(٢٦٦) عهد الله الى القرون ان يجيبوا الداعى ويعتزلوا المفتريات على الله من الاحزاب قبل ان يثقلهم غاشية وقت القيام،[٦٨] وكم من قرن عصوا رسالات ربهم؟ فاخذهم قهره بطمس ادبارهم، فانقلبوا الى

have been cast down in utter ruin, crawling in the Fire in hope of escape. It is prohibited in the First Tablet for the wicked to return to their homelands.[24] Those who have committed wickedness have imagined that the mercy of the horizon of glory will reach them without their taking firm hold of the Book of God. They will fear the snare of fate on the day when they are summoned from their homes to the court of dread. Soon at the moment of manifestation shall the deniers behold a scourge that cannot be opposed, nor in any way denied.

(267) God has placed seven paths in the world; on the seventh the reality of each wandering wayfarer is affirmed.[25] Those who follow the path shall consummate what God hath written for them in the primal inscription. Joys shall not keep them from the journey, nor the blazing heat of summer keep them from the good pleasure of the Lord of Command. Those who circle about the gate, who fear the might of God, who pray in the night season, who are patient in their cells, who give alms while their people are heedless, who are implacable in the holy war, wandering the earth although their spirits have risen to the all-highest spot, possessors of the greatest shekinah—these shall find from God the glad tidings of salvation.

(268) God has inscribed in the Book and decreed to the Faithful Spirit[26] that He will answer the prayers of all who are weighed down with gloom—of all who are pure yet seek to be darkened for the good pleasure of God—that He will aid the patient against the evil of the sons of devils, that He will clothe the evildoers in shirts of tar. The sons of grace will snatch from the ephemeral that which will give them immortality. Those who are forsaken will be kept far away and will prefer the ephemeral to that which could accompany them—to that which they could carry through the torments. The scourge of God shall take its vengeance upon each lying fugitive.

(269) The angels have heard the cries of the virtuous in their fear of God and beseech their Lord on their behalf: "O Master of the Kingdom of Might and Lord of the all-highest creatures! O Thou Who hast reared the pavilions of power and illumined all beings! Pray for them, for Thy good prayer giveth joy to each upright heart. Our Lord! There is a people who cry in the night season, who weep in Thy mihrabs, seeking blessings

مصرع السوء يدبون على النار وهم[٦٨] يتمنون الرجعى. وحرام فى الرقيم الأوّل عود الفاجرين الى الاوطان، ظن الذين اقترفوا الخطيئات ان تنالهم رحمة افق المجد دون اذ يأخذوا سفر الله بجد ويخشوا مكر القدر يوم القفول من الدار الى عرصة الهيبة، وسيرى الجاحدون عند البرزة سطوة لم يدفعها دافع ولا يبقى مع الانكار.

(٢٦٧) جعل الله فى البسيطة سبعا من المسالك، وعند السابع تقر عين كل سالك سيار. والذين ينهجون السبيل[٦٩] ليقضوا ما سطر الله عليهم فى الكتابة الاولى، ولا يمنعهم المسرات عن المسير، ولا تقعدهم حمارة القيظ عن السعى الى مرضات[٧٠] صاحب الأمر والذين يطوفون عند الباب ويخوفون حول الله والمصلّون فى الديجور، والصابرون فى المناسك، والمتصدقون فى غفلات قومهم، والصارمون فى الجهاد، والسايرون فى الارض وارواحهم معلقة بالمحل الاعلى، واصحاب السكينة الكبرى، سيجدون من الله البشرى بالخلاص.

(٢٦٨) وقّع الله فى السفر وقضى الى الروح الامين انه ليجيب دعوة كل مغلوب بالظلامة وكل ذى نظافة يطلب التظلم لرضاء الله، وانه لينصر الصابرين على بأس ابناء الشياطين، وليلبس الفاجر سربال القار، وابناء التوفيق يأخذون من الزائل ما يثبتهم، والمخذولون يحرمون عند البعاد ويختارون ما يزول عنهم على ما يصحبهم، فيعبرون به على العقبات، وسوط الله ينتقم من كل شارد أفّاك.

(٢٦٩) سمعت الملائكة صياح الابرار من خشية الله، فتضرعوا فيهمتة الى ربهم ان «يا صاحب العظموت، ورب الاعلين، وناصب سرادقات القدرة، ومضئ الاكوان! صلّ عليهم! ان صلاتك الخير يفرح بها كل قلب قوّام. ربنا! ان قوما صاحوا فى نجواهم وبكوا فى محاريبك

from the heaven of Thy glory. They have no idols and no ill-gotten property. They expend their efforts in Thy gracious path. Grant them a mighty portion from Thyself, and give them from Thee a sovereignty confirmed and illumined."

(270) God has answered the angels' prayer in behalf of those who work virtuous deeds, who are steadfast in worship, who associate nothing with Him, decreeing that when they reach the court of power, they will be cloaked in that in which the archangels are cloaked, the angels who stand beneath the stair of grandeur at the source of grace. He will aid them against the people of corruption before they are brought back to God's lofty gate. He will give them beauty[27] from His shining beauty, and all possessed of seeing eyes will humble themselves before them.

Section [nine]

[On the states of the wayfarers]

(271) Let us now return to the scientific objective that we had been considering. Know that if the exalted illuminations shine continually upon souls, the matter of the world will be submissive to those souls, and their prayer will be heard in the highest world. It will be ordained in the preordained fate that the prayer of an individual will be the cause of its answer in a certain thing. The propitious light from the all-highest world is the elixir of might and knowledge, so the world is submissive to it. An image of the light of God becomes established in the incorporeal souls, and a creative light becomes fixed in them. The evil eye is a dominant luminosity affecting and corrupting things.

(272) Lights of sundry kinds shine upon the brethren of incorporeality: a flashing light descending upon the beginners, shining and receding like the flash of a thunderbolt of pleasure; a stronger flashing light descending upon others, more like a terrifying thunderbolt, with which often a sound is heard like the sound of thunder or a roaring in the brain; a pleasant descending light whose descent is like warm water pouring upon the head; a light fixed for a long period, great in power, accompanied by a

طالبين بركات سماء جلالك، تبرؤوا من الطواغيت[٧١] وتجردوا عن السحت، وبذلوا جهدهم فى سبيلك الكريم، فاجعل لهم من لدنك حظا عزيزا، واجعل لهم من لدنك نصيرا منيرا».

(٢٧٠) استجاب الله دعوة الملائكة فى الذين يعملون الفاضلات ويصبرون على التعبد ولا يشركون به شيئا، انّهم اذا وردوا عرصة القدرة يغشيهم ما غشى المقربين الذين قاموا تحت درجة الكبرياء عند مصدر الجود، وينصرهم على اهلتض الفسوق قبل العود الى باب الله الرفيع، وليجعل لهم رواءا[٧٢] من روائه النير، فيخضع لهم كل ذى طرف حساس.

فصل
[فى احوال السالكين]

(٢٧١) ولنرجع الى المقصد الّذى كنا بسبيله من العلم. فاعلم ان النفوس اذا دامت عليها الاشراقات العلوية، يطيعها مادة العالم ويستمع دعاؤها فى العالم الاعلى، ويكون فى القضاء السابق مقدار ان دعاء شخص يكون سبب الاجابة فى شئ كذا. والنور السانح من العالم الاعلى هو اكسير القدرة والعلم، فيطيعه العالم. والنفوس المجردة يتقرر فيها مثال من نور الله، ويتمكن فيها نور خلاّق. والعين السوء هو نورية قاهرة نؤثر فى الاشياء فتفسدها.

(٢٧٢) واخوان التجريد يشرق عليهم انوار ولها اصناف: نور بارق يرد على اهل البدايا يلمع وينطوى كلمعة بارق لذيذ؛ ويرد على غيرهم ايضا نور بارق اعظم منه واشبه[٧٣] بالبرق إلاّ انه برق هائل، وربما يسمع معه صوت كصوت رعد او دوى فى الدماغ؛ نور وارد لذيذ يشبه وروده ورود ماء حار على الرأس؛ نور ثابت زمانا طويلا شديد القهر يصبحه

stupor in the brain; a light most pleasurable, not resembling a thunderbolt, but accompanied by a sweet and subtle joy moved by the power of love; a burning light moved by the motion of the power of might—when hearing drums and trumpets, it may result in things terrifying to the beginner, or in thought and imagination it may give him glory; a glittering light in a mighty blast, which in a drowning pleasure makes contemplation and vision more keen than does the Sun; a flashing light, greatly pleasurable, during which one seems to be suspended by the hair of the head for a long time; a propitious light by which one seems to be seized—it seems as though the hair of the head is grasped and one is dragged roughly and tormented with a pleasurable pain; a light with a seizing that seems to be fixed in the brain; a light, extremely pleasant, shining from the soul upon the entire spirit of the soul,[28] in which it seems as though something armors the body, and the spirit of the entire body might almost seem to have a luminous form; a light that begins as an assault, at the beginning of which a man imagines that something is being destroyed; a propitious light negating the soul, in which the soul appears to itself as something utterly suspended and wherein it beholds its own abstraction from dimensions, even if the one who experienced this had not known it beforehand; a light accompanied by the feeling of a weight almost too heavy to bear; a light accompanied by the power to move the body so great as to nearly tear asunder the joints.

(273) All of these are illuminations upon the managing light reflected upon the temple[29] and the spirit of the soul. These are the goals of the intermediate. These lights may bear them up, allowing them to walk on water and air. They may ascend to the heavens with their bodies and associate with one of the celestial masters. These are determinations of the eighth clime, in which are Jābulq, Jābarṣ and wondrous Hūrqalyā.[30]

(274) The mightiest state is the state of death, by which the managing light sheds the darknesses. If it has no remnant of attachment to the body, it will emerge into the world of light and be attached to the dominating lights. There will it behold all the veils of light as though transparent in relation to the glory of the eternal, the all-encompassing Light: the Light of Lights. It will become, as it were, placed within the all-encompassing Light. This is a station mighty indeed! Plato spoke from

خدر فى الدماغ؛ نور لذيذ جدا لا يشبه البرق، بل يصحبه بهجة لطيفة حلوة يتحرك بقوة المحبة؛ نور محرق يتحرك من تحرك القوة العزية، وقد تحصل من سماع طبول وابواق أمور هائلة للمبتدى، او لتفكر وتخيل يورث عزا؛ نور لامع فى خطفة عظيمة يظهر مشاهدة وابصارا اظهر من الشمس فى لذة مُغرقة؛ نور برّاق لذيذ جدا يتخيل كأنّه متعلق بشعر الرأس زمانا طويلا؛ نور سانح مع قبضة مثالية تترائى كأنها قبضت شعر رأسه وتجره شديدا وتؤلمه الما لذيذا؛ نور مع قبضة رائى كانها متمكنة فى الدماغ؛ نور يشرق من النفس على جميع الروح النفسانى، فيظهر كأنّه تدرع بالبدن شئ، ويكاد يقبل روح جميع البدن صورة نورية وهو لزيذ جدا؛ نور مبدأه فى صولة، وعند مبداه يتخيل الانسان كأنّ شيئا ينهدم؛ نور سانح يسلب النفس وبين معلقة محضة منها تشاهد تجردها عن الجهات، وان لم يكن لصاحبها علم قبل ذلك؛ نور يتخيل معه ثقل لا يكاد يطاق؛ نور معه قوة تحرك البدن حتى يكاد يقطع مفاصله.

(٢٧٣) وهذه كلها اشراقات على النور المدبر، فتنعكس الى الهيكل والى الروح النفسانى. وهذه غايات المتوسطين، وقد تحملهم هذه الانوار فيمشون على الماء والهواء. وقد يصعدون الى السماء مع الابدان فيلتصقون ببعض السادة العلوية. وهذه احكام الاقليم الثامن الّذى فيه جابلق وجابرص وهورقليا ذات العجائب.

(٢٧٤) واعظم الملكات ملكة موت ينسلخ النور المدبر عن الظلمات انسلاخا، وان لم يخل عن بقية علاقة مع البدن، إلاّ انه يبرز الى عالم النور ويصير معلقا بالانوار القاهرة؛ ويرى الحجب النورية كلها بالنسبة الى جلال النور المحيط القيوم نور الانوار كانها شفافة، ويصير كأنّه موضوع فى النور المحيط. وهذا المقام عزيز جدا، حكاه افلاطون

his own experience of this station, as did Hermes and the great sages. The Author of this Law[31] spoke of this station, as did many of those who divested themselves of the rank of humanity. Such people are always found throughout the ages. To each thing He hath appointed a measure, "and with Him are the keys to the unseen, which none knoweth save Him" [Qurʾān 6:59]. Whoso does not himself behold these stations, let him not gainsay the pillars of wisdom,[32] for that is ignorance and great folly. Whoso worships God sincerely and who dies from the darknesses and disdains to look upon them will behold what no one else can behold.

(275) Those lights in which there is an admixture of might are of use in matters dependent upon might, and the lights in which there is an admixture of love are of use in matters dependent upon love.[33] There are wonders among the lights! Whosoever is able to move his two faculties of might and love, his soul will hold sway over things exactly in accordance with that which corresponds to each faculty. Whoso ascends and thinks and endures will attain. Among the spiritual powers are stations, perils, terrors, and bewilderments. Each of these is known individually by those whose thought and opinion concerning divine and satanic matters is sound and whose resolve is steadfast toward the perceptibles that strengthen each faculty: the might that strengthens dominance and the love that strengthens attraction.

(276) The visionary will understand the implication completely, learning much from a few hints. He will have patience to be resolute in all matters, the secret of this patience being entrusted to the one who holds the authority to teach the Book. He will be characterized by nearness to God most high, a spare diet and little sleep, supplication to God to ease the path for him, and a heart made refined by refined thoughts. He will ponder the clues to God's holiness enshrined in beings. He will constantly recollect God's glory, which leads to these matters. He will be sincere in turning toward the Light of Lights, which is the basis of this realm, making his soul sing with the remembrance of God, the Master of the Kingdom—but worthy though this is, the sadness of the second state is more so—reciting the revealed pages, in haste in return to Him in whose hand is creation and command. All these are conditions.

عن نفسه وهرمس وكبار الحكماء من انفسهم. وهو ما حكاه صاحب هذه الشريعة، صلى الله عليه وسلم،[٧٤] وجماعة من المنسلخين عن النواسيت. ولا تخلوا الادوار عن هذه الأمور، وكل شئ عنده بمقدار «وعنده مفاتح الغيب لا يعلّمها إلاّ هو.»[٧٥] ومن لم يشاهد من نفسه هذه المقامات، فلا يعترض على اساطين الحكمة، فانّ ذلك نقص وجهل وقصور. ومن عبد الله على الاخلاص، ومات عن الظلمات، ورفض مشاعرها، شاهد ما لا يشاهد غيره.

(٢٧٥) وهذه الانوار ما يشوبها[٧٦] العزّ ينفع فى الأمور المتعلقة به؛ وما يشوبه المحبة ينفع فى الأمور المتعلقة بها وفى الانوار عجائب. ومن قدر على تحريك قوتى عزّه ومحبته، تتحكم نفسه على الاشياء بحسب كل قوة فيما يناسبها لا غير. والصاعد الفكور الصابر نائل. ومن الهمم المقامات والمحاذير والمهاويل والتحايير[٧٧] معينة لاصحاب الفكرة الصحيحة فى الآراء الالهية والشيطانية. وثبات الهمة بالمدركات الممددة لكل قوة بحسبها، تمد العز على القهر والمحبة على الجذب.

(٢٧٦) والمستبصر له العبرة التامة فيكثّر القليل، والصبر من عزم الأمور، والسر فيه مفوّض الى الشخص القائم بالكتاب. والقربة الى الله تعالى،[٧٨] وتقليل الطعام، والسهر، والتضرع الى الله عزّ وجل فى تسهيل السبل اليه، وتلطيف السر بالافكار اللطيفة، وفهم الاشارات من الكائنات الى قدس الله عزّ وجلّ، ودوام الذكر جلال الله يفضى الى هذه الامور؛ والاخلاص فى التوجه الى نور الانوار اصل فى الباب؛ وتطريب النفس بذكر الله صاحب الجبروت نافع على ان الحزن للحال الثانى افضل؛ وقرائة الصحف المنزلة، وسرعة الرجوع الى من له الأمر والخلق وكل[٧٩] هذه شرائط.

(277) Once the divine lights are dispersed[34] within a man, he is clothed in a robe of might and awe, and souls bend to his command. For seekers of the water of life, God hath a mighty spring! Who is there who will seek refuge with the light of One possessed of sovereignty and the Kingdom? Who is there who will hammer in longing upon the gate of divine glory? Who is there who will humble himself in the remembrance of God? Who is there who will go forth in search of God's guidance? No one who seeks His court will perish; neither will He disappoint the hopes of him who stands before His door.

[The Author's Exhortation]

(278) I exhort you, my brethren, to keep God's commandments, to shun what He abhors, to turn with all your being to God our Lord, the Light of Lights, to forswear every word and deed that does not profit you, to cut off every satanic thought.

(279) I exhort you to preserve this book, to keep it safe and guard it from those unworthy of it. God is my successor ruling over you! I completed its composition on the last day of the month of Jumādā al-Ākhira of the year 582,[35] on the day the seven planets were in the sign of Libra at the end of the daylight. Give it only to one well versed in the methods of the Peripatetics, a lover of the light of God. Let him meditate for forty days, abstaining from meat, taking little food, concentrating upon the contemplation of the light of God, most mighty and glorious, and upon that which he who holds the authority to teach the Book shall command.

(280) When the time for the book has come, let him immerse himself therein. He who studies it will learn that what escaped the Ancients and Moderns God has entrusted to my tongue. On a wondrous day the Holy Spirit blew it into my heart in a single instant, though its writing took many months due to the interruptions of journeys. It has great import. God will take vengeance upon him who strives against the truth. "God indeed is great, possessed of vengeance" [Qurʾān 3:4]. Let no one seek to peruse the mysteries of this book without repairing to my successor, he who possesses the knowledge of the Book!

(٢٧٧) واذا ذرت[٨٠] الانوار الالهية على انسان، كسته لباس العز والهيبة، وتنقاد له النفوس. وعند الله لطلاب ماء الحياة مورد عظيم. فهل من مستجير بنور ذى الملك والملكوت؟ فهل من مشتاق يقرع باب الجبروت؟ فهل من خاشع لذكر الله؟ فهل من ذاهب الى ربه ليهديه؟ ما ضاع من قصد نحو جنابه، ولا خاب من وقف ببابه.

[وصية المصنف]

(٢٧٨) اوصيكم اخوانى[٨١] بحفظ أوامر الله، وترك مناهيه، والتوجه الى الله مولانا نور الانوار بالكلية، وترك ما لا يعنيكم من قول وفعل، وقطع كل خاطر شيطانى.

(٢٧٩) واوصيكم بحفظ هذا الكتاب والاحتياط فيه، وصونه عن غير اهله، والله! خليفتى عليكم. فرغت من تأليفه فى آخر جمادى الآخرة من شهور سنة اثنين وثمانين وخمسمائة فى اليوم الّذى اجتمعت الكواكب السبعة فيه[٨٢] فى برج الميزان فى آخر النهار. فلا تمنحوه إلاّ[٨٣] لمن استحكم طريقة المشائين، وهو محب لنور الله، وقبل الشروع يرتاض اربعين يوما تاركا للحوم الحيوانات مقللا للطعام منقطعا الى تأمل نور الله[٨٤] عزّ وجلّ وعلى ما يأمره قيّم الكتاب.

(٢٨٠) فاذا بلغ الكتاب اجله، فله الخوض[٨٥] فيه. وسيعلم الباحث فيه انّه قد فات المتقدمين والمتأخرين ما يسر الله على لسانى منه. وقد القاه النافث القدسى فى روعى فى يوم عجيب دفعة، وان كانت كتابته ما اتفقت إلاّ فى اشهر لموانع الاسفار. وله خطب عظيم؛ ومن جحد الحق، فسينتقم الله منه «والله عزيز ذو انتقام».[٨٦] ولا يطمعن احد ان يطلع على اسرار هذه الكتاب دون المراجعة الى الشخص الّذى يكون خليفة عنده علم الكتاب.

(281) Know ye, my brethren, that the remembrance of death is ever essential, for "the other abode is life, did ye but know" [Qurʾān 29:64]. "Remember God often" [Qurʾān 8:45]. "If ye are Muslims, ye shall not die" [Qurʾān 2:132]. O God! O my Lord, my God, and the God of all things! Do with us as is worthy of Thee. Leave us not to ourselves nor entrust us to anyone save Thee for even the twinkling of an eye. Spread out before us, O Lord, the good things of this world and the next, and avert from us the evil of this world and the next. Shield us, teach us, aid us, purify us, perfect us, teach us, and make us happy in Thee, O Thou Who art our fairest hope and the answerer of our prayers, O Thou Who art most merciful of the merciful!

Praise be to God, worthy of thanksgiving and most pleasing, who emanates bounty and gives existence. He alone is due thanksgiving, forever and ever. Blessings be upon our master, Muḥammad, and his family good and pure—blessings without end, ever-increasing and spotless![36]

There is no power or might save in God, the exalted and almighty.
Praise be to the Lord of the worlds,
and blessings and peace be upon our master, Muḥammad,
his family, and his companions. Amen.
O God, blessed be our lord, Muḥammad, who is Thy servant,
Thy prophet, Thy friend, and Thy messenger, the unlettered prophet;
and blessed be his family and companions.

(٢٨١) واعلموا اخوانى! ان تذكر الموت ابدا من المهمات «وانّ الدار الآخرة لهى الحيوان لو كانوا يعلمون»،[٨٧] «فاذكروا الله كثيرا»،[٨٨] «ولا تموتن إلاّ وانتم مسلمون».[٨٩] اللهم! يا ربى ويا الهى واله كل شئ! افعل بنا ما انت اهله ولا تكلنا الى انفسنا ولا الى احد سواك طرفة عين. وابسط لنا يا رب! خير الدنيا والآخرة، واصرف عنا شر الدنيا والآخرة. واسترنا واخبرنا وانصرنا وطهّرنا وكمّلنا وعلّمنا واسعدنا بك، يا خير مأمول واكرم مسئول، يا ارحم الراحمين!

والحمد لله المشكور المقبول،[٩٠] فياض الجود وواهب الوجود، وله الشكر وحده ابد الآبدين، والصلاة على سيدنا محمد وآله الطيبين الطاهرين صلاة دائمة نامية زاكية.

ولا حولَ ولا قوة إلاّ بالله العلى العظيم، والحمدُ لرّب العالمين

وصلىّ الله على سيدنا محمد

وعلى آله وصحبه سلّم آمين.

اللّهم صلّ على سيدنا محمد عندك

ونبّيك وحبيبك ورسولّك النبى الأُمى

وعلى آله واصحابه وسلّم.

Notes to the English Text

Translators' Introduction

1. The major biographical sources on Suhrawardī which include references to Illuminationist philosophy are: Ibn Abī Uṣaybiʿa, *ʿUyūn al-anbāʾ fī ṭabaqāt al-aṭibbāʾ*, ed. A. Müller (Köningsberg, Ger.: al-Maṭbaʿa al-Wahbīya, 1884), 1:168; the edition of the same by N. Riḍā (Beirut: Dār Maktabat al-Ḥayāt, 1968), 641–46, which differs in part from Müller's; Ibn Yāqūt, *Irshād al-arīb*, ed. D. S. Margoliouth, 6:269–72 (Leiden: E. J. Brill, 1924); al-Qifṭī, *Tārīkh al-ḥukamāʾ*, ed. Bahman Dārāʾī (Tehran: Tehran University Press, 1347 A.H. /1967 C.E.), 345; Ibn Khallikān, *Wafayāt al-aʿyān*, ed. I. ʿAbbās (Beirut: Dār al-Thaqāfa, [1965]), 6:268–74; Ibn Faḍl Allāh al-ʿUmarī, *Masālik al-abṣār fī mamālik al-amṣār*, ed. F. Sezgin, Publications of the Institute for the History of Arabic-Islamic Science, Series C, 46, no. 9 (Frankfurt: Institute for the History of Arabic-Islamic Science, 1988), 86–93; and Shahrazūrī, *Nuzhat al-arwāḥ wa rawḍat al-afrāḥ fī tārīkh al-ḥukamāʾ wa al-falāsifa*, ed. S. Khurshid Aḥmed (Hyderabad, India: Dāʾirat al-Maʿārif al-ʿUthmānīya, 1976), 2:119–43.

There are two other editions of the Shahrazūrī text just mentioned: *Nuzhat al-arwāḥ wa-rawḍat al-afrāḥ: Tārīkh al-ḥukamāʾ*, ed. ʿAbd al-Karīm Abū Shuwayrib ([Tripoli]: Jamʿīyat al-Daʿwa al-Islāmīya al-ʿĀlamīya, 1988); and *Kitab nuzhat al-arwāḥ wa rawḍat al-afrāḥ: Tārīkh al-ḥukamaʾ*, ed. Muḥammad-ʿAli Abū Rayyān (Alexandria: Dār al-Maʿrifa al-Jāmiʿa, 1414 A.H./1993 C.E.), 600–622. The Abū Shuwayrib edition was done on the basis of two Istanbul manuscripts but is sharply criticized by Abū Rayyān (pp. 44–50). The seventeenth-century Persian translation of *Nuzhat al-arwāḥ* by Maqṣūd-ʿAlī Tabrīzī has recently been edited by M.-T. Dānish-Pazhūh and M. S. Mawlāʾī and published under the same title (Tehran: Shirkat-i Intishārāt-i ʿIlmī va Farhangī, 1986), and it differs—considerably, at times—from the Arabic text. Part of the notice on Suhrawardī in the Persian text just mentioned has been translated into English by W. M. Thackston, Jr., in *The Mystical and Visionary Treatises of Shihabuddin Yahya Suhrawardi* (London: The Octagon Press, 1982), 1–4. Thackston's translation is based on the partial edition of S. H. Nasr in Suhrawardī, *Opera Metaphysica et Mystica*, vol. 3, ed. Seyyid Hossein Nasr (Tehran: Institut Franco-Iranien, 1970). The Nasr edition includes the Arabic text as well as the Persian translation of Tabrīzī.

2. *Kharbanda,* a term that would imply a lowly mendicant.

3. He is to be distinguished from two other major Suhrawardīs of roughly the same period, both Sufi mystics: Abū Najīb ʿAbd al-Qāhir (d. 1168), the author of a popular short manual of Sufism called *Ādāb al-murīdīn* (Rule for novices), and Abū Ḥafṣ ʿUmar (1145–1234), nephew of Abū Najīb, author of the influential Sufi handbook *ʿAwārif al maʿārif* and founder of the Suhrawardīya order. Our Suhrawardī is often called al-Suhrawardī al-Maqtūl, "the executed Suhrawardī," to distinguish him from the other two.

4. There is a picture purporting to be of Suhraward in Suhrawardī, *Œuvres philosophiques et mystiques,* vol. 3, ed. Seyyid Hossein Nasr (1970; reprint, Paris: Adrien Maisonneuve, 1977), between 240 and 241. Its authenticity is questionable. The village of Suhraward actually lies southwest of Zanjān; cf. Ḥ. ʿA. Razmārā, ed., *Farhang-i jughrāfiyā'ī yi Īrān ābādīhā* (Tehran: Dayirah-i Jughrāfiyāʾi-i Sitad-i ʿArtish, 1328–32 A.H./1949–54 C.E.).

5. Ibn Abī Uṣaybiʿa, *ʿUyūn al-anbāʾ,* 2:23.

6. *Al-talwīḥāt,* paragraph 55, in *Œuvres,* 1:70–74; *The Philosophy of Illumination,* section 166, this volume. On the significance of the Sufis he mentions, see John Walbridge, *The Wisdom of the Mystic East: Suhrawardī and Platonic Orientalism,* SUNY Series on Islam (Albany: State University of New York Press, forthcoming).

7. The political aspects of Suhrawardī's thought and career are discussed in Hossein Ziai, "Suhrawardī wa-siyāsat," *Īrān-nāma* 9, no. 3 (1370 A.H./ 1991 C.E.): 396–410; Ziai, "The Source and Nature of Authority: A Study of al-Suhrawardī's Illuminationist Political Doctrine," in *The Political Aspects of Islamic Philosophy: Essays in Honor of Muhsin S. Mahdi,* ed. Charles E. Butterworth, Harvard Middle Eastern Monographs 17 (Cambridge, Mass.: Center for Middle Eastern Studies of Harvard University, 1992), 304–44; John Walbridge, *The Leaven of the Ancients: Suhrawardī and the Heritage of the Greeks,* SUNY Series on Islam (Albany: State University of New York Press, 2000), ch. 12; cf. Walbridge, "The Political Thought of Quṭb al-Dīn al-Shīrāzī," in *Political Aspects of Islamic Philosophy,* ed. Butterworth, 345–78.

8. Shahrazūrī, *Sharḥ ḥikmat al-ishrāq,* ed. Hossein Ziai (Tehran: Institute for Cultural Studies and Research, 1993), 16; cf. Quṭb al-Dīn Shīrāzī, *Sharḥ ḥikmat al-ishrāq,* ed. Asad Allāh Harātī (Tehran: n.p., 1313–15 A.H./1895–97 C.E.), 12, who repeats the explanation almost verbatim. On Suhrawardī's theory of knowledge, see Walbridge, *Leaven,* ch. 10, and Hossein Ziai, *Knowledge and Illumination: A Study of Suhrawardī's* Ḥikmat al-Ishrāq, Brown University Judaic Studies 97 (Atlanta: Scholars Press, 1990).

9. On Suhrawardī's views concerning his Greek predecessors, see Walbridge, *Leaven.* For his views concerning the "Orientals," see Walbridge, *Wisdom.*

10. Only the sections on metaphysics of the three works *Intimations, Apposites,* and *Paths and Havens,* each referred to by Suhrawardī as "The Third Science on Metaphysics" *(al-ʿilm al-thālith fī al-ilāhiyyāt),* have been edited and published in *Opera Metaphysica et Mystica,* vol. 1, ed. H. Corbin (Istanbul: Maarif Matbaasi, 1945).

11. Corbin develops this account of Suhrawardī's views in, for example, *Suhrawardī d'Alep, fondateur de la doctrine illuminative* (Paris: G. P. Maisonneuve,

1939); *Les Motifs zoroastriens dans la philosophie de Sohravardī* (Tehran: du Courrier, 1946); *En Islam iranien,* vol. 2, *Sohravardī et les platoniciens de Perse* (Paris: Gallimard, 1971); and the *prolégomènes* to his critical editions of Suhrawardī's works, found in *Opera,* vol. 1; *Opera Metaphysica et Mystica,* vol. 2, ed. H. Corbin (Tehran: Institut Franco-Iranien, 1954); and *Opera,* vol. 3. See also Corbin's translations of Suhrawardī's works: *L'Archange empourpré: Quinze traités et récits mystiques* (Paris: Fayard, 1976); and *Le Livre de la sagesse orientale: Kitāb ḥikmat al-ishrāq,* trans. Henry Corbin, ed. Christian Jambet (Paris: Verdier, 1986). For a comprehensive discussion of Corbin's views, see Daryush Shayegan, *Henry Corbin: La topographie spirituelle de l'Islam iranien* (Paris: Éditions de la Différence, 1990), especially 134–38, 192–201. On misconceptions of post-Avicennan philosophy by western historians, which we believe to have resulted in part from Corbin's "theosophical" terminology as well as from his emphasis on esoteric doctrine, see Hossein Ziai, "Explaining the Philosophical Meaning of Ṣadr al-Dīn Shīrāzī's 'Metaphysical Philosophy,' *Ḥikmat-e motaʿāliyeh,*" *Iranshenasi* 5, no. 2 (summer 1993): 354–64.

An interpretation similar to that of Corbin is given by S. H. Nasr, *Three Muslim Sages: Avicenna, Suhrawardi, Ibn Arabi* (Cambridge, Mass.: Harvard University Press, 1964), chapter 2; Nasr, "Suhrawardī," in *A History of Muslim Philosophy,* ed. M. M. Sharif (Wiesbaden, Ger.: Otto Harrassowitz, 1963), 1:372–98. Nasr also gives a religious significance to Suhrawardī's life and teachings. See, in this regard, Nasr, *An Introduction to Islamic Cosmological Doctrines* (Boulder, Colo.: Shambhala, 1978), chapter 12.

12. See Shahrazūrī, *Sharḥ ḥikmat,* e.g., 8ff, 60ff. Shahrazūrī makes extensive references to other texts by Suhrawardī in order to establish the process through which Illuminationist arguments are proven.

13. For a contrary view, see Mehdi Aminrazavi, *Suhrawardi and the School of Illumination,* Curzon Sufi Series (Richmond, Engl.: Curzon, 1996), reviewed by John Walbridge, *International Journal of Middle East Studies* 30, no. 4 (1998): 615–17; and Aminrazavi, "The Significance of Suhrawardī's Persian Sufi Writings in the Philosophy of Illumination," in *Classical Persian Sufism: From Its Origins to Rumi,* ed. Leonard Lewisohn (London: Khaniqahi Nimatullahi Publications, 1993).

14. For our views of the nature of Suhrawardī's project, see Ziai, *Knowledge,* especially 9–15, 20–31, and 38–39, which discuss the interrelations among his works; Ziai, "Shihāb al Dīn Suhrawardī: Founder of the Illuminationist School" and "The Illuminationist Tradition," in *History of Islamic Philosophy,* ed. Seyyed Hossein Nasr and Oliver Leaman, Routledge History of World Philosophies 1 (London: Routledge, 1996), 1:434–96; and John Walbridge, *The Science of Mystic Lights: Quṭb al-Dīn Shīrāzī and the Illuminationist Tradition in Islamic Philosophy,* Harvard Middle Eastern Monographs 26 (Cambridge, Mass.: Center for Middle Eastern Studies of Harvard University, 1992), especially chapters 2 and 3, which analyze the relationship between Illuminationist metaphysics and the Islamic Peripatetic tradition of Avicenna. See also Walbridge, *Leaven,* and Walbridge, *Wisdom.*

Suhrawardī's mature system has been characterized in many ways, for example: "reinplatonischen" (Carl Brockelmann, *Geschichte der arabischen Literatur,*

2d ed., [Leiden: E. J. Brill, 1943–49], 1:437–38; and *Geschichte der arabischen Literatur Supliment* [Leiden: E. J. Brill, 1937–42], 1:481–83); "néoplatonisme . . . exprimé au moyen d'unes termes métaphoriques 'lumière-ténèbres' " (B. Carra de Vaux, "La Philosophie illluminative," *Journal asiatique* 19, no. 1 [janvier–février, 1902]: 63); "avicenno-platonicienne" (Louis Massignon, *Recueil de textes inédits concernant l'histoire de la mystique en pays d'Islam* [Paris: Paul Guethner, 1929], 113); "Avicennian, Neo-Platonic" (Majid Fakhry, *A History of Islamic Philosophy,* 2d ed. [New York: Columbia University Press, 1983], 303–4); "la restauration de la sagesse de l'ancienne Perse," "théosophie orientale," "philosophie orientale," and "sagesse orientale" (Henry Corbin, *Histoire de la philosophie islamique* [Paris: Gallimard, 1964], 284ff).

Other scholars do recognize a systematically developed philosophy of Illumination—much of it in agreement with the Avicennan doctrine, but based on non-Aristotelian logical foundations—which in part is finally stated as a unified theory of knowledge. The new system is progressively formulated in texts ordered according to degree of complexity but agreeing in fundamental doctrines. This view was expounded by early twentieth-century scholars, who emphasized the significance of Suhrawardī's accomplishments in "philosophy of logic"—to use the modern term. See Max Horten, *Die Philosophie der Erleuchtung nach Suhrawardī* (Halle, Ger.: Strauss und Cramer, 1912), vii–x, 5–29. Muhammad Iqbal earlier noted the philosophical basis of Suhrawardī's thought in his *The Development of Metaphysics in Persia* (London: Luzac, 1908), 121–50 (he draws from the manuscript of Harawī's Persian commentary, "Anwāriyya," in Berlin at the Königlichen Bibliothek, *Bibliotheca Orientalis Sprengeriana,* Spr. 766). Noteworthy in this regard is a study by A. Dānā-Seresht, *Khulāsa-yi afkār-e Suhrawardī wa Mullā Ṣadrā* (Tehran: n.p., 1934), one of the few twentieth-century Persian works that recognizes the logical distinctions between the Peripatetic and Illuminationist systems (e.g., 9–15). On the influence of Suhrawardī's philosophical views on later Iranian philosophy, see Toshihiko Izutsu, *The Concept and Reality of Existence,* Studies in the Humanities and Social Relations (Tokyo: Keio Institute of Cultural and Linguistic Studies, 1971).

15. For medieval testimonies on Suhrawardī's accomplishments regarding the perfect synthesis of rational and intuitive knowledge, see Ibn Abī Uṣaybiᶜa, *ᶜUyūn al-anbāʾ* (Müller ed.), 1:168; Yāqūt, *Irshād,* 6:269; Shahrazūrī, *Nuzhat* (Aḥmad ed.), 2:119–43; and al Qifṭī, *Tārīkh* (Dārāʾī ed.), 345.

16. Shahrazūrī, *Nuzhat* (Aḥmad ed.), 2:124–25.

17. Hossein Ziai, Persian and English introductions to Shahrazūrī, *Sharḥ ḥikmat;* Ziai, "Muᶜarrifī wa-barrasī-i nuskhahā-yi khaṭṭī-i Shajara-yi ilāhīya . . ." *Irānshināsī* 2, no. 1 (spring 1369 A.H./1990 C.E.): 89–108.

18. See Walbridge, *Science.*

19. Sayyid Jaᶜfar Sajjādī, *Dāʾirat al-maᶜārif-i buzurg-i Islāmī,* s.v. "Ibn Kammūna."

20. Ibn al-Hirawī, *Anwārīya,* ed. Hossein Ziai, *Majmūᶜa-yi Muṭālaʾat-i Islāmī* 2 (Tehran: Intishārāt-i Markaz-i Īrānī-i Muṭālaᶜa-yi Farhang, Amīr Kabīr, 1358 A.H./1979 C.E.) On this movement, see Walbridge, *Wisdom,* ch. 5.

21. Ibn al-Khaṭīb, *Rawḍat al-taᶜrīf bi al-ḥubb al-sharīf,* ed. Muḥammad al-Kattānī (Rabat, Morocco: Dār al-Thaqāfa, 1981).

22. Published in *Opera,* vol. 2.

23. There have been two previous translations of *Ḥikmat al-ishrāq:* the French translation of Corbin, *Le Livre de la sagesse orientale,* cited above, and Sayyid Ja^c^far Sajjādī, *Ḥikmat al-ishrāq,* Intishārāt-i Dānishgāh-i Tihrān 1562 (Tehran: Dānishgāh-i Tihrān, [1976]). Corbin's translation, as has been mentioned, omits the logic but includes extensive translations from the commentary of Quṭb al-Dīn Shīrāzī and the supercommentary *(ta^c^līqāt)* of Mullā Ṣadrā.

24. The variant noted to section 115 of the Arabic text. Shahrazūrī, *Sharḥ ḥikmat,* 295 n. 413.

25. Helmut Ritter, "Philologika IX: Die vier Suhrawardi," *Der Islam* 24 (1937): 278 n. 17.

Shahrazūrī's Introduction

1. "Law" *(fiqh)* and "jurisprudence" *(uṣūl al-fiqh)* refer respectively to legal regulations and the principles by which they are deduced. Usually these terms refer specifically to Islamic law, but here they are used in a general sense.

2. Estimation *(wahm)* is the faculty by which the mind judges images without the use of pure intelligibles—for example, it is how an animal judges that a predator is dangerous.

3. *Metaphysics,* 1.3.983^{a}24–984^{a}23.

4. Cited in Shahrazūrī, *Nuzhat al-arwāḥ,* ed. M. ^c^A. Abū Rayyān, 614.

Suhrawardī's Introduction

1. Quṭb al-Dīn, *Sharḥ ḥikmat,* 12, writes: "Philosophy of illumination, i.e., the philosophy based on illumination, which is visionary experience *(kashf)*; or the philosophy of the Easterners—meaning the Persians. This amounts to the same thing since their philosophy is based on revelation and intuition. It is thus limited to the revelation of the lights of the intellects, their rays, and the outpouring upon the soul during its abstraction from the body. In philosophy, the Persians relied on intuition and revelation, as did the ancient Greeks with the exception of Aristotle and his school, who relied only on study and demonstration." The passage could also be translated "that I write *The Philosophy of Illumination,*" but this interpretation is not supported by the commentators, who agree in taking *ḥikmat al-ishrāq* as a common noun phrase rather than as the title of the book.

2. Intuition *(dhawq)* in Illuminationist terminology is the direct, instantaneous apprehension of the quiddities of things. It is a Sufi term used to describe mystical experience and literally means "tasting."

3. Quṭb al-Dīn, *Sharḥ ḥikmat,* 14, says that the *wāhib al-^c^ilm* is the active intellect.

4. *Al-talwīḥāt* (The intimations) is one of Suhrawardī's three major works written in the "Peripatetic style." Only the part discussing metaphysics is published. *Al-lamaḥāt* (The flashes of light) is a short summary of philosophy written in the Peripatetic mode.

5. Quṭb al-Dīn, *Sharḥ ḥikmat,* 16, remarks that the science of lights deals with the First Principle, the (celestial) intellects, and souls. That which is based upon it includes most of physics, some of metaphysics, and, in general, that which is known by intuition.

6. On Suhrawardī's attitudes toward the Greek philosophers, see John Walbridge, *Leaven,* where Empedocles, Pythagoras, and Plato are discussed.

7. Quṭb al-Dīn, *Sharḥ ḥikmat,* 17–18, lists four reasons for the use of symbolic language by the Ancients: to sharpen the reader's mind; to make the text suitable for both the elite and the masses; to conceal doctrines from those unworthy of or hostile to them; and to separate the intelligent students from the stupid. On the question of symbolic philosophical language in Suhrawardī's thought, see Walbridge, *Leaven,* 97–116.

8. Quṭb al-Dīn reads *al-ishrāq* for *al-sharq,* which would mean "the Illuminationist doctrine."

9. Three semilegendary ancient Persian sages: Jamasp was the vizier of Vishtaspa, the king who was Zoroaster's protector. Books on alchemy and astrology were attibuted to him in Islamic times. Frashostar was another early Zoroastrian mentioned in the Avesta. Bozorgmehr was a sixth-century Sassanian vizier famed for his wisdom. Books also circulated under his name. See Walbridge, *Wisdom,* ch. 3.C.

10. On Suhrawardī's attitudes toward Hermes, the ancient Persians, and also the Indians, see Walbridge, *Wisdom.*

11. Quṭb al-Dīn, *Sharḥ ḥikmat,* 20, says that they are the worlds of the intellect, the soul, and the body (or matter).

12. "Intuitive philosophy" is a (not wholly satisfactory) rendering of *taʾalluh,* which literally means "deification." "Mysticism" or "mystical philosophy" might also do.

13. Some manuscripts add, "and he will be the vicegerent of God," but this is evidently a gloss. The commentators tend to soften the political implications of this paragraph.

14. Some manuscripts add, "and unveiled."

15. That is, "axis." The Pole is the highest rank in the hierarchy of hidden saints of Sufi folklore.

16. These principles cover specific areas of Illuminationist doctrine and are identified by section headings in *The Philosophy of Illumination.* Lesser points of Illuminationist doctrine are called *daqīqa ishrāqīya,* "Illuminationist lemmas," and in one case a general principle is called *ḥikma ishrāqīya,* "Illuminationist wisdom." Other terms such as *nukta ishrāqīya* and *sunnat al-ishrāq* are used in a less technical way to identify special topics in Illuminationist philosophy.

17. Such principles are obtained by a soul "separated from body, which has a vision of the intellectual principles *(al-mabādiʾ al-ʿaqlīya)* and the apocalyptic lights," Quṭb al-Dīn, *Sharḥ ḥikmat,* 26.

18. The organon—that is, logic.

19. The commentators mention both Suhrawardī's "Peripatetic" works and Avicenna's standard works like the *Shifāʾ* and the *Najāt.*

20. This is probably an allusion to the arrangement of "Peripatetic" works of philosophy in Arabic, which were normally divided into parts dealing with

logic, physics, and metaphysics. This book contains only parts on logic and a "science of lights"—a pattern followed by later members of the Illuminationist school in their works.

Part One: The First Discourse

1. When there are no titles in Suhrawardī's text, they have been supplied whenever possible from Quṭb al-Dīn's commentary, *Sharḥ ḥikmat,* though sometimes in shortened form. The first five rules comprise the subject matter of the traditional *Isagoge.*

2. The standard Arabic terms for these three forms of signification are *dalālat al-muṭābaqa, dalālat al-taḍmīn,* and *dalālat al-iltizām* respectively. His use of unorthodox terminology, here and throughout the part dealing with logic, signals his intention to break with the logic of the Islamic world of his time.

3. Quṭb al-Dīn, *Sharḥ ḥikmat,* 37–38, disagrees with this on the grounds that the correlate may not be present in the mind.

4. Suhrawardī does not accept the standard notion in Islamic logic that all knowledge can be divided into conceptions and assents (terms that he quite deliberately does not use in this book). He adds a third category, "knowledge by presence." Quṭb al-Dīn, *Sharḥ ḥikmat,* 38–39, explains that in elementary logic one would ignore knowledge by presence, to which this analysis does not apply—which is why his commentary specifies that this is the "division between conception and assent in the manuals of logic."

5. Suhrawardī uses the term "image," *(mithāl)* and not the standard "form," *(ṣūra).*

6. Quṭb al-Dīn, *Sharḥ ḥikmat,* 44, gives the example of man in relation to animal.

7. The commentators here equate Suhrawardī's *ḥaqīqa,* "reality" or "real thing," with the standard term for quiddity or essence, *māhīya.* Cf. Quṭb al-Dīn, *Sharḥ ḥikmat,* 45, "every reality—that is, quiddity—whether in concrete things or in minds."

8. That which gives life to the animal is traditionally called the "animal soul."

9. The Peripatetic term is "genus."

10. In Peripatetic terms, this is the specific difference—the differentia. In this example it is the animal soul, which exists only in animals.

11. The Arabic word *nāṭiq,* "speaking," is used as the equivalent of "rational" in the phrase "rational animal" in Islamic philosophical texts.

12. An individual human being may or may not be laughing at a particular time. A concomitant accident is an attribute that is possessed by all members of a species without being part of the essence of the species.

13. The essence of a triangle—despite the derivation of English word—is to have three *sides.* The three *angles* are not part of the essence of a triangle, but every triangle necessarily has three angles. Suhrawardī is saying that the cause of all triangles having three angles must be the essence of the triangle. If the cause were something other than the essence, then a triangle could be conceived that did not have three angles. This can be made clearer by mentioning properties of triangles that do have causes external to the essence. For

example, if one of the angles of the triangle is greater than ninety degrees, this is due to some cause other than the essence of the triangle. Thus, in both mind and reality, there can be triangles with or without such an angle. Having three angles, however, is not such a variable property. Still, only the property of having three sides is part of the *essence* of a triangle; the property of having three angles is not.

14. Some manuscripts read "accidental."

15. Quṭb al-Dīn, *Sharḥ ḥikmat,* 53–53, explains that something can be identified by a series of attributes, each of which is unique to that thing: "Man is rational, laughing, etc." Alternatively, only some part of the definition might be peculiar to that thing: "Man is a rational animal," where "rational" is unique to man but "animal" is not. Finally, none of the elements may be unique to the thing defined, but in combination they may identify the thing: "A bat is a flying creature that bears its young alive."

16. That is, a lexical definition.

17. For instance, definition of "something black" must include two elements: blackness and the thing that is black.

18. Ibn Sīnā, *Al-ishārāt wa al-tanbīhāt,* 1.2.7.

19. Quṭb al-Dīn, *Sharḥ ḥikmat,* 58, identifies these three schools as being respectively, "the First Teacher [Aristotle] and his followers, the Peripatetics, who hold that the natural body is compounded of two non-sensible and simple parts: prime matter and form"; "some theologians and others"; and "the theologians who hold that the body is composed of indivisible parts [i.e., the Muslim atomists among the Mutakallimūn] and the Ancients who held that body is unchanging fixed magnitude." The theory of "the Ancients" (see sections 72–88) is Suhrawardī's own.

20. That is, the essentials.

21. Quṭb al-Dīn, *Sharḥ ḥikmat,* 59, explains that this formulation restricts it to the proximate genus and excludes the remote genus. This is because the more general is part of the less general, so that which is not a part of a part of the explanation of the thing itself must be the proximate genus.

22. For example, *Al-mashāriᶜ wa al-muṭāriḥāt* 1.2.1, published by Hossein Ziai as "Definition and the Foundations of Knowledge in Illuminationist Philosophy," in *Papers in Honor of "Ostād" Javad Mosleh,* ed. Borhan Ibneh Yousef (Los Angeles: Research and Education Center, 1993), 108-30.

23. Possibly a reference to Aristotle, *Analytica Posteriora,* 1.22.82^{b}39 or 2.3.90b15. This is Suhrawardī's first major dispute with the Peripatetics. He is challenging a major portion of the logical foundation of Peripatetic philosophy and offering an Illuminationist alternative.

Part One: The Second Discourse

1. Literally, "predicative."

2. *Modus ponens:* if ((if p, then q) and p), then q.

3. *Modus tollens:* if ((if p, then q) and not q), then not p.

4. That is, both (if ((if p, then q) and not p), then not q) and (if ((if p, then q), and q), then p) are invalid.

5. Some manuscripts read "blackness."

6. That is, exclusive disjunction, p or q, in which one and only one of the propositions can be true.

7. The term used is *ajzā'*, meaning "parts," but it is clear that what is meant are propositions. For example, the basic form of the exclusive disjunctive conditional proposition is p or q, but other propositions could be added—p or q or r, and so on.

8. For example, if ((p or q) and p), then not q.

9. For example, if ((p or q or r or s) and not p), then (q or r or s).

10. This is a problem concerning quantification of certain types of propositions, be they universal or particular to begin with. Thus, the proposition "Human is animal" can be quantified correctly both as a universal and as a particular proposition.

11. Suhrawardī is saying here that any proposition A is B should be specified either as universal (all A is B) or as a particular (some A is B) but should never remain simply as A is B.

12. Here the subject, Zayd, is a proper name and is thus particular.

13. The term *sūr* is a non-Aristotelian term, though not one unique to Suhrawardī. See Soheil M. Afnan, *A Philosophical Lexicon in Persian and Arabic* (Beirut: Dar El Mashreq, 1968), 131.

14. The Arabic "whenever" *(kullumā)* is here considered as an application of the universal quantifier "all" *(kull)* to a conditional proposition.

15. In the simplest sentences, Arabic omits the verb "to be" and sometimes uses a pronoun to mark the division between the subject and predicate.

16. The distinction is that, for example, "x is y" is called affirmative and "x is-not y" is called negative, but "x is non-y" and "non-x is y" are still considered affirmative and are given the name "infinite"—or in, Arabic, "modified" *(maᶜdūla)* because their copulas are affirmative.

17. This is the law of negation: not not p implies p.

18. *Mumkin* can be translated as either "possible" or "contingent." In Arabic, this term has the same ambiguity that the English "possible" has, in that it can mean either that which is not impossible or that which is neither necessary nor impossible. The term is uniformly translated "contingent" here, which accurately renders its technical Arabic meaning; but, of course, this makes Suhrawardī's explanation of the difference between popular and technical logical usage unnecessary.

19. Take the proposition "A is necessarily B." If this proposition be conditioned as "A is necessarily B, if B_t and B_s," then A itself is only possibly B when the time (t) and the state (s) are removed.

20. The proposition referred to here as the "definitely necessary" or "necessary at all times" combines the three modes with the temporal modalities "always" and "sometimes." In the language of contemporary formal logic, this is a type of "iterated modal proposition." By putting forth the notion of "reduction of proposition," Suhrawardī has in this section departed from the Peripatetics, notably Avicenna. The term *al-qaḍīya al-ḍarūrīya al-battāta* is coined by Suhrawardī himself and has no counterpart—despite the opinion of M.-T. Dānish-Pazhūh in his edition of Ibn Sahlān al-Sāwī, *Tabṣira wa du risāla-yi*

dīgar dar manṭiq (Tehran: Tehran University Press, 1958), 21—in the Aristotelian logical corpus. Where Aristotle states that "all propositions are convertible save only the particular negative" (*Prior Analytics* 1.46.52b7–8), he means "conversion" and not "reduction." Suhrawardī's "iterated modal proposition" reducing all propositions to necessary propositions is an innovation by him in the area of formal logic: $\Diamond p \rightarrow \Box \Diamond p$, where $\Box$ is the necessity sign and $\Diamond$ is the possibility sign. (In addition, the following, though awkward, are also iterated modal propositions according to Suhrawardī's scheme: $\neg \Box p \rightarrow \Box \neg \Diamond p$ and $\neg \Diamond p \rightarrow \Box \neg \Diamond p$.)

21. He is recapitulating his argument that negation and the modes of contingency and impossibility can be eliminated by incorporating them into the predicate. Thus, "necessarily all men are non-stone" and "contingently white."

22. From this perspective, the proposition called *muhmalat al-jiha,* "indefinite in mode"—which is also called *al-muṭlaqa al-^{c}āmma,* "universal absolute"—and the particular *(al-shākhiṣa)* and the indefinite, unquantified, are considered without value in logic. In general, all particulars are reduced to universals, all negatives are reduced to affirmatives, and every proposition is reduced to an iterated necessary modal. See Quṭb al-Dīn, *Sharḥ ḥikmat,* 86.

23. That is, if a necessary universal proposition is negated—"It is not the case that all men are mortal"—it follows that some man is not mortal but not that all men are not mortal.

24. Quṭb al-Dīn, *Sharḥ ḥikmat,* 92–93, has a long note explaining that this argument attacks the position of certain "moderns"—that is, Islamic philosophers.

25. See section 16, above. The "conjunctive syllogism" is the categorical syllogism, and the "exclusive syllogism" includes both the hypothetical and the disjunctive syllogisms. The first is the familiar syllogism of Aristotle's term logic. The second includes syllogisms of the types (if ((if p, then q) and p), then q) and (if ((p or q) and p), then not q), the first being hypothetical and the second disjunctive. Though we would consider the second class of syllogisms to belong to the propositional rather than term logic, Suhrawardī considers them to be a special case of term logic—syllogisms where both terms of the conclusion appear in the same premise.

26. A somewhat ambiguous statement, perhaps to be considered as follows: "The Sun is shining, then it is day; or the Sun is not shining, then it is not day," and so on.

27. Meaning the fourth figure of the syllogism, whose development was usually attributed to Galen and which was a subject of deep suspicion among medieval logicians. A valid example is: "No men are quadrupeds, all quadrupeds are animals; therefore some animals are not men."

28. A is B; B is C; therefore, A is C.

29. In the first type, *al-mūjiba al-ma^{c}dūla,* the subject, the predicate, or both are prefixed with negative particles, as in the Persian statement *"Ḥasan nā-bīnā ast,"* (Ḥasan is non-seeing), to use Avicenna's example. In the second type, called *al-sāliba al-ma^{c}dūla,* the whole proposition is denied. In other words, "A is non-B," "non-A is B," and "non-A is non-B" are all different from "It is not the case that A is B." Suhrawardī holds that the existence of A (or non-A) is assumed in the first type but not in the second.

30. In section 21 Suhrawardī had earlier formalized a single iterated necessary form of proposition, and here he is using it as the form for the premises. By incorporating quantification and negation into the terms, he is able to reduce all propositions to universal necessary affirmatives.

31. That is, the second and the third figures are appendages of the first.

32. Some manuscripts read, "the impossibility of part of its predicate."

33. That is, for one of them to be necessary and the other contingent.

34. Such as "All A are B, and all B are non-C; therefore, some B is non-C."

35. Aristotle, *Prior Analytics,* 1.3.25^{b}.

36. Suhrawardī uses the term *sharṭīyāt* to denote the conditional propositions like, "If p, then q." However, the constructions discussed in this section are pure and mixed hypothetical syllogisms that combine conditional propositions with categorical propositions.

37. This is the basic form of the hypothetical proposition: if ((if p, then q) and (if q, then r)), then (if p, then r), where in this specific case p, q, and r are all thought to be propositions reducible to the A-type.

38. See sections 16 and 21.

39. Some manuscripts read, "The simplest case is when the common term is . . ."

40. Aristotle, *History of Animals,* 1.11.492^{b}24, states that the river crocodile is the only animal that moves its upper jaw.

41. According to Quṭb al-Dīn, *Sharḥ ḥikmat,* 122, this was in contrast to certain scholars, presumably of the religious sciences, who set a fixed number of witnesses whose testimony would together establish certitude.

42. The argument is that all primary premises, and others of the same rank, are known "innately" and need only be conceived for the mind to assent to their validity. These premises are also called "self-evident" and "innate."

43. Suhrawardī is arguing that the well-known premises may be innate or acquired, the latter of which would have to be demonstrated in order to be accepted. His example, "Ignorance is abhorrent," is not known innately but will be readily accepted once the nature of ignorance is investigated. The contrasting premise that "Ignorance is bliss," while well known, is false. However, *"al-ḍiddān lā yajtamiʿān" (non coincidenta oppositorum)* is well known to be true but is also known innately and hence is among the primary premises.

44. A separate type called *maqbūlāt.* Such premises are not scientific and, as Quṭb al Dīn, *Sharḥ ḥikmat,* 126, states, are used in rhetoric, poetry, and sophistry.

45. Suhrawardī is making the point that although it is obvious that such a proposition is false, it may affect a person who hears it.

46. The usage of *ḥukm*—"predicate," "judgment," "state of affairs"—is theological, not philosophical.

47. Suhrawardī is criticizing the analogical reasoning used by Islamic theologians. The argument he is criticizing is as follows: Suppose we know that A is C and want to prove that A is D. This we can do if we know that for any x, if x is C, x is also D. For example, suppose we want to prove that the celestial spheres were created in time. Since we know that the spheres are bodies, we can reach our conclusion if we can show that anything that is a body is also created in time. Suhrawardī identifies two variants of this argument: (1) We can

do an induction showing that everything we examine that is C is also D and everything that is not-D is also not-C. In our example, then, all bodies that we examine are created in time, and everything that we know of that is not created in time—God, mathematicals, angels, and such—is also not a body. (2) We can choose a B that is both C and D. We can then show that C and D are always associated, whereas all other attributes of A are independent of D—that is, E, F, G, and so on, all occur independently of each other in other things. In each case, the validity of the argument is destroyed by the possibility that the correlation is by chance and that the real cause is some other factor—possibly a combination of attributes. Suhrawardī offers the further criticism that a single effect—heat, for example—may have more than one cause.

48. This is the distinction between knowledge of the fact *(hoti)* and knowledge of the reasoned fact *(dioti)* of Aristotle, *Posterior Analytics,* 1.13, the medieval distinction of demonstration *quia* and demonstration *propter quid.*

49. The real cause in this example of the burning stick—and therefore the middle term of its causal demonstration—is the stick's being touched by fire.

50. See Aristotle, *Posterior Analytics,* 2.1, although Suhrawardī's direct source is probably Ibn Sīnā.

Part One: The Third Discourse

1. *Al-mughālaṭāt,* one of the two terms used in Arabic for "sophistical refutations" (the other being the transliterated form *safsaṭa*), is the participle of the third form of the triliteral root *gh-l-ṭ,* one of the basic meanings of which is "to make or commit an error." Thus, the third discourse is devoted to a discussion of "errors" that occur in formal as well as material logic, and to a refutation of Peripatetic metaphysical principles considered to be false.

2. Quṭb al-Dīn, *Sharḥ ḥikmat,* 145, gives the example, "Some African is black" and "Some of the African is not black." The Arabic idiom makes it easy to confuse "some one" and "some of."

3. These are errors such as interpreting the assertion "All men can be fed with a loaf of bread" to mean that one loaf is sufficient to feed all mankind; cf. ibid., 145.

4. He means the fallacy of incorrectly assuming that a specific property of a thing is caused by a more general property shared by other things, then attributing the specific property indiscriminately to other things that share the general property.

5. *Iᶜtibārāt dhihnīya,* which Suhrawardī usually calls *iᶜtibārāt ᶜaqlīya.* He evidently wishes to stress that these are products of our minds and not real qualities abstracted from concrete things, and for this reason the term is translated "intellectual fictions" in John Walbridge, *Science of Mystic Lights,* especially 45–46. Another translation might be "second intentions," although both this term and "beings of reason," the term used in the text, have slightly different meanings in the Latin tradition.

6. That is, this thing man is not a universal, but the idea of man is.

7. That is, one errs by imagining that because fire burns, the image of fire formed in the mind should burn the one who has thought of it; but, since it

does not, one further errs by concluding that there is no such thing as the image of a thing existing in the mind.

8. The method called *al-lā-awlawīya* stipulates that when attributes of members of a group are being predicated, an attribution may lead to false conclusions if the group is not homogeneous.

9. Such an inference would be valid only if man and fish were of the same species under the genus animal, which they are not.

10. The argument is that we ought only to postulate things that are possible. For example, Quṭb al-Dīn, *Sharḥ ḥikmat,* 152, says that to postulate a god other than the one God would be a sophistical error, since it is not the case that a second God is possible just because we can suppose that there is one. It is generally held in the Islamic tradition that a second God is a rational impossibility.

11. The idea is that beardlessness cannot be said in the same way of a child and a grown man.

12. For example, there are differences of opinion about whether air can be said to be dark.

13. That is, one cannot infer that "All C is B" from "Some C is B."

14. In summary, whenever there is a true universal affirmative proposition, the definite affirmative is true as well as the specific; for example, "All humans are animal" implies that "Some humans are animal" and that "Zayd is an animal." But "It is not the case that all animals are man" does not imply the invalidity of "Some animals are man" or "Zayd is man."

15. Such an inference is valid when the parts and the whole differ only in quantity, as is the case with water.

16. The syllogism under discussion is, "What is in Zayd's sleeves (that is, his hands) is a multiple of two, and every multiple of two is even; therefore, what is in Zayd's sleeves is even." The view that Suhrawardī is refuting is evidently that it is possible to go directly from the major premise to the conclusion without explicit use of the minor premise, the minor premise being implicitly included in the major. However, Suhrawardī rejects this view concerning the syllogism. See Quṭb al-Dīn, *Sharḥ ḥikmat,* 160.

17. Aristotle, *Posterior Analytics,* 1.1.

18. Quṭb al-Dīn, *Sharḥ ḥikmat,* 162–63, gives the reading: "The reality of the thing cannot have alternating contradictory constituents, since the quiddity would change with each one of them; but it is possible for the existence of the thing to have alternating contradictory constituents." He mentions the reading in the text, which we derive from the Istanbul manuscript, as being that "of most of the manuscripts." The point is the same in both readings: that the essence of something cannot have contradictory constituents at different times, since that would change what the thing is, but one kind of thing can have quite different causes—for example, heat can be caused by a variety of processes.

Suhrawardī is saying that a thing cannot at different times have essential attributes that are contradictory to each other: a human cannot be at one time an animal that speaks and at another an animal that whinnies. On the other hand, a thing's existence may have incompatible constituents in its complete cause at different times. Since the cause consists of all aspects of the thing that cannot be taken as part of its existence, an example would be youth and old age, which may partly constitute a human being and, although contradictory, can at different times be part of the individual's cause. A simpler example would be the material from which a ring is made. See ibid., 162–63.

19. In this case, the term "law" may also be used.

20. That is to say, unlike the genus, the attributes that are true of all individuals of a species are also true of the universal corresponding to the species. The attributes that distinguish individuals of a species—the blackness of the African, for example—are due to external factors and are not essential. Cf. Quṭb al-Dīn, *Sharḥ ḥikmat,* 165.

21. The point is that a negation can be treated as an affirmative proposition, as he has already argued in section 21.

22. The point is evidently that nothing necessary can be said about contingents in propositions that do not specify the mode.

23. These are: *al-ḍarūrīya al-muṭlaqa, al-mashrūṭa al-ʿāmma, al-mashrūṭa al-khāṣṣa, al-waqtīya,* and *al-muntashira.* See Hossein Ziai, "Modal Propositions in Islamic Logic," *Bulletin of the Iranian Mathematical Society* 12 (winter 1980): 58–74.

24. "Ecthesis" is Aristotle's term for exposition, a logical operation in which an individual is selected to test a general rule. The use of the term D here is ecthesis.

25. Suhrawardī's contention has been that only the first figure, as a simple, straightforward form, is readily understood by people of simple common sense. Any other compound argument is considered unnatural and thus must be proven in reference to a simple argument such as the first figure.

26. Suhrawardī asserts the impossibility of any infinity whose members are actual, ordered, and simultaneously existent. Thus, there cannot be an infinite number of levels of being. Possible infinities include numbers (since they are not actual) and causal chains of temporal events (since they are not simultaneously existent). This principle is important and is often used by Suhrawardī and his followers, as in section 57 below.

27. This is less tautological than it sounds, since the Arabic word for "nonexistent" *(maʿdūm)*—literally "lacking," is unrelated to the word for "existence," which comes from a root meaning "to find."

28. Quṭb al-Dīn, *Sharḥ ḥikmat,* 185, explains that the issue is the implication of the fact that one can intellect a quiddity and yet doubt whether it exists. This is the argument Avicenna used to distinguish quiddity and existence. According to Suhrawardī, the followers of the Peripatetics—meaning the Avicennans—held that this meant that existence was added to quiddity in reference to concrete things. Their Illuminationist opponents countered that the same argument could be applied to the existence of a concrete thing as distinct from its quiddity—asking, in other words, if the thing's existence had an existence of its own, which would imply an infinite regress. This doctrine—that existence is a secondary intelligible—was later called "primacy of quiddity" and was one of the main doctrines by which the Illuminationists were distinguished from their opponents.

29. Islamic logicians were handicapped by the lack of an equivalent of "to be" in Arabic to render the logical copula. Thus, when the existential sense of

the copula is important, as here, the copula is rendered *yūjad,* "exists," followed a predicate, resulting in an Arabic sentence that is as awkward in Arabic as its English rendering suggests.

30. Meaning a being of reason.

31. Arabic distinguishes between *aswad,* "black," a descriptive adjective, and *sawād,* "blackness," a qualitative noun. Suhrawardī also occasionally uses *aswadīya,* "being black," to refer to the state of being of a black thing. As for color in general, he uses both *lawn,* "color," and *lawnīya,* "color-ness." Despite the awkwardness, these distinctions are maintained in the translation.

32. The argument is thus: Assume that the mental distinction of being a color and being black corresponds to a real distinction. Since there are different colors contingently, there is nothing in color-ness that requires that it be associated with blackness. Therefore, the blackness could be removed and replaced with whiteness, the color-ness remaining as a substratum—which is absurd in the same way that the independent existence of genera is absurd. Cf. Quṭb al-Dīn, *Sharḥ ḥikmat,* 197.

33. Reading *yataṣawwaru* with Quṭb al-Dīn, *Sharḥ ḥikmat,* 198.

34. That is, instances of nonbeing in cases where being is conceivable.

35. In effect, this is not a real definition.

36. "Blackness" renders *sawād* and "nigritude" *aswadīya,* the latter evidently meaning that by which blackness is blackness.

37. Some manuscripts read "predicates."

38. *Mumkinīya* and *imkān.* If there is a difference between the two, it would be that the first is the property of being contingent and the second that by which something is contingent; but Suhrawardī's point is that such abstract terms can be formed arbitrarily.

39. That is, blackness is also an intellectual attribute, in the sense that it is derived from the attribute black. Therefore, one can say that a substance is black, but not that a substance is blackness. However, it is more concrete than, say, contingency, which is not directly derived from something external to the mind.

40. Quṭb al-Dīn, *Sharḥ ḥikmat,* 206, entitled this section "Settling the disagreement between the Peripatetics, who hold that the body is compounded of prime matter and form, and the Ancients, who held that it was magnitude that accepted three dimensions."

41. Some manuscripts read, "yet extension does not admit of separation at all."

42. This view reflects the "receptacle" in Plato's *Timæus* 49A ff., which commentators from Aristotle on identified with space. Cf. Aristotle, *Physics,* 4.2.210^{a}11–18.

43. Suhrawardī means that the choice of technical terms is arbitrary and not subject to logical refutation.

44. Some manuscripts read, "have no real meaning except." Corbin's text reads, "We do not accept rarefaction and compression in the literal sense, since they are just . . ."

45. The experiment involves putting a tightly plugged bottle containing water into a fire. The bottle will break when the water boils.

46. That is, nonbodily forms like species and nature.

47. Quṭb al-Dīn, *Sharḥ ḥikmat,* 228, reads "nature."

48. Some manuscripts read "another, a corporeal substance."

49. Quṭb al-Dīn, *Sharḥ ḥikmat,* 233, attributes this view to the Peripatetics, who recognize distinction of species by differentia and distinction of individuals by accidents, but not distinction of individuals by intensity. Allowing distinction of substances by intensity is a characteristic Illuminationist doctrine.

50. Suhrawardī is attacking the ancient atomists and, more particularly, the Islamic kalam theologians, most of whom were atomists.

51. *Ṣanam;* literally, "idol," probably rendering the Platonic *eikōn.* The Platonic Forms are "lords of idols"—*arbāb aṣnām.* The notion is evidently that the species are the material imitations of a spiritual reality, corresponding to but not resembling their respective forms.

52. *Mithāl* (pl. *muthul*), is used in two senses here, as Quṭb al-Dīn, *Sharḥ ḥikmat,* 252, makes clear: the image in the mind and the Platonic Form. They are translated as "image" and "Form" respectively, but they are the same Arabic word. Normally Suhrawardī uses *ṣūra,* "form," for the mental image and for the material form, which transfers the ambiguity from Arabic to English. In this translation, "Form" *(mithāl)* in the Platonic sense is consistently capitalized to distinguish is from mental form *(ṣūra).*

53. "Inclination" is the body's natural motion or resistance to motion. Quṭb al-Dīn, *Sharḥ ḥikmat,* 258–59, summarizes the succeeding argument as follows:

> A is a body lacking all inclination that is moved by a particular force of ten cubits in an hour. B has a certain inclination and is moved by the same force ten cubits in two hours. The time of B's motion is half the time of A's motion. C is a body. The ratio of the inclination of B to the inclination of C is the same as the ratio of the times of B's and A's motion. Therefore, the inclination of C is half the inclination of B. The time of C's motion will thus be half the time of B's motion: one hour. Thus, A and C will each move the same distance—ten cubits—in response to the same force in the same time—one hour, despite the fact that C has an inclination and A does not.

54. Some manuscripts read "in its coarseness" for "naturally."

55. This view was associated with Plato and, more particularly, with writers on mathematical optics, such as Ptolemy.

56. Aristotle and the Peripatetics.

57. The gelatinous substance in the eyeball.

58. Physical vision and *mushāhada* ("intellectual apprehension") are two complementary principles of knowledge in Suhrawardī's system, so that he generalizes the principles he has established for vision when he works out his epistemology.

59. Literally, "points of articulation," the technical term in Arabic linguistics for the positions of the mouth by which the phonemes are articulated.

60. The point of this section is that the other senses can be brought within the same Illuminationist theory that he has just used to explain vision—a theory that he eventually uses to explain knowledge in general.

61. Other manuscripts read "Light of Lights."

Part Two: The First Discourse

1. Some manuscripts read "Light of Light."

2. "Evident" might also be translated as "manifest." Suhrawardī is arguing here that light is a self-evident conception and can thus be a basic concept of a science. He is also establishing, as a fundamental principle of his system, that our knowledge of the world is based on direct contact with real things—with lights as directly manifested to us.

3. These two Arabic terms, taking the place here of "necessary" and "contingent," have a double meaning: rich and independent, and poor and dependent.

4. Quṭb al-Dīn, *Sharḥ ḥikmat,* 286, explains that the Peripatetics thought that only that which could be illumined could be said to be dark. Thus, they held, against Suhrawardī, that air was not dark because it was transparent and could not itself be illumined.

5. Some manuscripts read "most dark states."

6. In being hidden, they are the opposite of being manifest, which is the primary quality of light.

7. That is, while substances are external entities, substantiality exists only in the mind.

8. That is, if there is any such thing as metaphysical light, it is something different from visible light.

9. Meaning, bodily. "Essence" here renders *dhāt,* which means both "self" and "essence" in the sense of the concrete being of the thing. The two meanings are not sharply distinguished in Suhrawardī's Arabic. This translation tends to use "essence" whenever there is any doubt.

10. Immaterial light and accidental light respectively.

11. According to Quṭb al-Dīn, *Sharḥ ḥikmat,* 300, a light is a light *in* itself if it is manifest, and it is a light *of* itself if it is manifest to itself—in other words, if it is self-conscious.

Part Two: The Second Discourse

1. Suhrawardī seems to deliberately avoid the use of the term *fayḍ,* "emanation," preferring more neutral terms like *ṣudūr,* "generation," and *ḥuṣūl,* "occurrence."

2. In other words, there must be some cause to explain the perfection of the Light of Lights, since other lights have the same quiddity of light and yet are not the Light of Lights.

3. "Bahman" is the New Persian and Arabic form of the name of the Avestan Vohu Manah ("Good Thought"), the first of the Zoroastrian archangels *(ameša spentas)* to be created by Ahura Mazda.

4. Suhrawardī is replying to the objection that the same argument could be used to prove the indivisibility of the earth.

5. Quṭb al-Dīn, *Sharḥ ḥikmat,* 230–31, explains that the daily movement of the outermost sphere, which the other spheres follow, cannot be by compulsion, since there is no sphere beyond it to drive it and since the motion of a lower sphere cannot drive the motion of a higher sphere.

6. "Ray" should be understood not as a line of light connecting the radiant existent with the thing it illumines but as an increase in illumination caused by the presence of the illumined thing before the radiant light.

7. Some manuscripts read "Principle."

8. The word means both a favorable omen and something that comes into the mind.

9. Meaning the light immediately above it that gives it being.

10. Literally, "masters of species idols," meaning the incorporeal lights that are the Platonic Forms of the various earthly species. It is synonymous with "lords of talismans," "talismans" being the earthly instances of the Platonic Forms: individual men or horses. Talismans and idols both are material representations of immaterial spiritual realities. This complex of terms stoutly resists being rendered by English equivalents that are both literal and clear.

11. This is a technical term for a fundamental Illuminationist principle stating that every existent must have a cause ontologically prior and superior to it. See section 164 below.

12. Some manuscripts read "archetypes of talismans."

13. Reading *muthul.* If it is read as *mithl,* the meaning would be "on something like the ranks of their sphere." Some manuscripts read, "on the ranks of their causes."

14. The sphere of the fixed stars, according to Quṭb al-Dīn, *Sharḥ ḥikmat,* 353.

15. Some manuscripts read "the sphere of fixed stars."

16. "Hūrakhsh" is the sun. "Shahrīr" is the Zoroastrian angel Xshathra Vairya, "Good Dominion," associated with the sky and metal.

17. "Risibility" is the ability to laugh, which is a property of all human beings but is not part of the essence of humanity.

18. Some manuscripts read "in the knowledge of humanity."

19. That is, the form of humanity.

20. According to Quṭb al-Dīn, *Sharḥ ḥikmat,* 365, these are the past and future contingents, which are manifest in the souls of the spheres.

21. Since bodies cannot cause bodies, this hierarchical order must be based on the causal relations among the lights.

22. That is, denying that there are more than ten immaterial intellects—or in other words, that the Platonic Forms exist.

23. The terms in this passage translated as "spiritual" and "kingly splendor" are words borrowed from pre-Islamic Persian and carry strong Zoroastrian connotations.

24. These are well-known Zoroastrian angels associated with nature.

25. Meaning, their material instances, such as individual men. The Arabic expression rendered here as "archetypes" is literally "masters of idols." See note 10 above.

26. Meaning, among the immaterial lights; cf. Quṭb al-Dīn, *Sharḥ ḥikmat,* 377.

27. Pseudo-Aristotle, "Theology of Aristotle," in *Aflūṭīn ᶜind al-ᶜArab,* ed. ᶜAbd al-Raḥmaān Badawī (Cairo: al-Nahḍa al-Miṣrīya, 1955), 22.

28. Meaning, the animal spirit.

29. Some dominating lights—Platonic Forms—are too low to require another light—a soul—to mediate between them and their individuals. This is the case for the forms of material elements.

30. This interjection is omitted in most manuscripts.

31. Suhrawardī is speaking of the lamp's wick and the walls that it illuminates, respectively.

Part Two: The Third Discourse

1. Quṭb al-Dīn, *Sharḥ ḥikmat,* 392, identifies them as the Ashᶜarites, those who believe in the distinction of God's essence and his attributes, such as life, knowledge, power, and will.

2. He means that there is no explanation for something coming into being from nonbeing if its cause has no beginning. The point at issue is whether the universe had a beginning in time.

3. By which Suhrawardī means the immaterial lights, according to Quṭb al-Dīn, *Sharḥ ḥikmat,* 358.

4. While the celestial spheres can express the full complexity of the world of lights, they cannot do so at one time and by a single set of planetary positions; they require all the positions of the planets over a period of time.

5. The conventional explanation of the movements of the spheres involved the imitation by each planet of one of the ten incorporeal intellects.

6. Quṭb al-Dīn, *Sharḥ ḥikmat,* 401, reads this word as "comparisons" and explains it as "intellectual comparisons, such as the comparison of the idols with their archetypes, including imitation by the spheres of the dominating lights."

7. The example given by the commentators is a quantity of two, which contains in some sense a quantity of one that is prior to it. The point of the argument as a whole is that positing a first moment to time implies a previous time, so that there can be no beginning to time.

8. Suhrawardī means that without some way of distinguishing the parts of time—as is done by relative priority and posteriority in relation to the present—there could be no moments in time, since there would be nothing to distinguish them.

9. In other words, the eternal pre-existence of the world implies an illegitimate actual infinity, so therefore the world had a beginning in time. Infinities, according to the philosophers of Suhrawardī's tradition, cannot be simultaneous, actual, and ordered. He is responding to the argument that past motions are implicitly existent in the present and therefore must be finite in number.

10. That is, this argument rests on the same disagreement about the status of past infinities as the argument in the previous paragraph.

11. Meaning, the archetypes, the Platonic Forms; cf. Quṭb al-Dīn, *Sharḥ ḥikmat,* 415.

Part Two: The Fourth Discourse

1. Meaning the sublunary material elements and what is generated from them, so named because the source of their light is always another.
2. Quṭb al-Dīn, *Sharḥ ḥikmat,* 418, infers that this means air.
3. That is, the Peripatetics.
4. Quṭb al-Dīn, *Sharḥ ḥikmat,* 421, says that one manuscript reads "comets and meteors" and that this reading is better, which it is.
5. The one whose argument is being cited—Avicenna, according to Quṭb al-Dīn, *Sharḥ ḥikmat,* 423.
6. Suhrawardī is referring to the formation of mineral deposits on the sides of wells.
7. Aša Vahišta (Avestan) or Ardwahišt (Middle Persian), the Zoroastrian archangel *(ameša spenta)* associated with fire.
8. Quṭb al-Dīn, *Sharḥ ḥikmat,* 434, explains that he means the incorporeal lights.
9. That is, the human soul and fire are the nearest counterparts in this world to the incorporeal lights and the rays of the incorporeal lights.
10. Meaning earth.
11. Esfandarmodh is the Avestan angel Spenta Armaiti, "Holy Devotion," who is associated with the primal element of earth in Zoroastrianism. "Womanliness" might well be translated as "the passive principle."
12. *Ṣīṣīya,* pl. *ṣayāṣī,* "fortress," an unusual word that Suhrawardī uses as the Illuminationist term for the human body.
13. Some manuscripts omit "It is Gabriel—upon him be peace!"
14. Persian for "Giver of the spirit."
15. The point, according to Quṭb al-Dīn, *Sharḥ ḥikmat,* 442, is that if souls, before their union with the body, were distinguished from each other by their intensity alone, the number of souls (which is infinite) would require that there be many souls of each degree of intensity.
16. The reason for their being made to control the fortresses is their perfection, which would already have been attained.
17. That is, by aid of the blood that it draws to itself.
18. Avicenna and his followers.
19. Another way to prove that they are different faculties would be to show that their location in the brain is different, which can be done by studying the effects of brain damage.
20. That is, the imagination (the storehouse of forms), the estimative faculty (which makes judgments concerning particulars), and the imaginative faculty (which combines and separates forms).
21. Quṭb al-Dīn, *Sharḥ ḥikmat,* 469, gives the example of deciding to spend the night alone with a corpse. There is a desire to flee that is different from the resolve to stay and that must have another cause.
22. From the body. In other words, the human soul does not necessarily behold the intelligible world before death.
23. Several manuscripts add "by the lights."

Part Two: The Fifth Discourse

1. Although the commentators, from whose works we took the section titles, used the term "reincarnation" *(tanāsukh),* Suhrawardī did not, carefully confining himself to the more neutral term "transference" *(naql).*

2. A play on words, since the word translated as "dependence" in the previous sentence means, literally, "poverty."

3. *Būdhāsuf,* from *bodhisattva,* is the Buddha. Quṭb al-Dīn, *Sharḥ ḥikmat,* 479, identifies "the Easterners" as the sages of Babylonia, Persia, India, and China, and the other mystics.

4. Meaning, the body of a nonhuman animal.

5. Other manuscripts read "loves the darknesses."

6. Other manuscripts read "not knowing its real abode."

7. Suhrawardī is attacking a standard Peripatetic objection to reincarnation: the difficulty of explaining how the number of souls of the newly dead can correspond to the number of bodies being born and needing souls. He avoids some of the difficulties by insisting that all human souls are newly created; that no animal souls are newly created, all animal souls being reincarnated human souls; and that there is thus no transmigration of animal or human souls to human bodies. The next difficulty is that there are always far more animals being born than human beings dying. Suhrawardī points out—correctly—that if the world is without beginning, there have been an indefinitely large number of human souls that have come into the world, thus supplying a sufficient number of souls to transmigrate to all the world's animals, large and small. The final difficulty of how the deaths and births precisely correspond and why there are no temporary surpluses and shortages of souls is solved by providence—by the relentless logic of the movements of the spheres.

It is not quite clear that Suhrawardī himself accepts reincarnation, but it was the view of his Platonist forebears and he certainly wishes to defend it as a legitimate point of view. It is probably because of the extreme unacceptability of the doctrine of reincarnation in the Islamic world that Suhrawardī expresses himself so cautiously, attributing the doctrine to the ancient nonmonotheistic religions of the East.

8. Quṭb al-Dīn, *Sharḥ ḥikmat,* 489, gives the example of Turkish soldiers, who correspond to the beasts of prey.

9. That is, the Peripatetics say that a new soul is emanated for every animal or human; but the Easterners say that though this is true of humans it may not be true of animals.

10. *Naql,* explained by Quṭb al-Dīn, *Sharḥ ḥikmat,* 491-92, as being "from man to animals only, and from them only to plants, and to minerals"—a form of transmigration that excludes the possibility of a reincarnated soul entering a human body. It would also seem to be a euphemism, avoiding the charged word *tanāsukh,* "reincarnation."

11. Quṭb al-Dīn, *Sharḥ ḥikmat,* 506, reads "higher" here and in the next sentence.

12. Meaning, transmigration of souls.

13. Some manuscripts add "and fixed."

14. Darband is now in Dagestan in Russia, and Miyānaj is in Iranian Azerbaijan, both in the general area that Suhrawardī came from.

15. Meaning the managing souls of the spheres.

16. It is later generally known as the "world of image," *ʿālam al-mithāl.*

17. Quṭb al-Dīn, *Sharḥ ḥikmat,* 517, reads "bodies."

18. Quṭb al-Dīn, *Sharḥ ḥikmat,* 523, reads "to the triumphal lights" and cites as another reading "to the victors in the race" (cf. Qurʾān 56:10). Quṭb al-Dīn says that in either reading the meaning is the celestial intellects. However, the last reading might be interpreted as meaning that the holy souls join other holy souls, for the "victors in the race" in the Qurʾān are the souls of the saints.

19. Quṭb al-Dīn, *Sharḥ ḥikmat,* 525, cites a manuscript reading "movements."

20. The seven planets; cf. Quṭb al-Dīn, *Sharḥ ḥikmat,* 538.

21. The sense of this invitation is obscure and not fully elucidated by the early commentators. Seemingly, it is an introduction to the following sections in which the Illuminationists' mystical quest is described in the language of the Qurʾān and its tradition." "Memory" or "Mention" (*dhikr,* in this text usually meaning "memory") and "Book" are titles by which the Qurʾān refers to itself. "Metaphor" *(mathal)* is the term used by the Qurʾān to refer to its own figurative language; but when vocalized as *muthul,* it means "Forms" or "archetypes" and has been used as a technical term by Suhrawardī. Thus, the following passages will tell what can be learned about the mystical quest from the celestial prototype of the Qurʾān, and they are full of Qurʾānic terminology. This passage, then, bears a double meaning and may be read both as "ponder the archetypes that can be apprehended in the memories of the celestial spheres" and as "ponder the true metaphors that can be read in the "Qurʾān."

22. *Adhkār:* this term is especially used for a kind of Sufi mystical prayer.

23. That is, the prophet.

24. The commentators explain that the "First Tablet" is the First Intellect and that the "homelands" of the wicked are their bodies (Quṭb al-Dīn, *Sharḥ ḥikmat,* 546).

25. Quṭb al-Dīn, *Sharḥ ḥikmat,* 547, explains that the "world" is the body and the seven paths are the five senses plus imagination and intellect.

26. Gabriel.

27. Quṭb al-Dīn, *Sharḥ ḥikmat,* 550, cites as an alternative reading "a cloak."

28. That is, the animal spirit.

29. Meaning, the body.

30. Fabulous cities of legend.

31. Muḥammad.

32. A term for the ancient sages.

33. Quṭb al-Dīn, *Sharḥ ḥikmat,* 558, explains that being illumined by a light mixed with might will tend to make one mighty among men, and being illumined by a light admixed with love will make one beloved.

34. Some manuscripts read "multiplied."

35. The evening of 15 September 1186 C.E., when there was such a conjunction. (We owe this information to John Bromberek.)

36. The manuscripts differ considerably in these last few lines.

Notes to the Arabic Text

المقدمة

(١) **ط**: اوهنت (٢) **ط**: ازالت (٣) القرآن المجيد، سورة التكوير [٨١]، آية ٢٣، ٢٤ (٤) **يش، ش، يو، ط**: انظم واضبط (٥) **ط**: فرشا وشتر. **يو**: فرشاوشر. **يش، ش**: فرشاوشير، + وفى بعض النسخ: فرشادشير. (٦) **يش، ش، يو**: بزرجمهر. **ط**: بوزرجمهر. (٧) **ط**: عن (٨) **ط**: ازراء باستاديه. **يش، ش، يو**: الازدراء باستاديه (٩) **ط**: استاذيه (١٠) **يش، ط**: اهل (١١) **ط**: + فى (١٢) **ط**: + وهو خليفة الله. **يو، س**: – وهو خليفة الله (١٣) **ط**: عن. **س**: من (١٤) **يش، ش، ط**: العالم عنه (١٥) **ط**: + مكشوفا. **يش، ش، س**: – مكشوفا (١٦) **ط**: كان. **س**: فيكون (١٧) **يش، ش، ط**: قارى هذا (١٨) **ط**: – ما فيه، + وحده (١٩) **يش، ش، ط**: نورية (٢٠) **ط**: يبتنى على هذه (٢١) **يش، ش، ط**: – العلوم الالهية (٢٢) **يش، ش، ط**: الفوايد

القسم الأوّل، المقالة الأولى

(١) **يش، ش، ط، ل، يو، س**: فيه (٢) **يش، ش، ط**: يخلو (٣) **س**: حيطة (٤) **ط، يو**: الى المثلث. **يش، ش**: الثلث (٥) **س، ط**: العرضى (٦) **ل، تح**: – بها (٧) **يش، ش، ط**: ولا يتصور الشركة فيها (٨) **ل**: المتساوى. **يو**: تمسم للتساوى. **يش، ش**: المتساوى، + وفى اكثر النسخ المتساوق (٩) **ط**: فيه (١٠) **ل**: الى (١١) **ط**: لتخصص (١٢) **ط**: وبما (١٣) **يش، ش، ط**: – الشئ (١٤) **ط**: – معنى (١٥) **ط**: – بالعوارض. **يش، ش**: تعريف الحقيقة بالعوارض

القسم الأوّل، المقالة الثانية

(١) **ط**: قولنا (٢) **ط**: كقولنا. **يش، ش**: قولنا (٣) **ط**: كقولنا. **يش، ش**: قولنا (٤) **ط**: سوادا (٥) **ط**: يكون (٦) **ط**: يتركب. **يش، ش**: يتركب منفصلة (٧) **ط**: يتركب (٨) **ل، س**: الحملية (٩) **يش، ش، يو، ل، س، ط**: فكان (١٠) **ط**: و (١١) **ل**: – هى كقولنا. **يش، ش**: + كقولنا (١٢) **ط**: فيقهر (١٣) **ط**: اللفظ الدال (١٤) **يش، ط**: للرابطة (١٥) **ط**: ربط (١٦) **ط**: صيّر (١٧) **ل**: لا يكون الا على ما هو ثابت فى عينى (١٨) **ط**: يوجب (١٩) **يش، ط**: كذلك (٢٠) **يش، ش، ط**: – ان (٢١) **يش، ش، ط**: يحتاج (٢٢) **يش، ش**: نقيضه (٢٣) **يش، ش، ط**: – يكون (٢٤) **ل، س**: – والعكس (٢٥) **ل، س**: – والعكس (٢٦) **يش، ش، ط**: كلاهما (٢٧) **ط**: فنجعل (٢٨) **ل، س**: جزء (٢٩) **ل**: سلب (٣٠) **ط**: للمحمول. **س**: من المحمول (٣١) **يش، ش، ط**: ينتج ان هذين القولين قضيتان موضوعاهما بالضرورة متباينان (٣٢) **يش، ش، ط**: وكذلك (٣٣) **ط**: والاخرى (٣٤) **ل**: الخبط (٣٥) **ط**: شئ (٣٦) **ط**: كقولنا (٣٧) **ط**: كان (٣٨) **ط**: طائر (٣٩) **ط**: البعض داخل (٤٠) **ط**: شئ (٤١) **ط**: – من (٤٢) **ط**: والشرطيات ايضا قد يؤلف. **س**: والشرطيات تؤلف منها (٤٣) **ط**: حالها (٤٤) **ط**: + والقريب ما اذا كانت؛ – كقولك (٤٥) **ل**: حقيقة (٤٦) **يش، ش، ط**: – كذب. **س**: + كذب (٤٧) **ل**: – ان (٤٨) **ل**: بعد ان تعيّنها (٤٩) **ط**: النفس فيه عن (٥٠) **ل**: – الحكم (٥١) **ل**: – معيّن (٥٢) **ط**: حجة (٥٣) **ط**: قد لا. **ش**: ايضا قد لا يكون (٥٤) **ش**: فمنه (٥٥) **يش، ش، ط**: كحكمنا (٥٦) **يش، ش، ط**: + ايضا (٥٧) **ش**: + فى اكثر النسخ ما لا يوثر بتصديق (٥٨) **يش، ط**: البراهين (٥٩) **ش**: اليقين (٦٠) **يش، ش، ط**: وجود. **س**: جواز (٦١) **يش، ش، ط**: + ونفسه. **س**: – ونفسه (٦٢) **ل**: اجزاء. **يش، ش**: – صفة (٦٣) **ط**: علل وشروط (٦٤) **يش، ش، ط**: – له (٦٥) **ط**: نقيض

القسم الأوّل، المقالة الثالثة

(١) **ط**: + مّا (٢) **يش، ش، ط**: + يكون (٣) **ل**: المغالطة (٤) **يش، ش، ط**: – وجود (٥) **ل**: قد يتصور مع المعية. **س**: فلا يتصور مع المعية (٦) **ط**: و (٧) **يش، ش، ط**: – مكان. **س**: + مكان (٨) **ط**: كقول القائل (٩) **ط**: جهة (١٠) **ط**: – فى، + متساوى (١١) **ل**: من (١٢) **س**: انه (١٣) **يش، ش، ط**: كذب الخاص ونفيه (١٤) **ط**: – ولا تشاركها الدائرة فى الحقيقة (١٥) **ل**: – تحته (١٦) **ل**: – المقدمة (١٧) **ل**:

– هو (١٨) **ط**: وطلب (١٩) **ط**: عموم (٢٠) **ط**: يكن (٢١) **يش، ط**: – لوجوده. **س**: + لوجوده. **ط**: + لحقيقته. **ش**: – لوجوده مختلفة، + مختلفة حقيقته (٢٢) **يش، ط**: – ولا يتصور ... البدل. **س**: + ولا يتصور ... البدل. **ش**: + ولكن يجوز ان يكون للشيء مقومات مختلفة لوجوده على سبيل البدل. **يش**: + لا يجوز (٢٣) **ل**: – الكلية (٢٤) **ط**: مواضع. **س**: مواقع (٢٥) **ط**: انه (٢٦) **يش، ش، ط**: لما (٢٧) **ل**: – يعرف (٢٨) **يش، ش، ط**: + ايضا (٢٩) **ط**: و (٣٠) **ل**: شاركت (٣١) **ط**: – والجوهرية (٣٢) **يش، ش، ط**: فيجب ويمتنع (٣٣) **ل**: بامر (٣٤) **يش، ش، ط**: واذا (٣٥) **س**: الجوهر. **يش، ش**: الجوهرية (٣٦) **ط**: + على (٣٧) **ط**: + في انه. **يو، س**: – في انه (٣٨) **ط**: فانا (٣٩) **يو، ل، س**: – في انه هل له وجود (٤٠) **ط**: او (٤١) **يو، ط**: لما (٤٢) **ط**: كانت. **س**: لكانت. **يش، ش**: فاذا لكانت (٤٣) **ل**: الاثنين (٤٤) **يش، ش، ط**: فالسواد (٤٥) **ط**: اضافاتها (٤٦) **ط**: فيه (٤٧) **ط**: محمولات (٤٨) **ط**: بأية (٤٩) **ل**: – فجمع البصر (٥٠) **ط**: اخذ. س: اتخذ (٥١) **ل**: صفتان محققتان (٥٢) **ط**: يقابله (٥٣) **س، ل**: قوله (٥٤) **ط**: فنمنع (٥٥) **ط**: في الصغر والكبر (٥٦) **يش، ش، ط**: اعنى (٥٧) **يش، ش، ط**: الاسامى. **يو، س**: الاسم (٥٨) **ط**: + فلا يشملها بالمعنى الحقيقى الا (٥٩) **ل**: تجويزات (٦٠) **ط**: مقدار (٦١) **يش، ش، ط**: + ان (٦٢) **ط**: + نفس . **س**: – نفس (٦٣) **يش، ش، ط**: حكموا. **يو، س**: يحكمون (٦٤) **ل**: يقولون (٦٥) **يش، ش، ط**: بيّن. **يو، س**: يبين (٦٦) **يش، ش، ط**: – عن الصورة (٦٧) **يش، ش، ط**: فان لقائل. **س**: اذ لقايل (٦٨) **يش، ش، ط**: الشكل. **س**: التشكل (٦٩) **ش**: الطبيعة (٧٠) **ش، ط**: تخصص. **يو، س**: يتشخص (٧١) **ط**: قالوه. **س**: قالوا (٧٢) **ط**: يدخل (٧٣) **ط**: جوهر مفارق وجوهر آخر جسمانى. **ش**: جوهر مفارق آخر جسمانى (٧٤) **يش، ش، ط**: يتغير فيها (٧٥) **ط**: الوجوه. **س**: جهاته (٧٦) **ل، س**: – لا (٧٧) **ط**: من (٧٨) **ط**: اكبر (٧٩) **ط**: علتها. **س**: عللها (٨٠) **يش، ش، ط**: العالم العقلى (٨١) **يش، ش، ط**: ولا (٨٢) **ط**: عارض له زايد على الماهية. **س**: زايد عارض للماهية. **يش، ش**: عارض له زائد الماهية (٨٣) **ط**: بيّن (٨٤) **ط**: + انما كان. **س**: – انما كان (٨٥) **ط**: او. **س**: و (٨٦) **ط**: وكما. **س**: فكما (٨٧) **ل**: – تحريك (٨٨) **يش، ش، ط**: – في (٨٩) **ط**: – الا. **س**: + الا (٩٠) **يش، ش، ط**: جسم. **س**: جرم (٩١) **ل، س**: – بغتة (٩٢) **يش، ش، ط**: + مما كان. **س**: – مما كان (٩٣) **ط**: غلظا. **س**: غليظا (٩٤) **يو، ط**: تخصص (٩٥) **يش، ش**: و (٩٦) **يش، ش، ط**: هو. **يو، س**: هى (٩٧) **ط**: الى غير النهاية (٩٨) **يش، ش، ط**: جوّز. **يو**: جاز

(٩٩) **ل**: أُخرى (١٠٠) **ل**: لكان (١٠١) **يش، ش، ط**: يسمع. **س**: يستمع (١٠٢) **ط**: وليس. **س**: فليس (١٠٣) **يش، ش، ط**: انها. **س**: هى (١٠٤) **ط**: – وكذا غيرها. **يش، ش، س**: + وكذا غيرها (١٠٥) **يش، ش، ط**: الانوار. **س**: النور

القسم الثانى، المقالة الاولى

(١) **ل، س**: النور (٢) **ط**: – تسعة (٣) **ل، س**: – ما هو (٤) **يش، ش، ط**: + فيه. **س**: – فيه (٥) **ط**: ما. **س**: بما (٦) **ش، ط**: + هو. **س**: – هو (٧) **ط**: + اكثر. **س**: – اكثر (٨) **ط**: كذلك لما. **س**: كذا ما (٩) **يش، ش، ط**: عن. **س**: من (١٠) **يش، ش**: مثال الأنانية [مع ن بعد الالف] فى النسخة المشهورة، ومثال الأنائية [مع همزة بعد الالف] كما على ما فى نسخة مكتوبة من نسخة مقروءة على المصنّف، رضى اللّه عنه، مقابل بها ايضا وهذه النسخة اصحّ، ولهذا غيّر تلك النسخة «الأنانية» [مع ن بعد الالف] حيث كان الى «الأنائية» [مع همزة بعد الالف]. (١١) **ط**: الشاعر. **س**: الشاعرين (١٢) **ل، س**: يرجع (١٣) **ط، س**: يثبت خصوص (١٤) **يش، ش**: – تعالى ان يكون هٰكذا (١٥) **ل**: – انه ... حقيقته (١٦) **ط**: بالذات. **س**: لذاته. **يش، ش**: + فى بعض النسخ فأنّه فياض بالذات (١٧) **يش، ش، ط**: – وهو محال. **س**: + وهو محال (١٨) **ط**: وتقرر. **س**: فيقرر (١٩) **يش، ش**: البرازخ (٢٠) **ط**: – عنه (٢١) **ط**: فى الحقيقة. **س**: بالحقيقة (٢٢) **ط**: + هو (٢٣) **يش، ش، ط**: بذاته. **س**: بنفسه (٢٤) **يش، ش، ط**: + آخر. **س**: – آخر (٢٥) **يش، ش، ط**: ولو. **س**: فلو (٢٦) **يش، ش، ط**: لان. **س**: فان (٢٧) **ط**: لان يعود. **س**: لعود هذا (٢٨) **يش، ش، ط**: + ايضا (٢٩) **يش، ش، ط**: – منها (٣٠) **ط**: ولا. **س**: فلا

القسم الثانى، المقالة الثانية

(١) **ط**: الظلمة. **س**: الظلمات (٢) **ط**: والارض. **س**: او الارض (٣) **ط**: والنور. **س**: فالنور (٤) **ط**: – هذه. **س**: + هذه (٥) **ط**: فوق (٦) **ط**: سلطنة. **س**: سلطة (٧) **ط**: + واحد. **س**: – واحد (٨) **ط**: تمكن. **س**: تتمكن (٩) **ط**: – كثرة (١٠) **ط**: الحجاب. **س**: الحجب (١١) **ط**: يقال (١٢) **ط**: قاعدة. **يش، ش، س**: فصل (١٣) **يش، ش، ط**: لحمد وثواب. **س**: لحمدة او ثواب (١٤) **ل**: – الحق (١٥) **يش، ش، ط**: فسيأتى. **س**: وسيأتى (١٦) **ط**: + عليها. **س**: – عليها (١٧) **يش، ش، ط**: سبقت. **س**: سلفت (١٨) **ط**: + هو. **س**: – هو (١٩) **يش، ش، ط**: النور (٢٠) **ط**: ومنه ما.

يش، ش: ومنه، + وفى بعض النسخ والى ما يكون (٢١) **يش، ش، ل**: – الترتيب (٢٢) **س**: فعُلم. **يش، ش**: وفى بعض النسخ فيعلم (٢٣) **يش، ش، ط**: جعل. **س**: يجعل (٢٤) **ط**: – والف والفين ومئة الف (٢٥) **ط**: + هيهنا. **س**: – هيهنا (٢٦) **يش، ش، ط**: قاهر واحد. **س**: قاهرة (٢٧) **ط**: – بعضها مع بعض (٢٨) **ط**: عدّا. **س**: عددا عددا (٢٩) **ط**: وبمشاركات (٣٠) **ط**: – اصحاب (٣١) **ط**: عن الاعلين (٣٢) **ط**: – مثل (٣٣) **يش، ش، ط**: العلل. **س**: الفلك (٣٤) **ط**: التصريف. **س**: التصرف (٣٥) **ط**: ضرورى. **س**: ضروريا (٣٦) **ط**: فى الكواكب. **س**: الكوكبية (٣٧) **ط**: اليها. **س**: اليه (٣٨) **ل**: + والذل (٣٩) **ط**: ازدواج. **س**: ازواج (٤٠) القرآن المجيد، سورة الذاريات [٥١]، آية ٤٩ (٤١) **يش، ش، ط**: + فلك. **س**: – فلك (٤٢) **ط**: ندركها. **س**: يدركها (٤٣) القرآن المجيد، سورة السبأ [٣٤] آية ٣ (٤٤) **ط**: فكذلك العلم. **س**: فالعلم (٤٥) **ط**: العلم (٤٦) **ط**: العلم بالانسانية. **س**: فى الانسانية (٤٧) **يش، ش، ط**: يجد (٤٨) **يش، ش، ط**: كان هو اولى. **س**: فهو اولى (٤٩) القرآن المجيد، سورة يوسف [١٢]، آية ٢٤ (٥٠) **ط**: المينوية (٥١) **يش، ش، ط**: متفقون. **س**: كانوا متفقين (٥٢) **ط**: الكثيرين. **س**: كثيرين. **يش، ش**: +فى بعض النسخ وليس اذا لم يقتض الانسانية الكثرة لا اقتضاء كثرتها يقتضى الوحدة، وفى بعض النسخ وليس اذا لم يقتض الانسانية الكثرة لا اقتضاء كثرتها الوحدة، والأوّل أُولى من الثانى (٥٣) القرآن المجيد، سورة ابراهيم [١٤]، آية ٤٨ (٥٤) القرآن المجيد، سورة النور [٢٤] آية ٣٥ (٥٥) **يش، ش، ط**: قبلت. **س**: يقبل (٥٦) **ط**: – ووجودها ... برزخى (٥٧) **ط**: مشاركة. **س**: متشاركة (٥٨) **س**: هيئته (٥٩) **ط**: شئ (٦٠) **يش، ش، ط**: بالاشدية. **س**: بالشدة (٦١) **يش، ش، ط**: – وقدرته

القسم الثانى، المقالة الثالثة

(١) **ط**: وهو. **س**: فهو (٢) **ط**: توقف. **س**: يتوقف (٣) **ط**: فلا يمكن. **س**: فلم يمكن. **يش، ش**: لا يمكن (٤) **ط**: الكوكب تارة راجع (٥) **ل**: فيكون (٦) **ش**: التشبيهات (٧) **ط**: لو (٨) **ط**: وحصل (٩) **ل، س**: يفيض (١٠) **يش، ش، ط**: يستدل. **س**: استدل (١١) **ط**: فلا (١٢) **ط**: + كلام. **س**: – كلام (١٣) **ط**: – وهو. **س**: + وهو (١٤) **ط**: بالعدم فيلزم منه ان يكون (١٥) **ط**: – ايضا. **س**: + ايضا (١٦) **ط**: حركات. **س**: حركة (١٧) **يش، ش، ط**: – وبما. **س**: + وبما (١٨) **س**: هوية

القسم الثانى، المقالة الرابعة

(١) **ط**: اما. **س**: فاما (٢) **يش، ش، ط**: لموضوعاتها. **س**: وموضوعاتها (٣) **يش، ش، ط**: هو. **س**: + وهو (٤) **ش**: + وفى بعض النسخ والشهب، وهذا اولى (٥) **ط**: + من. **س**: – من (٦) **يش، ش، ط**: فى هذا (٧) **ط**: الثلث. **س**: الثلاثة (٨) **يش، ش، ط**: اخو. **س**: اخ (٩) **ط**: – اليه. **س**: + اليه (١٠) **ط**: الحركات. **س**: الحركة (١١) **ط**: به يشبه. **س**: تشبه (١٢) **ش**: لأناث، + فى بعض النسخ حصّة الأناث، وهو أظهر واولى (١٣) **يش، ش، ل، س**: – يعنى جبرئيل عليه السلام (١٤) **ط**: لم يمكن. **س**: لم تكن (١٥) **ط**: وان. **س**: فان (١٦) **يش، ش، ط**: منها. **س**: فيها (١٧) **ط**: نور مدبر. **س**: نورا مدبرا (١٨) **يش، ش، ط**: الازال. **س**: الازل (١٩) **يش، ش، ط**: الحوادث. **س**: للحوادث (٢٠) **ط**: فلو. **س**: ولو (٢١) **يش، ش، ط**: يلزم. **س**: يلزمه (٢٢) **ش، ط**: استوفى (٢٣) **يش، ش، ط**: + ايضا. **س**: – ايضا (٢٤) **يش، ش، ط**: + يكن. **س**: – يكن (٢٥) **يش، ط**: فالنور. **ش**: فان النور (٢٦) **يش، ش، ل، س، ط**: –فصل [زاد كُربن عليه. م.] (٢٧) **يش، ش، ط**: ولا. **س**: فلا (٢٨) **ط**: فلا. **ش، س**: ولا (٢٩) **ط**: لا يتأتى. **س**: ما يأتى (٣٠) **ط**: + ان يكون. **يش، س**: – ان يكون (٣١) **ش**: + فى بعض النسخ تشبثا (٣٢) **ش**: + فى بعض النسخ في (٣٣) **ش**: + فى بعض النسخ ينسو (٣٤) **ش**: + فى بعض النسخ يقبل (٣٥) **يش، ش، ط**: ابداننا، **س**: بدننا (٣٦) **يش، ش، ط، ل، س**: – فصل. [زاد كُربن عليه. م.] (٣٧) **ط**: صياص. **س**: صياصى (٣٨) **ط**: – اصلا. **س**: + اصلا (٣٩) **ط**: فصور. **س**: فصورة (٤٠) **ش، ط**: ظهر (٤١) **يش، ش، ط**: مشاهدة (٤٢) **ل، س**: مثال. **يش، ش**: وللنور المدبر اشراق على مُثُل (٤٣) **يش، ش، ط**: ومبصرة للانوار. **س**: مبصرة

القسم الثانى، المقالة الخامسة

(١) **ل**: حقيقة. **يش، ش**: حقبة (٢) **ط**: مشتاق ... مشتاق. س: يشتاق ... يشتاق (٣) **ط**: – الحكماء. **يش، ش، س**: + الحكماء (٤) **يش، ش، ط**: اسفهبذ. **س**: اسفهبدى (٥) **يش، ش، ط**: – لمزاجها الاشرف. **س**: + لمزاجها الاشرف (٦) **ط**: عاشق للظلمات. **يش، ش**: عاشق الظلمات [غَسَقَ النورُ الاسفهبذىُ الظلمات، وظاهر أنّ «غاسق» صحيص، كما في النسخ «ل» و«س». م.] (٧) **ط**: مأواه. **س**: ما وراءه. **يش، ش**: – ماوراءه (٨) **ط**: ينجذب. **س**: منجذب (٩) القرآن المجيد: سورة الحجر [١٥]،

آية ٤٤ (١٠) **ل**: المتصرفة. **يش، ش**: المتفرقة، + فى بعض النسخ المستظلمة (١١) **ط**: صياص. **س**: صياصى (١٢) **ط**: الصيصية الانسية. **س**: الصياصى الانسانية. **يش، ش**: الصيصية الانسانية (١٣) **يش، ش، ط**: صيصية صامتة. **س**: الصيصية الصامتة (١٤) القرآن المجيد، سورة النساء [٤]، آية ٥٦ (١٥) القرآن المجيد، سورة السجدة [٣٢]، آية ٢٠ (١٦) القرآن المجيد، سورة الانعام [٦]، آية ٣٨ (١٧) القرآن المجيد، سورة المؤمن [٤٠]، آية ١١ (١٨) القرآن المجيد، سورة الدخان [٤٤]، آية ٥٦ (١٩) **ط**: صيصيته. **س**: الصيصية (٢٠) **ش**: + وفى بعض النسخ كمعلقات (٢١) **يش، ش، ط**: فكلما (٢٢) **ط**: قدسيا تقدس، **س**: قديسا بقداس (٢٣) **يش، ش، ط**: — عالم. **س**: + عالم (٢٤) **ط**: المشى. **س**: الشئ. **يش، ش**: شئ (٢٥) **ط**: ازهقته (٢٦) **ط**: ها. **س**: هذا. **يش، ش**: — نحو هذا (٢٧) **يش، ش، ط**: الصيصية. **س**: صيصيته (٢٨) **ط**: ثلث. **يش، ش**: ثلثة (٢٩) **ط**: — الغالبة. **س**: + الغالبة. **يش، ش**: العالية (٣٠) **يش، ش، ط**: + تعالى (٣١) القرآن المجيد، سورة الرعد [١٣]، آية ٢٩ (٣٢) القرآن المجيد، سورة مريم [١٩]، آية ٦٨ (٣٣) القرآن المجيد، سورة هود [١١]، آية ٩٤ (٣٤) **ط**: + ثابتة (٣٥) **ط**: — انهم. **س**: + انهم (٣٦) **ط**: — البرازخ. **س**: + البرازخ (٣٧) **ش، ط، س**: الاجساد. **يش**: الامثال (٣٨) **يش، ش، ط**: من. **س**: — من (٣٩) **ط**: فلا (٤٠) **ط**: انفتح. **يش، ش، س**: فانفتح (٤١) **ط**: نهاية. **يش، ش، س**: النهاية (٤٢) **ط**: — السابقين. **س**: — القواهر، + السابقين. **يش، ش**: + فى بعض النسخ بالسابقين (٤٣) **ط**: فقه. **س**: قد. **يش، ش**: فقد (٤٤) **ط**: يشهد. **س**: شهدت (٤٥) **ش**: + فى بعض النسخ عالمة بحركاتها (٤٦) **ط**: وان. **س**: فان (٤٧) **يش، ش، ط**: محفوظة. **س**: مضبوطة (٤٨) **يش، ش، ط**: + نفس. **س**: — نفس (٤٩) **ط**: بما. **س**: عما (٥٠) **ط**: — فوقها. **س**: + فوقها. **يش، ش**: وقواها (٥١) **يش، ش، ط**: لا يكون. **س**: ما كان (٥٢) **ل، س**: — فصل. **يش، ش**: + وفى بعض النسخ فصل (٥٣) **ط**: + فانها. **س**: — فانها. **يش، ش**: ما يلتقى الكاملون من المغيبات (٥٤) **ل، س**: — فتناجيهم بالغيب (٥٥) **يش، ش، ط**: فى مواجيدهم. **س**: بالمواجيد (٥٦) القرآن المجيد، سورة يوسف [١٢]، آية ١١١ (٥٧) **يش، ش، ط**: + عالم (٥٨) **يش، ش، ط**: + يبرز. **س**: — يبرز (٥٩) القرآن المجيد، سورة القمر [٥٤]، آية ٥٢–٥٣ (٦٠) **ط**: فليست (٦١) **ط**: — ما يدرك. **يش، ش**: من الذكر ما يدرك (٦٢) **يش، ش، ط**: + التقديس. **س**: — التقديس (٦٣) **يش، ش، ط**: ومطرح. **س**: مطلع (٦٤) **ط**: فقدّسهن. **س**: فقدّسها (٦٥) **ط**: —

في جولتها. **س**: + في جولتها (٦٦) **ط**: + فصل. **يش، ش، س**: – فصل [زاد كُربن عليه. م.] (٦٧) **ط**: يوم القيامة. **يش، ش، س**: وقت القيام (٦٨) **ط**: – هم. **يش، ش، س**: + هم (٦٩) **ط**: من السبل، **س**: ينهجون السبيل (٧٠) **ط**: + اللّه. **يش، ش، س**: – اللّه (٧١) **ط**: طواغيث. **يش، ش**: الطواغيت (٧٢) **ش**: + في اكثر النسخ رداء (٧٣) **يش، ش، ط**: + منه. **س**: – منه (٧٤) **ط**: – صلى ... سلم. **يش، ش، س**: + صلى ... سلم (٧٥) القرآن المجيد، سورة الأنعام[٦]، آية ٥٩ (٧٦) **ط**: يشوبها. **س**: يشوبه (٧٧) **ط**: + كلها. **يش، س**: – كلها (٧٨) **يش، ش، ط**: عز وجل (٧٩) **ط**: كل. **س**: وكل (٨٠) **يش، ش، ط**: كثرت. **س**: ذرت (٨١) **ل**: ما ضاع اخواني (٨٢) **يش، ش، ط**: – فيه. **س**: + فيه (٨٣) **ط**: + اهله عن. **س**: الا اهله لمن (٨٤) **يش، ش، ط**: التامل لنور اللّه. **س**: تامل نور اللّه (٨٥) **ط**: الحرص (٨٦) القرآن المجيد، سورة آل عمران [٣]، آية ٤ (٨٧) القرآن المجيد، سورة العنكبوت [٢٩]، آية ٦٤ (٨٨) القرآن المجيد، سورة الانفال [٨]، آية ٤٧ (٨٩) القرآن المجيد، سورة البقرة [٢]، آية ١٣٢ (٩٠) يش، ش، **ط**: المعبود. **س**: المقبول

Glossary

The glossary deals with technical philosophical terms, particularly those used frequently, whose meaning or nuance is not obvious from the context. Most proper names and terms used only once or twice are omitted, as are many conventional philosophical terms. Terms in ***bold italics*** *are defined elsewhere in the glossary.*

accidental light *(nūr ᶜāriḍ).* (1) A physical ***light;*** (2) a luminous ***accident*** in an ***immaterial light.***

accidents (adj. **accidental**) *(aᶜrāḍ, ᶜawāriḍ).* Attributes of a ***thing*** that are not **constituents** of it.

antecedent *(muqaddam).* The first ***term*** in a ***conditional proposition:*** "If Socrates is a man, then . . ."

apprehension [perception] *(idrāk).* The direct knowledge of something, whether through sensation or ***intuition.***

archetypes *(arbāb al-aṣnām, aṣḥāb al-aṣnām).* Literally, "lords of ***idols,***" referring to the ***Platonic Forms,*** so called because they possess copies or ***images*** in the material world that are like statues of them.

assent *(taṣdīq).* The acceptance of the truth of a ***proposition.***

barrier *(barzakh).* A physical body.

bearer *(ḥāmil).* The ***substance*** in which a ***state*** inheres. The term is equivalent to ***barrier, locus,*** and *matter.*

beholding *(mushāhada).* Direct ***intuition*** of an entity, whether through sensation or mystical experience; also translated as ***contemplation.***

beings of reason *(iᶜtibārāt ᶜaqlīya).* ***Conceptions,*** such as ***existence*** and ***necessity,*** abstracted from ***conceptions*** rather than ***concrete things*** and thus not necessarily corresponding to external entities.

Book, he who arises with the *(al-qāʾim* [or *al-qayyim*] *biʾl-kitāb).* The mystical successor of Suhrawardī as head of his order.

caliph *(khalīfa).* Literally, "successor"; also translated as ***vicegerent.*** Suhrawardī uses it not in its usual sense of the political leader of Islam but in the mystical sense of the spiritual ***vicegerent*** of God on earth. "The lesser and greater caliphates" are fire and man.

categorical proposition *(qaḍīya ḥamlīya).* A ***proposition*** in which a ***predicate*** is asserted of a ***subject:*** "All men are mortal"; "Socrates is white."

commanding light *(nūr isfahbad).* The human rational ***soul.***

common sense *(ḥiss mushtarak).* The ***faculty*** in which the impressions of the five external senses are combined.

compound proposition *(qaḍīya muttaṣila).* A ***proposition*** composed of two or more propositions to form either a ***disjunction*** or a ***conditional proposition.***

conception *(taṣawwur).* The knowledge of what something is, as distinguished from ***assent,*** which is a judgment about its truth.

concomitants *(lawāzim).* Properties that are invariably associated with a ***thing*** but without necessarily being parts of its ***essence.***

concrete things *(aʿyān).* Real entities outside the mind; the opposite of mental entities.

condition *(sharṭ).* A necessary but not sufficient reason for the ***existence*** of something that is itself not one of the four causes.

conditional proposition; compound conditional proposition *(qaḍīya sharṭīya; qaḍīya sharṭīya muttaṣila).* A ***proposition*** (or ***compound proposition***) of the form "If . . . then . . ."

consequent *(tālī).* The second, or "then," part of a ***conditional proposition.***

constituents *(muqawwimāt).* The parts of the ***quiddity.***

contemplation *(mushāhada).* See ***beholding.***

contingency, principle of the most noble *(qāʾidat al-imkān al-ashraf).* The ***Illuminationist*** version of the principle of sufficient reason: that the ***existence*** of something implies the ***existence*** of something of a higher ontological level.

contingent *(mumkin).* That whose ***existence*** is neither ***necessary*** nor ***impossible.***

contradictory *(naqīḍ).* One of a pair of ***propositions*** which, when asserted together, make a ***contradiction:*** "All men are mortal, and some men are not mortal."

contradiction *(tanāquḍ).* The assertion of two ***propositions*** that cannot both be true or both be false.

contrary *(ḍidd).* A ***proposition*** that cannot be true if its ***contradictory*** is true.

control *(taṣarruf).* The relation of a ***soul*** to its body.

conversion *(ʿaks).* The transformation of one ***proposition*** into a second whose ***subject*** is the ***predicate*** of the first and vice versa and which has the same affirmation or ***negation*** and the same truth value as the first: "All men are mortal" thus converts to "Some mortals are men."

dark state *(hayʾa ẓulmānīya).* A nonluminous ***accident,*** whether in ***immaterial light*** or bodies.

darkness *(ẓulm).* Lack of ***light,*** regardless of whether or not ***light*** is possible.

definite proposition *(battāta).* A ***proposition*** converted to a ***universal*** affirmative, with the ***mode*** and any ***negation*** made part of the ***predicate;*** an iterated modal.

definition *(taʿrīf)*. An expression that makes a ***conception*** known, whether by a process of ***essential definition, description,*** or explanation of the usage of a word.

definition, essential *(ḥadd)*. A ***definition*** that conveys the ***quiddity*** of the ***species*** by naming the proximate ***genus*** and the ***differentia;*** rejected by Suhrawardī.

demonstration *(burhān)*. A ***proof*** that yields certitude by means of valid syllogism and premises that are themselves known to be true. It is the sort of ***proof*** required in the sciences and may be either assertoric (proving that something is the case) or causal (proving the fact by showing its actual cause).

dependence *(faqr;* also *tawaqquf, ta'alluq)*. Contingency; the ***state*** of a ***thing***'s ***existence*** being dependent on another ***thing.***

description *(rasm)*. A ***definition*** identifying its subject by properties not ***essential*** to it: "Man is a laughing biped."

differentia *(faṣl)*. A property that distinguishes a ***species*** from other ***species*** in the same genus.

direction *(jiha)*. Extension in one dimension.

discursive philosophy *(baḥth)*. Philosophy based only on reason and not on the direct ***apprehension*** of the intelligible realm; the opposite of ***intuitive philosophy.***

disjunction *(istithnāʾ)*. A ***proposition*** composed of two ***propositions*** connected by "or." Suhrawardī and Islamic logicians recognize only exclusive disjunction: one of the ***propositions*** must be true, but not both.

dominance *(qahr)*. The relation of the higher ***immaterial lights*** to the lower, the reverse of which is love.

dominating lights *(qawāhir)*. The ***immaterial intellects*** that have no direct relation to material beings and are neither ***souls*** controlling bodies or ***spheres*** nor ***archetypes*** of ***species.***

dusky *(ghāsiq)*. Corporeal.

dusky substances *(ghawāsiq, al-jawāhir al-ghāsiqa)*. Bodies.

ecthesis *(iftirāḍ)*. A form of reasoning in which a hypothetical individual is introduced.

efficient cause *(fāʿil)*. The cause that immediately occasions the effect.

ego *(anāʾīya, inīya)*. The self-conscious thinking subject.

element *(ʿunṣur)*. One of the basic physical substances identified in Greek philosophy: earth, air, water, and fire. Suhrawardī does not recognize fire as an element, however.

emanation *(fayḍ)*. Creation by eternal ***generation*** from a higher being. Suhrawardī usually avoids this term.

enkindled *(qābis)*. ***Illuminationist*** equivalent of the term *elemental.*

essence *(dhāt)*. The ***thing*** in itself, not as it is known. In some contexts it is translated as ***self.***

essential *(dhātī)*. Anything that is a ***constituent*** of the ***thing***'s ***essence;*** the opposite of ***accidental.***

estimation, estimative faculty *(wahm, qūwa wahmīya).* The ***faculty*** by which the value of particulars is judged: "The wolf I see is dangerous."

evident *(ẓāhir).* The ***essential*** property of ***light.***

exalted lights *(al-aᶜlūn).* The higher ***dominating lights.***

exhaustive *(mustaghriq).* The ***Illuminationist*** term for a ***universal proposition.***

existence *(wujūd).* The act of being; to be distinguished from ***existent.*** According to Suhrawardī, existence in general is only a concept.

existent *(mawjūd).* Anything that is actual in some sense.

existential proposition *(al-qaḍīya al-baᶜḍīya).* A ***proposition*** whose ***subject*** includes only some of a class.

extreme (of a syllogism) *(ṭaraf).* Either of the two nonrepeated ***terms*** in a ***categorical syllogism.***

faculty *(qūwa).* A particular ability of the soul.

figure, image *(shibḥ).* A spatial ***form*** not embedded in matter, such as ***forms*** in mirrors, dreams, and the imaginal world; synonymous with ***forms, suspended.***

figure (of a syllogism) *(shakl).* One of the four classes of syllogism, depending on where the middle ***term*** is in the two premises. In the most useful figure—the first—the middle ***term*** is the ***subject*** of the major premise and the ***predicate*** of the minor premise.

form *(ṣūra).* The physical shape and function; the opposite of matter.

Forms, Platonic *(muthul aflāṭūnīya).* The celestial ***archetypes*** of natural kinds. In Suhrawardī's system, they are ***immaterial intellects.***

forms, suspended *(ṣuwar mu'allaqa).* ***Forms*** or ***figures,*** such as those in dreams, mirrors, and visions, that are not embedded in matter; synonymous with ***figure, image.***

fortress *(ṣīṣīya).* An animal or human body.

generation *(ṣudūr).* The process by which an ***existent*** of a lower ontological level comes to be from one of a higher ontological level.

genus *(jins).* A natural kind divisible into species.

godliness *(taʾalluh).* Mystical attainment.

horizontal order of lights *(al-anwār al-ᶜarḍīya).* The ***Platonic Forms,*** so called because they may differ in kind without differing in ontological level.

identity *(huwīya).* The concrete ***reality*** and ***essence*** of an entity.

idol, image *(ṣanam).* A ***sublunar existent*** considered in relation to its ***archetype.***

illumination *(ishrāq).* The influence upon an ***existent*** by an ***incorporeal*** or ***accidental light,*** the result of which is a luminous ***accident.***

Illuminationist *(ishrāqī).* The school of Suhrawardī, sometimes said by later Islamic writers—though not by Suhrawardī—to be the Islamic followers of the Stoics.

imagination *(khayāl).* The ***faculty*** of the animal ***soul*** that stores the sensible ***images*** when they are no longer present in sensation.

imaginative faculty *(mutakhayyila).* The ***faculty*** that combines sensible ***forms*** for the use of thought.

immaterial lights *(anwār mujarrada).* The ***lights*** that are not ***accidents*** in a material body or in another ***light;*** immaterial ***intellects.***

impediment *(māniᶜ).* Something that prevents the operation of a cause.

impossible *(mumtaniᶜ).* That which cannot exist. See also ***contingent*** and ***necessary.***

imprinting *(inṭibāᶜ).* A theory of sensation and knowledge, rejected by Suhrawardī, in which sensation or knowledge occurs by means of a material organ taking the ***form*** of the ***thing*** sensed or known. The term comes from an analogy of wax imprinted with the ***form*** of a signet ring.

incorporeal *(mujarrad).* Not embedded in matter.

indefiniteness *(ihmāl).* The failure to state explicitly whether a ***proposition*** is ***necessary, contingent,*** or ***impossible.***

independent *(ghanī).* Not dependent for its ***existence*** on something else.

individualizing *(shākhiṣ).* A meaning or word referring to a single individual.

infinite proposition *(qaḍīya maᶜdūla).* A ***proposition*** one of whose ***terms*** is of the form "non-x," as in "Non-man is not rational."

intellect *(ᶜaql).* The human ***faculty*** of pure reason; an ***incorporeal*** mind or ***immaterial light.***

intellection *(taᶜaqqul).* Rational cognition, understanding.

intelligibles *(maᶜqūlāt).* ***Conceptions*** that can be grasped by reason.

intensity *(shidda, ishtidād).* The property of having degrees of strength of being. Suhrawardī holds that it is a category and applies to ***substance.***

intuition *(dhawq).* The acquisition of supersensible knowledge directly, without the mediation of reason or thought.

intuitive philosophy *(taʾalluh).* Philosophy based in part on the direct ***apprehension*** of the ***intelligible*** realm; the opposite of ***discursive philosophy.***

invoke *(istidᶜāʾ).* Possess a ***state*** that necessitates the ***generation*** of something from some higher entity; refers particularly to the capacity of the human bodily constitution to necessitate the ***generation*** of a human ***soul.***

judgment *(ḥukūma).* The dialectical proof, without recourse to ***Illuminationist principles,*** of the invalidity of a non-***Illuminationist*** philosophical doctrine.

knowledge by presence *(ᶜilm ḥuḍūrī).* Knowledge acquired by ***apprehension,*** especially the ***intuition*** of supersensible entities.

light *(nūr).* That which is manifest in itself and manifests entities other than it. It is divided into ***immaterial light*** or ***intellect,*** luminous ***accidents*** in ***immaterial lights,*** and physical light in bodies.

Light of Lights *(nūr al-anwār).* The ***Illuminationist*** term for the Supreme Being.

locus *(maḥall).* The ***substance*** in which a ***form*** or quality exists.

locus of manifestation *(maẓhar).* The body in or by which an immaterial ***form*** is visible, such as the mirror for its ***images.***

lords of idols, of talismans *(arbāb).* ***Platonic Forms.***

love *(maḥabba).* The relation of lower ***lights*** to the higher ***lights.***

luminous *(nūrī, munīr).* Having or being ***light;*** the property of being manifest and manifesting another.

managing light *(nūr mudabbir).* A ***soul*** that is associated with a body, whether human or celestial.

matter, prime *(hayūlā).* In the philosophy of Aristotle, the ***constituent,*** with ***form,*** of bodies. Suhrawardī denies its existence.

meaning, general *(maʿnā ʿāmm).* ***Illuminationist*** term for a ***universal.***

mode *(jiha).* A ***proposition***'s degree of necessity: whether ***necessary, contingent,*** or ***impossible.***

nature *(ṭabīʿa).* The inner power of a corporeal ***substance*** by which it is what it is.

necessary *(wājib).* That which must exist. See also ***impossible*** and ***contingent.***

necessary (of propositions) *(ḍarūrī).* That which is not ***contingent;*** either it must exist or it must not exist.

Necessary Existent *(wājib al-wujūd).* The Avicennan term for the Supreme Being, equivalent to God and the ***Light of Lights.***

negation *(salb).* The denial of a ***proposition.***

Pahlavi *(fahlawī).* Pre-Islamic Persian.

particularities *(khuṣūṣīyāt).* The ***accidental*** properties that distinguish one member of a ***species*** from another.

passion *(ʿishq).* Intense—usually sexual—yearning, used as a technical term in Islamic mysticism and by Suhrawardī as a description of the relation of a lower ***light*** to a higher one.

perfection *(kamāl).* Complete actualization; closely related to ***intensity,*** and the opposite of deficiency.

Peripatetics *(Mashshāʾūn).* The followers of Aristotle, and usually the Avicennans in particular.

perpetual, enduring *(dawām).* Eternal throughout time.

philosopher *(ḥakīm).* Also translated as ***sage.*** On the root, see ***philosophy.***

philosophy *(ḥikma).* In accordance with later Islamic usage, Suhrawardī almost always expresses the concept of *philosophy* with the term *ḥikma,* which he also occasionally uses in a nontechnical sense for ***wisdom.*** In this work he does not use the loan words *falsafa* and *faylasūf,* which seem to have had bad connotations by his time.

pillars of philosophy *(asāṭīn al-ḥikma).* The theistic or "divine" philosophers among the Ancients, particularly Hermes, Empedocles, Pythagoras, Socrates, and Plato.

predicate *(maḥmūlāt).* What is said of the ***subject*** of a ***proposition.***

presence *(ḥuḍūr).* The property of being manifest without obstruction to something else. See ***knowledge by presence.***

principle *(qāʿida).* A general philosophical doctrine; in this work, usually a point of doctrine distinguishing the ***Illuminationist*** philosophy from the ***Peripatetic*** philosophy of Avicenna.

privations *(ᶜadamīyāt).* Properties that are really the absence of a quality, such as silence and rest.

proof *(ḥujja).* An argument of any kind, ranging from scientific ***demonstration*** to poetry.

propitious light *(nūr sāniḥ).* A luminous ***accident*** resulting from the ***Light of Lights*** illuminating another ***immaterial light.***

proposition *(qaḍīya).* A complete statement, which can be either ***categorical*** (consisting of a ***subject*** and a ***predicate***) or ***compound*** (a ***conditional proposition*** or ***disjunction***).

providence *(ᶜināya).* The concern of an ***immaterial light*** for its material ***talismans.***

proximate light *(nūr aqrab).* The first ***light*** generated from the ***Light of Lights.***

pure light *(nūr maḥḍ).* ***Incorporeal light.***

quantification sign *(sūr).* The "all," "some," or "no" governing the ***subject*** of a ***proposition.***

quantified (of propositions) *(maḥṣūr).* Having a ***quantification sign.***

quiddity *(māhīya).* What a ***thing*** is, considered apart from its ***existence*** or nonexistence.

ray *(shuᶜāᶜ).* The ***accidental light*** generated in a body or ***light*** by another ***light shining*** on it.

reality *(ḥaqīqa).* A synonym for ***essence.***

reincarnation *(tanāsukh).* Metempsychosis; ***transmigration*** of a ***soul*** to a different body after death.

relative *(iḍāfīyāt).* The ***accidental*** qualities of a ***thing*** being related to another ***thing.***

sage *(ḥakīm).* Usually translated as ***philosopher.***

self *(dhāt).* See also ***essence.***

self-consciousness *(ᶜilm bi-dhātihi, idrāk li-dhātihi,* or *li-nafsihi).* The self-awareness possessed by all ***incorporeal lights,*** including ***souls.***

separate intellects *(mufāraqāt).* Equivalent in Suhrawardī's system to ***immaterial lights.***

shadow *(ẓill).* That which is material considered in relation to the ***incorporeal lights.***

shining *(shurūq).* The act of a ***light*** illuminating something else.

signification, concomitant *(dalālat al-taṭafful).* The method of making a ***thing*** known by its correlate: "Man is a being capable of laughing." The usual Arabic term is *dalālat al-iltizām.*

signification, implicit *(dalālat al-ḥīṭa).* The method of making a ***thing*** known by terms exactly corresponding to it: "Man is a rational animal." The usual Arabic term is *dalālat al-muṭābaqa.*

signification, intended *(dalālat al-qaṣd).* The method of making a ***thing*** known by terms corresponding to only part of its meaning: "Man is a rational being." The usual Arabic term is *dalālat al-taḍammun.*

soul *(nafs).* An ***immaterial light*** associated with the body of an animal or human. See also ***managing light.***

species *(nawʿ).* The most specific natural class of ***things;*** a natural kind.

sphere *(falak).* One of the transparent globes that move the planets.

spirit *(rūḥ).* (1) Synonym for the intellect or ***immaterial light;*** (2) the *pneuma,* or animal ***soul.***

state *(hayʾa).* Properties of a ***substance;*** any of the categories except ***substance.***

subject *(mawḍūʿ).* The first ***term*** of a ***categorical proposition;*** that of which the ***predicate*** is said.

subsistent in *(ḥāll).* In a ***substance*** but not as a part of it.

substance *(jawhar).* An ***existent*** that is not a ***state*** in something else.

subtle *(laṭīf).* Transparent: the distinguishing property of the ***element*** air.

sufficient reason *(tarjīḥ, murajjiḥ).* The cause of a ***thing***'s existing as it is rather than not existing at all or existing with different properties.

syllogism, conjunctive or categorical *(qiyās iqtirānī).* A syllogism in which the middle ***term*** is the ***subject*** or ***predicate*** of both the major and minor premises—the usual form of the syllogism in Aristotelian ***term*** logic.

syllogism, exclusive or hypothetical *(qiyās istithnāʾī).* A syllogism in which one premise is of the form "if . . . then . . ." or "either . . . or . . ." and the other premise affirms or denies one part of the first premise.

talisman *(ṭilism).* Synonym of ***idol.***

temporal *(ḥādith).* An event or being in time.

term *(ḥadd).* The ***subject*** or ***predicate*** of a ***categorical proposition.***

thing *(shayʾ).* The most general class of entity.

translucent *(muqtaṣid).* Allowing the partial passage of ***light:*** the distinguishing property of the ***element*** water.

transmigration *(naql).* Synonym of ***reincarnation.***

transmutation *(inqilāb).* Transformation of one ***element*** into another.

unity *(waḥda).* The property of being one.

universal *(kullīya, kullī).* An idea that can apply to more than one entity.

universal proposition *(qaḍīya muḥīṭa).* A ***proposition*** whose ***subject*** is an entire class.

vacuum *(khalāʾ).* Space containing nothing.

veil *(ḥijāb).* Something that intervenes to prevent perception or ***knowledge by presence.***

vertical order of lights *(ṭūlī).* See ***dominating lights.***

vicegerent *(khalīfa).* See ***caliph.***

vision *(baṣar, ibṣār).* ***Apprehension*** of the visible.

wisdom *(ḥikma).* Variant translation of *ḥikma* when this term is not meant to imply the technical sense of *philosophy.*

Bibliography

Abū Rayyān, Muhammad-ᶜAlī. "Kayf Ubīḥ Dam al Suhrawardī al-īshrāqī." *Al-Thaqāfa* 702 (16 Ramadān 1371 A.H./9 June 1952 C.E.).

———. *Uṣūl al-falsafa al-ishrāqīya.* Beirut: Dār al-Ṭalaba al-ᶜArab, 1969.

Afnan, Soheil M. *A Philosophical Lexicon in Persian and Arabic.* Beirut: Dar El Mashreq, 1968.

Aminrazavi, Mehdi. "The Significance of Suhrawardī's Persian Sufi Writings in the Philosophy of Illumination." In *Classical Persian Sufism: From Its Origins to Rumi,* edited by Leonard Lewisohn, 259–83. London: Khaniqahi Nimatullahi Publications, 1993.

———. *Suhrawardi and the School of Illumination.* Curzon Sufi Series. Richmond, Engl.: Curzon, 1996.

Pseudo-Aristotle [Plotinus]. "Theology of Aristotle." In *Aflūṭīn ᶜind al-ᶜArab,* edited by ᶜAbd al-Raḥmān Badawī, 3–164. Cairo: al-Nahḍa al-Miṣrīya, 1955.

Brockelmann, Carl. *Geschichte der arabischen Literatur and Geschichte der arabischen Literatur Supliment.* 2d ed. 5 vols. Leiden: E. J. Brill, 1937–49.

Carra de Vaux, B. "La Philosophie illuminative." *Journal asiatique,* 9th ser., 19, no. 1 (janvier-février 1902): 63–94.

Corbin, H. *En Islam iranien.* Vol. 2, *Sohravardī et les platoniciens de Perse.* Paris: Gallimard, 1971.

———. *Histoire de la philosophie islamique.* Paris: Gallimard, 1964.

———. *History of Islamic Philosophy.* Translated by Liadain Sherrard. London: Kegan Paul International, 1993.

———. *Les Motifs zoroastriens dans la philosophie de Sohravardī.* Tehran: du Courrier, 1946.

———. *Suhrawardī d'Alep, fondateur de la doctrine illuminative.* Paris: G. P. Maisonneuve, 1939.

Dānā-Seresht, A. *Khulāsa-yi afkār-i Suhrawardī wa Mullā Ṣadrā.* Tehran: n.p., 1934.

Fakhry, Majid. *A History of Islamic Philosophy.* 2d ed. Studies in Oriental Culture 5. New York: Columbia University Press, 1983.

Horten, Max. *Die Philosophie der Erleuchtung nach Suhrawardī.* Halle, Ger.: Strauss und Cramer, 1912.

Ibn Abī Uṣaybiᶜa. *ᶜUyūn al-anbāᵓ fī ṭabaqāt al-aṭibbāᵓ.* 2 vols. in 1. Edited by A. Müller. Köningsberg, Ger.: al-Maṭbaᶜa al-Wahbīya, 1884.

———. *ʿUyūn al-anbāʾ fī ṭabaqāt al-aṭibbāʾ*. Edited by N. Riḍā. Beirut: Dār Maktabat al-Ḥayāt, 1968.

Ibn al-Hirawī, Muḥammad-Sharīf Niẓām al-Dīn Aḥmad. *Anwārīya*. Edited by Hossein Ziai. Majmūʿa-yi Muṭālaʾat-i Islāmī 2. Tehran: Intishārāt-i Markaz-i Īrānī-i Muṭālaʿa-yi Farhang, Amīr Kabīr, 1358 A.H./1979 C.E.

Ibn al-Khaṭīb, Lisān al-Dīn. *Rawḍat al-taʿrīf bi al-ḥubb al-sharīf.* Edited by Muḥammad al-Kattānī. Rabat, Morocco: Dār al-Thaqāfa, 1981.

Ibn Faḍl Allāh al-ʿUmarī, Aḥmad ibn Yaḥyā. *Masālik al-abṣār fī mamālik al-amṣār.* Edited by F. Sezgin. Publications of the Institute for the History of Arabic Islamic Science, Series C, 46, no. 9. Frankfurt: Institute for the History of Arabic-Islamic Science, 1988.

Ibn Khallikān, Shams al-Dīn Abū al-ʿAbbās Aḥmad. *Wafayāt al-aʿyān.* 8 vols. Edited by I. ʿAbbās. Beirut: Dār al-Thaqāfa, [1965].

Ibn Sahlān al-Sāwī. *Tabṣira wa du risāla-yi dīgar dar manṭiq.* Edited by M.-T. Dānish Pazhūh. Tehran: Tehran University Press, 1958.

Ibn Yāqūt, ʿAbd Allāh al-Ḥamawī. *Irshād al-arīb.* 7 vols. Edited by D. S. Margoliouth. Leiden: E. J. Brill, 1907–27.

Iqbal, Muhammad. *The Development of Metaphysics in Persia.* London: Luzac, 1908.

Izutsu, Toshihiko. *The Concept and Reality of Existence.* Studies in the Humanities and Social Relations. Tokyo: Keio Institute of Cultural and Linguistic Studies, 1971.

Madkūr, Ibrāhīm, ed. *Al-kitāb al-tidhkārī: Shaykh al-Ishrāq Shihāb al-Dīn al-Suhrawardī.* Al-Maktaba al-ʿArabīya 159. Cairo: Wizārat al-Thaqāfa, 1974.

Massignon, Louis. *Recueil de textes inédits concernant l'histoire de la mystique en pays d'Islam.* Paris: Paul Geuthner, 1929.

Nasr, S. H. *An Introduction to Islamic Cosmological Doctrines.* Boulder, Colo.: Shambhala, 1978.

———. "Suhrawardī." In *A History of Muslim Philosophy,* edited by M. M. Sharif, 1:372–98. Wiesbaden, Ger.: Otto Harrassowitz, 1963.

———. *Three Muslim Sages: Avicenna, Suhrawardi, Ibn Arabi.* Cambridge, Mass.: Harvard University Press, 1964.

Netton, Ian Richard. *Allāh Transcendent: Studies in the Structure and Semiotics of Islamic Philosophy, Theology, and Cosmology.* Exeter Arabic and Islamic Series 5. New York: Routledge, 1989.

al-Qifṭī, ʿAlī ibn Yūsuf. *Tārīkh al-ḥukamāʾ.* Edited by Bahman Dārāʾī. Tehran: Tehran University Press, 1347 A.H./1968 C.E.

Quṭb al-Dīn Shīrāzī, Maḥmūd ibn Masūd. *Sharḥ ḥikmat al-ishrāq.* Edited by Asad Allāh Harātī. Tehran: n.p., 1313–15 A.H./1895–97 C.E.

Razmārā, H. ʿA., ed. *Farhang-i jughrāfīyāʾī-yi Īrān.* 10 vols. Tehran: Dāyira-yi Jughrāfīyāʾī-yi Sitād-i Artish, 1328–32 A.H./ 1949–54 C.E.

Ritter, Helmut. "Philologika IX: Die vier Suhrawardi." *Der Islam* 24 (1937): 270–86; 25 (1938): 35–86.

al-Shahrazūrī, Shams al-Dīn Muḥammad. *Kitab nuzhat al-arwāḥ wa rawḍat al-afrāḥ: Tārīkh al-ḥukamāʾ.* Edited by Muḥammad-ʿAli Abū Rayyān. Alexandria: Dār al-Maʿrifa al-Jāmiʿa, 1414 A.H./1993 C.E.

———. *Nuzhat al-arwāḥ wa rawḍat al-afrāḥ fī tārīkh al-ḥukamā᾿ wa al-falāsifa.* Edited by S. Khurshid Aḥmed. 2 vols. Hyderabad, India: Dā᾿irat al-Ma[c]ārif al [c]Uthmānīya, 1976.

———. *Nuzhat al-arwāḥ wa rawḍat al-afrāḥ fī tārīkh al-ḥukamā᾿ wa al-falāsifa.* Trans. Maqṣūd-[c]Alī Tabrīzī. Edited by M.-T. Dānish-Pazhūh and M. S. Mawlā᾿ī. Tehran: Shirkat-i Intishārāt-i [c]Ilmī va Farhangī, 1986.

———. *Nuzhat al-arwāḥ wa-rawḍat al-afrāḥ: Tārīkh al-ḥukamā᾿.* Edited by [c]Abd al-Karīm Abū Shuwayrib. [Tripoli]: Jam[c]iyat al-Da[c]wa al-Islāmīya al-[c]Ālamīya, 1988.

———. *Sharḥ ḥikmat al-ishrāq.* Edited by Hossein Ziai. Tehran: Institute for Cultural Studies and Research, 1993.

Sharaf, Muḥammad Jalāl Abū al-Futūh. *Al-madhhab al ishrāqī bayn al-falsafa wa al-dīn fī al fikr al-Islāmī.* Al-maktaba al falsafīya. Cairo: Dār al-Ma[c]ārif, 1972.

Shayegan, Daryush. *Henry Corbin: La topographie spirituelle de l'Islam iranien.* Paris: Éditions de la Différence, 1990.

Suhrawardī, Shihāb al-Dīn Yaḥyā. *L'Archange empourpré: Quinze traités et récits mystiques.* Translated by H. Corbin. Paris: Fayard, 1976.

———. *The Book of Radiance: Partaw-Nāma.* Translated by Hossein Ziai. Costa Mesa, Calif.: Mazda Publishers, 1998.

———. *Hayākil al-nūr.* Edited by Muḥammad Abū Rayyān. Cairo: Al-Maktaba al Tijārīya al-Kubrā, 1957.

———. *Ḥikmat al-ishrāq.* Translated by Sayyid Ja[c]far Sajjādī. Intishārāt-i Dānishgāh-i Tihrān 1562 . Tehran: Dānishgāh-i Tihrān, [1976].

———. *Le Livre de la sagesse orientale: Kitāb ḥikmat al-ishrāq.* Translated by Henry Corbin. Edited by Christian Jambet. Paris: Verdier, 1986.

———. *Majmū[c]a-yi muṣannafāt-i Shaykh-i Ishrāq: Œuvres philosophiques et mystiques.* 3 vols. Edited by Henry Corbin (vols. 1 and 2) and Seyyid Hossein Nasr (vol. 3). Tehran: Académie Impériale Iranienne de Philosophie, 1976–77; Paris: Adrien Maisonneuve, 1977. Originally published as *Opera Metaphysica et Mystica.* Vol. 1: Istanbul: Maarif Matbaasi, 1945. Vol. 2: Tehran: Institut Franco-Iranien, 1954. Vol. 3: Tehran: Institut Franco-Iranien, 1970.

———. *Three Treatises.* Edited by Najaf-Gholī Ḥabībī. Lahore: Iran Pakistan Institute of Persian Studies, 1977.

Thackston, W. M., Jr. *The Mystical and Visionary Treatises of Shihabuddin Yahya Suhrawardi.* London: The Octagon Press, 1982.

Walbridge, John. *The Leaven of the Ancients: Suhrawardī and the Heritage of the Greeks.* SUNY Series on Islam. Albany: State University of New York Press, 2000.

———. "The Political Thought of Quṭb al-Dīn al-Shīrāzī." In *The Political Aspects of Islamic Philosophy: Essays in Honor of Muhsin S. Mahdi,* edited by Charles E. Butterworth, 345–78. Harvard Middle Eastern Monographs 17. Cambridge, Mass.: Center for Middle Eastern Studies of Harvard University, 1992.

———. Review of *Suhrawardi and the School of Illumination,* by Mehdi Aminrazavi. *International Journal of Middle East Studies* 30, no. 4 (1998): 615–17.

———. *The Science of Mystic Lights: Quṭb al-Dīn Shīrāzī and the Illuminationist Tradition in Islamic Philosophy.* Harvard Middle Eastern Monographs 26. Cambridge, Mass.: Center for Middle Eastern Studies of Harvard University, 1992.

———. *The Wisdom of the Mystic East: Suhrawardī and Platonic Orientalism.* SUNY Series on Islam. Albany: State University of New York Press, forthcoming.

Ziai, Hossein. "Definition and the Foundations of Knowledge in Illuminationist Philosophy." In *Papers in Honor of "Ostād" Javad Mosleh,* edited by Borhan Ibneh Yousef, 108-30. Los Angeles: Research and Education Center, 1993.

———. "Explaining the Philosophical Meaning of Ṣadr al-Dīn Shīrāzī's 'Metaphysical Philosophy,' *Ḥikmat-e motaᶜāliyeh." Iranshināsī* 5, no. 2 (summer 1993): 354–64.

———. *Knowledge and Illumination: A Study of Suhrawardī's Ḥikmat al-Ishraq.* Brown University Judaic Studies 97. Atlanta: Scholars Press, 1990.

———. "Modal Propositions in Islamic Logic." *Bulletin of the Iranian Mathematical Society* 12 (winter 1980): 58–74.

———. "Muᶜarrifī wa-barrasī-i nuskhahā-yi khaṭṭī-i Shajara-yi ilāhīya." *Irānshināsī* 2, no. 1 (spring 1369 A.H./1990 C.E.): 89–108.

———. "Shihāb al-Dīn Suhrawardī: Founder of the Illuminationist School" and "The Illuminationist Tradition." In *History of Islamic Philosophy,* edited by Seyyed Hossein Nasr and Oliver Leaman, 1:434–96. Routledge History of World Philosophies 1. London: Routledge, 1996.

———."The Source and Nature of Authority: A Study of al-Suhrawardī's Illuminationist Political Doctrine." In *The Political Aspects of Islamic Philosophy: Essays in Honor of Muhsin S. Mahdi,* edited by Charles E. Butterworth, 304–44. Harvard Middle Eastern Monographs 17. Cambridge, Mass.: Center for Middle Eastern Studies of Harvard University, 1992.

———. "Suhrawardī wa-siyāsat." *Irān-nāma* 9, no. 3 (1370 A.H./1991 C.E.): 396–410.

Index

About the Translators

JOHN WALBRIDGE, originally from the upper peninsula of Michigan, has a Ph.D. from Harvard University in Near Eastern languages and is presently associate professor of Near Eastern languages and of philosophy at Indiana University. He is the author of *The Science of Mystic Lights: Quṭb al-Dīn Shīrāzī and the Illuminationist Tradition in Islamic Philosophy* (1992) and *The Leaven of the Ancients: Suhrawardī and the Heritage of the Greeks* (2000), as well as two works on the Baha'i religion and two volumes of translations of the Arabic short stories and poems of Kahlil Gibran.

HOSSEIN ZIAI is currently director of Iranian studies at UCLA, where he has taught Iranian and Islamic studies since 1988. He received his B.S. from Yale in 1967 and his Ph.D. from Harvard in 1976. Dr. Ziai has published several books on Islamic philosophy, especially the Iranian Illuminationist tradition. These include *Knowledge and Illumination: A Study of Suhrawardī's* Ḥikmat al-ishrāq (1990), *The Book of Radiance* (1998; translation of Suhrawardī's *Partow Nameh*); and *The Ball and Polo Stick, or the Book of Ecstasy,* with W. M. Thackston (1999; translation of ʿArifi's *Halnamah*). He has also authored numerous articles and contributed many chapters to edited volumes.

A Note on the Type

The English text of this book was set in BASKERVILLE, a typeface originally designed by John Baskerville (1706–1775), a British stonecutter, letter designer, typefounder, and printer. The Baskerville type is considered to be one of the first "transitional" faces—a deliberate move away from the "old style" of the Continental humanist printer. Its rounded letterforms presented a greater differentiation of thick and thin strokes, the serifs on the lowercase letters were more nearly horizontal, and the stress was nearer the vertical—all of which would later influence the "modern" style undertaken by Bodoni and Didot in the 1790s. Because of its high readability, particularly in long texts, the type was subsequently copied by all major typefoundries. (The original punches and matrices still survive today at Cambridge University Press.) This adaptation, designed by the Compugraphic Corporation in the 1960s, is a notable departure from other versions of the Baskerville typeface by its overall typographic evenness and lightness in color. To enhance its range, supplemental diacritics and ligatures were created in 1997 for exclusive use in this series.

TYPOGRAPHY BY JONATHAN SALTZMAN

◆